GREEK AND LATIN POETRY OF
LATE ANTIQUITY

Although Greek and Latin poetry from Late Antiquity each poses similar questions and problems, a real dialogue between scholars on both sides is even now conspicuously absent. A lack of evidence impedes discussion of whether there was direct interaction between the two language traditions. This volume, however, starts from the premise that direct interaction should never be a prerequisite for a meaningful comparative and contextualising analysis of both late antique poetic traditions. A team of leading and emerging scholars sheds new light on literary developments that can be or have been regarded as typical of the period, and on the poetic and aesthetic ideals that affected individual works, which are both classicising and 'un-classical' in similar and diverging ways. This innovative exploration of the possibilities created by a bilingual focus should stimulate further explorations in future research.

BERENICE VERHELST is Assistant Professor in Ancient Greek at the University of Amsterdam. She is the author of *Direct Speech in Nonnus' Dionysiaca* (2017) and the editor of the fourth *Nonnus in Context* volume (2022).

TINE SCHEIJNEN is a postdoctoral researcher in the Department of Literary Studies (Greek section) at the Ghent University. She is the author of *Quintus of Smyrna's Posthomerica: A Study in Heroic Characterization and Heroism* (2018).

T0370542

GREEK AND LATIN POETRY OF LATE ANTIQUITY

Form, Tradition, and Context

EDITED BY

BERENICE VERHELST

University of Amsterdam

TINE SCHEIJNEN

Ghent University, Belgium

CAMBRIDGE
UNIVERSITY PRESS

Shaftesbury Road, Cambridge CB2 8EA, United Kingdom

One Liberty Plaza, 20th Floor, New York, NY 10006, USA

477 Williamstown Road, Port Melbourne, VIC 3207, Australia

314–321, 3rd Floor, Plot 3, Splendor Forum, Jasola District Centre, New Delhi – 110025, India

103 Penang Road, #05–06/07, Visioncrest Commercial, Singapore 238467

Cambridge University Press is part of Cambridge University Press & Assessment,
a department of the University of Cambridge.

We share the University's mission to contribute to society through the pursuit of
education, learning and research at the highest international levels of excellence.

www.cambridge.org
Information on this title: www.cambridge.org/9781009013673

DOI: 10.1017/9781009031769

First published 2022
First paperback edition 2023

A catalogue record for this publication is available from the British Library

Library of Congress Cataloging-in-Publication data
NAMES: Verhelst, Berenice, 1987– editor. | Scheijnen, Tine, editor.
TITLE: Greek and Latin poetry of late antiquity : form, tradition and context / edited by Berenice
Verhelst, Universiteit Gent, Belgium ; Tine Scheijnen, Universiteit Gent, Belgium.
DESCRIPTION: Cambridge ; New York, NY : Cambridge University Press, 2022. | Includes
bibliographical references and index.
IDENTIFIERS: LCCN 2022008928 (print) | LCCN 2022008929 (ebook) | ISBN 9781316516058
(hardback) | ISBN 9781009013673 (paperback) | ISBN 978100903169 (epub)
SUBJECTS: LCSH: Classical poetry–History and criticism. | BISAC: HISTORY / Ancient /
General | LCGFT: Literary criticism. | Essays.
CLASSIFICATION: LCC PA3019 .G74 2022 (print) | LCC PA3019 (ebook) |
DDC 881/.0109–dc23/eng/20220421
LC record available at https://lccn.loc.gov/2022008928
LC ebook record available at https://lccn.loc.gov/2022008929

ISBN 978-1-316-51605-8 Hardback
ISBN 978-1-009-01367-3 Paperback

Contents

Figures

Contributors

SILVIO BÄR is Professor of Classics at the University of Oslo. His research areas and interests include Greek epic (especially of the imperial period), tragedy, lyric, the novel, mythology, rhetoric, the Second Sophistic, intertextuality, transtextuality, diachronic narratology, and the reception of antiquity in English literature and popular culture. He has published widely on Quintus of Smyrna's *Posthomerica* and on the character of Heracles in Greek epic and beyond.

KATERINA CARVOUNIS is Assistant Professor in Ancient Greek Literature at the National and Kapodistrian University of Athens, Greece. Her main research interests include early Greek hexameter poetry, the Greek epic tradition (especially Homer, Quintus and Nonnus), and Greek literature in the Roman Empire. Among her recent publications is *A Commentary on Quintus of Smyrna, Posthomerica 14* (with Oxford University Press).

MARCELINA GILKA received her PhD from the University of Exeter. Her thesis examined the classical tradition and late antique reception of the mythical events leading up to the Trojan War. She has also taught a range of language and literature modules at Exeter and King's College London. Previously, she had completed a BA at Exeter and an MSt at Balliol College, Oxford. She currently works in Research Funding at Wellcome, managing grants related to cultural and social contexts of health.

EMMA GREENSMITH is Associate Professor of Classical Languages and Literature at the University of Oxford and a Fellow of St John's College. She specialises in imperial Greek literature, and is particularly interested in epic, poetics, and religious culture. Her recent book, *The Resurrection of Homer in Imperial Greek Epic: Quintus Smyrnaeus'*

Posthomerica and the Poetics of Impersonation (Cambridge Univeristy Press 2020), offers a new reading of the role of epic and the reception of Homer in Graeco-Roman culture. She has also written recent articles on Nonnus, Gregory of Nazianzus, and the Sibylline Oracles, and is editing a new Cambridge Companion to Greek Epic.

PHILIP HARDIE is a Fellow of Trinity College, Cambridge, and Honorary Professor Emeritus of Latin, University of Cambridge. His most recent book is *Classicism and Christianity in Late Antique Latin Poetry* (University of California Press).

HELEN KAUFMANN worked in Classics at universities in Switzerland, the US, and the UK before she came to Germany in 2019. She currently holds a Humboldt research fellowship at the University of Erlangen. Her research has focused on the Latin poetry of late antiquity, and she is the author of a commentary on Dracontius' Medea (Heidelberg 2006). She has also published articles on intertextuality, the reception of Statius and Vergil in late antiquity, and poetic unity and has more recently been working on the link between identity and place in the Latin poetry of the late Roman empire and post-Roman world.

CALUM MACIVER is senior lecturer in Classics at the University of Edinburgh. He has published on a wide range of the literatures (Greek and Latin) of the Roman Empire, especially Greek epic poetry. In the long term he plans to write a second monograph on Greek poetry of the Imperial period (with a focus on Nonnus' *Dionysiaca*), after his current shorter projects on Statius' Achilleid and Lucian of Samosata's literary aesthetics.

LAURA MIGUÉLEZ-CAVERO (Complutense University of Madrid) specialises in Late Antique epic poetry, mainly in Egyptian authors who wrote in Greek, such as Triphiodorus of Panopolis (she published a commentary on *The Capture of Troy* in 2013) and Nonnus of Panopolis (see her contributions to the Nonnus in Context conferences, as well as *Symbolae Osloenses* 93.1 [2019], *GRBS* 53.2 [2013], *Mnemosyne* 63.1 [2010], *GRBS* 49.4 [2009]). Her contribution to this volume seeks to broaden her horizons and understanding of how Christian poetry came into existence in the fourth and fifth centuries CE.

SOPHIA PAPAIOANNOU is Professor of Latin at the National and Kapodistrian University of Athens, Greece. Her research interests embrace Ancient Epic, Latin poetry and Roman Comedy, and ancient performance, and she has published widely on these topics. Recent publications include: *Intertextuality in Seneca's Philosophical Writings*, Routledge 2020 (co-edited with Myrto Garani and Andreas Michalopoulos); *Elements of Tragedy in Flavian Epic*, De Gruyter 2021 (co-edited with Agis Marinis); and most recently the *Brill's Companion to the Reception of Ancient Rhetoric* 2022 (co-edited with Andreas Serafim and Michael Edwards). Currently she is working on a book project that traces awareness of the Latin tradition in Nonnus' *Dionysiaca*.

AARON PELTTARI is Senior Lecturer in Classics at the University of Edinburgh, where he studies the literary culture of Late Antiquity and is editing the *Cambridge History of Later Latin Literature*. He has published *The Psychomachia of Prudentius* (Oklahoma 2019) and *The Space that Remains: Reading Latin Poetry in Late Antiquity* (Cornell 2014).

TINE SCHEIJNEN is a postdoctoral researcher at Ghent University (Belgium), where she obtained her PhD in 2016. Her research interests lie in the field of ancient, late antique and medieval Troy literature and heroism. She has published widely on Quintus of Smyrna, among which a 2018 monograph on *Quintus of Smyrna's Posthomerica, a Study in Heroic Characterization and Heroism* (Brill). She currently explores the reception and evolutions of heroic characterisation in Middle English Troy romances.

A. SOPHIE SCHOESS is Associate Lecturer in Classics at the University of St Andrews. Her research interests include late antique epic poetry, Greek and Latin intertextuality, the relationship between image and text in the ancient world, and the reception of classical myth from Late Antiquity through Modernity. Her doctoral thesis (University of Oxford, 2018) traced the reception of Ariadne's myth in literature and the visual arts from antiquity through the Renaissance. Her current research focusses on Christian interpretations and appropriations of classical myth in Late Antiquity and the Middle Ages.

BRIAN P. SOWERS is Assistant Professor of Classics at Brooklyn College of the City University of New York. His diverse research interests focus on early Christianity, late antique literature, and gender and reception studies. He has published on late Latin reading communities, early Christian female martyrs, saints, and poets (Perpetua, Felicitas, Thecla, Justina, Aelia Eudocia, Ausonius, and Proba) and the use of ancient literature to resist systemic racism and white supremacy in the US. His first book, *In Her Own Words: The Life and Poetry of Aelia Eudocia* (2020, Center for Hellenic Studies), examines the poetry of Aelia Eudocia, one of antiquity's best surviving female authors.

BERENICE VERHELST is Assistant Professor of Classics (UD) at the University of Amsterdam. She is interested in late antique epic and primarily specialises in the Greek authors, especially Nonnus' massive *Dionysiaca* and the shorter epyllia and ekphrastic poems of the so-called Nonnian poets. She has published (among other topics) on epic speech (*Direct Speech in Nonnus' Dionysiaca*, Brill 2017), allusions and inter-textuality in Nonnus and Ovid (*Latomus* 77.3 [2018]), genre and characterisation in Greek epyllia (*Symbolae Osloenses* 93.1 [2019] and on the Nonnian narrator (*Nonnus in Context III* [2020]; *Studies in Nonnus' Paraphrasis* [forthcoming]). She is also editing the fourth Nonnus in Context volume (Peeters, expected 2022).

Introduction
Walking the Wire: Towards an Inclusive Approach to Latin and Greek Late Antique Poetry

Berenice Verhelst and Tine Scheijnen

In the past few years, it has been possible to notice parallel developments in the study of both Latin and Greek late antique poetry, two neighbouring and growing scholarly fields. Recently published studies reveal an increased focus on the contemporary context and, in relation to that, on the 'otherness' of late antique aesthetics, when compared with the poetics of earlier periods that classically trained scholars have been taught to admire.[1] Long considered poetry of bad taste from a period of decline, late antique poetry fascinates classicists today mainly *because* of its otherness, its productive reception of the classical period, its innovations in terms of literary forms, and the creativity with which it responds to the 'seismic cultural changes'[2] of late antique society.

Although similar problems and questions arise in research on Greek and Latin poetry from Late Antiquity, a real dialogue across language-bound research specialties is today still conspicuously missing. Only a few scholars with exceptionally broad perspectives, like the late Alan Cameron, have in the past decades been able to stimulate an exchange of ideas across this invisible 'border'.[3] Monographs that integrate insights in the Greek *and*

As editors and in name of all contributing authors, we want to express our thanks to the participants of the Edinburgh conference and Ghent workshop and all others who advised us and offered help in the course of the project. We are very grateful to our MA Student Vic Vandendriessche for his invaluable help in creating the indices. Special thanks go to Calum Maciver and Aaron Pelttari, who together with Catherine Ware initiated this project, for entrusting it to us and for their invaluable assistance throughout.

This publication has been finalised with the support of a project grant (3G056118) and fellowship (12N6819N) of the Research Foundation Flanders (FWO). The Ghent workshop was organised with the financial support of the Research Foundation Flanders (grant K7.099.16N) and Ghent University's Faculty of Arts and Philosophy.

[1] Cf., on the Latin side, especially the monograph of Pelttari (2014) and the volumes edited by Formisano and Fuhrer (2014) and Elsner and Hernández Lobato (2017) – all on the specificity of Late Latin poetics. On the Greek side, cf. the volume edited by Carvounis and Hunter (2008), the important survey of Agosti (2012), and the more general contextualising approach of Miguélez-Cavero (2008), Agosti (2016), and the 'Nonnus in Context' conference series.

[2] McGill and Watts (2018: 26).

[3] Cf. the recent compilation of his work with revised and updated versions of his influential articles (Cameron 2016a).

the Latin tradition, like the work of Robert Shorrock and Karl Olav Sandnes, remain exceptional in their bilingual approach,[4] while collective volumes that shed light on both traditions (e.g. *Texts and Culture in Late Antiquity, Shifting Genres in Late Antiquity*, and the *Blackwell's Companion to Late Antique Literature*)[5] mostly do not initiate true dialogue between individual contributions that, with only a few exceptions, deal exclusively with either of the two languages.

How can we explain the limited interaction between these two neighbouring fields of study? Several factors reinforce one another. The first one is related to the marginal position of Late Antiquity in school and university curricula. There are exceptions to this pattern, and their number is growing, but, overall, classics programmes still tend to focus almost exclusively on the canonical authors of Classical Antiquity. Consequently, late antique authors are approached mostly by scholars who indeed have received background and training in both language traditions but limited to the classical period. Most scholars will only become acquainted with the late antique context at a later stage of their education, as part of their personal specialisation trajectory, which often results in a more selective focus on only one of the two late antique language traditions. A second factor, firmly rooted in the research tradition itself, is the so-called Latin Question. This delicate question concerning the degree of direct interaction in Late Antiquity between the two poetic traditions has become an obstacle to rather than an impetus for further investigations. The general hesitation as to whether it is plausible – let alone possible to prove – that late antique Greek authors knew of classical and near-contemporary Latin poetry thus far seems to have prevented a fruitful exchange of ideas.[6]

---

[4] Shorrock (2011) and Sandnes (2011). More recently, Goldhill's *Preposterous Politics* (2020) discusses works not only in Latin and Greek, but also in Hebrew and Aramaic.

[5] Scourfield (2007), Greatrex and Elton (2015), and McGill and Watts (2018).

[6] From the classical Latin poets, Vergil and Ovid are at the centre of the discussion, especially in combination with Quintus of Smyrna (probably third century) and Nonnus (mid-fifth century), respectively. For both authors, lively debates (e.g. Braune vs. Maas in 1935 for Nonnus; Keydell vs. Vian in the 1950s and 1960s for Quintus) have resulted in few decisive conclusions and a general tendency towards caution (e.g. Knox 1988 for Nonnus; Gärtner 2005 for Quintus) regarding the 'proven influence' of the Latin classical authors on the late antique epics, notwithstanding their apparent and widely recognised congeniality (e.g. Vian 1976: xxviii and Shorrock 2001: 20 for Nonnus; Maciver 2011 for Quintus). More recently, scholarship has started to explore alternative methods of reading these texts next to one another in meaningful ways (e.g. Paschalis 2014 for Nonnus; Carvounis 2019: lvii–lxv for Quintus). Cf. also Carvounis and Papaioannou (Chapter 1) and Schoess (Chapter 11) in this volume. From the body of late antique Latin poets, the author who is mentioned most often as a potential source of inspiration for near-contemporary Greek-writing authors is probably Claudian (ca. 400, Alexandria-Rome) (e.g. by Cadau 2015).

As a reaction to this situation and in an attempt to open a dialogue between the two fields, this volume wants to show that – especially in a collaborative setting – it is indeed possible to overcome the barriers created by personal specialisms, and that crossing these barriers is always valuable. The question whether and to which extent there was direct interaction between the two language traditions is only one of the possible lines of investigation. As we will explain later, it is never a prerequisite. Rather, and more broadly, this volume aims to shed new light on literary developments that can or have been regarded as 'typical' for Late Antiquity and on the poetic and aesthetic ideals that affect individual poems from this period. It is an exploration of the possibilities created by a bilingual focus seeking a deeper understanding of late antique poetry as a whole, and it aims to stimulate further such explorations in future research. Our goal is not to show late antique poetry as one unified literary current – which it is not – but rather to give a nuanced account of this complex reality.

A key question, which has repeatedly been raised but not fully answered, is whether and how the Greek and Latin poetic traditions are 'un-classical' in similar ways. Possible connections with the changing aesthetic ideals in the visual arts, which are not bound by language barriers, are suggested on both sides. For this reason, Michael Roberts' ground-breaking work *The Jeweled Style* on Late Latin poetry and late antique visual arts is also often quoted in studies on Greek poetry.[7] The popular metaphor of the 'jeweled' and 'mosaic' late antique style is indeed helpful to describe and understand aspects of style and poetic composition of both Latin and Greek poetry, but a closer investigation makes it equally clear that the interpretation and application of this metaphor varies significantly from study to study, depending on the specific qualities of the late antique poem it describes. What do they all have in common? Can we speak of a Greek 'jeweled style' with distinctive properties compared to the Latin 'jeweled style' defined by Roberts?

In order to answer such questions, a stronger dialogue is needed between scholars working on late antique poetry in both languages. Only then it is possible to come to a better understanding, not only of the shared developments, but also of the subtle differences between the two traditions, which are now often overlooked or simplified because of the lack of any comparative studies. Combined, they show the richness and creativity of the varied corpus of late antique Greek and Latin poetry.

The initiative for this book was taken at the 2015 Edinburgh conference 'Poetry and Aesthetics of Late Antiquity', organised by Aaron Pelttari,

---

[7] Roberts 1989, cited e.g. in Agosti (2012 and 2014) and Chuvin (2016).

Calum Maciver, and Catherine Ware. As is well known, the success of any dialogue depends on the zeal and ability of conversation partners to truly explore each other's perspectives. This is precisely what we as editors challenged the authors in this collaborative volume to do. In every chapter, Latin poetry and Greek poetry are discussed together. For most of the authors (both promising early career researchers and established scholars), adopting a bilingual perspective meant leaving the *terra firma* of their own research specialism. This idea was captured in the 'walking the wire' metaphor that became the motto of this book project and the preparatory Ghent workshop (2016). A 'safety net' in the form of a strong collaborative set-up provided working conditions for exploring the much less familiar 'wire' of the other language tradition. As editors of this volume, we want to thank all contributors for making this collaborative process possible and for their thorough and constructive feedback on each other's chapters.

Organisation and Scope

The scope of this volume is determined by three parameters: language (Greek and Latin), period (from ca. 200 to ca. 600 CE), and the opposition of poetry and prose. Each of these may seem to introduce unwelcome restrictions in a volume that, as a whole, pleads for abandoning hard divides between neighbouring fields of study. However, when applied to the particular divide between the study of Latin and Greek late antique poetry referred to above, these parameters define a domain that affords a stable common ground for starting the dialogue.

Late Antiquity is here defined with a broad scope in order to include early examples of certain late antique tendencies as well as late examples of continuity with the classical period. Cases in point are Nemesianus and Triphiodorus, both third-century poets writing in Latin and Greek, respectively, discussed in Chapter 3 as exemplary of late antique poetic self-reflexivity, and the sixth-century Latin poet Corippus, discussed in Chapter 5 as a late example of continuity with the classical period in terms of genre awareness. Whereas certain trends can be traced throughout the 'Long Late Antiquity',[8] it is also – perhaps primarily – a period of constant change. Juvencus' and Nonnus' biblical epics illustrate this point very well. They are similar along many lines, but in order to understand the subtle differences in their representation of internal audiences (Chapter 9), their

[8] Cf. Brown (1971). For reflections on the periodisation of Late Antiquity cf. Cameron (2002) and Marcone (2008).

specific temporal (early fourth vs. mid-fifth century) and geographical (Spain vs. Egypt) contexts are important factors, especially with respect to the position of Christianity in society.

The opposition between Spain and Egypt immediately also illustrates the wide geographical spread of the texts discussed in this volume. This spread can be (and has been) used as an argument against direct interaction between the two language traditions in this period of decentralisation, but they certainly did meet in the imperial courts of Rome and Constantinople (and Milan/Ravenna/Antioch). Claudian, as a Greek poet who moved to Rome in 393/4 and continued his poetical career in Latin, is one of the best-known and telling examples, but one might also think of Corippus, who in 566/8 presented his Latin panegyric epic at the Byzantine court of Justinus II in Constantinople. On the other hand, especially when thinking of other flourishing centres of late antique literature and education (e.g. Carthage and Alexandria), the geographical spread also raises the question of interaction with other language traditions and cultures, which could be an impetus to look at Late Antiquity with an even broader perspective.[9] To some, and certainly from some perspectives, Abbot Shenoute's Coptic writings (contemporary to Nonnus and active in the same region of Egypt) will seem more relevant for our understanding of Nonnus than Ovid, Claudian, or Juvencus, with whom he is paired in this volume.[10] These other languages and cultures are for classicists often a real blind spot. A more active scholarly dialogue between Classical studies and the fields of Coptic, Syriac, Hebrew, Persian, and so forth, studies is certainly a desideratum, and recent research projects and initiatives guide the way.[11]

The choice in this volume, however, to focus only on late antique poetry in the two 'classical' languages relates to the specific kind of questions that are asked. An important connecting thread throughout the volume is the previously mentioned creative reception of Classical Antiquity. The common ground of classical *paideia* undeniably links all late antique poetry in Latin and Greek. Dracontius' (late fifth-century Carthage) and Colluthus' (late fifth- and early sixth-century Egypt) treatments of the story of Paris

---

[9] Cf. Humphries' (2017) plea to look at Late Antiquity from a world history perspective.

[10] Agosti (2020) convincingly argues for taking Shenoute into account in Nonnus studies.

[11] E.g. the Ghent Novel Saints and Novel Echoes Projects (2014–2019 and 2019–2024 resp.; focus on Latin, Greek; Syriac, Persian, Arabic, and Western European vernacular traditions) and a recent conference organised in Turin (La cultura scritta dell'Egitto bizantino: produzione e circolazione di testi copti, greci e latini in una società multiculturale, December 2017). McGill and Watts' *Companion to Late Antique Literature* (2018) centres on Greek and Latin texts, but also includes introductory chapters on Syriac, Coptic, Armenian, Georgian, Middle Persian, and Arabian literature.

and Helen are exemplary: both poems present a very different, but characteristically late antique balance between continuity with and reaction against the literary past (cf. Chapter 10). One possible conclusion of this volume might be that it is the specific, often quite ambiguous relation to classical forms and subjects that makes these texts 'typically late antique'.

The choice to focus on poetry rather than prose is, in turn, connected to the idea of a late antique 'poetic revival' in both language traditions.[12] It also ties in with two other connecting threads in this volume: the late antique use of traditional and innovative poetical forms and the relation between poetry and society. For this period of rapid and fundamental socio-political and religious developments, it is interesting to see the inevitable correlation between this historical dimension and the literary developments, especially with respect to aesthetic ideals and reasons for writing poetry. These three central areas of interest (classical *paideia*, poetic form, and poetry in society) are reflected in the tripartite structure of this volume.

(1)   Part 1, 'A "Late" Perspective on The Literary Tradition' (Chapters 1–4), clusters chapters which focus on the engagement of late antique authors with their literary past. The constant dialogue with the past may in some cases also suggest intriguing patterns of influence (e.g. Nonnus and Ovid in the first chapter), but each poem's position in relation to this shared past certainly reveals much of its own poetic singularity. This section of the volume tackles issues of canonicity, belatedness, and (non-)referentiality by comparing and contrasting attitudes to the classical (Greek and Latin) past from late antique Greek and Latin perspectives. The last chapter deals with paratexts, a specific type of late antique engagement with the literary past, which reveals the dialogue between late antique practices of text edition (of older, by then canonical works) and contemporary poetical developments.

(2)   Part 2, 'Late Antique "Genres" and "Genre" in Late Antiquity' (Chapters 5–8) has a central focus on genre and poetic form. Whether Late Antiquity is considered as a period of generic innovation, flexibility, or instability, or as the period in which classical distinctions between genres were abandoned, the modern notion of 'genre', already problematic when applied to classical poetry, becomes even more difficult to conceptualise when late antique developments are taken into account. A general survey functions in

[12] Cf. (among others) Cameron (2004b), Roberts (2017), and Miguélez-Cavero (2008).

this section as an introduction, followed by two chapters which discuss particular poetic forms: cento poetry and epyllia.

(3) The diachronic perspective of the first section is, in the third and final section 'The Context of Late Antiquity' (Chapters 9–12), replaced with a primarily synchronic perspective, highlighting literary, socio-cultural, religious, and/or art-historical aspects of the context of the poems under consideration. The chapters in this section each address a different aspect of this context and contribute to an interpretation of late antique poetry on its own late antique terms by tracing characteristically 'late antique' developments. Striking examples are the defining importance of religious and socio-political contexts, but context can also be defined literarily or topically. Two chapters compare and contrast texts belonging to the same 'genre' and treating the same subject, while a third focusses on the late antique literary practice of allegorical reading and writing and discusses the development of epic personification allegory (leading up to the first full-blown allegorical epic, the *Psychomachia* of Prudentius, early fifth century). The final two chapters investigate the specifically late antique use of a traditional topos or theme (the comparison of a beautiful girl with a goddess; the theme of metamorphosis) in relation to contemporary art-historical and/or religious developments.

Subjects and Methods

Together, the chapters in this volume cover a broad spectrum of late antique poetic texts, which aims to be representative of the different genres, periods, and geographical contexts defined by the volume's scope in relation to its three main fields of interest. Critical readers may notice that certain authors are discussed several times and in great detail (e.g. Nonnus, Ausonius) whereas others are only briefly mentioned (e.g. Sedulius, Namatianus, Christodorus) or even entirely neglected in this volume (e.g. Paul the Silentiary). It was never the aim to present a survey of key authors and texts – if this would even be possible. The present selection of subjects was made with the aim of combining as many different approaches as possible, in order to show possible ways of creating dialogue not just between scholars working on late antique texts, but also between the texts.

The volume deliberately starts with the previously mentioned delicate question of direct interaction between the two traditions, the so-called Latin question of whether there is any influence to be discerned of the classical

Latin tradition on late antique Greek poetry (Chapter 1). Certainly, it is impossible to deny the difference between the general practice of Latin authors showcasing their Greek and Latin models alike and Greek authors tending to keep their literary world of reference monolingually Greek. Ausonius and Palladas, both fourth-century authors, are telling examples (Chapter 2). The absence of explicit references (the mentioning of names and works) does, however, not necessarily mean that there was no interaction or mutual interest at all. It suffices to think of the apparent ease with which the Greek poet Claudian became a successful learned Latin poet, or of the prominent position of Vergil as a 'second Homer' (416: ἄλλον Ὅμηρον) in Christodorus' *Description of Statues* (early sixth-century Constantinople). This volume is a plea for further investigation of potential nodes of contact between the two traditions, notwithstanding the difficulty of proving direct influence across language traditions. To achieve this goal, it is essential to look into possible traces of interaction with near-contemporary authors rather than only with the canonical authors of the classical period. Chapter 6, for instance, shows a possible connection within the cento-tradition between the fourth-century Latin centos of Ausonius and Proba and the fifth-century Greek *Homerocentones* of Eudocia.

This volume is also a plea to explore other paths. Even though it may never be possible to prove direct influence, late antique texts can meaningfully be read alongside one another. With variations in scope and method of analysis, roughly three alternative lines of approach are presented in this volume.

(1)   Several contributions adopt a comparative approach, juxtaposing texts with a certain degree of common ground, in order to lay bare the subtle (Chapter 9 on Nonnus and Juvencus) or not so subtle (Chapter 10 on Colluthus and Dracontius) differences. The added value of bringing these texts together primarily lies in the element of contrast, which helps to pinpoint singularities in each text and tradition (Chapter 2 on Ausonius and Palladas) and to connect these with particular socio-cultural, historical, or literary contexts. In Chapter 7, dealing with reflections on genre in late antique 'epyllia', the juxtaposition of Latin and Greek examples shows surprising similarities across the language divide (on the level of poetics they all metaphorically 'speak the same language'), but the comparison also highlights the variation between, and singularity of, each poem.

(2)   Other chapters trace specifically late antique poetical developments that may be considered as common to both literary traditions and

connected to shared elements of context, like the late antique visual aesthetics (Chapter 11) and the material culture of the late antique Mediterranean (Chapter 4 on paratexts). The most obvious catalyst of change in Late Antiquity is without any doubt the rise of Christianity. It has a direct impact on the literary scene with the introduction of new subjects and new genres, and with the scriptures as a new point of reference *par excellence* instead of/alongside Homer and Vergil. In Chapter 5, the rise of Christianity is put forward as one of the most important factors to explain the 'implosion' of the classical system of literary genres. '... Christianity increased the potential for literary expression and reached a wider range of audiences, thus easing some of the pressure inherent in the traditional system of poetic expression.'[13] Even in those texts that seemingly least reflect the new Christian world (e.g. Colluthus' *Abduction of Helen*), it is possible to trace elements that can be connected to it as a reflection of the contemporary Christianised socio-cultural reality (Chapter 10 on the role of children) and of the Christian appropriation of the 'classical' visual culture (Chapter 11).

(3) Lastly, several chapters use theoretical concepts and insights 'from the other side' of the scholarly divide between Latin studies and Greek studies in order to apply them, again primarily with a comparative angle, to both language traditions. This volume starts with a re-evaluation of the 'Latin Question' regarding Nonnus and Ovid (Chapter 1); it also deliberately ends with (among others) Nonnus and Ovid, but along a very different line of approach. The terminology developed in Ovidian scholarship regarding metamorphosis (e.g. on 'metamorphic landscapes') allows for discussing Ovidian metamorphosis in Late Antiquity (Latin and Greek, secular and Christian) without addressing the, in this respect irrelevant, question of direct Ovidian influence in the texts under consideration (Chapter 12). Similarly, Chapter 8 'borrows' from studies on the nature and functioning of personification allegory in Prudentius' *Psychomachia* in order to describe related (but less prominent) tendencies in Quintus' *Posthomerica*. The relative chronology in this case excludes Prudentian influence in Quintus, and also the reverse is unlikely, but by deliberately moving away from 'safe sources' and 'certain intertexts', the author manages to reveal what she calls 'conceptual nodes of interaction'. In Chapter 3, finally, a broader theoretical concept is

---

[13] Kaufmann in this volume, p. 114.

tackled (not connected to the study of one particular author, as in the other two cases), that of the 'nonreferential intertextuality'. This term was developed to describe the practice in Late Latin poetry of 'reus[ing] phraseology without requiring the reader to to apply any function from the context or content of the alluded text'. This chapter investigates whether it can be applied to the third-century Greek epics of Quintus and Triphiodorus.

Does intertextuality work differently in Late Antiquity, in comparison to earlier poetry? And is there a difference between the two language traditions in this respect? It is only one of several larger questions touched upon in this volume. To what extent is late antique poetry the product of a classicising culture? Can we speak of an implosion of the classical genre system? Do Christian poems and poems with non-Christian content address the same audience differently? This volume aims to raise even more questions than it attempts to answer, as incentives and possible starting points for ongoing dialogue in future scholarship on late antique poetry. At the end of the two conferences that were held in preparation of this volume, there was a strong feeling that bringing together scholars of Latin and Greek Late Antiquity in a collaborative setting was in itself a significant step forward.

These are exceptional times in which to be studying late antique poetry. Never before has late antique poetry received so much scholarly attention: new editions appear (often first editions or after century-long intervals), Late Antiquity conferences and workshops create regular occasions to meet up with specialists in the field, new journals and book series are being launched (e.g. *Studies in Late Antiquity* since 2017, *Mnemosyne Late Antique Literature* monographs since 2015), and Late Antiquity scholars team up in international research associations (THAT, GIRPAM, Late Latin Poetry Network, etc.). Such excellent working conditions are a reason for joy for all involved, but also, and importantly, they create a momentum of reflection on the methods and organisation of our research. This volume will have achieved its goal if it can stimulate this process by offering a variety of angles by which to approach the challenges ahead. Additionally, we hope that it can encourage further dialogue, both on paper and in the form of new conferences and collaborations.

PART I

A 'Late' Perspective on the Literary Tradition

CHAPTER I

Rivalling Song Contests and Alternative Typhonomachies in Ovid and Nonnus

Revisiting the Issue of Latin Influence on Greek Poetry in Late Antiquity

Katerina Carvounis and Sophia Papaioannou

Nonnus' *Dionysiaca*, more than any other extant text in the Greek and Latin epic tradition, is close to Ovid's *Metamorphoses* both in terms of theme, since the two poems share the same spirit of a world history that begins with a cosmogony and geographically covers a large territory of the known world, and in terms of structure, since they both favour an episodic narrative of multiple smaller or larger accounts which are sometimes only loosely connected to each other. Moreover, the theme of metamorphosis, which is present in each and every unit of Ovid's poem, operates similarly to the protagonistic character of Dionysus in Nonnus' epic, as catalyst that guarantees narrative coherence and smooth transition from one unit to the next.[1] And yet, the question of Nonnus' direct engagement with Ovid remains fraught with difficulties. Although convincing arguments regarding parallels and literary relationships between the two works have been put forward,[2] most scholars are still reluctant to make a positive statement on Nonnus' direct engagement with the Latin model. This reluctance or hesitation is well encapsulated in a note by Adrian Hollis, where he states that he is 'inclined to think that Nonnus did not read the *Metamorphoses*', but acknowledges 'an undeniable community of spirit between the two

---

[1] Philip Hardie in Chapter 12 of this volume offers a stimulating comparative study of the metamorphosis theme in Ovid and Nonnus.

[2] Critics arguing for Nonnus' direct engagement with Ovid include Braune (1935), D'Ippolito (1964), and Diggle (1970: 180–200); cf. Vian (1976: xlvi–xlvii). The case against direct engagement has been set out in detail in Knox (1988). The issue, as a whole, was revisited more recently by Paschalis (2014), who does not favour Nonnus' direct engagement with Ovid, but introduces his comparative reading of the myth of Actaeon in Ovid and Nonnus from a frank starting point: 'The parallel study of Ovid and Nonnus, independently of *Quellenforschung* and intertextual relations, would in my view prove more useful. It would shift attention to a more substantial comparison of Ovidian and Nonnian narratives and poetics in areas where there is common ground' (Paschalis 2014: 97).

poems' possibly owed to 'a similar temperament and a liking for the same kinds of Hellenistic poetry'.[3]

Hollis pinpoints the most important argument commonly raised against Nonnus' direct engagement with Ovid: it is indeed probable that both Ovid and Nonnus may be drawing on (now lost) Hellenistic works; although this argument cannot be countered, it does not rule out Ovidian influence *in addition to* Hellenistic (or other) influences. Throughout the Imperial period and into the Late Antiquity and beyond, Ovid's poetry was important among, and had certainly left a clear mark upon, poets composing within the Latin side of the tradition: in the fifth century, Rutilius Namatianus' *De Reditu* recounts his own journey from Rome to southern Gaul in 417 CE as a journey into exile recalling Ovid's exile poetry, and Dracontius' elegiac *Satisfactio*, in which he asks the Vandal king for forgiveness, echoes Ovid's plight and draws on the latter's works,[4] while St. Orientius' *Commonitorium* and, in the sixth century, Venantius Fortunatus' elegy *De Virginitate* are examples of Ovidian elegy used as a vehicle to convey Christian values.[5]

In the Greek side of the tradition, evidence from bilingual papyri marks Vergil's *Aeneid* as the most widely circulated literary text in Egypt between the fourth and sixth centuries;[6] yet there is evidence that Ovid, too, was read and appreciated by Greek-speaking readers in the early sixth century CE. As Fisher puts it, for John the Lydian at the first part of the sixth century, Ovid was a name familiar to a Greek readership aware of Latin *auctores*, and John himself referred to the Janus episode of *Fasti* 1.[7] Moreover, at the turn of the fourth to the fifth century, Nonnus' near-contemporary Claudian is an example of a poet born in Alexandria who subsequently moved to Rome and was well versed in both Greek and Latin, with fragments of his Greek *Gigantomachia* surviving alongside a Latin mythological epic (*De Raptu Proserpinae*), Latin verse panegyrics, and other compositions. Claudian is a bilingual and versatile author, and a particularly interesting case has been made for his reception of the 'apparent dissonance' between encomium and love poetry that resurfaces in

[3] Hollis (1994: 60 n. 16).
[4] Fielding (2014: 101–4 on Rutilius Namatianus' *De Reditu*; 104 on Dracontius' *Satisfactio*), with further bibliography.
[5] Fielding (2014: 106–7).
[6] Cf. Schubert (2013). It is worth noting that these translations were intended more as a crib to help readers understand the Latin language rather than to allow them to engage with the literary qualities of the text.
[7] Fisher (2011: 30–1). Yet in the same article, Fisher (2011: 29) believes that Nonnus did not know Ovid.

Ovid's *Ars Amatoria* 1.213ff, where Ovid depicts the triumphant return of Gaius Caesar, Augustus' adopted son, from the expedition against the Parthians and draws attention to the girls' admiration of, and questions about, the military exploits of the prince.[8] In celebrating the emperor Honorius' sixth consulship, Claudian describes the women of Rome gazing at the handsome emperor in his procession through the city and asking relevant questions (*VI Cons. Hon.* 560–74).[9]

There is, then, some evidence that Ovid was read by Greek-speaking authors and that there were bilingual poets in the period when Nonnus flourished. The fact that this evidence is scanty could potentially suggest that it points to the exception rather than the rule, and, therefore, to postulate direct engagement between a Greek-speaking author from the fifth century and an Augustan Latin poet on the basis of similarities or echoes may still seem tenuous, especially when considering that only a small portion of the wider tradition survives.[10] Furthermore, the affirmation of conscious intertextuality is a greater challenge in the cases of cross-linguistic literary interactions. Yet, when discussing Nonnus' version of a myth against other versions of the same myth in the literary tradition, to focus on one particular version from the epic tradition – even if that version comes from the Latin epic tradition, as we propose to do in the following discussion – does not amount to ignoring the rest of the literary tradition, but rather highlights points of contact that are too important to bypass.

In the first part of this chapter, we shall compare and contrast the dynamics within an extended song contest in Ovid's *Metamorphoses* 5 with the dynamics within a song contest in Nonnus' *Dionysiaca* 19. This Ovidian song contest relates in some detail an obscure myth that is referred to in Nonnus' Typhonomachy in *Dionysiaca* 1, so in the second part of this chapter, we shall turn to this Typhonomachy and focus upon the representation of the trickster Cadmus and his deception of Typhon in *Dionysiaca* 1. It will be argued that, for this representation, Nonnus' Cadmus is informed by Ovidian intertext, for several aspects of his conduct are justified only in light of the *Metamorphoses* narrative, while additional associations between Nonnus and Ovid can be identified in the

---

[8] Dewar (2002: 407–12). For this 'apparent dissonance' cf. Dewar (2002: 409).
[9] Dewar (2002: 409–10).
[10] Cf., for example, the conclusion drawn by Barchiesi (2005: 231): 'Allo stato attuale della discussione si può dire che Nonno è una fonte indipendente, non condizionata da Ovidio, e neppure risalente a un modello comune. Le somiglianze tra i due poeti vanno quindi interpretate nel quadro di una tradizione più vasta e complessa.'

narrative context of Cadmus' performance. It is thus hoped that this study may shed some new light upon scenes in Nonnus' *Dionysiaca* and invite further thought on reading later Greek poetry together with the Latin literary tradition.

1.1   The Song Contests in Ovid's *Metamorphoses* 5 and Nonnus' *Dionysiaca* 19

Let us take as our starting point two mythological narratives that feature as part of a song contest in Ovid's *Metamorphoses* 5.[11] A Muse reports to Minerva a song contest between Pierus' daughters and Calliope.[12] The description of the contest in battle-echoing vocabulary – the contest is for the Muse a 'battle of voices' (*proelia voce, Met.* 5.307) – reflects the subject of both songs.[13] The first (and shortest: 5.318–31) of the two songs is that of Pierus' daughters and deals with an episode from the Typhonomachy, which, typically for Ovid, is not a canonical part of this core theogonic legend, but an episode fitting for the Ovidian peritext: the daughters of Pierus sing of Typhon's routing of the Olympian gods, who, in an effort to rescue themselves, alter their forms assuming the 'pretend shapes' (*mentitis ... figuris*, 5.326) of animals and hide in Egypt. Unlike the Pierides' song, which is treated in a perfunctory 13 lines (first in indirect and then in direct speech: 5.319–31, cited in Section 1.2 below), the second song by Calliope is reproduced in full and takes up the next 333 lines (5.346–678). This is an account of Proserpina's rape by Dis and Demeter's search for her lost daughter. Its most complex narrative structure aside, the song of Calliope begins with the orthodox version of the Typhonomachy, according to which Typhon lost the Gigantomachy against the Olympians: *vasta Giganteis ingesta est insula membris | Trinacris et magnis subiectum molibus urget | aetherias ausum sperare Typhoea sedes* ('The huge island of Sicily had been heaped upon the body of the giant, and with its vast weight was resting on Typhoeus, who had dared to aspire to the heights of heaven,' *Met.* 5.346–8). Calliope's song thus begins by

---

[11]   In what follows, all English translations of Nonnus, Ovid, and Vergil are from the Loeb series by Rouse (1940), with slight adaptations, Miller and Goold (1984), and Fairclough and Goold (1999), respectively.

[12]   According to Ant. Lib. 9, this story was also related in Nicander's *Heteroeumena*. For two recent discussions of the Muse's retelling of this song contest to Minerva in Ovid's *Met.* 5 cf. Barchiesi (2002: 187–95, focussing on Ovid's narrative technique) and, more recently, Ziogas (2013: 88–94, from the perspective of the Muses in Hesiod's *Theogony*).

[13]   On the Hellenistic models for Ovid's account of the song contest cf. Hinds (1987: 14–15); cf. also Hinds (1987: 55), on Ant. Lib. 9 (report of Nicander).

applying the missing conclusion to the song of Pierus' daughters: she tells of Typhon's ultimate defeat by the gods and his punishment/imprisonment under Etna, where his unquenched frenzy explains why the landscape of Sicily is prone to volcanic eruptions and earthquakes (5.346–58).[14] The song of Calliope, then, starts by addressing Minerva's own preferences – she is, after all, the addressee of the story of the song contest – for traditional orthodoxy (Typhon's defeat) and punishment of arrogance, as it also becomes clear later on in the weaving competition between Arachne and Minerva herself in *Metamorphoses* 6.[15]

The setting of a song contest in the presence of a deity, the juxtaposition within that contest between a longer song and a shorter one, and the choice of Demeter's search for her daughter by at least one of the two contestants are features also shared with the contest organised by Dionysus in Nonnus' *Dionysiaca* 19 as part of the funeral games for the dead Staphylus, king of Assyria. The contest there is held between Erechtheus of Cecropia (i.e. Athens) and Oeagrus, who is Orpheus' father and Calliope's husband (*Dion.* 19.101; cf. *Dion.* 13.428–31). Erechtheus' song, like that of Calliope in *Metamorphoses* 5, is inspired by the myth of Demeter and Persephone (19.80–99), but aims to draw a parallel with the circumstances in the surrounding narrative: just as, in Athens, Celeus and his wife and son offered Demeter hospitality (ὡς Κελεὸς **ξείνισσε** βίου παμμήτορα Δηώ, 19.83) and the goddess subsequently gave them the corn (καί σφισι καρπὸν **ὄπασσεν**, 19.85), and, when Celeus died, offered words of consolation to his widow and son (παρηγορέουσα πάλιν θελξίφρονι μύθῳ, 19.89), so, too, Staphylus had offered Dionysus hospitality (οὕτω καὶ Διόνυσον ἑῷ **ξείνισσε** μελάθρῳ, 19.91) and the god gave his Bacchic gifts and the fruit of the vine in return (**ὤπασεν** εὔια δῶρα καὶ ἀμπελόεσσαν ὀπώρην, 19.93), and, when Staphylus died, lulled the sorrows of his widow and son.[16]

The detail that Demeter offered words of consolation to Celeus' bereaved family, which is not found elsewhere in the tradition, must be an innovation to correspond to Dionysus' relationship with Staphylus'

---

[14] Cf. Ziogas (2013: 87, n. 109): 'She [Calliope] also implicitly responds to the Pierid, who praised Typhoeus, but does not include his final defeat in her song.'

[15] Cf. Hill (1992: 153).

[16] That Demeter offered consolation with words (θελξίφρονι μύθῳ, *Dion.* 19.89) is not easy to interpret and finds no correspondence to the parallel drawn with Dionysus' consoling Botrys and Methe. Gerbeau and Vian (1992: 82) suggest that, although the text is allusive, it seems that Demeter teaches her host mysteries to comfort them just as Dionysus initiated Methe and her son to his own cult.

bereaved family members.[17] Yet there are further divergences from the traditional version of the myth adopted in the *Homeric hymn to Demeter* (and in *Met.* 5): the child is named Triptolemus (as in the version in Ov. *Fasti* 4.417–620: cf. *Fasti* 4.550), whereas he is Demophon in the *Homeric hymn to Demeter* (and in *Met.* 5),[18] with Triptolemus being one of the leading men of Eleusis (*Hom. hymn Dem.* 153–6).[19] Moreover, Nonnus' Athenian Erechtheus places Celeus in Athens, rather than in Eleusis, as he is known in the tradition from the *Homeric hymn to Demeter* onwards.[20]

More importantly for our purposes here, Nonnus' version is also markedly different from that of Ovid. In fact, there is hardly any overlap between the content of the accounts given by Calliope and Erechtheus (in the Ovidian and the Nonnian song contests, respectively) concerning Demeter's search for her daughter: Erechtheus' focus on the hospitality extended to the grieving Demeter is a point that, although important in the narrative of the *Homeric hymn to Demeter*, is only marginal in Calliope's extended version in *Metamorphoses* 5, where Demeter's hostess is an unnamed old woman, whose gesture to offer food to the goddess is condensed in two verses (*at inde | prodit anus divamque videt lymphamque roganti | dulce dedit, tosta quod texerat ante polenta*, 'Then out came an old woman and beheld the goddess, and when she asked for water gave her a sweet drink with parched barley floating upon it,' 5.448–50), and the focus then falls on the disrespectful behaviour shown to Demeter by a boy, whom the goddess transforms into a lizard (5.451–61).[21] Moreover, whereas Calliope had begun her song with a 'list of ἀρεταί linked by anaphora'[22] focussing on Ceres and her gifts, and culminating in the acknowledgement that *Cereris sunt omnia munus. | illa canenda mihi est* (5.343–4), Erechtheus' song is divided into two parts, with the first (slightly longer) part

[17] Gerbeau and Vian (1992: 81–2) also record the possibility that the poet may be preserving a local tradition.

[18] Cf. Richardson (1974: 236–7; n. on *Hom. hymn Dem.* 234), on Demophon's name.

[19] Cf. Richardson (1974: 194–6; n. on *Hom. hymn Dem.* 153), on the growing significance of Triptolemus and his association with Athens from an early stage in the tradition.

[20] It is relevant to note (with Barchiesi 2002: 193) that in the Ovidian version of Demeter's story offered within the song contest the Muse makes it clear that Athens is Pallas' city from the very start: '[Ceres] directed her light chariot to the city of Pallas' (*Tritonida . . . in urbem*, 5.645), and it is in Athens that Ceres meets Triptolemus. Cf. Barchiesi op. cit.: 'We can thus make a case that Pallas has a vested interest in the story she listens to, and that traces of her presence are visible in the narrative.'

[21] This incident (also reported in Ant. Lib. 24) seems to derive from Nicander's *Heteroeumena*: cf. Hinds (1987: 54–5 and 85) and Celoria (1992: 169–70). Cf. also Nic. *Ther.* 483–7 on Demeter and the gecko (ἀσκάλαβος: cf. the boy's name Ascalaphus in the Ovidian version) with Gow and Scholfield (1953: 179–80, n. on *Ther.* 483ff).

[22] Hinds (1987: 98).

(*Dion.* 19.82^b–90) outlining Demeter's relationship with Celeus' family, and the second part (19.91–6) making the connection with Dionysus' relationship to Staphylus' family in the narrative surrounding the song contest. For Erechtheus, then, this is not a song about Demeter alone; it is a song about Dionysus, who is being made Demeter's counterpart.[23]

As the second contestant in the *agon* in *Dionysiaca* 19, Oeagrus sings a very brief song (*Dion.* 19.102–3, δίστιχον ἁρμονίην ἀνεβάλλετο Φοιβάδι μολπῇ, | ταυροεπής, λιγύμυθος, Ἀμυκλαίῳ τινὶ θεσμῷ, 'Only a couple of verses he sang, a simple song of Phoebus, clearly spoken in few words after some Amyclaean style'),[24] which juxtaposes Apollo and Hyacinthus to Dionysus and Staphylus (19.104–5):

Εὐχαίτην Ὑάκινθον ἀνεζώγρησεν Ἀπόλλων,
καὶ Στάφυλον Διόνυσος ἀεὶ ζώοντα τελέσσει.

Apollo brought to life again his long-haired Hyacinthus: Staphylus
will be made to live forever by Dionysus.

Like Erechtheus' song, this one also pivots about a well-known story, which is that of the unfortunate death of Apollo's young *eromenos* and Hyacinthus' transformation into a flower with letters that mark the god's lament (*Al Al*) inscribed upon its petals.[25] Yet Oeagrus has added a twist that is not attested elsewhere in the mythological tradition, namely, that Apollo will resurrect Hyacinthus just as Dionysus (in the narrative context) will make Staphylus live forever. In both contests, a third party – the Nymphs in *Metamorphoses* 5 and the audience in *Dionysiaca* 19 – *unanimously* proclaims as winners of the contest Calliope and Oeagrus, respectively: *at Nymphae vicisse deas Helicona colentes* | **concordi** *dixere* **sono** ('Then the nymphs with one voice agreed that the goddesses of Helicon had won,' *Met.* 5.663–4); ἐπεφθέγξαντο δὲ λαοὶ | εὐφήμοις ἐπέεσσιν **ὁμογλώσσων ἀπὸ λαιμῶν** ('The people broke out into loud acclamations of propitious words with one voice and one tongue,' *Dion.* 19.106–7).

In each of the two songs dealing with familiar myths, a new twist has been added, which aims to bring the situation closer to that in the narrative context and the presiding god, Dionysus, as he is first aligned to Demeter and then compared to Apollo. The fact that the audience

---

[23] For complementary sides of Dionysus and Demeter, cf. Gerbeau and Vian (1992: 82–4).

[24] Gerbeau and Vian (1992: 84–5): 'Non sans humour, le prolixe Nonnos remplace ici ce chant par un simple distique, une de ces épigrammes dont il aime parsemer son poème. C'est pour lui l'occasion de célébrer le proverbial "laconisme" des habitants de Sparte.'

[25] Apollo's grief following the death of his *eromenos* is frequently paralleled in the *Dionysiaca* with that of Dionysus for the death of Ampelus (e.g. *Dion.* 11.329–30).

proclaims Oeagrus to be victorious gives more weight to Dionysus' victory over death in the latter poem, for he makes Staphylus immortal, than to his consolatory approach in the first poem, where he had been made counterpart to Demeter. Moreover, as Gerbeau and Vian point out, even within Oeagrus' distich a covert *syncrisis* is drawn between Apollo, who makes Hyacinthus live again (ἀνεζώγρησεν), and Dionysus, who confers immortality to Staphylus (ἀεὶ ζώοντα τελέσσει).[26] Therefore, through these particular accounts in the song contest and the verdict of the audience, Dionysus is distanced from, and even emerges as superior to, both Demeter and Apollo.[27] Oeagrus' song, then, takes Dionysus' dealing with mortal deaths a step further than Erechtheus' song had suggested, just as Calliope's song corrected the Typhonomachy as it had been represented by Pierus' daughters. It seems, then, that both the Ovidian and the Nonnian song contests contain competing songs, which are, at the same time, complementing each other in a narrative that is being unravelled before, and made relevant to, the judges and the presiding deity.[28]

1.2   The Song Contest in Ovid's *Metamorphoses* 5 and Nonnus' Typhonomachy in *Dionysiaca* 1–2

Beyond the composition of the song contest in *Dionysiaca* 19, the Ovidian song contest in *Metamorphoses* 5 may have further inspired Nonnus elsewhere in the *Dionysiaca* too. The subject matter of the song of Pierus' daughters – namely, the flight of the gods during the Typhonomachy – is mentioned at the start of the *Dionysiaca* to describe the dramatic circumstances at the moment when Cadmus enters the narrative in search of his abducted sister Europa (*Dion.* 1.140–5):

> Ἦλθε καὶ εἰς Ἀρίμων φόνιον σπέος, εὖτε κολῶναι   140
> φοιτάδες ἀρρήκτοιο πύλας ἤρασσον Ὀλύμπου,
> εὖτε θεοὶ πτερόεντες ἀχείμονος ὑψόθι Νείλου
> ὀρνίθων ἀκίχητον ἐμιμήσαντο πορείην
> ἠερίῳ ξένον ἴχνος ἐρετμώσαντες ἀήτῃ,
> καὶ πόλος ἑπτάζωνος ἱμάσσετο.   145

---

[26] Gerbeau and Vian (1992: 85).
[27] Cf. Otlewska-Jung (2014: 93): 'Clearly, Oeagrus' song wins not because of its poetic superiority, but because of its content and prophetic meaning: Staphylus indeed came back to eternal life as his name means "cluster of grapes". Moreover, in the two lines the god Dionysus is portrayed as winning against Apollo, the very god of music.'
[28] Cf. Zissos (1999) on Calliope structuring her song to please the Nymphs, judges of the song contest, and Hinds (1987: 128–33; with n. 25, p. 164), on listeners/judges within the text.

He came to the bloodstained cave of Arima, when the mountains had moved
from their seats and were beating at the gate of inexpugnable Olympus,
when the gods took wing above the rainless Nile, like a flight of birds far
out of reach, oaring their strange track in the winds of heaven, and the
seven zones of the sky were sore assailed.

The *Dionysiaca* opens with an illustration of the interfusion of genres that
underscores the whole epic.[29] Archaic epic intersects with Hellenistic
epyllion: Nonnus, like Ovid, introduces his work with a narrative that
draws primarily upon the theogonic tradition, specifically the
Titanomachy/Typhonomachy; yet there are also the heroic founder's
tradition, in the journey of Cadmus in search of his sister Europa, which
ends with a homecoming (the foundation of Thebes), and the epyllion
tradition, in the recollection of the story of Europa's rape and its best-
known Hellenistic version, Moschus' *Europa*.[30] These two storylines inter-
sect when Zeus, protagonist of the Typhonomachy, asks Cadmus to dress
up as a conventional pastoral figure – appropriate ambience, pipes and all –
to attract Typhon's attention with the music of his pipes, and distract him
with Eros' help, thus allowing Zeus to creep into the cave where the
thunderbolts are hidden (*Dion.* 1.387–407). The inspiration for this genre
intercrossing may be found, as we shall see, in Ovid's *Metamorphoses*.

Cadmus' journey takes place during the Typhonomachy at the time
when mountains had moved and the Olympian gods fled from their seats
in the shapes of birds, while the conclusion of the Typhonomachy at the
end of *Dionysiaca* 2 is signalled with the return of the Olympian gods back
to Olympus in their own true form: παλιννόστῳ δ' ἐνὶ μορφῇ | σὺν Διὶ
νικήσαντι θεοὶ νόστησαν Ὀλύμπῳ, | καὶ πτερόεν μίμημα μετηλλάξαντο
προσώπου ('With Zeus victorious, the other gods came home to
Olympus, in their own form came again, for they put off the winged
shapes which they had taken on,' *Dion.* 2.705–7).[31] When the hero enters

[29] For 'the play of genres' in Nonnus' epic cf. now Lasek (2016). On developments in poetic genre in
Late Antiquity, see Helen Kaufmann (Chapter 5 in this volume, especially pp. 108–9, for an
example from Nonnus' *Dion.*).
[30] Vian (1976 *passim*) records verbal echoes between Nonnus and Moschus; as Whitby (1994: 131
n. 11) notes, there is no extant treatment in Greek verse between these two poets.
[31] The flight of the gods is also included in Cadmus' deceptive song that he will later on sing to
Typhon: *Dion.* 1.521–4, θελγομένῳ δὲ Γίγαντι νόθος παρεσύρισε ποιμήν | **ἀθανάτων ἅτε φύζαν**
ἑῇ σύριγγι λιγαίνων, | καὶ Διὸς ἐσσομένην ἐμελίζετο γείτονα νίκην | ἑζομένῳ Τυφῶνι μόρον
Τυφῶνος ἀείδων ('The Giant was bewitched, while the false shepherd whistled by his side, as if
sounding the rout of the immortals with his pipes; but he was celebrating the imminent victory of
Zeus, and singing the fate of Typhon to Typhon sitting by his side').

the narrative at *Dionysiaca* 1.138, no indication is given that the Typhonomachy has already broken out and that it has reached a critical moment, as the Olympians' prospects look dismal. Typhon has already stolen Zeus' thunderbolts and sinews (1.154–5) and left the great god helpless, who is now armed only with his aegis, as he later on admits to Cadmus (1.381). The detail about the timing in this narrative – when the gods took wings and imitated the path of birds to fly away – may have belonged to a (now lost) Hellenistic text, but survives in the song of Pierus' daughters in Ovid's epic, which was mentioned at the start of this chapter (cf. Section 1.1 above). The leading sister from among Pierus' daughters pronounces this song, which is here set out in full (*Met.* 5.319–31):

> Bella canit superum falsoque in honore Gigantas
> ponit et extenuat magnorum facta deorum;   320
> emissumque ima de sede Typhoea terrae
> caelitibus fecisse metum cunctosque dedisse
> terga fugae, donec fessos Aegyptia tellus
> ceperit et septem discretus in ostia Nilus.
> huc quoque terrigenam venisse Typhoea narrat   325
> et se mentitis superos celasse figuris;
> 'dux' que 'gregis' dixit 'fit Iuppiter: unde recurvis
> nunc quoque formatus Libys est cum cornibus Ammon;
> Delius in corvo, proles Semeleia capro,
> fele soror Phoebi, nivea Saturnia vacca,   330
> pisce Venus latuit, Cyllenius ibidis alis.'

> She sang of the battle of the gods and giants, ascribing undeserved honour to the giants, and belittling the deeds of the mighty gods: how Typhoeus, sprung from the lowest depths of earth, inspired the heavenly gods with fear, and how they all turned their backs and fled, until, weary, they found refuge in the land of Egypt and the seven-mouthed Nile. How even there Typhoeus, son of earth, pursued them, and the gods hid themselves in lying shapes: 'Jove thus became a ram,' said she, 'the lord of flocks, whence Libyan Ammon even to this day is represented with curving horns; Apollo hid in a crow's shape, Bacchus in a goat; the sister of Phoebus, in a cat, Juno in a snow-white cow, Venus in a fish, Mercury in an ibis bird.'

Ovid's daughters of Pierus produce the only full version of this little-known episode of the flight of the gods from Olympus to Egypt, after transforming/disguising themselves into animals to escape Typhon.[32] In the extant narratives of the Typhonomachy, the flight of the gods in

---

[32] Cf. Griffiths (1960) for ancient sources for this story.

disguise, is absent: in Hesiod's account, Zeus' victory is swift; the conflict between the great god and Typhon both begins and concludes soon after the monster issues a challenge, and it is described in a mere five lines (*Theog.* 853–8), while Hyginus (*Fab.* 152.1) follows precisely the Hesiodic narrative.[33] The transformation and flight of the gods may have been included in the now-lost versions of Pindar and Nicander: Pindar's fragmentary *Prosodia* (fr. 91 Snell-Maehler)[34] likely mentions *in passim* the transformation of the gods as part of the battle with Typhon.[35] The account in Nicander's *Heteroeumena* (summarised in *Ant. Lib.* 28) offers the only other detailed version of the particular story prior to Ovid; notably, in Nicander's version neither Athena nor Zeus is among those gods who flee in panic.[36] In the Ovidian Pierides' reported account, however, the brief catalogue of the forms that the gods adopt is given in direct speech: Zeus himself is transformed into a ram and this transformation also receives a learned aetiology, for it explains why the Egyptian god Ammon is represented as a ram in Egyptian iconography,[37] and it thus becomes the most memorable of all divine transformations in this humiliating moment of the Olympians' career.

Nonnus' narrative, however, as if to understate the Ovidian connection, marginalises the cosmogonic earthquake that forced the Olympians to abandon their seats, transform themselves into animals, and flee (*Met.* 5.321–4), and emphasises instead the other consequences of the Typhonomachy, namely, the transposition of the mountains and the seven zones of the sky, for which he hastens to produce an explanation and thus assume a *detailed* Typhonomachy narrative. Furthermore, this thoroughly revised Typhonomachy is related, in Nonnus' narrative, from the start: the epic battle between Typhon and the gods begins when Zeus, seized by erotic passion for Plouto, left his thunderbolts out of guard – only to be stolen by Typhon (*Dion.* 1.145–62).[38] Plouto is mentioned in several later sources (including Hyginus, Anoninus Liberalis, Pausanias) as the mother

---

[33] On Typhon (Typhoeus) in Hesiod's *Theogony* and in the early literary tradition, cf. West (1966: 379–83).

[34] On the fragments of Pindar's *Prosodia*, cf. D'Alessio (1997: 39–40), on fr. 91, which mentions the animal transformation of Zeus during Typhon's attack. D'Alessio (1997: 40 n. 104), draws attention to the argument in Griffiths 1960 that, as D'Alessio *op. cit.* puts it, 'this *interpetatio graeca* of an Egyptian myth would not be unconceivable in the fifth century'.

[35] For a discussion of the gods' flight to Egypt cf. Vian (1976: 30–1).

[36] Moreover, as Gigli Piccardi (2003: 140–1) notes, in Nonnus' narrative the gods are transformed only into birds and not (as in Ant. Lib. 28) into other animals.

[37] *Unde recurvis | nunc quoque formatus Libys est cum cornibus Ammon* (*Met.* 5.327–8).

[38] Cf. Shorrock (2001: 35–6, with n. 34), on the juxtaposition of the stories of Europa and Typhon. Cf. also Kokorea (2014: 9–21), for Eros in the Typhonomachy.

of Tantalus by Zeus, but Nonnus is the only extant source that devotes some detail to Zeus' affair with Plouto, and which associates her seduction with the theft of his thunderbolts by Typhon.

Just as Nonnus undercut in *his* Typhonomachy the Ovidian flight of the Olympians, so too he undercuts Typhon's power when he makes him lack the proper skill to handle the thunderbolts effectively (*Dion.* 1.294–320); as soon as the thunderbolts realise that they have a different master, they lose their strength and refuse to obey (1.305–20). Meanwhile, Typhon has managed to wage war against all cosmic forces, planets, and constellations. These details in the narrative readily evoke the story of Phaethon as reported in Ovid's *Metamorphoses* 2.1–398, who causes his own version of a cosmogony, when he nearly destroys the universe upon losing control of the Sun's chariot. Like the thunderbolt of Zeus in the hands of Typhon, the horses of the Sun's chariot refuse to obey Phaethon's orders once they realise that he is not their master.

1.2.1   Typhon, Cadmus, and the Pastoral Context

The proximity between Ovid and Nonnus may be suggestive in these instances, but the ties acquire new meaning when seen in the context of Cadmus' successful deception of Typhon, an episode that seems modelled, as it will be presently argued, on Ovid's *Metamorphoses*, which also accounts for Zeus' suggestion that Cadmus face Typhon in the guise of a pastoral singer to bewitch the monster, thus allowing Zeus to reclaim his thunderbolts.[39]

Zeus (and Nonnus, who voices Zeus' anxieties here) is not particularly interested in specifying the pastoral type for Cadmus. As Harries has pointed out, there is '[a]n imprecision in poetic vocabulary' when Cadmus is termed interchangeably νομεύς, ποιμήν, αἰπόλος, βουκόλος, βοτήρ, and βούτης; moreover, Cadmus' musical instrument varies, as he handles, or is given to handle, a σῦριγξ, the πηκτίς, αὐλός, δόναξ or δόνακες, and the κάλαμοι, which obviously are not the same instruments.[40] The accumulation of all these terms carries a metapoetic

---

[39] Cadmus had also featured in the version of the Typhonomachy by Peisander of Laranda: Bezantakos (2015: 46, with n. 1), Vian (1976: xliv, 26–9).
[40] Cf. Harries (1994: 66), where he notes all those variant definitions of Cadmus' pastoral identity and his skillful playing of a variety of different musical instruments. Harries' discussion of the Cadmus episode (1994: 65–9) has bolstered crucially the present argument, as he argues for a modelling of Cadmus on the singing shepherds of Theocritus and, by association, substantiates the hero's metapoetical identity. For another reading of this episode cf. now Lasek (2016: 406–12, esp. 412): 'By invoking a whole arsenal of bucolic motifs and using exceptionally inexact

meaning, for it purports to evoke intertexts in the Hellenistic tradition where pastoral music is employed to enchant. For instance, as Harries, again, helpfully notes, in Theocritus we have several of those contexts: in *Idyll* 6 'the σῦριγξ-playing of the βούτης Daphnis makes the calves prance on the meadow' (6.43–5), and in *Id.* 20.28–31 'the playing of a βουκόλος on σῦριγξ, αὐλός or δόναξ makes the girls rush up to kiss him'.[41] As another example for this power of pastoral music coming from any available instrument Harries offers the following epigram attributed to Theocritus (5.1–4 = *HE* 3492–5 G-P):

> Λῆς ποτὶ τᾶν Νυμφᾶν διδύμοις αὐλοῖσιν ἀεῖσαι
>   ἁδύ τί μοι; κἠγὼ πακτίδ' ἀειράμενος
> ἀρξεῦμαί τι κρέκειν, ὁ δὲ βουκόλος ἄμμιγα θέλξει
>   Δάφνις κηροδέτῳ πνεύματι μελπόμενος.

> Will you, by the Nymphs, sing for me sweet music on the double pipes, and I will lift my lyre and strike up with you, while Daphnis, the cowherd, joins in and charms us with the breath of his wax-bound reeds?[42]

Different musical instruments are deployed here by a shepherd in a single instance for the single purpose that Cadmus is directed to fulfil, namely, to 'enchant' or 'bewitch' (θέλξει) his audience.[43]

As Harries notes, Nonnus toys here with the motif of the shepherd/enchanter known from the Hellenistic pastoral.[44] The 'imprecise vocabulary' that describes Cadmus' pastoral status is deliberate and means to overwhelm his audience: Cadmus should evoke every type of Hellenistic pastor who employs his music (on all possibly mentioned instruments) for enchanting purposes, with the obvious goal being to overwhelm Typhon with a massive attack of bewitching 'pastoralness'. Indeed, by wearing (any) shepherd's costume, Cadmus is automatically transformed into a pastoral singer, for literary *pastores* are typically gifted singers as well, endowed with the power of θέλξις.[45] In this new costume, Cadmus is instructed to enchant the mind of Typhon with the evil-repelling song of his witty syrinx: κερδαλέης σύριγγος ἀλεξικάκῳ σέο μολπῇ | θέλγε νόον Τυφῶνος (*Dion.* 1.394–5). A little later his pastoral music is to be his 'charmed shot' (θελγόμενον ... | ... βέλος, 1.404–5), creating 'madness from the mind-bewitching tune of Cadmus' (Καδμείης ... φρενοθελγέος

---

language (...), he [Nonnus] distracts the readers and lulls them into a false sense of security, allowing them to forget for a while that the fight for the destiny of the universe is raging on.'
[41] Harries (1994: 67).   [42] Translation by Gow (1952: 243), slightly adapted.
[43] Harries (1994: 67).   [44] Harries (1994: 67).
[45] Braden (1974: 868), renders this term as 'hypnosis'.

οἶστρον ἀοιδῆς, 1.406). As expected, a hundred or so lines later, Typhon is, indeed, totally bewitched: ὣς ὅ γε Κάδμῳ | θελγομένην μελέεσσιν ὅλην φρένα δῶκε Τυφωεύς (*Dion.* 1.533–4; cf. θελγομένῳ ... Γίγαντι, 1.521).[46]

And yet, the purpose of Cadmus' disguise is not only to enchant Typhon, but also to deceive him. Zeus devises with Cadmus a plan to overcome Typhon and, together with Pan, disguises/transforms Cadmus into a pastoral singer (*Dion.* 1.368–75): Pan builds a hut out of reed (πλέξας δ' ἐκ καλάμων καλύβην, 1.370), dresses Cadmus in shepherds' clothes (ποιμενίην ἐσθῆτα καθαψάμενος χροῒ Κάδμου, 1.372), and gives him 'deceiving pan-pipes' (καὶ δολίην σύριγγα φέρων εἰδήμονι Κάδμῳ, 1.374).[47] The shepherds of the pastoral tradition enchant but do not deceive, and the pastoral world identifies with innocence.[48] Deception is a motif associated more with narrative and the epic genre,[49] and, in our context, Nonnus' Cadmus has been inspired by the deception strategy of an epic shepherd in disguise, namely, Ovid's Mercury.[50]

1.2.2   Nonnus' Cadmus and Ovid's Mercury

In *Metamorphoses* 1.668–723, Mercury takes the form of a shepherd under very similar circumstances: he is sent by Jupiter to liberate Io who is guarded by the hundred-eyed monster Argus.[51] The situation of Mercury and Argus is strikingly similar to that of Cadmus and Typhon:

---

[46] Harries (1994: 67–8). Cf. also Shorrock (2001: 125–7), on the metapoetic associations invested in Cadmus the singer.

[47] On the importance of the disguised Cadmus and Typhon's penchant for music in Nonnus' Typhonomachy, cf. Bezantakos (2015: 99): 'Τὸ σπουδαιότερο στοιχεῖο στὴν παραλλαγὴ τοῦ Νόννου εἶναι ἀφ' ἑνὸς ἡ ὕπαρξη τοῦ Κάδμου, ὁ ὁποῖος, μεταμφιεσμένος σὲ ποιμένα καὶ παίζοντας τὴν σύριγγα, συμβάλλει ἀποφασιστικὰ στὴν νίκη τοῦ Διός, καὶ ἀφ' ἑτέρου ἡ εὐαισθησία τοῦ Τυφῶνος στὴν μουσικὴ (415 Γίγας φιλάοιδος), ἡ ὁποία τελικῶς τὸν ὁδηγεῖ στὴν καταστροφή.' On the emphasis on Cadmus' deception, cf. Bezantakos (2015: 212; n. on *Dion.* 1.410–14).

[48] Harries (1994: 67), summarily pairs δόλος and θέλξις: 'And to what end? The aims are defined clearly enough: δόλος and θέλξις, deception and enchantment.'

[49] However, cf. Gutzwiller (2006: 15–16), for the capacity of the *syrinx* both to charm and to delude; cf. Longus *Daphnis and Chloe* 1.27; Bacchylides 19.35–6.

[50] This connection has been tentatively explored by Hardie (2005: 127–8): 'As often, Nonnus' poetic games strike the Ovidian with a beguiling sense of familiarity. The similarity between the story of the fake shepherd's musical enchantment of Typhoeus and the story in *Met.* 1 of the bewitchment of Argos by Mercury disguised as a pastoral musician has been noted by others.' Cf. also Vian (1976: 27, with n. 3: 'La ruse de Cadmos rappelle à certains égards celle dont Hermès s'est servi pour endormir Argos au son de la flûte: la narration d'Ovide présente des analogies avec le récit de Nonnos') who pursues further, however, the links between the motif of an enchanted monster and oriental theologies (Vian 1976: 26–9).

[51] In *Dion.* 1.341–3, when Hera beholds Zeus in the form of a bull, carrying Europa on his back, she wishes Argus were still alive. Hermes' killing of Argus is mentioned in Nonn. *Dion.* 25.25–7 as an example to Dionysus of the toils that other gods had to undergo in order to reach Olympus.

both Argus and Typhon are monstrous creatures (the former has a hun-dred eyes and the latter has numerous hands), and they both guard something that Zeus/Jupiter really wants. Like Cadmus, Mercury changes his guise: he sheds his traditional dress of the winged sandals and hat, so Argus will not recognise him, and puts on the attire of a shepherd (*hac agit ut pastor per devia rura capellas | dum venit abductas et structis cantat avenis*, 'With this, in the character of a shepherd, through the sequestered country paths he drives a flock of goats which he has rustled as he came along, and plays upon his reed pipe as he goes,' *Met.* 1.676–7), in ways that recall pastoral poetry in general and Vergil's *Eclogues* in particular, for, aside from tending to goats, Mercury notably plays the reed flute (*Met.* 1.677, cited above), which is familiar already from Tityrus' performance at *Eclogues* 1.2 (*silvestrem tenui Musam meditaris avena*, 'wooing the woodland Muse on slender reed') and elsewhere in bucolic poetry.[52]

Ovid's Mercury succeeds in putting the hundred-eyed Argus to sleep, not through his sleep-bearing rod (*virgam ... | somniferam, Met.* 1.671–2),[53] but through his narrative of Pan's amatory pursuit of the nymph Syrinx, which ends with the latter's transformation and thus becomes the *aetion* for the panpipes. The amatory pursuit of an innocent female by a lustful god was the very theme of the two tales reported in *Metamorphoses* 1 immediately before this episode (namely, the stories of Daphne and Io),[54] and also of several others to follow in *Metamorphoses* 2 (Callisto and Europa herself, whose rape is the springboard episode for the *Dionysiaca*): repetition is crucial because it is what defines Mercury's pastoral θέλξις.

Nonnus' Cadmus and Ovid's Mercury are, moreover, joined by the fact that their respective performances are self-referential, for both are trickster figures who usurp the role of the poet. Mercury assumes the role of Ovid as he narrates yet another story of a young girl's seduction and metamorpho-sis before the narrator undercuts Mercury's tale to complete the story with what the disguised god *would* have said.[55] Mercury's performance enchants the monstrous Argus and puts him to sleep with variant versions of the

[52] On the bucolic element in this Ovidian episode featuring Mercury and Argus, cf. Barchiesi (2005: 223).
[53] Fredericks (1977: 245), where he further points out that Mercury uses his rod only to deepen Argus' sleep (*Met.* 1.715–16).
[54] Note also that in the archetypal literary model for Nonnus' story of Europa's rape, Moschus' epyllion *Europa*, Io's seduction is the topic of the ekphrasis on Europa's basket.
[55] Cf. Murgatroyd (2001: 621), for a contrast between Mercury's detailed and leisurely style and the livelier narrative given by Ovid after Argus has fallen asleep.

same story of deception and with the music of his pan-pipe (1.689–716); and what is particularly successful is the story of the origin of the pan-pipe, which Argus asks to hear out of curiosity. The poet-singer in this instance is a trickster who sings about his own art to make his listener nod, drop his guard, and betray the charge entrusted to him.

Nonnus' Cadmus is twice paralleled to a traditional poetic figure: Cadmus himself and the power of his song on Typhon are explicitly compared in *Dionysiaca* 2.9–19 to the Sirens and the power of their song on the sailors respectively:[56]

> Ὁ δὲ πλέον ἡδέι κέντρῳ
> ἤθελεν εἰσαΐειν φρενοθελγέα ῥυθμὸν ἀοιδῆς.   10
> ὡς δ᾽ ὅτε τις Σειρῆνος ἐπίκλοπον ὕμνον ἀκούων
> εἰς μόρον αὐτοκέλευστον ἀώριος εἵλκετο ναύτης,
> θελγόμενος μελέεσσι, καὶ οὐκέτι κῦμα χαράσσων
> γλαυκὸν ἀκυμάντοισιν ὕδωρ λεύκαινεν ἐρετμοῖς,
> ἀλλὰ λιγυφθόγγοιο πεσὼν ἐπὶ δίκτυα Μοίρης   15
> τέρπετο πηδαλίοιο λελασμένος, ἄστρον ἐάσσας
> Πλειάδος ἑπταπόροιο καὶ ἄντυγα κυκλάδος Ἄρκτου·
> ὡς ὅ γε κερδαλέης δεδονημένος ἄσθμασι μολπῆς
> πηκτίδος ἡδὺ βέλεμνον ἐδέξατο πομπὸν ὀλέθρου.

But all the Giant wanted was to hear more and more of the mind-bewitching melody with its delicious thrill. When a sailor hears the Siren's perfidious song, and bewitched by the melody, he is dragged to a self-chosen fate too soon; no longer he cleaves the waves, no longer he whitens the blue water with his oars unwetted now, but falling into the net of melodious Fate, he forgets to steer, quite happy, caring not for the seven starry Pleiades and the Bear's circling course: so the monster, shaken by the breath of that deceitful tune, welcomed with delight the wound of the pipes which was his escort to death.

The poetic caliber of the Nonnian Cadmus seems to be matched by that of Typhon, a Γίγας φιλάοιδος (*Dion.* 1.415), for they both feature parallel portrayals as singers who are contestants of the same calibre: παντοίην ἀλάλαζεν **ὁμοφθόγγων** ὄπα θηρῶν (Typhon, 1.157) ~ ὀξὺ δὲ τείνων | Κάδμος **ὁμοφθόγγων** δονάκων ἀπατήλιον ἠχώ (1.409–10).

Moreover, Cadmus is paralleled to a traditional poetic figure within the false story that he devises before Typhon and which he uses to deceive the monster (*Dion.* 1.489–92): he claims that he defeated Apollo with his harp (ἐρίζων |

---

[56] Harries (1994: 68) notes that the vocabulary relevant to θέλγειν distinguishing Cadmus defines also the Homeric Sirens; this enforces the association between their respective songs and underscores the metapoetic possibilities of Cadmus' agonistic performance and conquest of Typhon.

Φοῖβον ἐμῇ φόρμιγγι παρέδραμον, 1.489–90), but that Zeus destroyed his lyre-strings to honour his son, Apollo (1.490–2). In this respect too, the plight of Pierus' daughters in the Ovidian song contest in *Metamorphoses* 5 becomes relevant, as they were punished following their challenge to the Muses by being turned into magpies (*Met.* 5.664–78). The Muses traditionally stand as the guardians of poetic memory, with Calliope offering the canonical ending to the Typhonomachy, whereas Pierus' daughters had given an alternative version of the Typhonomachy that focussed on the flight of the Olympians and their transformation into animals. In this respect, the composition of Pierus' daughters stands as an inversion of the traditional encomium served by a traditional epic reproduction of the same story;[57] in other words, the Pierides seem to imply that the long literary tradition of the Gigantomachy/ Typhonomachy is false, and they corroborate the veracity of their own version by means of an impeccable Egyptian aetiology (*Met.* 5.327–8, cited above).

A comparable intervention in the canonical narrative of the Typhonomachy is feared by the Nonnian Zeus too when, prior to assigning Cadmus the mission to recover his thunderbolts, he expresses his fear that a victory by Typhon will equal a revision of the myths of Greece and, therefore, a dismissal of all earlier literary, indeed textual, versions of the Gigantomachy/ Typhonomachy: δείδια μυθοτόκον πλέον Ἑλλάδα, μή τις Ἀχαιῶν | ὑέτιον Τυφῶνα καὶ ὑψιμέδοντα καλέσσῃ | ἢ ὕπατον, χραίνων ἐμὸν οὔνομα ('I fear Hellas even more, that mother of romances – what if one of that nation call Typhon Lord of Rain, or Highest, and Ruling in the Heights, defiling my name!' *Dion.* 1.385–7). True enough, when Typhon hears the shepherd Cadmus playing his pipes, he initially invites him in a contest, but then asks the disguised shepherd to strike up an 'epinician hymn' (1.488) that would legitimise and canonise his victory over the Olympians – his new version of the Typhonomachy; and the witty Cadmus tells him the deceptive story of another music contest between Apollo and himself (1.489–92). In this deceiving story, Cadmus promotes himself as a non-conformist poet who is punished by the guardians of the literary establishment (Apollo, god of music and poetry, and, of course, Zeus), by being silenced through permanent damage of his musical

[57] Hardie (1986) discusses how in Greek and Roman poetry allusions to the Gigantomachy are politically loaded; they evoke other struggles, historical and mythological, and align the protagonists with the two opposite sides, Zeus, who embodies order, and Typhon/Giants, who embody disorder. In Augustan poetry, specifically Vergil, the Giants and Typhon are typical embodiments of disorder, while a series of other forces, including Jupiter, though not as prominently, identify with order. By the time of the *Metamorphoses* – and even earlier in Hor. *Carm.* 3.4 – with the identification of Augustus with Zeus a given, the Gigantomachy becomes part of the poetics of the Augustans; it is an allusion for traditional epic, which the Augustans refuse to follow (cf. Hor. *Carm.* 3.4).

instrument—not unlike the punishment of Pierus' daughters in Ovid's *Metamorphoses*.

1.3   Conclusion

The consideration of two song contests in Ovid's *Metamorphoses* and in Nonnus' *Dionysiaca* has sought to draw attention to the notion of complementarity between the two songs within each contest: Ovid's Calliope in *Metamorphoses* 5 begins by adding the missing ending to the Pierides' song, while Nonnus' Oeagrus in *Dionysiaca* 19 takes the comparison between Dionysus and another Olympian that has already been formulated a step further. Moreover, although the longer song in both song contests is inspired by the Demeter-Persephone myth, there is no common ground between the two accounts of this myth, with Nonnus' Erechtheus in *Dionysiaca* 19 focussing entirely on the hospitality extended to Demeter, which remains marginal in Calliope's version.

As Hardie has noted, the complementary Typhonomachies in the Ovidian song contest seem to be combined within Cadmus' song before Typhon himself in Nonnus' own version of the Typhonomachy:[58] θελγομένῳ δὲ Γίγαντι νόθος παρεσύρισε ποιμήν | ἀθανάτων ἅτε φύζαν ἑῇ σύριγγι λιγαίνων, | καὶ Διὸς ἐσσομένην ἐμελίζετο γείτονα νίκην | ἑζομένῳ Τυφῶνι μόρον Τυφῶνος ἀείδων (*Dion.* 1.521–4).[59] It has been shown in the second part of this chapter that, in (re-)writing the Typhonomachy, Nonnus seems to have been inspired by Mercury's defeat of Argus in *Metamorphoses* 1 with music and narrative, as well as disguise and deception, eventually leading in both cases to the monster's defeat.

There were, to be sure, earlier Greek renderings of Hermes' killing of Argus, while Eros' role is, indeed, manifold in the Greco-Roman literary tradition.[60] But it is hoped that the juxtaposition in this study of specific episodes from Ovid with parallel (and not necessarily similar) episodes in Nonnus' *Dionysiaca* will make less audacious the claim that this important poet in the Latin side of the tradition in the world of Late Antiquity is too important to overlook when reading later Greek epic poetry.

---

[58] Hardie (2005: 125, with n. 19).   [59] The translation is cited on p. 21 (above).

[60] For Hermes' killing of Argus and the use of music, cf. Maehler (2004: 208), who draws attention to the reference to the Muses (Πιερίδες) in Bacchylides 19.35–6, and to pan-pipes in Soph. *Inachos* fr. 269c *TrGF* and in Io's frenzied vision in Aesch. *PV* 566–75 (with Griffith's n. on Aesch. *Prom.* 574).

CHAPTER 2

Greek and Roman Epigrammatists in the Later Imperial Period
Ausonius and Palladas in Dialogue with the Classical Past

Silvio Bär

Heiner Marti zum Gedenken

Drawing on a centuries-old tradition, but at the same time being open for experimentation and new developments, the literary epigram is perhaps the most versatile ancient literary genre of all. It was at home in the Greek and in the Roman world from the earliest days, and remained so uninterruptedly throughout all periods up until the Byzantine era and the European Renaissance, respectively. Within this triangle of tradition, longevity, and versatility, epigrammatists have always used their genre as a testing ground for the recollection and construction of their literary past. Indeed, since the Hellenistic period, the epigram was used as a medium for the writing of literary history and canons, as well as for literary polemics.[1] For example, Hellenistic funerary epigrams on authors of the classical past were employed as a means of constructing identity and bridging the gap between the past and the present.[2] Similarly, the Roman epigrammatist Martial devised what has been aptly named his 'epigrammatic canon' by establishing his position through references to the main authors of his past such as Cicero, Vergil, and Catullus.[3]

This chapter takes a comparative approach towards the corpus of two eminent representatives of the epigrammatic genre from the later imperial period: Decim(i)us Magnus Ausonius on the Roman side, and Palladas of Alexandria on the Greek side.[4] There are several reasons for the choice of

I wish to thank the two editors, Berenice Verhelst and Tine Scheijnen, as well as Sophia Papaioannou and Brian Sowers for their perspicacious comments and feedback during various stages of the writing process. Without their help, I would not have been able to develop this chapter in the right direction.

[1] Cf. e.g. Gabathuler (1937) and the chapters in part IV of the volume by Bing and Bruss (eds. 2007). On literary polemics in Hellenistic epigrams, cf. Cairns (2016: 125–86).

[2] Cf. e.g. Bolmarcich (2002) on Hellenistic funerary epigrams on Homer. Cf. also Skiadas (1965) on Homer in the Greek epigrammatic tradition in general.

[3] Cf. Mindt (2013a, 2013b).

[4] Textual editions used: Kay (2001) for Ausonius, Beckby (1965²) for Palladas. All translations from Greek and Latin are my own (exception: for Ausonius I use Kay's translation, with modifications).

these two authors. First, they are (roughly) contemporaries, both having lived during the fourth century CE (traditionally, both have been dated to the late fourth century; Palladas has recently been predated to a few decades earlier, but this new dating has not been universally accepted).[5] Second, both share a similar background insofar as both were schoolteachers (*grammatici*).[6] Third, they are both, inter alia, authors of scoptic epigrams and thus share common ground within the broad spectrum of the epigrammatic genre.[7] Furthermore, their epigrammatic corpus is comparable in quantity, too: the number of Palladas' existing epigrams amounts to a total of ca. 160 poems in the *Greek Anthology*,[8] whereas Ausonius' *œuvre* comprises 121 epigrams. Finally, it has even been suggested that Ausonius may be intertextually indebted to Palladas in some of his epigrams. (This point, however, is only tangentially relevant for the argument of my chapter, given its comparative, rather that intertextual, approach.)[9] In sum, this common ground provides a basis for comparison and, potentially, allows for some generalisations. To this end, several epigrams by Ausonius and Palladas are analysed and discussed. Concerning Ausonius, the selection is limited to five epigrams which contain *nominatim* references to one or more classical authorities from the literary past (henceforth I call this type of epigram a '*nominatim* reference epigram'). In essence, I argue that Ausonius' dialogue with the literary past is characterised by a discourse about the value, validity, and reliability of classical authors and authorities from the Greek and the Roman world. For this purpose, Ausonius uses various techniques, amongst which the tension between acknowledged and anonymous sources, the inclusion of potentially invented 'fake sources', and a recurring

---

There is disagreement as to whether Ausonius' *praenomen* was Decimus or Decimius (cf. Coşkun 2002: 182–5).

[5] The traditional dating of Palladas to the later fourth century CE stems from Bowra 1959: 91–5. Kevin Wilkinson, the editor of the latest papyrus findings, the 'New Palladas' (= P.CtYBR inv. 4000), predates Palladas to the early fourth century (Wilkinson 2012: 41–57; Wilkinson 2015). However, the established dating has been defended by most scholars since then (cf. especially Benelli 2016 and Cameron 2016b, with further references).

[6] Cf. Kaster (1988: 100–6, 247–9, 327–9).

[7] Cf. Zerwes (1956: 292–320) for Palladas and Szelest (1976) for Ausonius.

[8] Cf. Zerwes (1956: 4–7, 414–21). This corpus is now supplemented by the 'New Palladas' (cf. n. 5 above).

[9] Kay (2001: 18) mentions four cases where 'Ausonian epigrams may be derived from, may be the model for, or may share the same source as pieces by Palladas'. Those who accept the earlier dating of Palladas (on which cf. n. 5 above) may be inclined to accept a direct 'dependence' of Ausonius on Palladas (but the risk of circular argumentation is high in this case). On other Greek models of Ausonius, cf. e.g. Munari (1956), Benedetti (1980: 9–14), Cameron (1993: 80–84) and Kay (2001: 13–19).

discussion of Greek versus Roman authorities prevail. In contrast, Palladas constructs a *persona* of himself which resorts to Greek authorities only and, especially, to Homer. Therefore, for Palladas a slightly different approach is taken here: I restrict myself to a selection of Homeric epigrams, some of which mention Homer by name, whereas others refer to him by other means. As is demonstrated, Homer and the Homeric epics were to a large extent appropriated in order to construct Palladas' personal voice, whereas the actual discourse about classical authors and authorities remains comparatively flat and limited as compared to Ausonius.

2.1 Ausonius: From Questioning Authorities to Faking Sources

In the epigrammatic corpus of Ausonius, we find six *nominatim* reference epigrams: *Epigr.* 12 (Cicero), 35 (Sappho), 72 (Ovid, Pliny), 73 (Lucilius, Pythagoras), 75 (Afranius), and 103 (Sappho). In what follows, five of these epigrams are discussed in order of their appearance in Ausonius' collection. (*Epigr.* 35 is omitted because of its brevity.)

Epigr. 12 takes the form of an interrogative dialogue between the spectator of two statues and the two statues which the speaker contemplates:

'Cuius opus?' 'Phidiae, qui signum Pallados, eius,
    quique Iovem fecit, tertia palma ego sum.
sum dea.' 'quae?' 'rara et paucis Occasio nota.'
    'quid rotulae insistis?' 'stare loco nequeo.'
'quid talaria habes?' 'volucris sum; Mercurius quae   5
    fortunare solet, trado ego, cum volui.'
'crine tegis faciem.' 'cognosci nolo.' 'sed heus tu,
    occipiti calvo es.' 'ne tenear fugiens.'
'quae tibi iuncta comes?' 'dicat tibi.' 'dic, rogo, quae sis.'
    'sum dea cui nomen nec Cicero ipse dedit;   10
sum dea quae facti non factique exigo poenas,
    nempe ut paeniteat: sic Metanoea vocor.'
'tu modo dic, quid agat tecum.' 'quandoque volavi
    haec manet; hanc retinent quos ego praeterii.
tu quoque dum rogitas, dum percontando moraris,   15
    elapsam disces me tibi de manibus.'

'Whose work [are you]?' 'That of Pheidias, he who made the statue of Pallas,
    I'm his!
And he made the Jupiter; I'm his third-best piece.
I'm a goddess!' 'Which one?' 'Opportunity, infrequent, and known to few.'
    'Why are you standing on a wheel?' 'I can't stand still.'

'Why have you got winged sandals?' 'I am very swift. Whenever I want,
 I hand over the good fortune which Mercury customarily creates.'
'You cover your face with your hair.' 'I don't want to be recognised.' 'But,
 good heavens,
 the back of your head is bald!' 'So I can't be caught as I make off.'
'Who is the companion with you?' 'Let her tell you.' 'Please tell me who you
 are.'
 'I am a goddess to whom even Cicero himself did not give a name:
I am the goddess who exacts punishment for what has and has not been
 done,
 so that one truly regrets it. Hence I am called Metanoea.'
'Now you again please, tell me what she is doing with you.' 'Whenever I've
 flown away,
 she stays behind. Those whom I've passed by hold on to her.
You too, while you're asking all these questions and procrastinating with
 your interrogation,
 will discover that I have slipped through your hands.'

This epigram is closely related to a Greek epigram by Posidippus (*Anth. Plan.* 16.275) which consists of a similar dialogue between a statue of Καιρός, crafted by Lysippus, and an anonymous speaker who questions the statue as to its provenance and appearance. As Kay (2001: 98–9) puts it, '[t]he similarities between Ausonius and Posidippus are so close that coincidence is not credible'. In essence, Ausonius introduces three significant changes as compared to the Greek original:[10] first, a change of sculptor (Pheidias instead of Lysippus); second, a gender shift from a male (Καιρός) to a female (*Occasio*) statue; and, third, the addition of a second statue (*Metanoea*). Whereas Cicero is prominently mentioned as the 'non-translator' of the Greek personification of Μετάνοια, Ausonius does not acknowledge the fact that the translation of Καιρός as Latin *Occasio* does in fact date back to Cicero (*Off.* 1.142). Therein we can see an implicit comment on the speaker's attitude towards Cicero: for one, Cicero is clearly attributed the role of the principal classical authority when it comes to the translation of Greek terms and concepts into Latin. For another, though, he is silenced in the one case he ought to be credited, and mentioned when he cannot be given credit as a translator. This may be read as a smug comment *ex silentio* by Ausonius on Cicero's reputed authority: Cicero is introduced and referenced as an authority, but at the same time his authority is undermined; indirectly, Ausonius thus seems to state that he is in fact a better translator than Cicero.

---

[10] For a detailed comparison, cf. Benedetti (1980: 109–25) and Kay (2001: 97–103).

The next epigram to be discussed is not concerned with the assessment of a classical translator, but rather with the validity and authority of classical authors as literary sources (*Epigr.* 72):

Vallebanae (nova res et vix credenda poetis,
    sed quae de vera promitur historia)
femineam in speciem convertit masculus ales
    pavaque de pavo constitit ante oculos.
cuncti admirantur monstrum, sed mollior agna   5
    * * * * * * * * *
'quid stolidi ad speciem notae novitatis hebetis?
    an vos Nasonis carmina non legitis?
Caenida convertit proles Saturnia Consus
    ambiguoque fuit corpore Tiresias.   10
sensit semivirum fons Salmacis Hermaphroditum,
    vidit nubentem Plinius androgynum.
nec satis antiquum, quod Campana in Benevento
    unus epheborum virgo repente fuit.
nolo tamen veteris documenta arcessere famae: 15
    ecce ego sum factus femina de puero.'

At Vallebana (a strange matter and one barely credible to poets,
    but one that comes from a true report)
a male bird changed to female form
    and a peacock became a peahen before the eyes [of onlookers].
All wondered at the portent, but one smoother than a lamb [said]:
    * * * * * * * * *
'Why are you uncomprehending in the face of something strange but
    attested, you blockheads?
    Don't you read Ovid's poems?
Consus, Saturn's offspring, changed Caenis' sex,
    and Tiresias had a body of indeterminate sex.
The fount Salmacis experienced Hermaphroditus the half-man,
    and Pliny witnessed an androgyne marrying.
Nor is it all that long ago that one of the youths in Campanian Beneventum
    suddenly became a girl.
Yet I don't want to adduce my proof from old reports:
    look at me, I was a boy and have turned female.'

The latest news about the alleged sex change of birds in the city of Vallebana, reported by an anonymous speaker, is supported by references to several mythical examples of gender reversal. This evidence is given in direct speech by another, embedded, anonymous speaker – a person who, as the punchline at the end of the poem shows, has undergone a sex change him-/herself. As the embedded speaker indicates, several of the mythical

examples are taken from Ovid's *Metamorphoses* and, in one case, from
Pliny's *Naturalis historia* (two authors who are well known for their
treatment of marvels).[11] In contrast, the last (and latest) example, that of
a teenage boy who was turned into a girl in the city of Beneventum, comes
from an anonymous, and thus unattested, source.[12] Hence, the embedded
speaker navigates between the juxtaposition of, and dichotomy between,
well-known literary sources from famous classical writers and an anonymous (and thus potentially invented) source. This dichotomy between
well-known and unknown (= invented?) sources serves several ends: first, it
undermines the credibility of the reported sex changes, which are 'a strange
matter and one barely credible to poets' (*nova res et vix credenda poetis*,
line 1).[13] Indeed, since the city of Vallebana is not attested elsewhere, it
may well be a fictional place, the mention of which serves to introduce
the overarching idea of the 'fake source'.[14] Second, the aforementioned
dichotomy also in parts challenges the validity of classical authorities: in a
similar way to *Epigr.* 12, where Cicero is given credit at the wrong
moment, here the credit given to Ovid and Pliny is put into perspective
by the addition of an anonymous source – a source which may not exist
at all.

The next epigram to be considered also (*mutatis mutandis*) adopts the
theme of transformation, here in conjunction with pederasty (*Epigr.* 73):

'Pythagora Euphorbi, reparas qui semina rerum
     corporibusque novis das reduces animas,
dic, quid erit Marcus iam fata novissima functus,
     si redeat vitam rursus in aeriam?'
'quis Marcus?' 'feles nuper pullaria dictus,   5
     corrupit totum qui puerile secus,
perversae Veneris postico vulnere fossor,
     Lucili vatis subpilo †pullo premor†.'
'non taurus, non mulus erit, non hippocamelus,
     non caper aut aries, sed scarabaeus erit.'   10

---

[11] For the sources, cf. the commentaries by Green (1991: 406) and Kay (2001: 211–13). On
paradoxography in Augustan literature, cf. the volume by Hardie (2009). On *mirabilia* in Pliny's
Naturalis historia, cf. Naas (2011).

[12] Cf. Kay (2001: 213).

[13] It must be noted, though, that the phrase *nova res* is a conjecture (cf. the *apparatus criticus* at Green
1991).

[14] Cf. the commentaries by Green (1991: 406) and Kay (2001: 210) for speculation about the
city's localisation.

'Pythagoras [son] of Euphorbus, since you re-arrange the building blocks of
  nature
  and bring back souls to give to new bodies,
tell me, what will Marcus be, who has just experienced his final hour,
  if he should come back to life above the ground?'
'Which Marcus?' 'The one who recently was called the chicken-chasing
  polecat,
  who corrupted all the boy gender,
the digger of unnatural sex by violence at the back entry,
  the "chicken-plucker and molester" of the bard Lucilius.'
'He won't be a bull, he won't be a mule, he won't be a hippocamel,
  nor a goat nor a ram, but he will be a dung beetle.'

The epigrammatic speaker stages himself in a dialogue with Pythagoras;
the latter, in the form of an embedded speaker, talks about a recently
deceased gay man called Marcus who will be reborn as a dung beetle
because, in his previous life, he enjoyed the faecal pollution of his sexual
organ that resulted from active anal intercourse. Here, Ausonius resorts
once more to the opposition between famous and obscure, and again he
raises questions about the credibility and validity of classical literary
authorities. On a first level, the irony lies in the fact that none less than
the great Pythagoras himself – the main philosophical authority on
reincarnation – is quoted as providing information about something as
low and vulgar as the destined rebirth of a man in the form of a dung
beetle because of his predilection for anal sex. The ironic tension between a
high-brow witness and a low-brow topic is mirrored in the contrast
between the temporal distance that sets Ausonius and Pythagoras apart.
In addition to this tension, the situation is made more complex by the
speaker's mention of Gaius Lucilius, the father of Roman satire, 'whose
poetry was mythologised by subsequent Roman satirists as the benchmark
of the genre' (Rosen 2012: 22) and who, inter alia, was also known as the
author of pederastic epigrams.[15] Due to the fragmentary state of the
transmission of Lucilius' work, we do not know whether Ausonius is
referring to an epigram that really existed or whether he has invented a
'fake source' as (possibly) in *Epigr.* 72. The name of the pederast may
imply the latter since Marcus is an extremely common Roman *praenomen*;
therefore, the reader is invited to feel a tension between the reference to a
supposedly accurate source and the lack of accuracy when it comes to the

[15] Ausonius also refers to Lucilius in the preface to his elegiac poem *De herediolo* ('On the little
patrimony'), where it is stated that this text was written 'in the style of Lucilius' (*Luciliano stilo*; on
the textual problem, cf. Green 1991: 282).

source's actual traceability.[16] Finally, a third authority is invoked indirectly in line 2 via the phrase *corporibusque novis*, which hints at the proem of Ovid's *Metamorphoses*: *In nova fert animus mutatas dicere formas | corpora* ('My mind compels me to speak of forms that were changed into new | bodies', *Met.* 1.1–2). Through this allusion, Ausonius not only provides a reference to the most canonical text of transformation, but he also establishes a further connection between himself and Pythagoras because the *Metamorphoses* treats the life and deeds of Pythagoras at great length (*Met.* 15.60–478). Thus, Ovid's *Metamorphoses* can be regarded as an intermediary between Pythagoras' time and Ausonius' time.

In *Epigr.* 73, Ovid is only casually present; in *Epigr.* 103, however, he is at the very centre. This epigram is presented, again, in the form of a dialogue, and it foregrounds the question of literary models as a question of Greek versus Roman authorities:

'Suasisti, Venus, ecce, duas dyseros ut amarem.
    odit utraque; aliud da modo consilium.'
'vince datis ambas.' 'cupio, verum arta domi res.'
    'pellice promissis.' 'nulla fides inopi.'
'antestare deos.' 'non fas mihi fallere divos.'   5
    'pervigila ante fores.' 'nocte capi metuo.'
'scribe elegos.' 'nequeo, Musarum et Apollinis expers.'
    'frange fores.' 'poenas iudicii metuo.'
'stulte, ab amore mori pateris, non vis ob amorem?'
    'malo miser dici quam miser atque reus.'   10
'suasi quod potui: <tu> alios modo consule.' 'dic quos.'
    'quod sibi suaserunt Phaedra et Elissa dabunt,
quod Canace Phyllisque et fastidita Phaoni.'
    'hoc das consilium?' 'tale datur miseris.'

'Look, Venus, you've persuaded me, unlucky in love as I am, to love two
    girls.
    They both hate me. Now give me different advice.'
'Win them both over with gifts.' 'I'd like to, but I've straitened
    circumstances at home.'
    'Ensnare them with promises.' 'There's no trust in the poor.'
'Testify before the gods.' 'It is not right for me to deceive the gods.'
    'Mount watch outside their doors.' 'I'm afraid of getting arrested at night.'
'Write elegies.' 'I can't, I'm inexperienced with the Muses and Apollo.'
    'Break down their doors.' 'I fear the punishment of the law.'
'You fool, you're prepared to die of love, but not for love?'
    'I'd rather be called unhappy than unhappy and charged with a crime.'

---

[16] I owe this point to Sophia Papaioannou.

'I've given you what advice I can. You should ask others for advice now.'
  'Tell me who.'
  'Phaedra and Elissa will give you the counsel they gave themselves,
as will Canace and Phyllis and the one who was scorned by Phaon.'
  'So that's your advice?' 'Such [advice] is given to wretches!'

This epigram is a direct response to the preceding *Epigr.* 102, in which
Venus promises the speaker (who, as in *Epigr.* 73, bears the run-of-the-mill
praenomen Marcus) that she is going to resolve his problem of loving and
hating the wrong two girls by making him fall in love with both. According
to *Epigr.* 103, Venus has fulfilled Marcus' wish, but only partially; now he
loves both girls, but they both reject him. Therefore, in the rest of the
epigram Venus gives Marcus various pieces of advice about how he should
win both, but Marcus rejects every single piece until Venus loses her
patience and directs him to other authorities. Both epigrams recognisably
play with topoi from Roman, and especially Ovidian, love elegy.[17] On a
metapoetic level, the dialogue between Venus and Marcus, and the latter's
repudiation of the former's advice, can be read as a dialogue between Ovid
and Ausonius in which the latter refutes the former as his model. This
metapoetic quality becomes particularly obvious at two points: first, in line
7, Marcus rejects Venus's advice that he should write elegies by self-
ironically replying: 'I can't, I'm unexperienced with the Muses and
Apollo' (*nequeo, Musarum et Apollinis expers*). Second, when Venus finally
loses her temper, she sneeringly recommends that Marcus seek advice
elsewhere: namely, from women who all committed suicide because of
unfulfilled love. Whereas the first four (Phaedra, Elissa, Canace, and
Phyllis) are mythical figures, the last one is Sappho who, according to an
ancient myth, threw herself off a rock because her love for a man called
Phaon was unrequited.[18] This orientation towards figures from the Greek
world may, at first sight, be read as a metapoetic statement in favour of
Greek over Roman models. However, upon closer consideration, the line of
thought is more complex, and more witty: as Kay (2001: 271) points out in
his commentary, 'all the exemplars of advice which Venus gives are also
featured amongst Ovid's *Heroides* [. . .], except for Sappho, who appears in
the pseudo-Ovidian *epistula Sapphus*, which Ausonius [. . .] might have
considered genuinely Ovidian'. Seen from this angle, the shift from
Roman to Greek authorities turns out to be a dead end: eventually, Venus
states that Marcus will not escape Ovid's authority on love matters, and
similarly, Ausonius will not be able to do without the Ovidian model. The

---

[17] Cf. Kay (2001: 267–8).   [18] On the various sources of these stories, cf. Kay (2001: 271–2).

Greek loanword *dyseros* ('unlucky in love'), spoken by Marcus in the first line of *Epigr.* 103, ties in with this interpretation: it is an intertextual reference to Theocr. *Id.* 1.85, where Priapus thus addresses Daphnis. At first glance, Ausonius' use of this adjective may appear as a mere reference to the supposed shift from Roman to Greek models. However, as noted, there is no path that leads away from the Roman models after all. This is, ultimately, reflected in the word *dyseros* itself, which denotes love that has gone the wrong way.[19] Similarly, it would be a move in the wrong direction for a Roman author to resort to Greek instead of Roman models.

The last epigram which shall be discussed here is *Epigr.* 75. Here again, we encounter the idea of the 'fake source':

> Praeter legitimi genitalia foedera coetus
> repperit obscenas veneres vitiosa libido,
> Herculis heredi quam Lemnia suasit egestas,
> quam toga facundi scaenis agitavit Afrani
> et quam Nolanis capitalis luxus inussit.   5
> Crispa tamen cunctas exercet corpore in uno:
> deglubit, fellat, molitur per utramque cavernam,
> ne quid inexpertum frustra moritura relinquat.

> Beyond the procreative unions of legitimate sex,
> vicious libido has discovered obscene ways of love-making –
> that which lack of alternatives on Lemnos forced on Hercules' heir,
> that which eloquent Afranius' played in Roman dress paraded on stage,
> and that with which their heady decadence branded the people of Nola.
> But Crispa practises them all with one body:
> she masturbates men, fellates them and is pounded by them at both passages,
> lest she should die in vain and leave anything untried.

This epigram ties in with the widespread tradition of epigrammatic obscenity by enumerating, in the form of a priamble, three sexual practices that were considered unnatural: masturbation, anal intercourse, and *fellatio*. As a climax, a woman called Crispa is reported for being notorious for practising all three of them. For our purposes, it is again illuminating to note how Ausonius oscillates between closeness and openness when acknowledging his literary sources.[20] The first example is that of the mythological figure Philoctetes who, abandoned and alone on the isle of Scyrus, was compelled to beat his own meat. Interestingly, according to Martial in his epigram 2.84, Philoctetes was not a masturbator, but a

---

[19] Cf. the commentary at Theocr. *Id.* 1.85 by Gow (1952: vol. II, 19). The adjective occurs again at Theocr. *Id.* 6.7 with reference to Polyphemus who is in love with Galatea.
[20] For details, cf. the commentaries by Green (1991: 408) and Kay (2001: 219–22).

passive homosexual. Both sexual practices have in common that they were considered unmanly, and were therefore viewed as unnatural within the Roman classification system of sexual behaviour because they were non-penetrating and non-vaginal.[21] Both traditions 'may go back to Greek comedy', as Green (1991: 408) notes. However, it is also possible that Ausonius deliberately toys with Martial, his major model, by virtually inventing a different sexual deviation for Philoctetes and thus feeding back into the idea of the 'fake source'.[22]

The second example is a reference to the Roman comic author Lucius Afranius (second century BCE), and it is the only *nominatim* reference in this epigram. Afranius is a representative of the native Roman comedy, the *fabula togata*.[23] According to Quintilian, he was notorious for the depiction of pederasty on stage (*Inst.* 10.1.100), and it is possible that Quintilian's authority cemented this judgement and that Ausonius here reads Afranius through the lenses of Quintilian.[24] Finally, the source of the third example is again unacknowledged, as was the first example. However, again in Quintilian we can find a potential allusion to Nola as a place where *fellatio* was notoriously practised: at *Inst.* 8.6.53, the orator Marcus Caelius Rufus is quoted as having said that Clytemnestra was 'a Coan at the dining-coach, a Nolan in the bedroom' (*in triclinio coam, in cubiculo nolam*). According to Kay (2001: 221), a pun may be at work here 'where "nolam" stands for "Nolanam"'. In sum, we can state that besides Afranius who is acknowledged by name, Ausonius relates two further literary models that remain hidden between the lines. In the case of Martial, a deliberate deviation from the model's authority may be at work. Quintilian, in turn, may actually serve as the principal model on the two other occasions.

2.2 Palladas: Constructing One's *Persona* With, Through, and Against Homer

In contrast to Ausonius, Palladas refers to authors from the classical past considerably more often, and his references are solely restricted to Greek figures. His *nominatim* reference epigrams include figures such as Homer

---

[21] On the Roman 'classification system' of sexual behaviour, cf. e.g. Parker (1997) and Williams (2010²).
[22] I owe this point to Sophia Papaioannou.   [23] Cf. Manuwald (2011: 263–6).
[24] Cf. Welsh (2010: 121): 'Ausonius certainly did not know the works of Afranius at first hand, but instead derived his quotations and references to the playwright from intermediate sources.' Ausonius refers to Afranius again in the prefatory letter to the *Cento Nuptialis*, where he juxtaposes him with Plautus.

(*Anth. Pal.* 6.61; 9.165; 9.166; 10.47; 10.50), Callimachus (*Anth. Pal.* 9.175), Pindar (*Anth. Pal.* 9.175; 10.51), Plato (*Anth. Pal.* 10.45; 11.305), Pythagoras (*Anth. Pal.* 10.46), Isocrates (*Anth. Pal.* 10.48), and Menander (*Anth. Pal.* 10.52; 11.263). As far as Homer is concerned, further epigrams can be found where the dialogue with Homer is not established via a reference to the author by name, but, rather, through other means such as the mention of Homeric characters, settings, or the citation of Homeric phrases.[25]

In what follows, I discuss a selection of the Homeric epigrams that can be regarded as representative of Palladas' use of Homer. As is going to be demonstrated in the course of the subsequent analysis, these epigrams exhibit a number of characteristics and techniques which are typical of the construction of Palladas' *persona* in dialogue with the classical past and which can invite a comparison with Ausonius' methods and techniques. Thematically, they centre on three different areas. One recurring topic is Palladas' role as a schoolteacher and his embitterment about its dullness and the low pay.[26] Furthermore, he connects Homer and Homeric references to his (at times excruciating) misogyny.[27] Eventually, he also adopts the centuries-old tradition of resorting to Homer for the sake of adding credibility to one's point (which I henceforth call the '*iam Homerus*-motif').[28] Let us begin by looking at an example of the first type (*Anth. Pal.* 9.173):

Ἀρχὴ γραμματικῆς πεντάστιχός ἐστι κατάρα·
    πρῶτος 'μῆνιν' ἔχει, δεύτερος 'οὐλομένην',
καὶ μετὰ δ' 'οὐλομένην' Δαναῶν πάλιν 'ἄλγεα' πολλά·
    ὁ τρίτατος 'ψυχὰς εἰς Ἀίδην' κατάγει·
τοῦ δὲ τεταρταίου τὰ 'ἑλώρια' καὶ 'κύνες' ἀργοί,   5
    πέμπτου δ' 'οἰωνοὶ' καὶ 'χόλος' ἐστὶ 'Διός'.
πῶς οὖν γραμματικὸς δύναται μετὰ πέντε κατάρας
    καὶ πέντε πτώσεις μὴ μέγα πένθος ἔχειν;

The beginning of grammar is a five-versed curse:
    The first one offers 'wrath', the second 'ruinous',
and after 'ruinous' again the many 'pains' of the Danaäns.
    The third one brings down 'the souls into Hades';
The [topic] of the fourth one is the 'preys' and the swift 'dogs',
    the [topic] of the fifth one is the 'birds of prey' and the 'anger of Zeus'.

---

[25] On Homer in Palladas, cf. Zerwes (1956: 385), Skiadas (1965: 153–7), and Guichard (2017).
[26] On the role and the social standing of the *grammaticus* in later antiquity, cf. e.g. Kaster (1988), Cribiore (2001: 185–219) and Maurice (2013: 10–13).
[27] On Palladas' misogyny, cf. Zerwes (1956: 36–61) and Henderson (2009).
[28] Cf. Skiadas (1965: 63–75) on Homeric authority in the Greek epigrammatic tradition.

Now, how can a grammarian, after five curses
   and five cases, not feel great pain?

As Guichard (2017: 159) rightly points out, this 'epigram makes direct reference to school practice, specifically the teaching of the Greek inflection', and thus has a *Sitz im Leben* in imperial scholastic practice. Its actual wit, though, consists of the speaker's toying with the reader's expectations of the subject of the contempt. Typically, one would expect that this sort of mindless memorisation would be a curse to the pupils; however, only in the last distichon is it revealed that, in fact, it is the teacher himself who 'feels great pain' (line 8). Notably, Palladas expresses his negative emotion by resorting to the Homeric phrase μέγα πένθος (*Il.* 1.254; 4.417; 7.124; 17.139; *Od.* 17.489). By doing so, he ironically comments on the inevitability of his destiny: as much as he hates his profession, he needs it because it is only through Homer that he is able to make a living (however modest that might be).[29]

The perhaps most persistent leitmotif of several of Palladas' epigrams is his misogyny. In *Anth. Pal.* 9.168, his contempt for women takes the form of a complaint about his wife – which, in turn, is linked again to the hatred of his profession and the scholastic practice of teaching inflection on the basis of the first lines of the *Iliad*:

> 'Μῆνιν οὐλομένην' γαμετὴν ὁ τάλας γεγάμηκα
>   καὶ παρὰ τῆς τέχνης μήνιδος ἀρξάμενος.
> ὤμοι ἐγὼ πολύμηνις, ἔχων τριχόλωτον ἀνάγκην,
>   τέχνης γραμματικῆς καὶ γαμετῆς μαχίμης.

> 'The ruinous wrath' I, wretch, married for my spouse,
>   although I already begin with wrath by my profession.
> Oh me, full of wrath, with my thrice-detested constraint
>   of my profession as a grammarian and of a war-like spouse.

Here, Palladas acrimoniously appropriates Achilles' wrath and makes it the focus of his own *persona* both in his professional and his private life. The epigram's wit lies in the adjective πολύμηνις ('full of wrath'), which is an obvious pun on the Homeric πολύμητις ('of many counsels') – one of the standard epithets of Odysseus in Homer. Palladas thus turns himself into a virtual anti-Odysseus: in contrast to Odysseus, who leads an adventurous life and gets to see the world, but ultimately wishes only to return home

---

[29] Further similar epigrams are *Anth. Pal.* 9.169 and 9.174, where Palladas expresses his contempt for his profession along with his frustration for the bad pay by way of reference to Homer and the scholastic practice. On Palladas' poverty, cf. also *Anth. Pal.* 11.302 and 11.303; discussion in Zerwes (1956: 62–81).

and be reunited with his wife, Palladas is trapped in his daily routine, and
there is nothing he would like more than to escape his much-hated job and
his equally despised wife.

The misogyny continues in *Anth. Pal.* 9.166, where Helen and
Penelope are invoked as paradigms of the viciousness and deceitfulness
of women:[30]

Πᾶσαν Ὅμηρος ἔδειξε κακὴν σφαλερήν τε γυναῖκα,
    σώφρονα καὶ πόρνην ἀμφοτέρας ὄλεθρον.
ἐκ γὰρ τῆς Ἑλένης μοιχευσαμένης φόνος ἀνδρῶν
    καὶ διὰ σωφροσύνην Πηνελόπης θάνατοι.
Ἰλιὰς οὖν τὸ πόνημα μιᾶς χάριν ἐστι γυναικός,   5
    αὐτὰρ Ὀδυσσείῃ Πηνελόπη πρόφασις.

Homer has shown that each woman is evil and deceptive,
    a ruin both the chaste one and the whore.
For, from adulterous Helen killing among men [arose],
    and death through the chastity of Penelope.
The Iliad is a work due to one single woman,
    but Penelope is the cause of the Odyssey.

Helen is the one who caused the Trojan War. Penelope, in turn, is called a
cause of evil, too, since she is accused of being responsible for Odysseus'
slaughter of her suitors. Thus, both promiscuity and chastity ultimately
had the same devastating effect, as is expressed in the confrontation
between the antipodal terms σώφρονα καὶ πόρνην ('the chaste one and
the whore') in line 2. The contrast between the centuries-old cliché of
Helen as the embodiment of evil, deception, and the cause of mass
destruction is contrasted with the unexpected *ad hoc* penalisation of
Penelope for her chastity. Palladas thus employs a similar technique to
that of Ausonius: namely, the juxtaposition of, and dichotomy between, an
age-old and well-known literary source or topos and an anonymous (and,
thus, potentially invented) one.[31] Moreover, indirectly the epigram makes
Helen and Penelope also the cause of the Homeric epics and thus turns the
acid criticism into implicit praise.[32]

In *Anth. Pal.* 9.165, misogyny comes again in Homeric (as well as
Hesiodic and Euripidean) terms. The eternal feud between Zeus and

---

[30] On this epigram, cf. also Skiadas (1965: 154–5) and Guichard (2017: 160–61).
[31] I owe this point to Sophia Papaioannou.
[32] Cf. Skiadas (1965: 155). Linguistically, this is highlighted by the ambiguity of the term πόνημα in
line 5, which can denote a burden, but also a literary work (on the latter meaning cf. *Anth. Pal.*
4.3.42 [Agathias]).

Hera serves as a paradigm for all women's devastating effects upon men, which ultimately leads to the untimely death of the latter:

Ὀργὴ τοῦ Διός ἐστι γυνὴ πυρὸς ἀντιδοθεῖσα
  δῶρον ἀνιηρὸν τοῦ πυρὸς ἀντίδοτον·
ἄνδρα γὰρ ἐκκαίει ταῖς φροντίσιν ἠδὲ μαραίνει
  καὶ γῆρας προπετὲς τῇ νεότητι φέρει.
οὐδ᾽ ὁ Ζεὺς ἀμέριμνος ἔχει χρυσόθρονον Ἥρην,   5
  πολλάκι γοῦν αὐτὴν ῥίψεν ἀπ᾽ ἀθανάτων
ἠέρι καὶ νεφέλῃσι μετήορον· οἶδεν Ὅμηρος,
  καὶ Δία συγγράψας τῇ γαμετῇ χόλιον.
οὕτως οὐδέποτ᾽ ἐστὶ γυνὴ σύμφωνος ἀκοίτῃ,
  οὐδὲ καὶ ἐν χρυσέῳ μιγνυμένη δαπέδῳ.   10

The wrath of Zeus is woman, a gift given in exchange
  for fire, the grievous antidote of fire:
She burns and quenches man with her concerns,
  and she brings untimely old age to his youth.
Not even Zeus is free of sorrow with gold-enthroned Hera,
  for, often he has thrust her away from the immortals
and [made her] hang in the air and in the clouds. Homer knows of it,
  who also described Zeus in his anger against his spouse.
Thus a woman is never in accordance with her consort,
  not even if she were to have sex with him on a golden floor.

Guichard (2017: 162) points to several Homeric quotes and subtexts, as well as allusions to passages from Hesiod and Euripides. Through these citations and allusions, significant intertexts are evoked. To begin with, in line 2 the phrase δῶρον ἀνιηρόν echoes *Od.* 17.220 πτωχὸν ἀνιηρόν, the context of which is important: *Od.* 17.220 is spoken by the evil goatherd Melanthios and is directed against Odysseus, who is disguised as a beggar. Thus, by qualifying women a 'grievous antidote of fire' (δῶρον ἀνιηρὸν τοῦ πυρὸς ἀντίδοτον), Palladas refers to a highly abusive Homeric context and underlines his contempt. Second, two Homeric allusions point to intertexts that feature Zeus and Hera: the phrase χρυσόθρονον Ἥρην (line 5) quotes *Il.* 1.611 χρυσόθρονος Ἥρη, a line which comes from the scene where the couple withdraws to bed, happily reunited after a divine feast on Olympus. In contrast, the phrase ἐν χρυσέῳ [. . .] δαπέδῳ (line 10) stems from an opposing context – namely, from *Il.* 4.2 χρυσέῳ ἐν δαπέδῳ, which marks the beginning of the divine council where Zeus attacks and ridicules Hera. Hence, Palladas ironically alludes to two different Homeric contexts that both feature Zeus and Hera, one in a positive light, the other in a negative light. By doing so, he incorporates the entire scope of possible

relations between husband and wife. Finally, lines 2–4 echo both Hes. *Op.*
57–8 and Eur. fr. 429 *TrGF*.[33] The lines at *Op.* 57–8 are spoken by Zeus
to Prometheus in response to the latter having stolen the fire from the
gods; the gift which the humans are going to receive in exchange for the
fire is Pandora, the prototypical evil woman. Eur. fr. 429 *TrGF* stems from
a choral passage from the lost *Hippolytos Kalyptomenos* in which the women
call themselves a greater fire that was created in place of 'ordinary' fire.
This passage, in turn, suggests an allusion to *Op.* 57–8. In sum, Palladas
here again employs a technique similar to that of Ausonius, namely, the
juxtaposition of acknowledged/open (< Homer) and unacknowledged/
hidden (< Hesiod, Euripides) source.

The explicit reference to Homer and a Homeric *hapax legomenon*
provides the backdrop of an ironic role transferal and a metapoetic statement in *Anth. Pal.* 6.61:[34]

Ὦ ξυρὸν οὐράνιον, ξυρὸν ὄλβιον, ᾧ πλοκαμῖδας
    κειραμένη πλεκτὰς ἄνθετο Παμφίλιον,
οὔ σέ τις ἀνθρώπων χαλκεύσατο, πὰρ δὲ καμίνῳ
    Ἡφαίστου χρυσέην σφῦραν ἀειραμένη
ἡ λιπαροκρήδεμνος, ἵν' εἴπωμεν καθ' Ὅμηρον,   5
    χερσί σε ταῖς ἰδίαις ἐξεπόνησε Χάρις.

Heavenly razor, happy razor, with which Pamphilion
    clipped her plaited locks and dedicated them!
Not one of the humans forged you, but at the side of the furnace
    of Hephaestus, lifting her golden hammer,
Charis with the bright headband – to say it according to Homer –
    wrought you with her very own hands.

This epigram harks back to a characteristic type of Hellenistic votive
epigram that evokes the dedication of small, but precious, objects along
with the metapoetic association of equally small, but artistically refined,
poetry in favour of pompous and orotund epic.[35] The preciousness of the
object described is emphasised by its provenance in Hephaestus' smithy, as
well as by its creator Charis, Hephaestus' wife. It is, however, only via the

---

[33] Hes. *Op.* 57–58: τοῖς δ' ἐγὼ ἀντὶ πυρὸς δώσω κακόν, ᾧ κεν ἅπαντες | τέρπωνται κατὰ θυμὸν ἑὸν
κακὸν ἀμφαγαπῶντες ('But to them I will give an evil in exchange by which they will all | take
pleasure in their heart, embracing their very own evil'). – Eur. fr. 429 *TrGF*: ἀντὶ πυρὸς γὰρ ἄλλο
πῦρ | μεῖζον ἐβλάστομεν γυναῖ– | κες πολὺ δυσμαχώτερον ('For, in place of fire, as yet another fire, |
a greater one, we women have been created, | much harder to fight against').

[34] On this epigram, cf. also Guichard (2017: 164).

[35] On Hellenistic votive epigrams, cf. e.g. Fantuzzi and Hunter (2004: 291–338). *Anth. Pal.* 6.61
constitutes a direct continuation of *Anth. Pal.* 6.60, where Pamphilion's dedication of her hair to
Isis is reported.

Homeric quote in line 5 that the epigram's full potential becomes apparent: λιπαροκρήδεμνος is a Homeric *hapax legomenon* which is used at *Il.* 18.382, in a context that is both similar and dissimilar to that of our epigram. In *Iliad* Book 18, the creation of Achilles' shield by Hephaestus is narrated; thus, a context is evoked which deals with a much larger object and, accordingly, a considerably longer text. In other words, the grandiosity of one object (Achilles' shield) and its genre (epic) is contrasted with the tininess of the other object (Pamphilion's razor) and its corresponding genre (epigram). Moreover, *Il.* 18.382 refers to a scene where Charis appears in order to tend to Thetis who is visiting. Thus, a further point of irony lies in the conversion of Charis' role: in *Iliad* 18, she is Hephaestus' wife and acts as a servant for Thetis; contrastingly, in Palladas' epigram she assumes the role of Hephaestus by creating the object of art herself, as is explicitly emphasised in the last line.

The last epigram to be considered provides an example of the *iam Homerus*-motif in combination with two quotes from the *Iliad* (*Anth. Pal.* 10.47):

Ἔσθιε, πῖνε, μύσας ἐπὶ πένθεσιν· οὐ γὰρ ἔοικεν
   γαστέρι πενθῆσαι νεκρόν, Ὅμηρος ἔφη·
καὶ γὰρ ὁμοῦ θάψασαν ὀλωλότα δώδεκα τέκνα
   σίτου μνησαμένην τὴν Νιόβην παράγει.

Eat and drink with closed lips in your sorrow, for it isn't appropriate
   to mourn for a dead with your stomach, [as already] Homer said:
For he puts forward one who buried her twelve children, deceased at the
   same time,
and who remembered her food: Niobe!

The quote in line 2 is an almost literal citation of *Il.* 19.225: γαστέρι δ' οὔ πως ἔστι νέκυν πενθῆσαι Ἀχαιούς ('but it is by no means possible for the Achaeans to mourn for a dead with their stomach').[36] There, Odysseus reacts to Achilles' call for a return to battle without having eaten by appealing to his sense of responsibility, arguing that there is no point in the warriors fighting unfed even if Achilles himself wishes to do so. Through this quote, the epigrammatic speaker assumes the role of Odysseus. The epigram may thus be understood as relating back to *Anth. Pal.* 9.168.3, where Palladas stages himself as an anti-Odysseus through the adjective πολύμηνις. The second distichon of the epigram, then, is an allusion to (and partial quote from) *Il.* 24.602–3: καὶ γάρ τ

---

[36] Cf. also Guichard (2017: 165).

ἠΰκομος Νιόβη ἐμνήσατο σίτου, | τῇ περ δώδεκα παῖδες ἐνὶ μεγάροισιν
ὄλοντο ('for, even the fair-haired Niobe remembered her food, | although
all of her twelve children had died in her halls'). These words are spoken by
Achilles, who reminds Priam of the necessity to eat and drink by reference
to a mythical example. Intratextually, the passage relates back to *Il.* 19.225:
Achilles – who has finally found peace and put his anger aside – has
internalised Odysseus' admonition and now passes it on. Palladas, in turn,
refers to both passages and combines them into one epigram; the two
separate character speeches are merged into a single voice – that of the
author Homer: Ὅμηρος ἔφη ('Homer said').

2.3   Summary and Conclusion

Ausonius' dialogue with the classical past can, in essence, be divided into
two areas. The first main aspect is the way he initiates a discourse about the
authority and the value of the classical past and its representatives. Classical
authors and their authority are implicitly questioned on several occasions;
this concerns Cicero and his role as a translator of Greek terms into Latin
(*Epigr.* 12), Ovid and Pliny who turn out to be almost useless (*Epigr.*
72 and 103), and Pythagoras who is ironically employed as an authority in
a highly obscene context (*Epigr.* 73). In addition (and in close connection)
to this, Ausonius also discusses the relation of Greek versus Roman authors
and sources: *Epigr.* 12 is a free translation of an epigram by Posidippus; in
Epigr. 103, the shift from Roman to Greek models is only superficial,
whereas Ovid remains the principal classical authority beyond the surface.
In sum, we can conclude that Ausonius' discourse about the classical past
and the authority of its representatives is surprisingly complex and differ-
entiated; he does not suggest a straightforward answer, and most notably,
he prioritises Roman over Greek authorities but at the same time also
questions the former.

    The second area is the way Ausonius negotiates the value and validity of
literary sources and models as such. We noted several instances where a
tension is created by explicitly acknowledged sources versus implied,
anonymous, hidden ones. In *Epigr.* 72, an unacknowledged source is
juxtaposed with Ovid and Pliny; in *Epigr.* 73, Ovid is alluded to by way
of an intertextual reference, whereas Pythagoras and Lucilius are mentioned by name; in *Epigr.* 75, Afranius is acknowledged, but Martial and
Quintilian are made at least equally important (if not more so) by way of
intertextual hints. Furthermore, this aspect is reinforced by what I chose to
call 'fake sources': textual allusions which raise suspicions about the

credibility and authenticity of a model, such as the place name of Vallebana in *Epigr.* 72, a dodgy reference to Lucilius in *Epigr.* 73, and an unclear relation to Martial in *Epigr.* 75. Thus, Ausonius feeds back into the question about the relation between the classical past and the present; to how far an extent literary models and sources are valuable and reliable for an epigrammatic author of his period; and to what extent the classical past and its recollection is a mere construct, an invention, a fantasy.

Palladas, then, is conspicuously different from Ausonius in both content and tone. For reasons of scope and focus, this analysis had to be selective and was therefore restricted to Homeric epigrams. Content-wise, Palladas often focusses on his role as a schoolteacher as well as his excessive misogyny. Thus, in contrast to Ausonius, Palladas constructs a considerably more tangible *persona* of himself in his epigrams. Viewed from this 'personal' angle, his relation to Homer is twofold: as a *grammaticus*, he clearly has an ambivalent attitude towards Homer, whose works constitute the source of his living although Homer himself is the cause of Palladas' dissatisfaction. In his role as a misogynist, however, Palladas displays a less ambivalent attitude towards Homer – in these epigrams, he resorts to the *iam Homerus*-motif by (ab-)using Homer as a paradigm and justification for his misogyny. On one occasion, Palladas even goes so far as to stylise himself as a counterpart to a Homeric character: as an anti-Odysseus who does not wish to return to – but, rather, wants to be released from – his wife (*Anth. Pal.* 9.168).

From a more technical perspective, it can be noted that Palladas creates Homericity both through *nominatim* references as well as via verbal and structural intertextuality. One specific technique is that of the scholastic practice of teaching inflection on the basis of the first lines of the *Iliad* – in these cases, we are faced with a triangle of a personal voice, a concrete *Sitz im Leben*, and an idiosyncratic literary technique. Another literary technique – often used by Ausonius, too, as discussed above – is that of the juxtaposition of acknowledged and unacknowledged sources or topoi. This technique is clearly more at home in the work of Ausonius, but it can be found in Palladas on two occasions as well: namely, in *Anth. Pal.* 9.166 (the stereotype of the destructive Helen paired with an analogous *ad hoc* penalisation of Penelope) and in *Anth. Pal.* 9.165 (Homer as an acknowledged *nominatim* model versus Hesiod and Euripides as hidden sources).

It goes without saying that any generalisation which is deduced from this comparison between Ausonius and Palladas can only be tentative and provisional. Further studies will have to take into consideration more authors and larger corpora. It could, for example, be rewarding to expand the analysis to Ausonius' *Epitaphia heroum qui bello Troiano interfuerunt* ('Epitaphs on the heroes who participated in the Trojan War'), a collection of epigrams many of which engage with the Homeric tradition and its reception in Roman epic (Vergil), or to the *Epigrammata Bobiensia*, a collection of Latin epigrams attributed to various (partly unidentified) authors, the latest of which are dated to the age of Ausonius, and some of which have been identified as imitations of epigrams by Palladas. Another epigrammatist appropriate for this type of study could be Christodorus of Coptus, author of the 'Description of the statues in the public bath-gymnasium of the so-called Zeuxippus' in Constantinople (late fifth century CE); this epigrammatic catalogue of museal statues features numerous characters from the classical past of both Greece and Rome. As the analysis in this chapter has shown, there are considerable differences in the approaches to the literary past between Ausonius and Palladas. Further research, going beyond individual authorial differences, will have to contemplate the question as to whether there is a typically Roman versus Greek way of dealing with the classical past in later imperial epigrammatic poetry.

CHAPTER 3

Allusion and Referentiality in Late Antique Epic

Calum Maciver

Nam quis non Nioben numeroso funere maestam
Iam cecinet?

For who is there now who has not sung of
Niobe distraught at those deaths so numerous?

Nemesianus, *Cynegetica* 15–16.

Nemesianus begins his didactic poem on hunting (published 283–4) with
a *recusatio*, listing the catalogue of themes associated with the writing of
epic that he will avoid; he will seek other fields now that he has been
inspired with new cups from the nourishing font of the Muses (lines 4–5).[1]
His first mythological example truly is a clichéd one, and the reader might
well ask who indeed had not sung of Niobe.[2] This type of self-reflexivity
and advertisement of the tradition, characteristics of genre and assertions
of uniqueness of poetic enterprise, is much more typical of late antique
poetry in Latin than in Greek. Even in Nonnus' *Dionysiaca* (fifth century),
an epic more blatantly self-referential than any other Imperial Greek
poem, the poet's engagement is with Homer above all, and nowhere does
he explicitly mention his Imperial predecessors. Such intertextual behaviour marks out Greek poetry as decidedly different from the interactive
discourse so identifiable on the Latin side.

Scholarship on late antique poetry is burgeoning (this statement has itself
become a clichéd feature of work published in the past two decades), but
even in this respect there is a disparity in the nature of the work done between
the Greek and the Latin sides. One could go so far as to assert that the playful

I would like to express my thanks to the editors (and organisers of the conference in Ghent, as well as
the participants) for their input and for the production of this volume.

[1] For recent discussion of the proem and *recusatio* at the beginning of the *Cynegetica*, cf. Jakobi (2014:
53–77).
[2] Niobe as a repeated mythological paradigm features, for example, in the two largest extant Greek
epic poems of the Imperial period, in Quint. Smyrn. 1.291–304, and Nonnus' *Dion.* 2.159–60,
12.79–81, 130–2, 28.428–9, 48.406–8, 417, 424–32 and 455–6.

reflexivity so much more transparent in the Latin poetry of Late Antiquity has produced a similar type of scholarship, whereas on the Greek side the studies in the last two decades have tended to reflect the more conservative nature of Greek verse of the Imperial period (that is not to disparage such work, which has certainly breathed life into an area so long sidelined or undermined).[3] The trend in studies of late antique Latin poetry has been to articulate a poetics peculiar to late antique verse, exemplified above all by *The Jeweled Style*, the influential study by Michael Roberts. There has been a concentration of studies, more recently, on the nature of intertextuality in late antique verse. Pelttari (2014) and Kaufmann (2017, in an important collection of essays on the poetics of late antique Latin literature), in particular, have demonstrated that the intertextual strategies of referentiality so typified by Augustan poets do not always have the same functions in late antique verse in contrast to the evident intricacies of their Classical forebears. Late antique poets are more prone to quote and reuse phraseology without requiring the reader to apply any function from the context or content of the alluded text. Quotations, according to this theory, can be just quotations, advertisements of redeployment without any textual interaction to be further interpreted. Such allusions have been termed nonreferential. It is of course up to the reader, in the end, to decide which allusions are simply nonreferential, and this essential subjectivity will inevitably result in varying lines of interpretation concerning the validity of 'nonreferentiality'.[4]

As the editors discuss in the Introduction, the primary aim of this volume is to bring together into a single setting scholars from both the Latin and Greek sides, to share practices and to investigate potential areas of overlap. In this chapter, I will bring to Greek epic some of the recent work done on the intertextuality of late antique Latin verse. My focus, above all, will be on referential and non-referential intertextuality. I shall attempt to unpack some of the many 'cfs' which recur in commentary of Imperial Greek epic. So often similar patterns or phraseology are flagged in commentaries without further comment, the implication often being that the phraseology is simply that, and therefore not referential. For my case study in this chapter I shall examine allusions to Apollonius Rhodius in Triphiodorus' poem, and show that seemingly nonreferential allusions are in fact vital for understanding of Triphiodorus' poetic programme. I will

---

[3] That recent work on Nonnus is beginning to change this trend is no surprise: cf. e.g. the recent *Brill's Companion to Nonnus* (Accorinti ed., 2016), and the collection edited by Spanoudakis (2014b). Pivotal in studies of Quintus was the collection of essays edited by Baumbach and Bär (2007).

[4] For further discussion, cf. Section 3.2 (below); see the caveats expressed by Kaufmann (2017: 159) on allusions as mere formal features.

then explore whether recent scholarship on 'nonreferential intertextuality' can help elucidate one of the most contested allusions in Imperial Greek verse, namely, the in-proem in Book 12 of Quintus' *Posthomerica*. By choosing Triphiodorus and Quintus, I am restricting my discussion to near-contemporary poems with similar themes and practices (both concern the Trojan war and are characterised by overt and sustained imitation of Homeric language, motifs, and patterns). It is important, first, to explore, by way of introduction, some of the programmatic statements in late antique verse which seem to play on Hellenistic (and Augustan) metapoetics for the creation of poetic identity. I shall show that the 'jeweled style', a facet widely acknowledged to characterise late antique Latin verse, can be applied as a label too to Greek epic, through discussion of Triphiodorus' ekphrasis of the Wooden Horse in the *Iliou Halosis*.

3.1 Programme and Tradition

There are a number of ways of formulating labels for the poetics and aesthetics of late antique Latin verse, based on studies of the past fifty years. Most frequently one reads the label 'Alexandrian' or 'neo-Alexandrian'. The current trend in late antique Latin studies, however, is against understanding late antique verse as having an aesthetic which mimics the type of allusive engagement and poetics of exclusivity characterised by Alexandrian poetry.[5] Often Hellenistic poetic programme and Callimachean polemics are used to point to how late antique poetry is not Hellenistic. Rather, Alexandrian ideals are appropriated to voice a poetics of overuse and 'tiredness'. A passage in Ausonius, in particular, reflects this reuse of Alexandrian imagery for this very purpose (*Epistle* 4.20–8):

> Nam populi coetus et compita sordida rixis
>   fastidientes cernimus
> angustas fervere vias et congrege volgo
>   nomen plateas perdere.
> Turbida congestis referitur vocibus echo:
>   'Tene!', 'feri!', 'duc!', 'da!', 'cave!'
> Sus lutulenta fugit, rabidus canis impete saevo
>   Et impares palustro boves.
> Nec prodest penetrale domus et operta subire;
>   Per tecta clamores meant.[6]

---

[5] Cf., in particular, Pelttari (2014: 4), *contra* Charlet (1988).
[6] Green (1991: 611–12) for discussion of this passage; he compares, in particular, line 25–8 with Horace *Epist.* 2.2.74–5.

For I am weary at the sight of throngs of people, the vulgar brawls at the cross-roads, the narrow lanes a-swarm, and the broadways belying their name for the rabble herded there. Confused Echo resounds with a babel of cries: 'Hold!' – 'Strike!' – 'Lead!' – 'Give!' – 'Look out!' Here is a mucky sow in flight, there a mad dog in fell career, there oxen too weak for the waggon. No use to steal into the inner chamber and the recesses of your home: the cries penetrate through the house.[7]

This contrast between life in the rowdy city and the sanctuary of the countryside is a metaphor for poetic endeavour. Now Ausonius/the narrator of the poem discerns the narrow paths (*angustas vias*), the Callimachean ways of elite, learned poetry (στεῐ̣ι̣ϳγοτέρην, *Aet.* 1.28) in contrast to the broad ways of cyclical epic (οἶμον ἀνὰ πλατύν, *Aet.* 1.27), packed with the mob (cf. Hor. *Carm.* 3.1.1–4), which were supposed to serve as a contrast to the type of poetry Alexandria, and post-Alexandrian receptions, so characterised. Now the mob is clamouring to get in, and is choking those narrow ways so as to make them trodden rather than untrodden. The echo of voices (an allusion both to Callim. *Epigr.* 28 and Ov. *Met.* 3 (tale of Echo and Narcissus), and above all the house of *fama* in *Met.* 12) is packed with commands – so many are the programmatic, poetic agendas of the past, that the poet does not know where to turn. Ausonius attempts to mark out his own new paths, but this is only illustrated and described against (and within) the programmatic paths of the past: Alexandrian paths are no longer 'Alexandrian'. To warn against the past is to express the past, even if that advice is to scorn the (now) clichéd strictures of Alexandria.

The trend of the past three decades in the study of late antique Greek verse has pointed to the apparently Alexandrian nature of the epics of Quintus, Triphiodorus, and Nonnus,[8] but more recent studies have shown that Alexandrian allusion need not imply adherence altogether to Alexandrian poetic strictures.[9] The most recurrent label, in addition to 'Alexandrian' is the 'jeweled style', which has taken hold since the foundational study by Roberts.[10] Recently, similar aesthetics have been identified for Greek verse of Late Antiquity, and in particular the poetry of

---

[7] Translation of Evelyn-White (1919).
[8] Cf. in particular Bär (2007), Maciver (2012b), Maciver (2020), and Acosta-Hughes (2016).
[9] I refer in particular to Greensmith's study of Quintus' in-proem (2018), whose arguments I include in Section 3.3 (below), in my own discussion of that passage.
[10] Roberts (1989).

Nonnus.[11] A very notable example occurs in Triphiodorus, too, in the description of the eyes of the wooden horse (69–72):

ὀφθαλμοὺς δ' ἐνέθηκε λιθώπεας ἐν δυσὶ κύκλοις
γλαυκῆς βηρύλλοιο καὶ αἱμαλέης ἀμεθύσσου·   70
τῶν δ' ἐπιμισγομένων διδύμης ἀμαρύγματι χροιῆς
γλαυκῶν φοινίσσοντο λίθων ἑλίκεσσιν ὀπωπαί.

He inserted eyes made of stone in the two circular holes,
Made of blue beryl and blood-red amethyst.
From the sparkle of the twin colour of the two when mixed together
The eyes were ruddy with the gleam of the blue stones.

The significance of these particular stones, and in particular their colour, is clear.[12] The wooden horse is closely tied in with the recurrent metaphor, propounded throughout by Triphiodorus, of the horse, and the horse/chariot race, as metonymic of the *aoide* that Triphiodorus has composed.[13] The wooden horse's function is very much a case of *ut pictura poesis*. Triphiodorus uses these particular jewels not only to reflect the quality of his own poem and poetry,[14] whereby just as onlookers behold the beauty of the blending of these colours, so too do readers appreciate the aesthetics of the poem itself.[15] It is no accident, either, that the poet has described beryl with the adjective used commonly for the sea (γλαυκῆς, 70),[16] and applies to the gem amethyst the adjective *bloody*, αἱμαλέης. In my discussion below on the connections between Triphiodorus and Apollonius, I show how closely paralleled the wooden horse is with the ship Argo. The metaphor of a ship reaching its destination built into the horse, which

[11] The recent *Brill's Companion to Nonnus* (Accorinti ed., 2016), for example, contains a number of studies which, as Roberts did for Latin poetry, usefully compare artistic aesthetics and Nonnus' verse. Cf., in particular, the contribution of Kristensen.

[12] Miguélez-Cavero (2013b: 156–76, and in particular 172–5) has detailed discussion of intertextuality. Cf., too, her discussion at p. 87. For the significance of gems in Nonnus' *Dionysiaca*, cf. Frangoulis (2003) and Faber (2016: 449–50).

[13] I discuss Triphiodorus' poetics more fully below (Section 3.2). The proem, in particular (lines 1–5), and the programmatic epilogue (664–7) are key in this respect. For further discussion, cf. Miguélez-Cavero (2013b: 127–34) and my own article on Triphiodorus' poetics (Maciver 2020).

[14] The fact that he carefully alludes to Posidippus' own poem on gems (6.3) in this description, as well as other poems which foreground the beauty of precious stones (e.g. Dionysius Periegetes 1119), points to emphasis placed on literary and intertextual quality as symbolised by these gem-eyes.

[15] Cf. Roberts (1989: 69) on the particular late antique aesthetics inherent in such descriptions: 'Poetic descriptions are not concerned with documentary reality. They may exaggerate and distort, exploiting the greater flexibility of their medium, but these distortions will tend to emphasise in the object described exactly those qualities that the observer of Late Antiquity was most inclined to notice and admire.'

[16] Beryl itself is, according to Pliny *NH* 37.20.76, the same colour as the sea. (I follow the note of Miguélez-Cavero 2013b: 174 here.)

itself is a metaphor of the poem reaching its own *terma*, is symbolised in the beryl. The bloody amethyst, in addition to the traditional association with wine,[17] connotes too the other aspect of the horse, namely, the ambush (*lochos*, line 2), which itself is a recurrent application of the horse throughout the poem.[18] The mixing of the colours of the gem-eyes is implicitly paralleled within the poem itself: for example,[19] the description of Enyo at 559–61, in the midst of battle, applies sea imagery and bloodiness:

παννυχίη δ' ἐχόρευσεν ἀνὰ πτόλιν, οἷα θύελλα,
κύμασι παφλάζουσα πολυφλοίσβου πολέμοιο
αἵματος ἀκρήτοιο μέθης ἐπίκωμος Ἐνυώ.

And all night there danced in the city Enyo, revelling
Like a storm churned up with the waves of crashing
War, drunk with unmixed blood.

Enyo is drunk with blood, and is like a squall stirred by the sea's waves – though Triphiodorus has transferred the Homeric epithet commonly attached to sea instead to war here (πολυφλοίσβου πολέμοιο) – perhaps to emphasise the mixing of maritime and polemical imagery. This description of the personification of war puns on amethyst, in that μέθης not only echoes verbally ἀμεθύσσου, but points to the traditional use of amethyst as protection against drunkenness; the fact that Enyo is *drunk* with blood points especially to the description of the amethyst eye of the horse as bloody (αἱμαλέης).[20] Triphiodorus' 'jeweled style', an emblem of his poem's qualities, has a specific programmatic function within the poem, too, like the wooden horse itself.

3.2   Beyond the 'CF': Triphiodorus and Apollonius Rhodius

It is indisputable that the 'Latin side' is ahead of the 'Greek side' in articulating a template and function for intertextuality in late antique poetry. Recent studies by Pelttari,[21] and in 2017 by Kaufmann, have demonstrated well that late antique Latin authors deploy nonreferential allusion, to a greater extent than their Classical counterparts:[22] that is, to

---

[17] So Miguélez-Cavero (2013b: 174).   [18] Full discussion below in Section 3.3.
[19] Cf., too, the descriptions at 391–2 and 542.
[20] On amethyst as a protection against drunkenness, cf. the note in Miguélez-Cavero (2013b: 174). On Triphiodorus' propensity for punning, cf. Miguélez-Cavero (2013b: 86).
[21] Pelttari (2014: 126–30) summarises the trends of studies on allusion in late antique Latin poetry and then establishes new ground in our understanding of the role of the reader in the intertextual process (pp. 131–60).
[22] Pelttari (2014: 130–7).

follow Kaufmann's recent reformulation of the phenomenon, there are 'allusions of this kind [that are] purely formal features, that is, elements of the texture of the poem, by themselves expressing adherence to the classical poetic tradition but irrelevant for the content of the new poem'.[23] A later poet alludes to an earlier text, the allusion is as close to indubitable as any allusion can be, either through use of a rare word, or by quotation of whole lines or half-lines, but the content or context of the text alluded jars with and brings nothing to the content and/or context of the alluding text. I shall show that the same nonreferentiality of allusion applies to late antique Greek Poetry.

I begin first, however, with two examples of referential allusion to Apollonius' *Argonautica* in Triphiodorus, where one could easily argue for instances of nonreferential allusion. Triphiodorus uses the Argo as an intertextual symbol for the wooden horse in a number of places in the extended ekphrasis, and goes as far as to compare the size of the horse to a curved ship (63: ὁπόσον νεὸς ἀμφιελίσσης).[24] It is not, however, the Argo but rather the magical horse in *Argonautica* 4 that is especially alluded to by Triphiodorus in the intertextual fabric of the ekphrasis of the horse. At *Argon.* 4.1364–8 a horse leaps out of the sea, huge in size, and runs off across the desert, leaving a trail. Following this, the Argonauts are able to carry their ship and find the sea. The initial description of the portentous horse as it leaves the sea is referenced at Triphiodorus 58 and 67:

ἔνθα τὸ μήκιστον τεράων Μινύῃσιν ἐτύχθη.
ἐξ ἁλὸς ἤπειρόνδε **πελώριος** ἄνθορεν **ἵππος**   1365
ἀμφιλαφὴς χρυσέῃσι **μετήορος αὐχένα** χαίταις·
ῥίμφα δὲ σεισάμενος γυίων ἄπο νήχυτον ἅλμην
ὦρτο θέειν πνοιῇ ἴκελος πόδας.

Then was wrought for the Minyae the strangest of portents. From the sea to the land leapt forth a monstrous horse, of vast size, with golden mane tossing round his neck; and quickly from his limbs he shook off abundant spray and started on his course, with feet like the wind.

~

ἤδη καὶ βουλῇσι θεῆς ὑποεργὸς Ἐπειός
Τροίης ἐχθρὸν ἄγαλμα **πελώριον ἵππον** ἐποίει.
καὶ δὴ τέμνετο δοῦρα καὶ ἐς πεδίον κατέβαινεν
Ἴδης ἐξ αὐτῆς, ὁπόθεν καὶ πρόσθε Φέρεκλος   60

---

[23] Kaufmann (2017: 159).
[24] There seems to be an allusion to the building of the raft by Odysseus in *Od.* 5.249–50 in line 63, μέγεθος τορνώσατο τέκτων.

νῆας Ἀλεξάνδρῳ τεκτήνατο, πήματος ἀρχήν.
ποίει δ᾽ εὐρυτάτης μὲν ἐπὶ πλευρῆς ἀραρυῖαν
γαστέρα κοιλήνας, ὁπόσον νεὸς ἀμφιελίσσης
ὀρθὸν ἐπὶ στάθμην μέγεθος τορνώσατο τέκτων.
αὐχένα δὲ γλαφυροῖσιν ἐπὶ στήθεσσιν ἔπηξε   65
ξανθῷ πορφυρόπεζαν ἐπιρρήνας τρίχα χρυσῷ·
ἡ δ᾽ ἐπικυμαίνουσα **μετήορος αὐχένι** κυρτῷ
ἐκ κορυφῆς λοφόεντι κατεσφρηγίζετο δεσμῷ.

And now following the goddess's instructions Epeius her worker
Made the mighty horse, a statue of doom to Troy.
First he cut the logs and brought them down
From Ida itself, from where, before, Phereclus
Made the ships for Alexander, the beginning of the trouble.
He hollowed out the belly and made it
Fit the broadest sides, as big as a curved ship
Which the craftsman shapes off true to its length.
He fixed the neck on the hollow chest
And sprinkled the purple-edged mane with tawny gold.
The horse gloried from its height in the round neck
And was sealed from its head with a crested band.

The allusion has been noted before.[25] Like other allusions to Apollonius in
Triphiodorus, at first notice there scarcely seems to be a connection
between the two passages beyond the fact that a horse is described in
both. From the same passage commentators have noted, for example, that
ἐπὶ πλευρῆς ἀραρυῖαν at line 62 near-quotes *Argon.* 1.946 (ἐπὶ πλευρῆς
ἀραρυῖαι) but there in Apollonius describes the many arms fitted to the
bodies of the Earthborn of Kyzikos who dwell on the Mountain of Bears
(941).[26] The content and context there in Apollonius have no bearing on
or function in elucidation of the ekphrasis of the horse in Triphiodorus. It
is a clear allusion back to Apollonius but the underlying point of the
reference is unclear. This type of allusion may therefore be called with
some confidence 'nonreferential'.[27] In the case of the portent of the horse
of Poseidon from *Argon.* 4 quoted, however, Triphiodorus is careful to
embed the passage within his ekphrasis. The adjective πελώριος is used of
ἵππος only twice, here in these two passages. Similarly, only Triphiodorus

---

[25] E.g. Miguélez-Cavero (2013b: 167 and 172), Gerlaud (1982: 113) and Vian (2011: 397) but
without further discussion.
[26] Vian (2011: 397).
[27] Cf. Pelttari (2014: 131): 'The link between the context of their text and its hypotext is
undetermined. In this, the practice of late antique poets diverges from that of classical poets.'

and Apollonius use the adjective μετήορος in relation to αὐχήν.[28] The manes of both horses are made of gold. A plausible reason for Triphiodorus' careful allusion to this *live* horse, a divinely sent portent to allow the Argonauts to continue their journey home, is to emphasise the lifelikeness and size of his own horse (something the poet is careful to reiterate throughout the ekphrasis and which he encapsulates at 103–5)[29] and the divine sanction for its composition and success in its aim.[30] Moreover, this is an ekphrasis alluding to an ekphrasis,[31] and therefore the nature and quality of Apollonius' description encourage Triphiodorus' readers to put his own ekphrasis to the test, and judge how his ekphrasis compares, and the extent to which his horse excels that of Apollonius. This in itself would give justification to calling this allusion more than a mere formal feature, that is more than 'expressing adherence to a tradition but irrelevant for the content of the new poem',[32] yet the context in Apollonius casts further significance on the alluding passage in Triphiodorus. Peleus rejoices at the sight and tells his companions that their mother is no other than the ship Argo itself, saying (4.1372–4):

'μητέρα δ' οὐκ ἄλλην προτιόσσομαι ἠέ περ αὐτήν
νῆα πέλειν· ἥ γάρ, κατὰ νηδύος αἰὲν ἔχουσα
νωλεμές, ἀργαλέοισιν ὀϊζύει καμάτοισιν.'

'I observe that our mother is none other than
The ship itself. For she kept us in her womb
Without fail, and groans aloud in her grievous labour.'

Peleus observes that the Argo is pregnant with them in her womb and endures the pains of birth. In Triphiodorus, the careful collocation of the wooden horse with ship imagery throughout the poem, and especially the explicit comparison with a ship (lines 63–4) at the beginning of the ekphrasis, gains further relevance for interpretation of the wooden horse through Peleus' exclamation. The wooden horse is represented as a

---

[28] It is interesting to note that Triphiodorus uses μετήορος elsewhere only in describing the flaming torch which Helen holds from her chamber aloft to signal to the ships to return from Tenedos to sack Troy: σέλας πυρσοῖο μετήορον, line 522. The intratext is significant in that the holding aloft of the flame and the return of the ships is one half of the strategy, the other being the ruse of the lofty horse and the pouring out of the Greeks from on high. Note the emphasis in the immediate context on the eagerness of the Argives, who see the torch, to reach an end of war (σπεύδοντες, 524 and πολέμοιο τέλος, 525), echoing the programmatic emphasis on speed and the finishing post in the proem (τέρμα πολέμοιο, 1, and σπεύδοντι, 3).

[29] Esp. 105: εἴ μιν ζωὸν ἔτετμεν.   [30] E.g. Lines 2 and 56–7.   [31] Cf. Hunter (2015: 265–6).

[32] Kaufmann (2017: 156).

pregnant animal in Triphiodorus, at 135–6, 200, 308, 357 and above all in
the extended metaphor spoken by Cassandra at 379–90,[33] in addition to
the recurrent pun on the dual meaning of λόχος as both ambush and
childbirth.[34] Athene herself is midwife (390: μαῖα πολυκλαύστοιο τόκου
πτολίπορθος Ἀθήνη). The metaphors of ship and creature pregnant with
warriors, formulated in Triphiodorus for the wooden horse, are found
combined in Apollonius in the identification of the Argo as childbearing
mother to the Argonauts, by means of the allusion to the simile to the
portentous horse. The Argonauts carry the Argo in the trail left by the
horse to reach their *telos* of arriving at the sea and completing their
homeward journey, and similarly the horse in Triphiodorus will carry
the Argives in its belly and give birth to them and so bring about their
long-awaited aim of the sack of Troy, the poem's programatically self-
proclaimed finishing-post, *terma* (lines 1 and 667).

   The description of the builder of the wooden horse includes an epithet
which recalls the epithet of the builder of the Argo in the *Argonautica*, too.
The ekphrasis in Triphiodorus is prefaced with a description of Epeius as
under-worker of Athene (ἤδη καὶ βουλῆσι θεῆς ὑποεργὸς Ἐπειός, line 57).
Before Triphiodorus, in epic, it is used only by Dionysius Periegetes 342,[35]
and most notably by Apollonius at *Argon.* 1.226, of Argus the son of Arestor
and builder of the Argo: Ἄργος τε θεᾶς ὑποεργὸς Ἀθήνης.[36] The contexts of
the two passages are entirely dissimilar, yet the quotation of θεᾶς ὑποεργός
brings Apollonius markedly into the reader's mind. The function of the
allusion is the same as the reference to the portentous horse in *Argonautica*
4 – in the construction of the wooden horse there is to be read a synonymity
with the construction of the Argo. Both are Athena's devices, and both have
famous artificers who construct their renowned objects as the goddess's
subcontractors. Through careful allusion to key moments and terms in the
Argonautica, Triphiodorus draws Apollonius' Argo into the interpretation of
the nature and function of his wooden horse.

---

[33] Cf., for further discussion, Miguélez-Cavero (2013b: 31 and esp. 334–6). For the metaphor of the
    pregnancy of the Trojan horse in the tradition before Triphiodorus, cf. the study by Rodari (1985).
[34] For the significance of λόχος as ambush in Triphiodorus and its literary origins, cf. Gerlaud (1982:
    103–4) and Miguélez-Cavero (2013b: 120–1). On the double meaning, cf. above all Paschalis
    (2005: 97–8) and Miguélez-Cavero (2013b: 16, 63).
[35] Dionysius seems to be alluding to Apollonius, but the context in Dionysius makes it unlikely that
    Triphiodorus is alluding in this way to both poets, let alone to Apollonius *through* Dionysius.
[36] The parallel is noted by Gerlaud (1982: 112) and Miguélez-Cavero (2013b: 167), who also points
    to the original expression in the third song of Demodocus at *Od.* 8.493: τὸν Ἐπειὸς ἐποίησεν
    σὺν Ἀθήνῃ.

This twofold use of Apollonius' *Argonautica* in the intertextuality employed by Triphiodorus is similarly found in allusions to Medea. Silence comes over the Trojans and their city on the eve of destruction, and the barking of dogs is not heard (503–5):

ἡσυχίη δὲ πόλιν κατεβόσκετο, νυκτὸς ἑταίρη,
οὐδ᾽ ὑλακὴ σκυλάκων ἠκούετο, πᾶσα δὲ σιγή
εἰστήκει καλέουσα φόνον πνείουσαν αὐτήν.

Quiet, Night's co-worker, greedily devoured the city.
Not to be heard was the barking of puppies, and utter Silence
Stood calling upon Slaughter who breaths Battle.

As Malcolm Campbell indicates,[37] 'when abstractions gang up like this there is no hope for a city'. The final attempts of Cassandra to show the Trojans the folly of their decisions have been ignored and scorned, and the city's celebrations have been doused with fateful slumber. All is ready for the sacking of the city. In *Argonautica* 3, the whole city sleeps *except* Medea who lies awake worrying about the trial Jason will face the next day. The description of the onset of night seems to be behind Triphiodorus' description (*Argon.* 3.744–51):

Νὺξ μὲν ἔπειτ᾽ ἐπὶ γαῖαν ἄγεν κνέφας, οἱ δ᾽ ἐνὶ πόντῳ
ναυτίλοι εἰς Ἑλίκην τε καὶ ἀστέρας Ὠρίωνος   745
ἔδρακον ἐκ νηῶν, ὕπνοιο δὲ καί τις ὁδίτης
ἤδη καὶ πυλαωρὸς ἐέλδετο, καί τινα παίδων
μητέρα τεθνεώτων ἀδινὸν περὶ κῶμ᾽ ἐκάλυπτεν,
οὐδὲ κυνῶν ὑλακὴ ἔτ᾽ ἀνὰ πτόλιν, οὐ θρόος ἦεν
ἠχήεις, σιγῇ δὲ μελαινομένην ἔχεν ὄρφνην·   750
ἀλλὰ μάλ᾽ οὐ Μήδειαν ἐπὶ γλυκερὸς λάβεν ὕπνος.

Then Night drew darkness over the earth, and on the sea
Sailors from their ships looked towards the Bear
And the stars of Orion, and now the traveller
And the gatekeeper longed for sleep, and the pall
Of Slumber wrapped the mother whose children were dead.
Nor was there any more barking of dogs in the city, nor the sound
Of men's voices, but silence held the blackening gloom.
But not indeed upon Medea did sweet sleep come.

Here in the *Argonautica*'s narrative it is the eve of an important day. Jason must face the trial of the bulls set for him by Medea's father. Medea cannot sleep because of the knowledge she has of forthcoming events and is in

---

[37] Campbell (1985: 493) on line 505, where he discusses these abstractions as 'beings'.

turmoil whether she should help Jason in his task. In Triphiodorus, it is precisely the Trojans' lack of knowledge of the imminent danger for their city which makes this allusion to Apollonius so markedly functional in drawing a contrast between the anxiety of Medea and the ignorance and celebration of the Trojans. The verbal parallels are clear: οὐδ' ὑλακὴ σκυλάκων ἠκούετο (504 – the only occurrence of the non-Homeric ὑλακή in Triphiodorus) recalls οὐδὲ κυνῶν ὑλακὴ ἔτ' ἀνὰ πτόλιν (749), especially as both emphasise the drawing in of night under silence (σιγή).[38] Beyond the superficial connection between the passages of nightfall, the contrasting states of sleep and wakefulness emphasise the blindness of the Trojans to the impending doom.[39]

3.3   Quintus' Sheep and Nonreferentiality

Triphiodorus, then, applies Apollonian intertextuality at key moments in his narrative with significant impact on how the reader unpacks the poem, even if, at first, that intertextuality appears to be a confluence of similar phrasing with little connection in content or context. I turn, now, to Triphiodorus' near contemporary Quintus of Smyrna to raise the possibility that he deploys non-referential allusions in situations which scholars previously have taken as vital to an understanding of Quintus' poetics. Quintus' epic was famously termed anti-Callimachean by his greatest commentator, Francis Vian.[40] There are instances in his poem of the type of intertextual engagement which one would find in the Alexandrian poets: for example, there is the extremely cogent example at *Posthomerica* 5.239,[41] at the beginning of Odysseus' first speech in the *hoplon krisis*, where he describes Ajax in terms which evoke the description of Thersites in *Iliad* 2. Odysseus applies to Ajax the very adjective used by the primary narrator in the *Iliad* to describe Thersites' speaking style, namely ἀμετροεπής. It occurs in poetry in only these two places (*Il.* 2.212 and *Quint. Smyrn.* 5.239). Thus, in his opening nomination of his

---

[38] For further discussion of the parallel, and of the significance of the passage in Triphiodorus, cf. Miguélez-Cavero (2013b: 385–6).

[39] Triphiodorus has carefully inserted a further Hellenistic reference within the Apollonian allusion. κατεβόσκετο (503), of the quiet which devours the city, occurs only here in Triphiodorus and previously in hexameter verse at line 125 of Callimachus' *Hymn to Artemis*, used to describe the plague that infects the cattle of the city against which Artemis has turned her anger because of the citizens' wrongdoing.

[40] Vian (1963: xl). A brief discussion of Quintus and possible Callimachean elements can be found at Maciver (2012b: 67).

[41] I have fuller discussion at Maciver (2012c: 616–20).

antagonist Ajax he alludes to the Iliadic setting in which he punished a speaker who had no right to speak, and who was in status far below the level of Odysseus himself or the other kings. James and Lee, in their commentary on Book 5, state that 'for once Quintus achieves all the allusive wit of Callimachus'.[42] James and Lee imply that such 'Callimachean' moments in the *Posthomerica* are the exception rather than the rule, and even the most ardent proponent of an Alexandrian type of engagement with the literary tradition by Quintus cannot deny that, for the most part, Quintus' poetic agenda is rather different from, for example, Nonnus' thorough and careful activation and realignment of Hellenistic poetics.[43]

Quintus' Callimachean moments are occasional and have therefore attracted a greater degree of attention than other sections of his epic. This is especially the case with the programmatic Muse-invocation in Book 12. The most recent study is the groundbreaking article by Greensmith (2018), which has entirely shifted scholarly discourse away from Quintus as a 'Homeric' poet who is 'Callimachean' too, to something much more nuanced. To contextualise: Quintus' *Posthomerica* has no proem at the beginning of the poem; it begins exactly where the *Iliad* ends ('after godlike Hector had been killed by the son of Peleus …', line 1), an indication in itself of the direct continuation of the *Iliad* which the *Posthomerica* poses as, evident not only in this apparently seamless transition, but in the overwhelmingly Homeric nature of the epic's linguistic fabric.[44] Every aspect of the *Posthomerica* bespeaks the Homeric epics which it so closely imitates.[45] It is no surprise, therefore, that there is nothing in the in-proem of Book 12 which could not be applied, traditionally, to the poet of the *Iliad*. It is a pseudo-autobiographical vignette with the conceit of articulating the voice of Homer himself, but there are infiltrations of non-Homeric elements, in particular allusions to Hesiod and Callimachus, which allow the reader to get a glimpse of a *persona* which has betrayed his belated identity. The narrator invokes the Muses immediately before cataloguing the heroes who enter the recently constructed wooden horse (12.306–13):

---

[42] James and Lee (2000: 93).
[43] On Nonnus' Alexandrian poetics, cf. Acosta-Hughes (2016) and Hollis (1994).
[44] On the (hyper-)Homeric nature of the *Posthomerica*, cf. my overview in Maciver (2012a: 3–27).
[45] The Homeric nature of the *Posthomerica* makes the evident non-Homeric elements, especially the ethical framework, all the more noteworthy and apparent. This is especially the case with the recurrent wisdom sayings in the poem, which I discuss at Maciver (2012a: 87–123).

τούς μοι νῦν καθ᾽ ἕκαστον ἀνειρομένῳ σάφα, Μοῦσαι,
ἔσπεθ᾽ ὅσοι κατέβησαν ἔσω πολυχανδέος ἵππου·
ὑμεῖς γὰρ πᾶσάν μοι ἐνὶ φρεσὶ θήκατ᾽ ἀοιδήν,
πρίν μοι <ἔτ᾽> ἀμφὶ παρειὰ κατασκίδνασθαι ἴουλον,
Σμύρνης ἐν δαπέδοισι περικλυτὰ μῆλα νέμοντι   310
τρὶς τόσον Ἕρμου ἄπωθεν ὅσον βοόωντος ἀκοῦσαι,
Ἀρτέμιδος περὶ νηὸν Ἐλευθερίῳ ἐνὶ κήπῳ,
οὔρεϊ οὔτε λίην χθαμαλῷ οὔθ᾽ ὑψόθι πολλῷ.

Tell me clearly now, Muses, in answer to me, the names of
Each one who went inside the cavernous horse.
For you inspired me with all my song,
Before the soft down was spread over my cheeks,
As I was shepherding my renowned flocks in the plains of Smyrna,
Three times as far from Hermos as you can hear a shout,
Around the temple of Artemis in the garden of Freedom,
On a mountain neither too low nor too high.

It is not my intention here to rehearse all of the interpretations applied to
this passage.[46] Instead, I shall concentrate solely all on περικλυτὰ μῆλα
νέμοντι of line 310. μῆλα νέμοντι is a quotation of Callimachus *Aetia* fr.
2.1–2:

ποιμένι **μῆλα νέμοντι** παρ᾽ ἴχνιον ὀξέος ἵππου
Ἡσιόδῳ Μουσέων ἑσμὸς ὅτ᾽ ἠντίασεν (...)

When the band of Muses met the shepherd Hesiod tending his sheep by the
footprint of the fiery horse ...

Greensmith encapsulates the current scholarly *communis opinio* on this
allusion to Callimachus and the other epic forebears in this passage: 'By
alluding to the figures of Homer, Hesiod and Callimachus Quintus finds a
coded way to chart his literary inheritance.'[47] There are two current views,
however, on how this Callimachean engagement here, in particular, functions. One view, set forward in particular by Bär,[48] and promoted too in
my own work,[49] argues for reading this allusion as a template for how the
Posthomerica as a whole is to be read: that is, Homeric above all in its
imitation, but that Homer is received by way of Alexandria, and that only
an Alexandrian type of reader will be able to engage fully with the
Alexandrian allusiveness offered by Quintus, *à la* Callimachus. The problem with this interpretation is that allusive engagement in Quintus of this

---

[46] For full discussion cf. Greensmith (2018).   [47] Greensmith (2018: 3).   [48] Bär (2007).
[49] Esp. Maciver (2012b).

type is rarer than these studies seem to suggest.[50] Greensmith's recent re-evaluation of the in-proem has surely corrected the exaggerated apparent Callimachean practice of Quintus offered by myself and above all Bär. Greensmith is right to suggest that Quintus mobilises 'Alexandrian techniques [in the in-proem] ... to defend a defiantly non-Alexandrian poem'.[51] Greensmith has demonstrated that Quintus' engagement in the in-proem with Callimachus' programmatics is far more sustained than previously thought, and argues that Quintus deploys such engagement for a polemical purpose, to affirm his own poetics of conservative Homeric-imitativeness in the face of (traditional) demands for innovation and otherness. The insertion of Callimachean references in his most programmatic of passages is a proclamation that a poet can be both Homeric and un-Homeric unashamedly, that sustained and blatant Homericity need not exclude the voice of others from the literary tradition, including those of Alexandria.[52]

What follows is not to deny the validity of Greensmith's claims, but only to offer an alternative reading (or rather, *non*-reading) of the key Callimachean allusion in the in-proem. Labels such as programme imply a template, in miniature, to enable the reader to unpack the poet's poetic agenda and interpret the rest of the poem accordingly.[53] Triphiodorus' proem offers such a template without any disguise, to the extent that the proem is answered by the epilogue towards the end of the poem (lines 664–7) which itself emphasises further the metaphor both of the horse race and of the poetics of brevity raised in the poem's first five lines. The rest of the poem reiterates this programme with insistence, to the extent that the programme becomes more dominant than the poem about which it is being programmatic. Quintus' epic, however, avoids such obvious self-reflection within the main body of the poem, given its design as a 'Homeric' bridging between the *Iliad* and the *Odyssey* – this is 'still' Homer, and overt Callimachean reference or practice would not be in keeping with this agenda.[54] I want to argue that it is possible to read the quotation of the *Aetia* as partially nonreferential in

---

[50] Having read Quintus yet again, in great detail, for my forthcoming English translation of the *Posthomerica*, I am more than ever convinced that this interpretation of the in-proem which I previously offered is too assertive and does not reflect the tendency of the poem as a whole.

[51] Greensmith (2018: 4).

[52] As Greensmith (2018: 37) puts it, Quintus confronts 'his Homeric affiliation proudly and without apology, [and] he finds a way to redefine it as a discrete epic agenda – a *post* post-Homeric poetics'.

[53] The most cogent discussion of the function of such in-proems is still that of Conte (1992).

[54] That is undoubtedly why the *Posthomerica* lacks overt reflection on its poetics. However, it is not strictly speaking correct to assert that the *Posthomerica* avoids Alexandrian practices on the whole – cf. Greensmith (2018: 8–10).

function. In his only 'autobiographical', reflexive moment, the poet fills his invocation with allusions to invocations. All of these allusions have a refer- ential function to an extent. The allusion to *Iliad* 2 and the invocation before the catalogue of ships (2.484–93) fits the context in Quintus, in that the narrator is about to catalogue the heroes who enter the horse. The allusion to Hesiod *Theog.* 22–8 is the most dominant in the passage, given its focus on poetic initiation for a shepherd tending flocks. The Callimachean allusion references Hesiod, and reinforces Quintus' own allusion to Hesiod, and is as close to a naming of a poetic predecessor as Quintus comes, given that *Hesiod* is named there at *Aet.* Fr. 1.2. The two lines in Callimachus also point to the location of Hesiod: he was tending his sheep by the trace, or print, of the fiery, or swift, horse (1.1: παρ' ἴχνιον ὀξέος ἵππου). The insertion of the Callimachean reference, then, has the dual function not only of nominating Hesiod but also of playing with the notion that a *horse* was associated with Hesiod's own initiation. Quintus' own initiation is reported in conjunction with the most critical moment in his own epic, the completion of the wooden horse, which portends the sack of Troy. Quintus reinforces the homage he pays to Hesiod (and Homer too) by emphasising that the sheep he tends, the symbol for his own poetry, are περικλυτά (310) – renowned sheep because of the source from which he receives them.[55]

The impact of the Callimachean allusion could end there – that is the extent of its referentiality. The inclination of scholars has been to find further metapoetic significance for the reference, despite (to state it only in very general terms) the un-Callimachean fabric of the poem as a whole. I would like to posit that in typical epic type-scenes Quintus alludes to famous earlier epic type-scenes of the same kind, to underscore the nature and inheritance of the type-scene he is constructing, as if to assert 'this is a Muse invocation'. Thus, this allusion to Callimachus is referential only in the sense that it is an allusion to an initiatory/invocatory poetic scene – both the alluding text and the alluded text share this characteristic, but further referentiality is not present. To illustrate the point further, take the ekphrasis of the shield of Achilles in *Posthomerica* 5. Quintus opens his description in typical (one could argue, clichéd) terms:

Ἀμφὶ δὲ πάντη   5
δαίδαλα μαρμαίρεσκεν ὅσα σθένος Ἡφαίστοιο
ἀμφὶ σάκος ποίησε θρασύφρονος Αἰακίδαο.

---

[55] I discuss this in more detail at Maciver (2012b: 66). For further significances for the adjective, cf. Greensmith (2018: 33–6).

> The ornate
> Designs glittered in all directions, as many as Hephaestus' skill
> Had crafted on the shield of the bold-minded grandson of Aeacus.

The adjective δαίδαλα in particular draws attention to the first description of the same shield, where the Homeric narrator describes Hephaestus making the whole shield cunning in its design (*Il.* 18.482, ποίει δαίδαλα πολλά).[56] Yet there is a further reference in lines 4–5, to Moschus *Europa* 43: ἐν τῷ δαίδαλα πολλὰ τετεύχατο **μαρμαίροντα**. Only in Quintus and Moschus is the adjective δαίδαλα used in conjunction with the verb μαρμαίρω in the same sentence. Both authors are alluding to Homer, but Quintus has once again included a Hellenistic reference within his more overt inclusion of Homeric intertextuality, in the most Homeric of all scenes in the poem, the description of the arms of Achilles. Yet the Moschus reference does little to further understanding or interpretation of the Posthomeric shield. Moschus' ekphrasis is a basket, one which belonged to Europa's ancestors, each of whom was abducted. Quintus has simply woven a reference to another ekphrasis within an ekphrasis, to emphasise that this *is* a post-Homeric, post-Hellenistic ekphrasis. This is a nonreferential allusion, beyond the similarity in that both sets of phrasing are ekphrastic and both allude to the Iliadic shield. Just as Quintus carefully inserts a Hellenistic reference (or references) within his Homeric (/Hesiodic) Muse-invocation, so here does he include this clear allusion to Moschus' own ekphrasis, without any obvious implication in extending or varying the meaning of the textual *locus* in Achilles' shield which has embedded the allusion. 'The poet alludes to a specific antecedent but does not ask the reader to interpret a given hypertext through the context of its hypotext.'[57]

3.4 Learning From Latin

My purpose in this chapter has been to appropriate some of the most up-to-date evaluations and techniques used of late antique Latin verse and bring them to bear on reading of (early) late antique Greek verse. I have attempted to show that Greek authors play with the overlapping aesthetics of art and text, and in particular the 'jeweled style', just as been demonstrated for Latin verse. There is certainly more to be done on that level of study of Greek texts, especially in terms of episode and disconnection of

---

[56] I discuss the Homeric reference, and discuss the intertextuality of the shield more fully, at Maciver (2012a: 43–8).
[57] Pelttari (2014: 137).

continuous narration. I have also discussed examples of referential allusion
in Triphiodorus in cases which have previously been posited (one assumes,
given no contextual discussion is given in the previous scholarship I cite) as
nonreferential allusion. Snippets of quotation of phraseology are often
mere quotation without further function in Greek epic, as is the case too
in Latin verse of Late Antiquity, but there are abundant examples of
allusion in Greek verse which need to be re-evaluated as referential, as
I showed is the case for Apollonian allusion in Triphiodorus and the
identification, above all, of the wooden horse with the Argo in the
Argonautica. I ended my analysis with a return, once again, to the in-
proem in Quintus *Posthomerica* 12, to argue that the frequently discussed
Callimachean quotation need not have the mannered programmatic function which has been applied to it by recent scholarship. Greek authors,
especially Quintus, allude to famous passages of type-scenes, such as
ekphrases and invocations, to underscore the fact that the reader is reading
that type of scene in the *Posthomerica*, as well as to point to the place in the
literary tradition, post-archaic, post-Classical, and post-Hellenistic (to use
modern applications of terms to literary periods), in which epics such as
those by Triphiodorus and Quintus are written.

Why is it that scholarship on late antique Latin verse is more abundant,
technical in its advances on how to approach these texts as a whole,
literary-theoretical, and (arguably) more developed as an evolving disci-
pline than scholarship on Greek verse of the same periods? The go-to
author by rights on the Greek side tends to be Nonnus, in that his more
overt reactionary responses to tradition and his more blatant programmatic
playfulness and 'otherness' attract scholars of Hellenistic poetry.[58] Yet
Nonnus is *unlike* the other epics which precede him, and the relative lack
of surviving texts in the Imperial period on the Greek side, and the
chronological and geographical range which separates the works which
survive, from Dionysius Periegetes to Musaeus and Colluthus, mean that a
cohesive formulation of aesthetics, shared characteristics, and interaction
for these works is very difficult. That is the primary reason for choosing
Triphiodorus and Quintus for this chapter, given their similarity of styles
and subject matters, as well as date. The two sides, Greek and Latin, of late
antique verse have similarities, and the scholarly trends for Latin verse can
be brought to illuminate Greek verse of similar periods.

---

[58] The authors found in the collection edited by Hopkinson (1994c), and as well as more recent edited
collections on Nonnus, prove this point.

CHAPTER 4

Speaking from the Margins
Paratexts in Greek and Latin Poetry

Aaron Pelttari

A paratext is the written or material enclosure that mediates a text to its readers.[1] Paratexts include such elements as titles, indices, dedications, prefaces, and illustrations. In the modern world, paratexts range all the way from authorial prefaces to the publisher's marketing information printed on a dust jacket. As many modern examples could show, the relation between text and paratext is often unstable. Because paratexts regularly change from one edition to the next, the author is usually regarded as less responsible for the paratexts than for the text itself. In the same vein, the impermanence of paratexts and their intermediate status mean that they provide precious insight into the literary cultures in which they are formed. Greek and Latin paratexts from Late Antiquity display a remarkable degree of similarity even though it is usually not possible to detect direct influence one way or the other.

This chapter is focussed on the paratextual elements that seem to have been most prominent in Late Antiquity and that are most recoverable today: titles, section headings, summaries, prefaces, and illustrations. In the sections on summaries and illustrations, I have included some material produced in Late Antiquity for earlier texts, both because it is indicative of the literary culture of Late Antiquity and because so few contemporary summaries or illustrations have survived for ancient poetry of any period. Usually, I have restricted the discussion to paratextual elements that could reasonably be attributed to the work of an author or to a contemporary editor.

Why privilege the author, especially when the very impermanence of paratexts clearly reveals that authors do not control their texts? I engage in a philological and historical mode of writing that seeks to uncover the layers in the history of a text. Of course, meanings arise through individual interactions, and authorial paratexts are subjective interpretations that

---

[1] The term 'paratext' was defined and studied by Gérard Genette (1987). For a collection of studies on Latin paratexts, cf. Jansen (2014).

need not carry more weight than any other interpretation. Indeed, non-authorial paratexts often have just as much of an impact on the reception of a text as any author's interpretation. But most non-authorial paratexts from antiquity cannot be located with any precision in space or time, and any historical study of Greek and Latin literary culture depends on relatively specific information about where and when the texts in question were written. Indeed, many of the paratexts considered here have often been ignored because they were thought to be much later and anonymous additions to the original text. Exploring authorial paratexts allows us to distinguish and differentiate some of the earliest layers of the text.

But why privilege the text? Intermediality confronts the fact that texts are just one of the means by which we interact with each other and with the world. Indeed, the kind of images that below are presented as illustrations were often independent from texts or even subordinated texts to their own ends. The entire question was treated by Michael Squire in *Image and Text in Graeco-Roman Antiquity* (2009). Even more, Ildar Garipzanov has argued that images became increasingly prominent in Late Antiquity (2015). And Optatianus Porfyrius provides an incredible example of how image and text were combined in the fourth century.[2] The choice to focus on texts is only pragmatic here, and much could be gained by reading Greek and Latin poetry in light of intermediality.

4.1   Titles

We will begin with the title after the author, in accordance with ancient practice.[3] By the Hellenistic period titles were given to individual poems and to collections of poems, and the practice continued throughout antiquity.[4] The new Posidippus papyrus demonstrates that collections of epigrams could even include section headings. Posidippus' poems are divided in that copy into sections such as λιθικά, οἰωνοσκοπικά, ἀναθεματικά, etc.[5] In the first century in Rome, Martial provides explicit and lively evidence that titles were added for the epigrams in his *Apophoreta* (14.2):

---

[2] Cf. Squire and Wienand (2017).
[3] *In exponendis auctoribus haec consideranda sunt: poetae uita, titulus operis* ... Serv. *Aen.* 1 praef. (Thilo 1). On such preliminary schemata of interpretation, cf. Mansfeld (1994).
[4] Cf. Fredouille (1997), Schröder (1999), and Del Mastro (2014).
[5] Cf. Johnson (2005: 71) and Krevans (2005).

Quo vis cumque loco potes hunc finire libellum:
  versibus explicitumst omne duobus opus.
lemmata si quaeris cur sint adscripta, docebo:
  ut, si malueris, lemmata sola legas.

You can finish this book at whatever point you wish:
  every piece is unfurled in two verses.
I'll tell you, if you ask, why the lemmata were written in:
  so that, if you prefer, you may read only the lemmata.[6]

The passive *adscripta* can suggest the impersonality of paratexts, and their distance from the author. Indeed, Martial clearly imagines that some readers will not proceed through the book from beginning to end. In Late Antiquity, Ausonius mentioned explicitly, in a prose preface, that the only thing he liked about the *Cupido cruciatus* was its title.[7] Furthermore, there can be no doubt that the titles of Commodian's eighty *Instructiones* are original, since they are spelled out as acrostics in the text. For example, the titles of the first three of Commodian's *Instructiones* are *Praefatio*, *Indignatio dei*, and *Cultura daemonum*.

Despite their widespread use, titles were not found with every poem or work, and extant titles are often later additions. In his commentary on the Psalms, Jerome notes that the individual Psalms had titles in Hebrew, Greek, and Latin, and he explicitly says that they are part of scripture (Jerome, *tract. in psalm.* I, p. 12):[8]

> Multi putant titulos ad psalmos non pertinere, et hoc qua ratione aestiment, nesciunt. Si quidem non haberentur in Hebraeis et Graecis et Latinis voluminibus, recte putarent: nunc vero cum in Hebraicis habeantur libris . . . miror eos hoc velle dicere, quod aliquid in scriptura sine causa sit.

> Many think that the headings do not pertain to the Psalms, and they do not know why they think this. If they were not included in the Hebrew and Greek and Latin volumes, they would judge correctly: however, since they are included in the Hebrew books. . . . I am amazed that they try to say this, that any part of scripture should exist for no reason.

For example, the heading for Psalm 5 (the one under discussion here) is *Victori pro hereditatibus canticum David* according to Jerome's translation from the Hebrew. We can see, therefore, that titles were an interpretable component of the text and should not be surprised that Jerome regularly discusses them in his commentaries.

---

[6] All translations are my own. [7] *Mihi praeter lemma nihil placet*, Auson. *Cupido cruciatus* praef.
[8] On this passage and the titles of the Psalms, cf. Schröder (1999: 196–8).

Although titles were already common in many genres, in Late Antiquity new titles continued to be added even to old texts. For example, Horace's poems were graced with descriptive headings in Late Antiquity. They included such information as the poem's addressee, topic, metre, and rhetorical category.[9] Likewise, titles are found for *Eclogues* 4, 6, and 10 in two manuscripts, the Palatine Vergil (*Pal. lat.* 1631) and the Roman Vergil (*Vat. lat.* 3867).

4.2   Section Headings

Subsections and section headings could also be an important component of poetic texts. As poems came to be written in codices, books of poetry came to be divorced from the physical dimensions of earlier papyrus rolls. Indeed, the division of longer works into books apparently began only in the fourth century BCE, and we should not be surprised that the length and use of book divisions did not remain constant throughout antiquity.[10] One result of the later developments was that poets divided a longer text into shorter book units in order to distinguish sections within the work. For example, the anonymous *Carmen adversus Marcionitas* (dated to the middle of the fifth century[11]) is divided into five books, despite the fact that the entire poem is only 1,302 lines long, with an average book length of 260 lines. The entire work is much shorter than just book 5 of Lucretius' *De rerum natura* (1,457 lines), and not much longer than Prudentius' one-book *Apotheosis* (1,140 lines, including both prefaces). The reason for the book divisions of *Carmen adversus Marcionitas* becomes clear at the beginning of book five, where the author uses them to break down and summarise the contents of the work as a whole (5.1–18). Likewise, Alcimus Avitus probably added titles to the five individual books of his *De spiritalis historiae gestis*, which were written around the turn of the sixth century.[12] The manuscripts give the following titles for each book (the number of lines for each book is given in parentheses):

1. *De initio mundi* (325).
2. *De originali peccato* (423).
3. *De sententia dei* (425).
4. *De diluvio mundi* (658).
5. *De transitu maris rubri* (721).

[9] Cf. Schmidt (1997: 223–4). For a study of the rhetorical terms used, cf. Färber (1937).
[10] For the early history, cf. Higbie (2010).   [11] Pollmann (1991: 33).
[12] Cf. Hecquet-Noti (1999: 31).

Because the length of books had become separated from the material realities of the papyrus roll, authors could use book divisions in a more flexible way to structure the work in its various parts.

Book divisions could also be discarded, or the vocabulary modified. Nonnus' *Paraphrase of the Gospel of John* appears without divisions in the manuscripts and as a single book of 3,653 hexameters. Book divisions no longer followed the format and length that had been common for poetry written on papyrus rolls and that had been made canonical through the scholarly activities of the Hellenistic world. More surprisingly perhaps, and in the opposite direction, the 48 parts of Nonnus' *Dionysiaca* were labelled ποιήματα, including in a surviving portion of the papyrus codex *Π* (Berolinensis P. 10567) from the sixth century.[13] At over 20,000 lines, the poem is enormous. The flexibility afforded by large codices was an impetus for authors to experiment with new ways of structuring their books and of marking the formal divisions within their poems.

Section headings are clearly related to the indices and capitula that were first used for technical writing but were also taken up by Diodorus Siculus and Dionysus of Halicarnassus in the first century BCE and by Aulus Gellius in his miscellany of the second century CE.[14] There are only a few examples from antiquity of continuous poetic texts being divided into subsections. David Butterfield has argued that the *capitula* extant in the seventh–eighth century archetype of Lucretius' *De rerum natura* are the result of a compli-cated process of revision beginning as early as the second or third century: in the first phase, someone apparently added marginal annotations in Greek and then someone else added further marginal annotations in Latin; around the fourth or fifth century, those marginal headings were transferred to indices for books 4–6; finally, the headings were transferred directly into the text (and not the margins) in rubricated capitals.[15] Although these headings were clearly not devised by Lucretius, their eventual placement within the body of the text shows that section headings for long and continuous poetic texts were not alien to the literary culture of Late Antiquity.

But good evidence also exists for some section headings composed by the original author in Late Antiquity. The headings in Ausonius' *Cento Nuptialis* are unproblematic, and they are already regarded as authentic.

---

[13] Cf. Vian (1976: lxi).
[14] On the earliest summaries, cf. Friderici (1911). On the historians, cf. Irigoin (1997). On lists and tables of contents, see Riggsby (2019), which was published after this chapter was written.
[15] Butterfield (2013: 136–202).

They divide the poem into the following sections: *Praefatio, Cena nuptialis, Descriptio egredientis sponsae, Descriptio egredientis sponsi, Oblatio munerum, Epithalamium utrique, Ingressus in cubiculum, Parecbasis,* and *Imminutio.* The final heading is especially noteworthy, as being a playful reference to the 'deflowering' of the bride and to the poem's explicit sexual content. More controversial than these headings are two examples from the works of Gregory of Nazianzus and Prudentius. We will consider Prudentius first because the situation with his *Apotheosis* is less complicated.

4.2.1   The Apotheosis *of Prudentius*

The *Apotheosis* was divided into at least six sections in the archetype of the surviving manuscripts. I list them below with the number of the line that they precede and citing their manuscript sources.[16] I have ignored minor and insignificant variants.

> 1. *Contra heresim quae patrem passum adfirmat*] *ATES,* omisit *B*
> 178. *Contra unionitas*] *ATES,* omisit *B*
> 321. *Adversum Iudaeos*] *ATES,* omisit *B*
> 552. *Contra homuncionitas*] *ATES,* omisit *B*
> 782. *De natura animae*] *ATES,* omisit *B*
> 952. *Adversum fantasmaticos qui Christum negant verum corpus habuisse*] *ATES,* omisit *B*
> 1062. *De resurrectione carnis humanae*] *S, De resurrectione* addidit *E, De resurrectione carnis* addidit *T,* omisit *A* (*B* hic deest)

The witness of the manuscripts and their coherence with the text of *Apotheosis* support the view that these headings are authentic.

The archetype of the manuscripts of Prudentius was produced either in the fifth or the sixth century. Johannes Bergman puts the archetype in the fifth century, and the headings appear in three out of the four secondary branches of his bipartite stemma codicum.[17] Only *B* (Ambros. D 36 sup) does not include the headings, and we should not be surprised that some scribes or editors would have preferred the clean and classical look of running text without headers.[18] Cunningham is more conservative: he believes that the tradition is too contaminated to be represented by a traditional stemma, and so he argues that five manuscripts or groups of

---

[16] I use the text and sigla of Cunningham's edition (1966) because there is nothing else relevant in Bergman's fuller edition (1926).

[17] Bergman (1926: xxiv).

[18] On the clean, classical look of luxury papyri from Oxyrhynchus, cf. Johnson (2004: 156–7).

manuscripts together represent the text as it was in the sixth century.[19] Again, *B* is the only one of his cited manuscripts that does not include the section headings for *Apotheosis*. Ms *A* (Paris. lat. 8084) has been dated to the first half of the sixth century, both on palaeographical grounds and on account of the signature in it of one Vettius Agorius Basilius, who was formerly identified as Vettius Agorius Basilius Mavortius (consul in 527) but should instead be seen as a relation of the consul.[20] Since the section headings must have been present already in the examplar of ms *A* and in the archetype of all extant manuscripts, then we are not far from the omnibus edition of Prudentius' works for which he wrote a preface in the year 404.

The section headings were probably written with the *Apotheosis* and not as an addition made by some early editor, for three reasons: the poem is structured as a loose collection of theological arguments; the headings come at meaningful points in the poem; and the wording of the headings suggest that they were written by a learned observer of theology who also innovated linguistically. That the structure of *Apotheosis* is accumulative rather than systematic is stated explicitly in the first two lines of the poem (*Apotheosis* 1–2):

> Plurima sunt sed pauca loquar, ne dira relatu
> dogmata catholicam maculent male prodita linguam.

> There are many [heresies], but I will name a few so that the teachings that are terrible to recall will not stain my catholic tongue producing them foully.

A poet who says that he will pick a few heresies from many would also be prone to separate the ones he chose under different headings. Although we have seen that not all manuscripts agree on the number of section headings, they do seem to mark and clarify significant breaks in the text. The first section ends with a brief conclusion (175–7) and resumes after the break with two vocatives and two imperatives that mark the beginning of the new section against the Sabellians: *Cede profanator Christi, iam cede, Sabelli* (178). The section *Adversum Iudaeos* (321) is different. Since the section builds slowly through a detailed introductory paragraph, the transition to a new opponent would not be entirely clear if the heading did not mark this as the beginning of a new topic. In contrast, the beginning of the next section clearly marks the transition from the polemics against the Jews: *Sunt qui Iudaico cognatum dogma furori / instituunt ...* (552–3). While the last two section breaks occur at logical joints in the text, the

---

[19] Cunningham (1966: xx).   [20] Cameron (1998).

headings improve the clarity of the argument. Although the *Apotheosis* could certainly be analysed in different ways, the breaks introduced by these headings match the key divisions in the text suggested by modern scholars.[21] A final reason to regard the headings as authentic is that the use of distinctive vocabulary – *unionita*, *homuncionita*, and *phantasmaticus* – points to a composer for the headings who was learned and creative. I have found the word *unionita* elsewhere only in the *Indiculus de haeresibus* wrongly attributed to Jerome: *Sabellius, qui et Patripassianus, idem et unionita* (39). I found *homuncionita* used before the sixth century only in Eusebius Vercellensis *De trinitate* 3.47, Arnobius Iunior *Praedestinatus* 1.76, and in the same *Indiculus de haeresibus* 42. The word *phantasmaticus* occurs once in Augustine (*Contra Faustum Manichaeum* 20.15), once in Isidore (*Etym.* 8.9.7), once in the Letters of Leo the Great (*Epist.* 124.6), and once in a scholium to the *Odes* of Horace (Hor. *gloss.* Γ ad *Carm.* 2.1.17).[22] For the sake of comparison, a search of the *Library of Latin Texts* (Series A and B) for *patripassianus* yields 36 hits.[23] A search for the name Sabellius yields 253 relevant passages. Either an editor somehow chose three very rare words to use in summarising the contents of this poem, or Prudentius himself selected the precise vocabulary to denote the competing theologies confronted in the separate sections of *Apotheosis*.

The clear testimony of the manuscripts of Prudentius, the coherence of the headings themselves, and their place within the text of *Apotheosis* make me confident that they go back to Prudentius, or at least to his circle (a copyist, editor, dedicatee, etc.).[24]

Whether or not one regards the headings as genuine may not make a huge difference for one's interpretation of the poem, but they do say a lot about its composition. In contrast to basic ideas of the classical poem as a single whole, the *Apotheosis* was structured as a series of individual sections.

4.2.2   The Poemata arcana *of Gregory of Nazianzus*

A different kind of evidence comes from Gregory's so-called *Poemata arcana* (Τὰ ἀπόρρητα). Although not all of his reasons are fully convincing, Rudolf Keydell has suggested that Gregory's work influenced

---

[21] Garuti (2005: 13–15) and Rank (1966: 18–31).   [22] Keller (1904: 381).
[23] The precise search term was 'patripassian*', and the search was run in July 2016.
[24] Compare C. T. Mallan's conclusions on the indices to Cassius Dio: since they were composed by a contemporary with interests similar to those of Dio, the likeliest conclusion is that they were made by the author (2016: 722–3).

Prudentius' Christian didactic poetry (*Apotheosis* and *Amartigenia*).[25] The *Poemata arcana* (the title was apparently added by the Byzantine commentator Nicetas David) have been printed by modern editors as a collection of eight poems, but there are good reasons to consider the work instead as a single poem totalling 713 lines but divided into eight subsections.[26] Indeed, Keydell argued in the paper already cited that the eight sections comprise together one didactic poem (*Lehrgedicht*), but he insists on calling each of them an individual poem, presumably because even he did not consider the possibility that the headings could be subheadings rather than titles for individual poems. In what follows, I will consider the poem section by section to review the evidence for thinking that Gregory structured the work as one continuous poem in eight parts. If my suggestions are convincing, then we have more reason to think that late antique poets used section headings, and we should pay closer attention to the titles and headings preserved in medieval manuscripts.

The first section, Περὶ ἀρχῶν, begins with a proem that starts from the clichéd image of a poet embarking on a voyage (*Poemata arcana* 1.1):

Οἶδα μὲν ὡς σχεδίῃσι μακρὸν πλόον ἐκπερόωμεν.

I know that we set out in skiffs on a long voyage.

The long voyage must be the entire work, especially since we will see that Gregory returns to this image later. Keydell thinks that the proem and the invocation of the Spirit in lines 22–4 were originally separate from the rest of this section, namely, lines 25–39 on the trinity.[27] As with Prudentius' *Apotheosis*, there is more than one way to divide the poem. Nevertheless, I suspect that the title Περὶ ἀρχῶν was chosen because it is vague enough to cover all of the poem's different beginnings.

The first words of the second section, Περὶ Υἱοῦ, are clearly linked to what comes before: Υἱέα δὲ πρώτιστον ἀείσομεν (2.1). Keydell pointed out that most of the sections are grammatically tied to the previous sections, and the δέ here is a good example.[28] Although it could also work for a looser collection of poems, πρώτιστον shows that the sections are definitely ordered. Even Donald Sykes, who views the sections as separate

---

[25] Keydell (1951). On the similarities and differences between Gregory and Prudentius, cf. Evenepoel (1994).
[26] Unlike most of Gregory's poetry, the *Poemata arcana* have benefitted from a full and reliable modern edition and commentary (Moreschini and Sykes 1997). As Moreschini explains (1997: ix), the eight poems were transmitted in the manuscripts as a single group but printed by Migne (Patrologia Graeca 38) as his *Carmina* 1.1.1–5 and 1.1.7–9.
[27] Keydell (1951: 318–19).   [28] Keydell (1951: 315).

poems, notes that πρώτιστον 'indicates the first major theme of the sequence of poems' and that the first section is 'treated as a proem to the whole'.[29]

The third section, Περὶ Πνεύματος, is more intriguing. The first two lines effect the transition, but they also gesture towards the dissonance of having one whole work divided into various sections (3.1–2).

Θυμέ, τί δηθύνεις; καὶ Πνεύματος εὖχος ἄειδε
μηδὲ τέμῃς μύθοισιν ὃ μὴ φύσις ἐκτὸς ἔθηκε.

My heart, why do you delay? Sing also the praise of the Spirit
but do not divide with words what nature has not separated.

The reference to dividing (literally 'cutting') clearly refers to the trinity, but Gregory's words could also refer to the transition in the poem to a new section. The unity of the poem through its different divisions would then be reflected in the unity of the trinity.

We can survey most of the other transitions more briefly. Section four (Περὶ κόσμου) is also linked to what came before (4.1):

Εἰ δ' ἄγε[30] καὶ μεγάλοιο Θεοῦ κτίσιν ὑμνείωμεν.

Come, let us also sing the creation of almighty God.

Section five (Περὶ Προνοίας) begins with an adverb, Ὧδε ('In this way') that refers back to the previous discussion of creation. Section seven (Περὶ ψυχῆς) begins Ψυχὴ δ' ἐστὶν ἄημα θεοῦ ('The soul is the breath of God'): as Sykes points out, the exact phrase appears as a transition within another of Gregory's poems, at Carm. 1.2.15.151–2 (PG 37.777A). Lastly, section eight begins with Δεῦρ' ἄγε καί ('Come now'). These transitions link the sections of Gregory's poem together as parts of a larger whole.

The transition between sections five and six deserves a closer look. Section six (Περὶ λογικῶν φύσεων) begins with an apparently abrupt simile introduced by Οἵη δ'; the simile extends for the first seven lines and compares the highest light of God to a sunbeam illuminating a rainbow. The expected transition between sections actually came at the end of section five, with an allusion to the stars as the fifth element that happens to match the place of that section (fifth) within the poem[31] and then with the following metapoetic reference to the poet's journey (5.70–1):

---

[29] Moreschini and Sykes (1997: 95).

[30] In his review of the edition of Moreschini and Sykes, Ian Tompkins (1999) notes that this same phrase was used by Gregory to introduce a new argument, rather than a new poem, at Carm. 1.2.1.56 (PG 37.526).

[31] Line 69 mentions the fifth element and also describes the planets as having a circular course (περίδρομον οἶμον ἔχοντες). That looks like a metapoetic reference to the form of the sections.

ἡμεῖς δ' ἡμετέρην ὁδόν ἄνιμεν.[32] ἐς λογικὴν γάρ 70
σπεύδομεν, οὐρανίην τε φύσιν καὶ δέσμιον αἴης.

But we will return to our path, for we hasten to the rational
nature that is both heavenly and bound to earth.

The rational nature bound to earth is certainly the human soul, and that is
the subject of section seven; section six, 'On rational natures', provides an
overview but then focusses on the heavenly spirits – that is, the angels and
demons. Therefore, Gregory describes in these lines his journey through
sections six and seven – and we have confirmation that the parts of the
poem are being thought of as a unity.

The middle of section six includes an extended passage in which the poet
says he is uncertain whether he should continue his theme and then
compares his situation to that of a traveller who pauses in fear before
crossing a river and continues only out of necessity (6.27–35). The difficulty
is that Gregory must now explain the source of evil in the world, and he
wants to be sure that God (who is good) not be associated in any way with
evil. As above, the mention of a traveller recalls the ship metaphor from the
beginning of the *Poemata arcana*, and the hesitation makes much more
sense here if we understand Gregory as having come to a crucial moment in
the entire work, rather than pausing in such a dramatic way so soon after
beginning section six. If the whole series of poems are seen as a study of a
quasi-Neoplatonic great chain of being, then it becomes apparent that the
crucial moment is the point at which change and sin entered the world.

The end of section seven transitions again from sin and failing to the
introduction of the salvation that is the subject of the eighth and final section,
'On the covenants and the appearance of Christ' (Περὶ Διαθηκῶν καὶ
Ἐπιφανείας Χριστοῦ). The transition recalls the nautical imagery from the
first section and clearly presents the sections as a continuous whole (7.122–9):

ὡς δ' ὑπ' ἀήταις
χειμερίοις παλίνορσος ἀλίπλοος ἦλθεν ὀπίσσω,
αὖθις δ' ἠὲ πνοιῆσιν ἐλαφροτέρῃσι πετάσσας
ἱστίον ἢ ἐρέτῃσι μόγῳ πλόον αὖθις ἄνυσσεν, 125
ὣς ἡμεῖς μεγάλοιο Θεοῦ ἀπὸ τῆλε πεσόντες,[33]
ἔμπαλιν οὐκ ἀμογητὶ φίλον πλόον ἐκπερόωμεν.
τοίη πρωτογόνοιο νεόσπορος ἦλυθεν ἄτη
δειλοῖσιν μερόπεσσιν, ὅθεν στάχυς ἐβλάστησε.

---

[32] The manuscripts are split between ἄνιμεν and ἄνομεν.
[33] ἀποτῆλε πλέοντες is the reading of ms *Cu*, but Moreschini and Sykes both prefer ἀπὸ
τῆλε πεσόντες.

> As a sailor of the sea
> comes back once more under the winter winds,
> and again spreads out the sail to gentler breezes
> or completes his difficult voyage again with oars,
> so we, who have fallen far from our great God,
> must complete our journey once more with difficulty.
> The newfound woe of our first parent came like this
> upon wretched mortals, from here its crop has sprung.

The voyage that Gregory will complete is, allegorically, the poem that is now almost finished. The port in which he finds temporary relief is the break between sections seven and eight. The journey finishes with the last section in which Gregory describes the solution to sin offered by Christ. The image of a traveller on foot recurs at the end of section eight (8.93–5), and anaphora in lines 8.97–9 marks the end of the entire poem.[34]

In summary, formal elements and internal references to the poem's progress and structure confirm that the *Poemata arcana* was written as a single poem. Although Keydell recognised the unity of the poem, he did not realise that the headings of the individual sections should be read as subheadings.[35] As far as the meaning and interpretation of the work, there may not be much difference, in theory, between a single poem divided into sections and a closely related series of poems. But the only reason to regard these as individual poems was that scholars had not realised that there are contemporary parallels in Latin for the use of section headings in a continuous poem, and this has important implications for how poetry was written and read in the fourth century and beyond.

4.3   Summaries

Summaries and *argumenta* are closely related to section headings. Many diegeses, hypotheses, and summaries by other names were produced already in the Hellenistic period.[36] They were usually in prose and produced for popular or important works. The early imperial *tabulae Iliacae* 6B and 12F include verse summaries of different parts of the *Iliad*, and hypotheses in verse were being appended to dramatic texts by

---

[34] The function of the anaphora was pointed out by Keydell, who also notes that this figure is rare in Gregory (1951: 317).

[35] Despite the title of his article, Keydell makes it clear that he does not think the poem is really unified: 'Richtig wäre es gewesen, auf die formale Verbindung zu verzichten und selbständige Gedichte nebeneinanderzustellen. Da Gregor sie beibehielt, wurde das Ganze zum Lehrgedicht und erhielt ein entsprechendes Proömium. Aber ein Zwitter ist es geblieben' (Keydell 1951: 320).

[36] Cf. Van Rossum-Steenbeek (1998) and Cameron (2004a: 52–62).

Late Antiquity if not before.[37] Even more, *Anthologia Palatina* 9.385 is a summary of the *Iliad* in 24 verses, with each successive verse forming an acrostic of the alphabet from alpha to omega.[38] The game was also played in Latin and for Vergil. Extant examples include *Anthologia Latina* 1 and 2 (Riese = SB 1–2), 591–602, 634, 653–4, 672a, 717, 720a, and 874.[39] All of these summaries were produced long after their texts had become canonical.

A *perioche* survives for the forty-eight books of Nonnus' *Dionysiaca*. On the basis of metrical, stylistic, and thematic similarities, Simon Zuenelli has argued that the 48 distichs of the *perioche* were probably written by the author himself; even more, the fact that the summary for book 17 does not match the received text suggests to him that the *perioche* was written for a hypothetical earlier draft of the poem.[40] Less controversial, perhaps, is an inference we can make from the transmission of the *perioche*: the fact that it is divided in the manuscripts into two parts and copied out before books 1 and 25 implies that the long poem was published in two separate volumes.[41] The writer of this summary, whoever it was, is playing a paratextual game to present a new epic as an instant classic, in line with the works of Homer and Vergil. If it is the work of Nonnus, he would be the only author from antiquity known to have composed a verse summary of his own poem.

4.4 Verse Prefaces

Metrically distinct prefaces to longer individual poems became common in the fourth century. These prefaces show the influence of various earlier forms, including proems, comedic prologues, epigrams, and the rhetorical *prolalia*. Twelve of Claudian's prefaces survive, for individual Latin poems and all in elegiac couplets.[42] Prudentius' five longer books in dactylic hexameters are all preceded by prefaces in various metres, including two in iambic trimeters. This corresponds to the normal practice among later Greek authors of hexameter poems, which were often prefaced by iambic trimeters influenced by the vocabulary and diction of Greek comedy.[43]

---

[37] Cf. Zuenelli (2016: 578–9) and Squire (2011b: 96–7).
[38] Ludwich (1887) edits a similar verse summary of the *Odyssey*.
[39] Cf. Gioseffi (2012) and McGill (2018).   [40] Zuenelli (2016: 585–8).
[41] As pointed out by Claudio De Stefani (2016: 672).
[42] Felgentreu (1999) is a thorough study of them.
[43] Cf. Viljama (1968: 68–97), Cameron (1970b), and Miguélez-Cavero (2008: 112–14). Lukas Dorfbauer (2012) has convincingly argued that Prudentius was influenced directly by Claudian.

The earliest examples are preserved on two sets of papyri: *P.Vindob. gr.* 29788a-b + 29474 (= Heitsch 27 + 28) contain fragmentary iambics that apparently introduced an encomium in honour of one Maximus; they have been dated to the third or probably the fourth century.[44] The other set of papyri (*P.Berol.* 10559 + 10558 = Heitsch 30 and 31) contain two fragmentary poems in which separate iambic prefaces introduce encomia in praise of either one or two professors of law in Beryto (Beirut).[45] The obvious inference is that Claudian borrowed the idea of writing separate verse prefaces from the example of Greek rhetorical poets. And these earlier Greek poets had apparently begun including iambic prefaces to their praise poetry either in the third or the fourth century. Despite a common beginning, the two traditions quickly diverged. Most notably, Claudian's example of using elegiacs was quickly followed by Sedulius, Sidonius, Venantius Fortunatus, and Corippus. Outliers in Latin include Dracontius' *Romulea* 1 (a preface in iambic septenarii to his poem on *Hylas*) and Priscian's preface in iambic trimeters to his panegyric for Anastasius, of which at least the latter would have been directly influenced by the Greek practice. Beyond metrical differences, the traditions also diverge in their most prominent themes and in the intertexts employed. Many more examples could be mentioned, but these prefaces have been studied before, and this is enough to demonstrate that the Latin tradition of writing separate prefaces probably descended from the Greek practice but that both traditions then followed their own separate ways.

The spread of authorial prefaces surely contributed to the popularity of book epigrams in the Middle Ages, the Byzantine occurrences of which are being studied in the Database of Byzantine Book Epigrams currently under construction at Ghent University.[46]

4.5 Illustrations

Diagrams were produced early on for scientific and technical texts, and Greek scribes of the Hellenistic period were probably influenced by earlier Egyptian practices.[47] And, in the first century BCE, Atticus and Varro each published collections of author portraits.[48] However, for Greek or Latin literary narratives, the earliest examples of images in extant papyri are

---

[44] Cf. Miguélez-Cavero (2008: 52–3) and Zumbo (2007: 2.1063–75).
[45] Cf. Heitsch (1963–1964: 94–9).
[46] The database and explanatory materials are hosted at www.dbbe.ugent.be.
[47] Weitzmann (1970²: 57–69).   [48] Cf. Small (2003: 129–34).

dated to the second century CE, and this is probably when Greek and Roman narratives first began to be accompanied by illustrations.[49] This thesis is still controversial, but I find Michael Squire's arguments on this point convincing. Because individual genres each developed in their own way and attracted illustrations at different times, we should be wary of assuming from parallel evidence that literary narratives were illustrated in antiquity before the second century. Indeed, the fact that eventual illustrations of comedy or epic were influenced by paintings and mosaics does not prove in any way that such images were included in books at an early date. Instead, the evidence suggests that the earliest images in Greek or Latin books accompanied technical texts and that their later adoption in literary narratives was influenced by their use with low or popular forms of narrative. A particularly intriguing early example is *P. Oxy.* xxii 2331 (middle of the third century), which contains two columns of poetry on Heracles and three line drawings in colour of the hero's labours. Gideon Nisbet has put forward the enticing suggestion that the papyrus presents a 'true mixed-media narrative' in which 'the reader is presented with two stories, not one' (2002: 16).[50] The images (Fig. 4.1) are inserted without frames within columns of text, and they seem to present an ironic counterpart to the laudatory narrative.

By the fifth century at the latest, lavish illustrations were being produced in codices of canonical and authoritative narrative texts. Extant examples include the surviving portions of the Vatican Vergil (early fifth century), the Roman Vergil (late fifth century), the Ambrosian *Iliad* (fifth–sixth century), and several examples with parts of the Christian scriptures (beginning in the fifth century).[51] The dates are estimates, but they provide a rough guide. Also extant are some illustrations in medieval codices that probably derive from late antique exemplars: from the fourth century in the case of Oppian of Apamea's *Cynegetica*, from the fifth century for the comedies of Terence, and from the fifth–sixth century for the *Psychomachia* of Prudentius.[52] The codex was better suited to thick painting, which would easily flake when unrolling a scroll, and the page format quickly came to accommodate large-scale images, although the earlier in-column format continued to be used. As Kurt Weitzmann has pointed out, the common use in codices of images with borders and of

[49] Cf. Geyer (1989: 29–55) and Squire (2011b: 129–39).
[50] Cf. also Nisbet (2011). For a broader view and some comparative evidence, cf. Stramaglia (2007).
[51] Cf. Bandinelli (1955), Wright (1993), Lowden (1999), and Wright (2001).
[52] Cf. Stettiner (1895–1905), Woodruff (1929), Spatharakis (2004), and Wright (2006).

Figure 4.1   *P. Oxy. xxii 2331; courtesy of the Egypt Exploration Society and the University of Oxford Imaging Papyri Project.*

scenes with full landscapes does not seem to have any earlier precedent in bookrolls (1970²: 52).

We are considering illustrations as paratexts, standing beside the text as a form of mediation and presentation. As such, it is implicit that illustrations are not subservient to the text or inferior to it. The interplay between word and image is a two-way process, and we should expect each medium to serve its own purposes. Indeed, the popular genre of verse tituli for images real or imagined already attests to the dynamic interplay between poetry and pictures.[53] The illustrated codices give full evidence of their images functioning as paratexts in the full sense. For example, the Vatican Vergil offers a remarkable illustration of Aeneas looking back at Dido as he leaves Carthage (Fig. 4.2). Dido, a thin and ghastly figure, gestures towards the departing ships. The round enclosure of the sea is shadowy and harsh. The sailors, and especially Aeneas, are shapeless and dark. And all of this is in sharp contrast to the light colours of the sky, the beach, and the building in the foreground. The scene no doubt reflects the artist's view of the

[53] On the *Tituli historiarum*, cf. Lubian (2014).

Figure 4.2   *Vat. Lat. 3225, fol. 39v, following Aen. 4.583; ©2021 Biblioteca Apostolica Vaticana; reproduced by permission of Biblioteca Apostolica Vaticana, with all rights reserved.*

pathos surrounding Aeneas' departure, and so it works as an interpretation of the text. Likewise, the images preceding each of the surviving *Eclogues* in the Roman Vergil present a kind of guide to the text, as they foreground the personae speaking in each poem: Meliboeus and Tityrus in the first eclogue; the poet in the second; Palaemon, Menalcas, and Damoetas in the third; and so on. Ancient critics often discussed the difference between speeches attributed to characters and the poet's speaking *in propria persona*, and so these images would function as a handy guide to this aspect of each

Figure 4.3 *Vat. Lat. 3867, fol. 14r, beginning of Ecl. 6;* ©2021 *Biblioteca Apostolica Vaticana; reproduced by permission of Biblioteca Apostolica Vaticana, with all rights reserved.*

poem.[54] This explains why essentially the same author portrait (Fig. 4.3) is found before *Eclogues* 2, 4, and 6. I have not found exact equivalents to these scenes in the surviving Greek illustrated codices, but the frames, techniques, and imagery employed are the same whether the text is written in Greek or Latin, and that suggests a certain level of continuity between highly skilled artisans engaged in making books around the Mediterranean.

The *Cynegetica* and the *Psychomachia* are the only poems composed in Late Antiquity for which there is good evidence of illustrations created in the same period. It seems likely *prima facie* that the *Cynegetica* attracted

[54] On personae in ancient criticism, cf. Nünlist (2009: 116–34).

Figure 4.4   *Paris. Lat. 8085, fol. 55v, beginning of Psychomachia; courtesy Bibliothèque nationale de France.*

illustrations because its subject matter was close to the kind of technical and zoological treatises that had often been illustrated. The *Psychomachia* would fit several categories of illustrated books: scripture, magical texts, and quasi-technical psychology. The illustrations could also have been a way to put this foundational Christian epic in the same category as the works of Vergil and Homer. Nevertheless, there has been essentially no study of the illustrations to the *Psychomachia* in almost ninety years, in part no doubt because of the complications of Prudentius' manuscript tradition and because of the problems with reconstructing from Carolingian copies an exemplar dated to the fifth or sixth century. However, the illustrations open up, radically, the experience of the text; and it is remarkable that the extant *Psychomachia* images may derive from a version created already in the fifth century. We can see the effect of the illustrations already on the first page of a version copied in the ninth century (Fig. 4.4), in which the poem is overtaken by three large, dramatic, and complicated images. In the Middle Ages, the images present the poem as a classic worthy of the same diligence as Homer or Vergil, the same reverence as scripture, and the same caution as a scientific or technical treatise. If illustrated copies of Vergil and Homer were not in fact created until the later fourth century, then this would suggest that the illustrations to the *Psychomachia* derive from a time when images were first being combined in a book with high epic poetry.

4.6   Conclusion

Because paratexts are always on the border, they are usually attributed to the work of scribes and editors rather than individual authors, and so it is less likely that we will be able to identify in them the work of individuals or of direct influences between Greek and Latin. Nevertheless, extant paratexts do reveal a considerable degree of overlap between the Greek and Roman literary cultures of Late Antiquity, and especially in the use of headings, prefaces, and illustrations. In both East and West, we see that authors and scribes extended each of these categories in the fourth and fifth centuries as they came to use them for their own and contemporary poems. Such a shared movement towards paratexts points to a shared desire to interpret the text, or at least to play with the impossibility of writing a text that is already interpreted.[55] While the paratext provides a way out of the text and gestures at an escape from the text, it is an escape that can never come because the paratext also remains a text with a history. To put it another way, the author is already a reader, and even an authorial paratext is an act of interpretation. And while we can see a remarkable degree of similarity between large-scale developments in Latin and Greek in Late Antiquity, individuals constantly adapted paratexts to suit their own particular uses.

---

[55] On the role of the reader in late antique Latin poetry, cf. Pelttari (2014).

PART 2

Late Antique 'Genres' and 'Genre' in Late Antiquity

CHAPTER 5

The Implosion of Poetic Genre in Late Antiquity

Helen Kaufmann

Late Antiquity saw significant developments in poetic genre. Genres such as biblical epic, ekphrastic epic, epithalamia, and hymns first appeared or became particularly popular in that period, at times in forms that differed considerably from their classical counterparts. Furthermore, late antique poetic genre appears to be particularly flexible and open to change, as is evident from works such as Rutilius Namatianus' *De reditu suo* (early fifth century), a hybrid of an *itinerarium*, νόστος, and elegy or the Greek *Iambi ad Seleucum*, an iambo-didactic letter of the fourth-century bishop Amphilochius of Iconium.[1]

Scholars have accounted for what happened to genre in Late Antiquity in various ways: Fontaine (1975: 760–9, 775–7 and 1977: 438–52), for example, referred to it as 'mélange des genres' (1975) 'et des tons' (1977) ('blend of genres and tones'); Ludwig (1977: 304–50) as 'Transformation der klassischen Gattungen' ('transformation of classical genres'); Herzog (1977: 381–400) discussed a range of transformative processes from 'Verdrängung' ('replacement') and 'Kontrafaktur' ('rivalry through contrast') to 'Verschmelzung' ('amalgamation') and 'Christianisierung' ('Christianisation'); Garzya (1984: 19) pointed to the reduced importance of generic ethos;[2] and Young (2004: 254) suggested that '[l]ittle of [fourth- and fifth-century Christian literature] can be analysed neatly according to

---

I would like to thank the organisers, Calum Maciver, Aaron Pelttari, and Catherine Ware, and audience of the *Poetry and Aesthetics of Late Antiquity* conference (Edinburgh, September 2015) for their favourable reception of this chapter as well as the audience and the organisers, Berenice Verhelst and Tine Scheijnen, of the Ghent workshop *Walking the Wire* for further comments and suggestions. I am particularly grateful to Mary Whitby, Aaron Pelttari, Laura Miguélez-Cavero, Ruth Parkes, and Berenice Verhelst for their suggestions.

[1] On the former cf. Fo (1989: 54–6) and Brocca (2003), on the latter Oberg (1973) and Dijkstra (2016: 162–4).

[2] 'In epoca tardoantica la sensibilità nei riguardi dell' ethos dei singoli generi si attenua notevolmente [. . .]. Le motivazioni sono diverse per il greco et per il latino [. . .]: il resultato è il medesimo: una "eintönige Stilisierung".'

the classical genres'.[3] Without denying the merits of these and other characterisations of genre, I propose the metaphor of implosion to describe poetic genre in Late Antiquity, arguing that the classical order of poetic genre imploded in Late Antiquity and transformed into a more flexible and open system in which classical understandings of genre existed alongside generic innovations while the overall importance of genre as a category decreased.

An implosion is caused by a reduction of the pressure inside a hollow body of sturdy material. Whereas the material remains unchanged throughout the process, the original shape of the object is transformed into something less symmetrical, but still related to the original. The steel sculptures designed by the German-Dutch artist Ewerdt Hilgemann (b. 1938) and produced by creating a vacuum inside symmetrical shapes can illustrate this.

Hilgemann's 2011 sculpture *Three Graces* (Fig. 5.1), for instance, retains the hardness of steel and a resemblance to its former symmetrical cuboids, but the sculpture as a whole and in its parts has lost a number of right angles and has become asymmetrical as well as more organic than it was. Three aspects of this metaphor make it particularly suitable for my discussion of poetic genre: (1) the consistency of the material, (2) the resemblance between the old and new appearance of the shapes, and (3) the reduced pressure as the cause of the implosion and of the change. This is how the analogy between a physical implosion and the implosion of poetic genre works in more detail: (1) the material constituting poetic genre in Late Antiquity remains the same: subject matter, metre, and reference to exemplary models. (2) If steel stands for the material that constitutes genre, the shapes stand for the genres themselves. At this point, however, the metaphor is prone to misunderstandings: I am not suggesting that the classical genre system is rigid like the steel cuboids

---

[3] Late Latin poetic genres have also been discussed among others by Fontaine (1976), Fontaine (1981), Fontaine (1988), Basson (1996), Pollmann (2001), Consolino (2003), Consolino (2005), Wasyl (2011), Pollmann (2012), Kuhn-Treichel (2016), Pucci (2016), and Lefteratou and Hadjittofi (2020), late Greek genres by Hollis (2006) and Gador-Whyte (2013). The most recent research project in the field was the 2017 workshop series *Modulations and Transpositions: The Contexts and Boundaries of 'Minor' and 'Major' Genres in Late Antique Christian Poetry* organised by Fotini Hadjittofi and Anna Lefteratou at the universities of Lisbon and Heidelberg, which resulted in the publication of Hadjittofi and Lefteratou (2020). I regret that that publication has reached me too late to engage in a proper dialogue with it as I developed the argument of this chapter in 2015, though I have updated it to refer to the discussions in that volume and other recent publications.

Figure 5.1   *E. Hilgemann, Three Graces (2011). Reproduced by permission of the artist. Photo by Wolfgang Lukowski, Frankfurt.*

before the implosion nor that late antique genres look like the organic shapes after the implosion. Rather, I propose that the classical genre system comes across as rigid and static through its generic discourse and that classical poets reinforce the existing system through generic innovations and experiments, increasing the pressure inside the cuboids, so to speak, to see how far each genre can be expanded before the cuboids explode. Furthermore, the overall shape and distinctive features of classical genres continue to be manifest after the implosion, as the late antique genre system is still framed in the classical discourse while at the same time being marked by generic innovations that bypass the classical genre system as though it was no longer important. Last, (3) the loss of internal pressure that led to the implosion of poetic genre in Late Antiquity was caused by historical and cultural circumstances such as Christianity with its new subject matters and poetic tradition. Nevertheless, the implosion affected Christian and non-Christian, Greek and Latin poetry alike with the result that the poetic genre system in Late Antiquity as a whole allowed classical understandings of genre to coexist alongside generic innovations and alongside the decreased importance of genre as a category.

At the heart of this chapter is the late antique system of poetic genre after it imploded. From that point, it continued to make use of the classical genre discourse and at the same time developed into a new organic form. The chapter starts with classical genre discourse, a definition of poetic genre based on three genre markers repeatedly used by ancient authors: appropriate subject matter, exemplary model, and metre. The subsequent section demonstrates how authors in Late Antiquity continued the classical genre discourse by using traditional genre markers: appropriate subject matter (Agathias and Dracontius), references to exemplary models (Corippus, Nonnus, Jerome, Isidore of Seville, and Sozomenus), and metre (Socrates and Prudentius). This confirmation of traditional genre is counterbalanced in the third section, which explores generic innovations in late antique poetry in the form of generically unique works (Endelechius and Gregory of Nazianzus), genre mixing (Nonnus, *Heptateuch*, and Sedulius), and new genres (hymns). The conclusion revisits the causes of the implosion of poetic genre.

This chapter contributes to the argument of the volume by showing that late antique poetic genre is distinct from its classical predecessor (despite its close relation), and that it underwent a comparable transformation in both halves of the Roman empire, as a result of which the implosion of genre can be observed in both late Greek and Latin poetry.

5.1 The Classical Discourse on Poetic Genre

There have been countless attempts to define classical genre, as well as criticisms of such definitions.[4] At the heart of the matter is the discrepancy between theory and practice or between a static genre system, in which each genre follows clearly defined rules, and one open to change and to the transgression of rules. This discrepancy is inherent in poetic genre and leads to the question of whether genre exists at all, and if so, for whom: the poet or the reader? At least as far classical poetic genre is concerned, however, poets' commitment to genre confirms not just its existence but also its use as a device to communicate meaning. In practice, the poets largely treat genre as malleable while – paradoxically – subscribing to the view of genre as a static system in metapoetic passages, a view also popular with ancient and modern scholars alike.[5] In other words, even though in practice poetic genre was far from static, the classical generic discourse pretended that it was – as though genres resembled clearly defined, rigid steel cuboids. An illustration of this paradox is Horace's prescriptive comment in his generically ambivalent *Ars Poetica* (a combination of a letter and didactic poem): He claims that the 'law of genre' forbids the poet to do certain things (135: *pudor vetet aut operis lex*).[6] In the classical discourse that views genre as static, poetic genre is typically defined on the basis of various markers such the poet's character, generic models, metre, appropriate subject matter, and *Sitz im Leben*.[7] Explicit references to such markers describe genre as static, while implicit deviation from them can characterise it as a dynamic category. In this section I present three generic markers – appropriate subject matter, metre, and generic models – as constituting genre in classical literary criticism.

The notion of appropriateness takes various forms in the ancient critical discourse. Aristotle in his *Poetics* (1459b31–60a5 and 1460a11–18), for example, discusses the natural fit of different metres to subject matters and

---

[4] For discussions of ancient genre as a concept, cf. Rossi (1971), Conte (1991: 145–73), Depew and Obbink (2000: 2–13), Barchiesi (2001), Harrison (2007: 1–33), Harrison (2013), and Pollmann (2012: 103–10). For criticisms, e.g. Rosenmeyer (1985) and Rotstein (2010: 3–16). For more general discussions of genre as a concept, cf. Fowler (1982), White (2003), and Zymner (2003).
[5] Farrell (2003).   [6] Cf. Farrell (2003: 394–5).
[7] For the relation between the poet's character and genre, cf. e.g. Arist. *Poet.* 1448b, 24–7, for *Sitz im Leben*, itself a modern term, but the concept was arguably already present in classical texts that make their own performance explicit (e.g. Greek hymns), cf. Depew (2000). The other three markers will be discussed in more detail below, but for their importance as generic markers, cf. Rosenmeyer (1985) on generic model, Harrison (2007: 23) on metre, and Harrison (2013: 2) on appropriate subject matter.

of certain subject matters to specific genres such as epic or tragedy. Horace (*Carm.* 1.6.9–12) follows this line of thinking when he argues that lyric is unsuitable for Agrippa's desired subject matter:

> Pudor
> imbellisque lyrae Musa potens vetat
> laudes egregii Caesaris et tuas
>   culpa deterere ingeni.

> Modesty and the Muse who is in charge of the unwarlike lyre forbid us to impair the praises of outstanding Caesar and of yourself by fault of our talent.[8]

The genre of Horace's lyric poetry is expressed by reference to the 'Muse in control of the unwarlike lyre' (*imbellisque lyrae Musa potens*), which contrasts with poetry praising Augustus and Agrippa, as that would have included praise of military achievements (cf. *Carm.* 1.6.3: *navibus aut equis*).

References to exemplary models, on the other hand, are at the heart of Quintilian's list of poetic genres (*Inst.* 10.1.46–72 and 85–100), for example 10.1.61 or 10.1.96:

> Novem vero lyricorum longe Pindarus princeps spiritu, magnificentia, sententiis, figuris

> Of the nine lyric poets Pindar by far surpasses the others in inspiration, magnificence, sayings, and figures

> ~

> [Iambi] acerbitas in Catullo, Bibaculo, Horatio (quamquam illi epodos intervenit) reperiatur

> The bitterness [of the iamb] may be seen in Catullus, Bibaculus, and Horace though in him the epode [i.e. the arrangement of his iambs in couplets] tones it down

According to Quintilian, Pindar is the figurehead of lyric poetry while Catullus, Bibaculus, and Horace have been particularly successful with iambic invective. In both statements, Quintilian combines reference to exemplary models with other generic markers: the poets' characters when he describes them as 'lyric poets' (*lyrici*) and metre when he refers to the iamb.

Such references to multiple generic markers are not unusual: Ovid, for instance, combines the notion of appropriate theme with that of metre as he starts his *Amores* with war, arms and hexameter before turning to Cupid and elegiacs (*Am.* 1.1.1–4):

---

[8] All translations are my own.

Arma gravi numero violentaque bella parabam
   edere, materia conveniente modis.
Par erat inferior versus – risisse Cupido
   dicitur atque unum surripuisse pedem.

I was preparing to publish arms and violent wars in serious metre, with the
matter corresponding to its metre. The even verse was equal – but Cupid
allegedly laughed and secretly took away one foot.

In the first couplet, Ovid details the subject matter (*materia*) of his
proposed poem as 'arms' (*arma*) and 'violent wars' (*violenta bella*) and
twice stresses that his subject matter fits his choice of metre, by calling the
metre 'serious' (*gravi numero*) and by explicitly connecting the two (*materia conveniente modis*). Cupid's intervention leads both to a change of
subject matter – from war to love, from seriousness to laughter – and of
metre as the god turns each other hexameter into a pentameter, which
results in elegiac couplets.

    Finally, Horace neatly links the three generic markers of appropriate
material, metre, and generic model in his *Ars poetica* (73–9):[9]

Res gestae regumque ducumque et tristia bella
quo scribi possent numero, mostravit Homerus.
Versibus impariter iunctis querimonia primum,   75
post etiam inclusa est voti sententia compos;
quis tamen exiguos elegos emiserit auctor,
grammatici certant et adhuc sub iudice lis est.
Archilochum proprio rabies armavit iambo.

Homer has shown in what metre the exploits of kings and leaders and
sorrowful wars can be written. Lamentation was first framed in sequences
of lines of unequal length, later also the sentiment expressing vows was
included in them: Yet scholars dispute who the first exponent was to produce
slight elegiacs, and the case is still before the judge. Rage armed Archilochus
with its very own iambus.

In this passage, Horace first associates Homer with the deeds of kings and
leaders (*res gestae regumque ducumque*) and wars (*tristia bella*) and suggests
that Homer chose the metre fitting these topics (*quo scribi possent numero
monstravit*). Later, Horace neatly links iambic poetry with rage and its
generic model Archilochus. The close association between metre, theme,
and generic model is highlighted by the condensation of the three markers
into one line and by the qualification of the iambus as *proprius* (*proprio . . .*

---

[9] Cf. Harrison (2007: 4–6) for further discussion.

iambo), which includes the aspects of 'belonging [to rage]' and 'character-istic [of rage]'. By contrast, the lengthy discussion of elegiacs in the middle of the passage (75–8) remains vague as the first proponent of the genre is unknown.

Thus, in classical literary criticism, poetic genre appears to be clearly definable on the basis of markers such as generic model, metre, and appropriate subject matter used individually or in combination. In practice, the consistent use of such generic markers defined genre for centuries to come and enabled a dialogue between poets and readers concerning poetic genre where the poets worked with the generic expectations of their readers.[10]

5.2   The Classical Discourse on Poetic Genre in Late Antiquity

Poetic genre continued to be conceptualised in Late Antiquity according to the classical definition based on generic markers.[11] This section presents examples from late antique Latin and Greek poetry that reflect the classical discourse.

5.2.1   Appropriate Subject Matter

The link between genre and subject matter continues to be made in late antique poetry, for example, in Agathias' preface to his *Cycle*, a sixth-century collection of epigrams by contemporary poets. This preface has three parts: one in iambic trimeter addressed to the reader, a second in hexameter – containing a panegyric of the emperor,[12] a dedication, and a

---

[10] Fowler (1982: 36) goes even further by stating genre is 'the basis of the conventions that make literary communication possible'.

[11] There is also continuity between other classical and late antique definitions of genre, for example, between Plato's (*Resp.* 3.392d–394d) and Aristotle's (*Poet.* 1448a19–28) division of poetry into narrative and dramatic mimesis and a mixture of both forms and the tripartite division in Diomedes' *Ars Grammatica* (fourth century) (I 482.14–17 Keil: *Poematos genera sunt tria. Aut enim activum est vel imitativum, quod Graeci dramaticon vel mimeticon, aut enarrativum vel enuntiativum, quod Graeci exegeticon vel apangelticon dicunt, aut commune vel mixtum, quod Graeci κοινόν vel μικτόν appellant*, 'There are three poetic genres. For genre is either [first] active or imitative, which the Greeks call dramatic or mimetic, or [second] expository or demonstrative, which the Greeks call descriptive or narrative, or [third] sharing features with several genres or mixed, which the Greeks call common or mixed') and Isidore of Seville's *Etym.* (seventh century) (8.7.11: *Apud poetas autem tres characteres esse dicendi: unum, in quo tantum poeta loquitur [...]: alium dramaticum, in quo nusquam poeta loquitur [...]: tertium mixtum*, 'In poetry there are three kinds of speaking: One in which only the poet speaks [...], the second, dramatic, kind, in which the poet never speaks [...] and the third mixed kind'); cf. Lefteratou and Hadjittofi (2020: 15).

[12] Scholars have identified the emperor as Justinian (e.g. McCail 1969: 94–6) or Justin II (Cameron 1966; cf. also Cameron 1993: 69–75).

description of the content of the collection – and last an epigrammatic part in elegiacs. The following excerpt is the beginning of the iambic section and establishes a relationship between poet and readers while focusing on food, a topic typical of 'low' genres such as comedy, epigram, and satire (Agathias, *Cycle* praef. [*Anth. Pal.* 4.3] 1–4):

οἶμαι μὲν ὑμᾶς, ἄνδρες, ἐμπεπλησμένους
ἐκ τῆς τοσαύτης τῶν λόγων πανδαισίας,
ἔτι που τὰ σιτία προσκόρως ἐρυγγάνειν·
καὶ δὴ κάθησθε τῇ τρυφῇ σεσαγμένοι·

I think, gentlemen, that, filled from such a substantial banquet of words, you still belch out the food in your satiation: Indeed, you sit packed with dainties.

Metaphorically speaking, the poet offers his readers a rich banquet by way of his collection, but the food topic also fits the iambic metre,[13] both in the context of the small iambic genre of late antique Greek prefaces and that of comedy, a link strengthened by the many verbal echoes from Aristophanes.[14] When Agathias addresses the potential criticism of plagiarism (29–31), for example, he quotes directly from Aristophanes' *Knights* (*Eq.* 57: αὐτὸς παρέθηκε τὴν ὑπ᾽ ἐμοῦ μεμαγμένην 'he himself served what I had kneaded'):

ἴσως ἐρεῖ πρὸς ἄλλον· 'ἀρτίως ἐμοῦ
μάζαν μεμαχότος μουσικὴν τε καὶ νέαν,
οὗτος παρέθηκεν τὴν ὑπ᾽ ἐμοῦ μεμαγμένην.'

[Someone] might say to another: 'I recently kneaded fresh poetical dough, and what he serves is of my kneading.'

Thus, while Agathias chooses a subject matter that fits the late antique genre of iambic prefaces, he also uses it (and metre) to establish a link to comedy and, in particular, to comic prologues, which in turn helps to understand the new late antique genre of Greek iambic prefaces to hexameter panegyric.[15] In sum, Agathias' preface shows a classical understanding of genre by its display of appropriate material, here food in iambics, but it is also an example of generic innovation as it significantly contributes to establishing the Greek genre of iambic prefaces.

In the *prooemium* of *Romulea* 10, the North African poet Dracontius (end of fifth century) associates the second part of the Medea myth –

---

[13] Cf. West (1974: 31).   [14] Cf. Viljamaa (1968: 88–90).
[15] Iambic prefaces to hexameter poems were common in Greek imperial panegyric as were quotes from Aristophanes in these prefaces; cf. Viljamaa (1968: 68, 88–90).

Jason's marriage with the new bride and Medea's revenge – with tragedy
by referring to Melpomene, the Muse of tragedy (Drac. *Romul.* 10.20–5).

> vel quod grande boans longis sublata cothurnis   20
> pallida Melpomene, tragicis cum surgit iambis,
> quando cruentatam fecit de matre novercam
> mixtus amore furor dotata paelice flammis,
> squamea viperei subdentes colla dracones
> cum rapuere rotis post funera tanta nocentem.   25

And [we will sing] what pale Melpomene, raised on high buskins, cries out in
grand style, as she rises with tragic iambs, when fury mixed with love turned a
mother into a stepmother spattered with blood and the rival received flames
for her dowry, when snake-dragons submitting their scaly necks [to the yoke]
took the culprit away in a chariot after such great murders.

In this passage, Melpomene is associated with grand style (*grande boans*),
tragic metre (*tragicis ... iambis*), pallor (*pallida*),[16] and the traditional
content of earlier Medea tragedies such as the murder of the new bride
and of Medea's children. This looks like an example of classical genre
discourse, but the very passage introduces a short epic (*Romul.* 10), which
is (partly) based on the tragic material presented here. Thus, at the same
time as linking Medea's revenge and murder with tragedy in accordance
with a classical understanding of genre, Dracontius integrates the tragic
material into his epic. This makes the passage also an example of genre
mixing (cf. Section 5.3.2 below). Nevertheless, in the two passages discussed in this section, specific subject matters (food, Medea's revenge) and
tones (humorous, grand) characterise the genres under discussion, iambic
preface and tragedy, respectively.

5.2.2   Exemplary Generic Models

Like classical poetry, late antique poetry is full of references to exemplary
generic models. The epic poets Corippus (sixth century) and Nonnus (fifth
century), for instance, refer to (Vergil and) Homer as model(s) for their
works. In the preface to his *Iohannis*, Corippus puts himself into the
tradition of Homer and Vergil, who have made heroes immortal through
their poetry (Coripp. *Ioh.* praef. 7–16):

---

[16] Either the pallor of the mask or that caused by the tragic recitation; cf. Kaufmann (2006: 123 with
n. 126).

Quis magnum Aeneam, saevum quis nosset Achillem,
 Hectora quis fortem, quis Diomedis equos,
quis Palamedeas acies, quis nosset Ulixem,
 littera ni priscum commemoraret opus? 10
Smyrnaeus vates fortem descripsit Achillem,
 Aeneam doctus carmine Vergilius:
meque Iohannis opus docuit describere pugnas
 cunctaque venturis acta referre viris.
Aeneam superat melior virtute Iohannes, 15
 sed non Vergilio carmina digna cano.

Who would know great Aeneas and cruel Achilles, who strong Hector and Diomedes' horses, who Palamedes' wit, who Ulysses if literature did not record the deed of long ago? The poet from Smyrna described strong Achilles, learned Vergil in his poem Aeneas: And John's deed taught me to compose accounts of battles and tell all his acts for the benefit of future generations. John, superior in manliness, surpasses Aeneas, but I am not singing songs worthy of Vergil.

However, there are two twists in the parallelism between poets and heroes: first, Justinian's *magister militum* John Troglita surpasses Aeneas, whereas Corippus feels inferior to Vergil and, second, Achilles', Hector's, and Aeneas' deeds would have been forgotten if it had not been for epic poetry, whereas John's deeds made Corippus an epic poet in the first place. This second twist highlights the panegyric nature of the *Iohannis*, as the poet's inspiration from his hero complements the epic models of Homer and Vergil.[17]

Nonnus of Panopolis also explicitly refers to Homer as his model in the opening of the second half of his poem (25.8–9).[18] In addition, his *Dionysiaca* in 48 books appear to correspond to the sum of 24 books of the *Iliad* plus 24 books of the *Odyssey*,[19] all the more so because his reference to Homer comes not long after an episode about a half-finished piece of weaving (24.242–326) – a metaphor to indicate the poet's intention to add another 24 books to the first Homeric set of 24.

Christian writers likewise adopted the practice to refer to generic models. Jerome, for example, equates David with several classical lyric poets (*Epist.* 53.8.17),[20] and Isidore of Seville derives various classical

---

[17] In a similar way the references to Vergil and Homer in Juvencus' preface are interrupted by Christ's intervention (Juvencus 1–27); cf. Green (2006: 15–23).
[18] τελέσας δὲ τύπον μιμηλὸν Ὁμήρου | ὕστατον ὑμνήσω πολέμων ἔτος ('fulfilling the choice of Homer as a model for imitation I will only sing of the last year of the war').
[19] On Nonnus and Homer, cf. Hopkinson (1994b).
[20] *David, Simonides noster, Pindarus et Alcaeus, Flaccus quoque, Catullus et Serenus, Christum lyra personat* ('David, our Simonides, Pindar and Alcaeus, also Flaccus, Catullus, and Serenus, calls out Christ on his lyre').

metres and genres from biblical authors when he claims that Moses wrote in hexameter before Pherecydes and Homer, that David sang the first hymn, Salomon the first epithalamium, and Jeremiah the first lament.[21] According to Sozomenus (Sozom. *Hist. eccl.* 5.3–4), a certain Apolinarius even turned the Old Testament into classical poetry using the generic models of Homer, Euripides, Menander, and Pindar:[22]

ἡνίκα δὴ Ἀπολινάριος οὗτος εἰς καιρὸν τῇ πολυμαθίᾳ καὶ τῇ φύσει χρησάμενος, ἀντὶ μὲν τῆς Ὁμήρου ποιήσεως ἐν ἔπεσιν ἡρῴοις τὴν Ἑβραϊκὴν ἀρχαιολογίαν συνεγράψατο μέχρι τῆς τοῦ Σαοὺλ βασιλείας, καὶ εἰς εἰκοσιτέσσαρα μέρη τὴν πᾶσαν πραγματείαν διεῖλεν, ἑκάστῳ τόμῳ προσηγορίαν θέμενος ὁμώνυμον τοῖς παρ' Ἕλλησι στοιχείοις κατὰ τὸν τούτων ἀριθμὸν καὶ τὴν τάξιν. ἐπραγματεύσατο δὲ καὶ τοῖς Μενάνδρου δράμασιν εἰκασμένας κωμῳδίας. καὶ τὴν Εὐριπίδου τραγῳδίαν, καὶ τὴν Πινδάρου λύραν ἐμιμήσατο. καὶ ἁπλῶς εἰπεῖν, ἐκ τῶν θείων γραφῶν τὰς ὑποθέσεις λαβὼν τῶν ἐγκυκλίων καλουμένων μαθημάτων, ἐν ὀλίγῳ χρόνῳ ἐπενόησεν ἰσαρίθμους καὶ ἰσοδυνάμους πραγματείας, ἤθει τε καὶ φράσει καὶ χαρακτῆρι καὶ οἰκονομίᾳ ὁμοίᾳ τοῖς παρ' Ἕλλησιν ἐν τούτοις εὐδοκιμήσασιν.

Then the Apolinarius mentioned before made use of his wide knowledge and talent at the right time and composed the old Hebrew history books up to Saul's kingship in the form of heroic books instead of Homer's poetry and divided the whole subject matter into 24 parts, assigning each volume the name of one of the Greek letters according to their number and order. He also produced comedies resembling Menander's plays and imitated Euripides' tragedy and Pindar's lyric. To put it simply: By taking the material of the so-called encyclopaedic knowledge from the holy scripts, in a short time he brought forth works identical in number and strength and similar in kind, expression, type, and structure to those exemplary works famous among the Greeks.

The story is also transmitted in Socrates' *Church History* and discrepancies between the two versions, for example, Sozomenus' one Apolinarius vs. Socrates' two Apolinarii (father and son), as well as other uncertainties have cast doubt on the reliability of the account.[23] However, even if the account bears little resemblance to what happened, the story shows that

---

[21] *Etym.* 1.39.11: *omnibus quoque metris prior est. hunc primum Moyses in cantico Deuteronomii* [Deut. 32–3] *longe ante Pherecyden et Homerum cecinisse probatur*; 1.39.17: *hymnos primum David prophetam in laudem Dei conposuisse ac cecinisse manifestum est*; 1.39.18: *haec [epithalamia] primum Salomon edidit in laudem Ecclesiae et Christi*; 19: *threnos, quod Latine lamentum vocamus, primus versu Ieremias conposuit super urbem Hierusalem.*
[22] Cf. McLynn (2014) for the historical context.   [23] Cf. Speck (1997) and Agosti (2001a: 70–1).

genre definitions in Late Antiquity continued to include exemplary generic models.

5.2.3 Metre

Socrates' version of the Apolinarian poetry project (Socrates, *Hist. eccl.* 3.16.3) focuses on metre rather than exemplary model when he states that each metre was represented in Apolinarius' poetic version of the Old Testament:

ὁ μὲν γὰρ εὐθὺς γραμματικὸς ἅτε τὴν τέχνην γραμματικὴν Χριστιανικῷ τύπῳ συνέτατтε τά τε Μωυσέως βιβλία διὰ τοῦ ἡρωικοῦ λεγομένου μέτρου μετέβαλεν καὶ ὅσα κατὰ τὴν παλαιὰν διαθήκην ἐν ἱστορίας τύπῳ συγγέγραπται. καὶ τοῦτο μὲν τῷ δακτυλικῷ μέτρῳ συνέτατтε, τοῦτο δὲ καὶ τῷ τῆς τραγῳδίας τύπῳ δραματικῶς ἐξειργάζετο, καὶ παντὶ μέτρῳ ῥυθμικῷ [λυρικῷ Hansen] ἐχρῆτο, ὅπως ἂν μηδεὶς τρόπος τῆς Ἑλληνικῆς γλώττης τοῖς Χριστιανοῖς ἀνήκοος ᾖ.

For the former (Apolinarius the Elder), as he was a grammarian, wrote a grammar of a Christian manner: He also rendered the Books of Moses into so-called heroic verse and changed everything that is written in a historical manner in the Old Testament. He turned some of this into dactyls and other into a drama of a tragic kind. He made use of every rhythmical [lyrical] metre so that every kind of Greek expression would be heard among the Christians.

The literary transformation envisaged here works in two directions: on the one hand, the prose of the Old Testament is turned into various poetic genres and, on the other, traditional Greek poetry is Christianised through Apolinarius' use of its metres.

A more complex use of metre to define lyric can be found in Prudentius' *Cathemerinon* (9.1–3):[24]

Da, puer, plectrum, choraeis ut canam fidelibus
dulce carmen et melodum, gesta Christi insignia!
Hunc Camena nostra solum pangat, hunc laudet lyra.

Give me, boy, the plectrum that I sing the sweet and melodious song, the famous deeds of Christ, in constant trochees! Our Camena should record only him, him our lyre praise.

Here, the genre of lyric poetry is signalled by *plectrum*, *lyra*, *dulce carmen et melodum*, and the metre is indicated by *choraeis . . . fidelibus*. Furthermore, the hymn is written in trochaic tetrameter catalectic, a metre closely related

---

[24] For the discussion of the following lines, cf. Smolak (2000) and O'Daly (2012: 261).

to trochaic *septenarius* (*versus quadratus*), which in turn was associated with praise of military triumph[25] and – through Hilary of Poitiers' third *Hymn* – in particular with Christ's battles over Satan and sin.[26] Thus, the reference to metre in this hymn declares the hymn's allegiance not only to lyric poetry but also to panegyric on martial deeds and to hymnic praise of Christ's victory.

All the passages discussed in this section show that the classical discourse on genre is well attested for late antique poetry. Genres are framed as clear-cut categories based on metre, famous generic representatives, or generically appropriate subject matter. Some of the texts, however, go beyond a classical understanding of genre: Dracontius by incorporating the tragic subject matter of Medea's revenge into his epic, and Prudentius by using a specific lyric metre to include a hymnic victory praise. These exemplify both generic continuity and innovation.

5.3   Generic Innovations in Late Antiquity

While the classical discourse on genre continued into Late Antiquity, various generic experiments and major genre developments took place at the same time. The two strands of generic thinking taken together represent the genre system after its implosion when traditional genre discourse coexisted alongside generic innovations. The latter are explored in this section, and I argue that their manifestations – generically unique works, genre mixing, and new genres – went hand in hand with a reduced importance of genre itself.

For various reasons, this point is harder to argue than the previous one about continuity. First, hardly any late antique poem falls neatly into only one of the proposed categories of generic innovation, namely, generically unique works, genre mixing, and new genres. Instead, a poem might, for example, be a generically unique work and at the same time show genre mixing. In addition, poems might also combine generic innovation with a classical understanding of genre, as has already been obvious in the passages from Agathias, Dracontius (cf. Section 5.2.1 above), and Prudentius (cf. Section 5.2.3 above). While the latter case, in fact, illustrates the metaphor of generic implosion well, as that reflects both continuity and innovation, I have divided generic innovations into the three

---

[25] Cf. Smolak (2000: 216–17).
[26] Hil. *Hymn.* 3.2–3 (*proelia, | per quae primum satanas est Adam victus in novo*); cf. O'Daly (2012: 262).

subcategories mentioned in order to cover a good range of new concepts, but with the caveat that the categories themselves present an artificial selection and do not accurately represent the poetic practice.

A second challenge to this part of the argument is that – like late antique poetry – classical poetry is also full of generic innovations: There are generically unique works (e.g. Callimachus' *Aetia*, Ovid's *Fasti*), new genres (e.g. Latin love elegy), and many instances of genre mixing (e.g. Theocritus 22, Propertius 4). Furthermore, these generic innovations likewise combine with the classical understanding of genre as stable and unchangeable.[27] The crucial difference between these and the late antique generic innovations is that the latter coincide with a generally decreased importance of genre. This combination is reflected in the relatively organic shapes after the implosion caused by decreased pressure within the containers, whereas in the classical system, the innovations reinforce the traditional generic boundaries up to a point where they are close to exploding – rather than imploding – because of the increased pressure on them.

However, and this is the third problem in the argument, it is difficult to maintain that genre itself was considered less important in Late Antiquity than before, not only because absence of generic thinking is less conspicuous than its presence, but also because, in many cases, playing down generic boundaries can be read either as an attempt at abolishing them or as an attempt at (playfully) reinforcing them. The example from Nonnus' *Dionysiaca* 15 (cf. Section 5.3.2 below) will illustrate this in more detail. On the other hand, late antique readings of contemporary poetry support the idea of decreased importance attributed to genre. Symmachus, for example, praises various aspects of Ausonius' *Mosella* in a letter to the poet (Symm. *Ep.* 1.14) – for example, the fish catalogue, Ausonius' geographic accuracy – but does not discuss the genre of the work, quite in contrast to the intense modern discussions about it (cf. Section 5.3.1 below). Furthermore, Sidonius Apollinaris praises Claudianus Mamertus' hymn with a detailed description that first uses generic markers (*Epist.* 4.3.8: style, metre, appropriateness), but ends in comparing the composition metaphorically to a gem and a horse to state that it transgresses generic boundaries (*Epist.* 4.3.9):

> Excrescit amplitudo proloquii angustias regulares et tamquam parvo auro grandis gemma vix capitur emicatque ut equi potentis animositas, cui

---

[27] Cf. Farrell (2003).

frementi, si inter tesqua vel confraga frenorum lege teneatur, intellegis non tam cursum deesse quam campum.

The breadth of what you proclaim transcends narrow rules: Just like a large gem in a small gold setting it can hardly be contained and it flashes out like the spirit of a powerful horse, which neighs if it is held back by the rule of the bridle in wild and rough country, and – as you know – does not lack speed but space.

As Mamertus' hymn has not survived, we do not know how generically innovative it was, but according to Sidonius, its conventional aspects were by far surpassed by its transgeneric quality. By reverting to metaphors to express that quality, Sidonius implies that the hymn did not reinforce generic boundaries but surpassed them, and that genre definitions are irrelevant to understand it. Thus, these samples of late antique literary criticism confirm that poetic genre itself was not considered as important as, for example, in Hellenistic or Augustan times.

In summary, the difficulties inherent in this part of the argument – coexistence of generic innovations and classical understandings of genre, similarities between classical and late antique generic innovations and low visibility of decreased importance of genre – do not weaken its overall plausibility as long as the various manifestations of poetic genre are understood as aspects of one and the same genre system and decreased importance of genre is accepted as a concomitant of generic innovation.

5.3.1 Generically Unique Works

One manifestation of generic innovations consists of poems that are generically unique or single representatives of new genres. An example of this is Endelechius' *De mortibus boum* (*Anth. Lat.* 893 Riese), a fourth-century bucolic poem featuring a conversation between the herdsmen Bucolus, Aegon, and Tityrus, but written in lyric (second asclepiads) stanzas and incorporating the stance of didactic poetry, in particular Vergil's *Georgics*, and Christian preaching.[28] On the Greek side, Gregory of Nazianzus' autobiography is also generically unique as it is written in iambic trimeter, the only Greek autobiography in verse[29] and the only autobiography at all in iambic trimeter.[30] Some scholars have seen an

---

[28] Cf. Schmid (1953: 123–4), Barton (2000), Green (2004b: 23–8), and Schierl (2016).
[29] Gregory's closest model seems to have been Libanios' *or.* 1; cf. Jungck (1974: 13–14, 151).
[30] Jungck (1974: 13–14).

indication of the poem's invective[31] or didactic[32] nature in Gregory's choice of iambs, others argue that iambs were simply the most convenient and most prosaic metre.[33] Gregory himself characterises the metre as τῆς ἀνίας φάρμακον, | παίδευμα καὶ γλύκασμα τοῖς νέοις ἅμα, | τερπνὸν παρηγόρημα ('a remedy of sorrow, playful instruction and sweetening for the youth at the same time, a delightful consolation': *De vita sua* 2.1.11.7–9). Παίδευμα ('instruction') as well as the combination of γλύκασμα ('sweetening') with φάρμακον ('remedy') and παρηγόρημα ('consolation') may point to didactic,[34] though the description of poetry as a remedy against sorrow is also found in Archilochus (fr. 13 W), the generic model of Greek iambic poetry, and in Hellenistic poetry (e.g. Theoc. 11.1).[35] However, Gregory's autobiography is not particularly didactic or iambic, and the medical metaphor might best be understood as a non-generic reference to the nature of poetry.[36]

Other examples of generically unique works include Ausonius' *Mosella*, a hymn-panegyric-ekphrasis-didactic epic, idyll, or travel satire,[37] the Greek *visio Dorothei*, a hexameter narrative about Dorotheus' vision,[38] Prudentius' *Peristephanon* 10, a tragedy in the form of a hymn,[39] Lactantius' *De ave Phoenice*, a descriptive allegorical narrative,[40] Dracontius' *Satisfactio*, an elegiac plea and penitential poem,[41] and Christodorus' *Ekphrasis*, which includes elements of epigram and epyllion.[42] All of these works are generically unique without making their generic innovation the subject of their works.

5.3.2 Genre Mixing

In classical scholarship, genre mixing has been described by various terms, examples including Kreuzung der Gattungen,[43] generic enrichment,[44] and by applying the concept of generic modes.[45] The generic interactions

---

[31] The long invective part against Maximus the Cynic in 2.1.11.750–1037; cf. Agosti (2001b: 230–3) and Hawkins (2014: 163–9).
[32] E.g. Cameron (2004b: 333–9).
[33] E.g. Jungck (1974: 14) and Milovanovic-Barham (1997: 502).
[34] E.g. Lucr. 1.935–50; cf. Cameron (2004b: 333).   [35] Cf. Hawkins (2014: 53–9).
[36] For Gregory's use of generic markers including metre and exemplary models in other generically open poems, cf. McDonald (2020) and Kuhn-Treichel (2020), respectively.
[37] Cf. Gruber (2013: 28–35) and Scafoglio (1999: 267–9).
[38] Cf. Miguélez-Cavero (2008: 61–2), Kessels and van der Horst (1987), and Miguélez-Cavero (2013a).
[39] Cf. Henke (1985), Palmer (1989: 192–3), and Fux (2005).   [40] Cf. Roberts (2017: 377–8).
[41] Cf. Falcone (2020).   [42] Cf. Bär (2012).   [43] Cf. Kroll (1924: 202–24).
[44] Cf. Harrison (2007: 11–18).   [45] Cf. Fowler (1982: 106–18).

described by these terms tend to be marked as such and problematised. By comparison, in late antique poetry, genre mixing can be marked or implied, and it means the incorporation of a generically distinct passage into a text characterised by a dominant genre. For example, in the *prooemium* of Dracontius' *Romul.* 10.26–9 discussed above (cf. Section 5.2.1), the Muses of tragedy and pantomime invite Calliope, the Muse of epic, to take over right at the beginning of the short epic.[46] A similar case is the following passage from Nonnus' *Dionysiaca*, in which the bucolic mode is embedded into epic. Here, the herdsman and singer Hymnus has died and is lamented by a song in stanzas with a refrain (*Dion.* 15.399–416):

Βούτης καλὸς ὄλωλε, καλὴ δέ μιν ἔκτανε κούρη.
παρθενικὴ ποθέοντα κατέκτανεν, ἀντὶ δὲ φίλτρων
πότμον μισθὸν ἔδωκε, ποθοβλήτου δὲ νομῆος
αἵματι χαλκὸν ἔβαψε καὶ ἔσβεσε πυρσὸν Ἐρώτων—
Βούτης καλὸς ὄλωλε, καλὴ δέ μιν ἔκτανε κούρη—
καὶ Νύμφας ἀκάχησεν, ὀρειάδος οὐ κλύε πέτρης,
οὐ πτελέης ἤκουσε καὶ οὐκ ἠδέσσατο πεύκην
λισσομένην· 'μὴ πέμπε βέλος, μὴ κτεῖνε νομῆα.'
καὶ λύκος ἔστενεν Ὕμνον, ἀναιδέες ἔστενον ἄρκτοι,
καὶ βλοσυροῖς βλεφάροισι λέων ὠδύρετο βούτην·
'Βούτης καλὸς ὄλωλε, καλὴ δέ μιν ἔκτανε κούρη.
ἄλλο λέπας δίζεσθε, βόες, μαστεύσατε, ταῦροι,
ξεῖνον ὄρος· ποθέων γὰρ ἐμὸς γλυκὺς ὤλετο βούτης.'
θηλυτέρῃ παλάμῃ δεδαϊγμένος. εἰς τίνα λόχμην
ἴχνος ἄγω; σώζεσθε, νομαί, σώζεσθε, χαμεῦναι.
'Βούτης καλὸς ὄλωλε, καλὴ δέ μιν ἔκτανε κούρη.
χαίρετέ μοι, σκοπιαί τε καὶ οὔρεα, χαίρετε, πηγαί,
χαίρετε, Νηιάδες, καὶ ἐμαὶ δρύες.

The beautiful herdsman has perished, a beautiful girl has killed him! A maiden killed the one who desired her; instead of love-charms she gave him death as his reward, she dipped her bronze in the blood of the love-smitten herdsman, and extinguished the flame of Desires – the beautiful herdsman has perished, a beautiful girl has killed him! – and she distressed the nymphs, she did not give ear to the mountain rock, she did not listen to the elm and did not respect the prayer of the pine, 'Don't shoot your missile, don't kill the herdsman!' The wolf bewailed Hymnus, the ruthless bears

---

[46] Drac. *Romul.* 10.26–9: *te modo, Calliope, poscunt optantque sorores: | dulcior ut venias (non te decet ire rogatam) | ad sua castra petunt* ('the sisters ask you in particular, Calliope, wish and demand that you come to their camp more sweetly [it's not fitting for you to go after their request]'). Berenice Verhelst discusses the similar situation described in the *prooemium* of Dracontius' *Orestis tragoedia* (cf. Chapter 7).

bewailed him and the lion with bristling eyelids lamented the herdsman: 'The beautiful herdsman has perished, a beautiful girl has killed him! Look for another crag, cattle, seek a mountain elsewhere, bulls; for my sweet herdsman has perished of desires.' He has been torn apart by a woman's hand. To which thicket shall I lead my footsteps? Take care, pastures, take care, beds on the ground! 'The beautiful herdsman has perished, a beautiful girl has killed him! Goodbye, peaks and mountains, goodbye, springs, goodbye, Naiads, and my trees!'

The bucolic nature of this passage is highlighted by the refrain and by nature's lament after the death of a herdsman/singer.[47] At the same time, the genre mixing is played down by the introduction of the song as it is said to have seemingly come out of the mouth of a mourning cow (15.397–8): καὶ ἔστενεν ἀχνυμένη βοῦς | ποιμένος ἀσπαίροντος, ἔοικε δὲ τοῦτο βοῆσαι ('and the cow groaned for grief over the panting herdsman, and seemed to cry out these words'). We learn that the bucolic lament did not really happen, it was just an illusion and furthermore a rather ridiculous idea that a cow could sing such an elaborate lament. With this introductory statement, bucolic is sent out of the epic before it can assert its place there, and since the existence of the bucolic lament is denied at the very moment it is introduced into the epic, the whole passage looks like a playful attempt at genre mixing, a far cry from questioning the status of the *Dionysiaca* as an epic or even super-epic.[48]

In other, particularly Christian, poetry, secondary genres are integrated with little or no attention drawn to their differences. The anonymous *Heptateuch* from the fifth century (attributed to the so-called Cyprianus Gallus), for example, includes three lyrical songs in an overall epic format:[49] *Exod.* 507–42 (the song of Moses and Mirjam after the Israelites crossed the Red Sea), *Num.* 557–67 ('spring up, oh well'), and *Deut.* 152–278 (Moses' praise of God).[50] In the Bible, the first and the third passages are poems inserted into the prose text. Hence, the *Heptateuch* poet reflects their tone and their poetical status within the prose text by turning them into lyric so that they stand out in the hexameter epic. However, the uniqueness of this type of genre mixing jars with the lack of meta-generic discourse that would draw attention to it.

---

[47] Cf. Theoc. 1.64–145 (Thyrsis' lament of Daphnis) with Harries (1994: 74–6), Harries (2006: 529–36), and Miguélez-Cavero (2008: 168–70).
[48] Cf. Shorrock (2001: 20–2), Miguélez-Cavero (2008: 167–80), and Lasek (2016).
[49] Cf. Smolak (2001: 20) and Schmalzgruber (2016: 41–2).
[50] Incidentally, the third of these passages, Moses' second song, which according to Isidore quoted above (under Section 5.3.2) shows that Moses invented the hexameter, is in hendecasyllabi in *Hept.*

By contrast, other Christian poets explicitly put themselves into a cross-generic tradition. Sedulius, for example, first contrasts his epic *Carmen paschale* with the works of pagan poets of different genres (*Carm. Pasch.* 1.17–19):

> Cum sua gentiles studeant figmenta poetae
> grandisonis pompare modis, tragicoque boatu
> ridiculove Geta seu qualibet arte canendi

> Since pagan poets attempt to parade their fictions in grand modes and renew the cruel contagions of wicked deeds in tragic shouting, in the manner of the ridiculous Geta or some other kind of poetry

Here, Sedulius sets off his work against pagan drama, tragedy (*tragicoque boatu*), and comedy (*ridiculove Geta*[51]), perhaps following an apologetic tradition.[52] In the subsequent positive argument, he puts himself in the lyric tradition of biblical poetry, namely, the psalms founded by David (*Carm. Pasch.* 1.23–24):[53]

> Ego, Daviticis assuetus cantibus odas
> chordarum resonare decem

> I, used to sound out the songs of the ten-stringed lyre in the form of David's psalms

By choosing the lyric poet David as his model, Sedulius ranks David's biblical context above considerations about poetic genre, incidentally contrary to his predecessor, the first Latin New Testament poet Juvencus, who compared his own epic to those of Homer and Vergil (Juvencus 1–27) using generic models to reinforce the genre of his work. Thus, on account of his allegiance to the Bible, Sedulius chooses a lyric model for his epic albeit without drawing attention to this as a mixing of genres.

Given the popularity of epic in late antiquity, it is not a coincidence that all examples of genre mixing discussed in this section have come from epic. However, the type of genre mixing described here, in which a dominant genre incorporates a second genre, explicitly or implicitly, but without problematising the process, is not restricted to epic: Endelechius' *De mortibus boum*, for instance, incorporates lyric and didactic into pastoral, as mentioned above, and the anonymous *Metaphrasis Psalmorum* (fourth

---

[51] There is a slave by this name in each of Ter. *Ad.* and *Phorm.*; for Geta as a reference to comedy cf. Green (2006: 162–3) and Springer (2013: 24).
[52] E.g. Lactant. *Div. inst.* 6.20.27–8; cf. Green (2006: 163).   [53] Cf. Smolak (2001: 20–1).

or fifth century) combines the psalms of the Septuagint with Homeric language and imagery from didactic epic.[54]

5.3.3 New Genres

Identifying new genres is inherently difficult in a literary culture full of references to past traditions and in a system that is open to change, for in practice, any late antique poetic genre had previously already existed in a related form. The question thus is not which poetic genres are new in Late Antiquity, but whether the late antique and the classical forms of a genre are distinct enough for the later manifestations to be considered a new genre. For example, panegyric epic (e.g. Claud. 8; Coripp., *In laudem Iustini minoris*) might be considered a new late antique genre or a development of earlier epic with panegyric passages (e.g. Verg. *Aen.*).[55]

The most likely candidates for new poetic genres in Late Antiquity seem to be biblical paraphrases/epics (e.g. Juvencus; Nonnus, *Paraphrase*) and hymns (e.g. Hilary of Poitiers; Synesius of Cyrene)[56] even though they, too, have earlier generic roots: biblical paraphrases/epics in classical epic and rhetorical paraphrases,[57] and late antique hymns in earlier literary hymns (e.g. the *Homeric hymns* or Hor. *Carm.* 1.35).[58] In this section, it will be argued that hymns do constitute a new genre in Late Antiquity because they are only loosely connected to the generic tradition and to each other (despite some cross-references[59]), which reflects the decreased importance of genre identified above as typical for late antique generic innovations.[60] Hymns also exemplify a genre that works across the Greek and Latin linguistic divide. One of the earliest Christian hymns in Latin (third or first half of fourth century), the so-called *Psalmus Responsorius*, for

---

[54] On the former cf. n. 29 above and on the latter Faulkner (2020).
[55] Cf. Schindler (2009), Ware (2012: 18–31) and Ware (2016) for the late Latin texts.
[56] Other contenders are further sub-forms of epic such as ekphrastic epic (e.g. Christodorus' *Ekphrasis of the statues in the public gymnasium called Zeuxippos*, Paulus Silentiarius' *Description of Hagia Sophia*, cf. Elsner 2002: 9–15) and epithalamia (cf. Horstmann 2004 for the late Latin tradition). I have excluded centos, as with Pollmann (2004) and others I consider cento to a be poetic technique rather than a genre (though cf. also McGill 2005: xvif., Whitby 2007: 197–8, Rondholz 2012: 1–15, Prieto Domínguez 2010 and Garambois-Vasquez and Vallat 2017).
[57] Cf. Herzog (1975: 60–8; 155–211) for the former and Roberts (1985a: 61–74) for the latter. For the late antique Greek tradition, cf. Agosti (2001a), Hose (2004 25–33), and Whitby (2016) and, particularly on the genre of Nonnus' *Paraphrase*, Accorinti (2020) and Hadjittofi (2020).
[58] Cf. Lattke (1991) and Malick-Prunier (2017).
[59] E.g. from Prudent. *Cath.* 9 to Hil. *Hymn.* 3, as mentioned above (under Section 5.2.3).
[60] For a similarly brief survey of late antique poetic hymns, see Lefteratou and Hadjittofi (2020: 10–11).

example, contains very close parallels to the second century prose *Protevangelium Jacobi* written in Greek. This hymn was written in abecedarian fashion,[61] very unclassical in language and metre,[62] supposedly sung in church services and containing the story of Mary[63]. In the following extract, Mary alerts Joseph that she is about to give birth, and Joseph leads her into a cave (*Psalm. Resp.* ed. Roca-Puig [1965: 52–5]):[64]

> 'Urguet me valde, iosep, – dicit –
> quod in utero fero, foris prodire.'
> respicit locum, spelunc{h}am vidit;
> tenebros{a}e et obscur{a}e, sic illoc ibit.   55

'What I carry in my womb, Joseph, very much puts pressure on me to come out.' He looked around the place and saw a cave; dark and obscure, in this way he went there.

The elliptical text of the hymn becomes clearer against the background of the passage in the *Protevangelium Jacobi* (*Protevangelium Jacobi* 17):

> Ἰωσήφ, κατάγαγέ με ἀπὸ τοῦ ὄνου, ὅτι τὸ ἐν ἐμοὶ ἐπείγει με προελθεῖν.'
> καὶ κατήγαγεν αὐτὴν ἐκεῖ καὶ εἶπεν αὐτῇ· ποῦ σε ἀπάξω καὶ σκεπάσω σου
> τὴν ἀσχημοσύνην, ὅτι ὁ τόπος ἔρημός ἐστιν;' καὶ εὗρεν ἐκεῖ σπήλαιον καὶ
> εἰσήγαγεν αὐτήν.

'Joseph, take me off the donkey, for that which is in me presses me with its urge to come out.' And he took her down there, and said to her: 'Where shall I take you, and give shelter to your grace-lacking state since the place is deserted?' And he found a cave there, and led her into it.

We learn from the comparison of the texts that Joseph chooses the cave as shelter for Mary because the area is deserted, and that he led her there rather than just disappearing in it on his own, as the hymn seems to suggest. Thus, the *psalmus responsorius* is grounded in the Greek New Testament and (probably) in religious practice instead of being rooted in a literary hymn tradition. Later in the fourth century, Ambrose also linked his hymns closely to the church liturgy,[65] but he composed them in a higher literary register[66] and in a fixed form of eight four liners in

---

[61] The text breaks off after stanza M.
[62] Cf. Roca-Puig (1965: 76–96), who characterises it as *clausulae*.
[63] On its date, language, form, and *Sitz im Leben*, cf. Freund (2016).
[64] The text has been transmitted on a papyrus. In editions of papyri braces ({}) stand for letters that the editor considers redundant. For the adverbial uses of *tenebrose* and *obscure*, see Roca-Puig (1965: 129).
[65] Cf. Ambr. *epist.* 75A,34 and Evenpoel (1993: 52–3) on the practical purpose of his hymns.
[66] Cf. Den Boeft (2007: 88–90).

acatalectic iambic dimeter.[67] This metre had not previously been used in stanzas,[68] nor did it become the standard metre for late antique hymns despite the fact that Ambrose's hymns were well known and Prudentius used the metre in some of his hymns (though never for eight stanzas). In fact, Prudentius innovated the genre through his two lyric collections of metrically and thematically varied hymns *Cathemerinon* and *Peristephanon* by increasing poetic register again and choosing an organisational principle and thematic focus, respectively.

Late antique hymns in the East show great diversity, too. For example, Synesius of Cyrene wrote hymns in lines described by scholars either as stichic telesilleans[69] (a metrical innovation itself and an unusual metre for hymns[70]) or ἀπόκροτα (a mixture of anapaests and iambs, adapted from Mesomedes' hymnic use of this metre).[71] Either way, Synesius regarded his use of the metre as innovative (Syn. *hymn.* 6.1–6):

> πρῶτος νόμον εὑρόμαν
> ἐπὶ σοί, μάκαρ, ἄμβροτε,
> γόνε κύδιμε παρθένου,
> Ἰησοῦ Σολυμήιε,
> νεοπαγέσιν ἁρμογαῖς   5
> κρέξαι κιθάρας μίτους.

As the first I have found a mode to strike the strings of the lyre with newly composed modulations to praise you, blessed, immortal, famous son of the virgin, Jesus of Jerusalem.

Synesius presents himself as an innovator, 'the first ... to find' (πρῶτος ... εὑρόμαν) and as a potential model for later poets in the tradition that considered the inventor of a genre (πρῶτος εὑρετής) to become a generic model. However, later in the fifth century, Proclus composed philosophical and theurgical hymns in hexameters,[72] and Romanus Melodus' hymns in the sixth century combine biblical narratives and Greek lyric poetry with Syriac genres.[73]

Thus, overall, late antique hymns feature a great variety of metres and subject matters. They form a genre open to transformations and, like other instances of generic innovations, draw little attention to their generic definition or the development of the genre across the centuries.

---

[67] Cf. Evenepoel (1993: 51–2); Den Boeft (1993 and 2007).   [68] Den Boeft (1993: 78–9).
[69] *Hymns* 6–8; cf. Lacombrade (1978: 85).
[70] Cf. *PMG* 935, a hymn on the mother of the gods (perhaps Hellenistic), written in stanzas of three telesilleans and one reizianum, mentioned by West (1982: 142).
[71] Cf. Baldi (2012: 116–26).   [72] Cf. Van den Berg (2001) and Agosti (2015).
[73] Cf. Van Rompay (1993) and Gador-Whyte (2013).

5.4 Conclusion

I have argued that in both halves of the late Roman empire traditional understandings of poetic genre and generic innovations coincided with a generally low importance assigned to poetic genre, and I have likened this to the state of the generic system after it imploded – while the classical genre system would reflect the pre-implosion state in the metaphor. The difference between the two systems is not between old and new genres or genre systems, but between a traditional generic discourse in which the generic system appears to be well organised and fixed, combined with innovative poetic practice that reinforces this thinking, and a late antique system which partly continues the classical framework and partly introduces generic innovations while at the same time reducing the importance of genre as a concept.

As we know, implosion is caused by a decrease of internal pressure. In the case of poetic genre, this loss of pressure within the genre system might have been due to the new subject matters (stories of the Old and New Testaments) and poetic traditions (in particular, David and the psalms) that came with Christianity and the Bible;[74] second, the long-fought ideological battle to bring the classical literary tradition and Christianity together;[75] and third, perhaps a reduced focus on *aemulatio* on the part of the poets.[76] Even though the first two proposed causes are closely connected to the spread of Christianity in the Roman empire, the implosion of poetic genre is not the direct result of Christianisation. Rather, Christianity increased the potential for literary expression and reached a wider range of audiences, thus easing some of the pressure inherent in the traditional system of poetic expression. As a consequence, the implosion of poetic genre in Late Antiquity increased the generic freedom of poets and decreased their use of genre as a device to communicate with their audiences. Hence, the audience or readership of a late antique poem is required to approach it with an open mind and go beyond genre by paying attention to all the features of the poem to establish its meaning.

---

[74] Cf. Pollmann (2012).
[75] More heavily fought in the West than in the East; cf. e.g. Wyss (1949) and Evenepoel (1993).
[76] Such has been proposed by Pelttari (2014: 154–60) in the context of late Latin intertextuality.

CHAPTER 6

Common Texts, (Un)Common Aesthetics
The Greek and Latin Cento in Dialogue

Brian Sowers

One can no longer speak of Greek and Latin centos as a marginalised poetic form.[1] Scholarly interest in and treatments of cento poetry are at an all-time high, and, if the current trend continues, it has not yet reached its zenith. Within the past few decades, some two dozen critical editions and monographs dedicated entirely or in large part to Homeric and Vergilian centos have come to print and represent the collective work of Italian, French, German, Spanish, and Anglophone scholars.[2] Within circles interested in late antique literature, centos are hardly obscure; in fact, some cento authors, Ausonius and Proba in particular, are well known outside these circles.

The readership of this volume is undoubtedly familiar with the defining features of cento poetry, so I will not recapitulate them in any detail here. Simply, a cento is a patchwork poem composed from hemistichs or whole lines of pre-existing poetry, typically, though not exclusively, the corpora of Vergil and Homer.[3] Some centos date to the classical period, but most were written during Late Antiquity and hail from across the empire: Gaul, Italy, North Africa, Constantinople, and Palestine each claimed at least one cento poet. If centos spanned the late Roman empire, they also, in keeping with late antique aesthetics, crossed generic boundaries; examples of such poetic hybrids or bricolage include epic epithalamia, Gospel epics, epic tragedies, and tragic Gospels.[4]

---

[1] Hinds (2014: 172). All translations in this chapter are my own.

[2] More complete bibliographies can be found in Schottenius Cullhed (2015), Hinds (2014), Rondholz (2012), Malamud (2011), Sandnes (2011), Prieto Domínguez (2010), Formisano and Sogno (2010), Bažil (2009), Harich-Schwarzbauer (2009), Schembra (2007b), and McGill (2005).

[3] For an example of a non-Vergilian/Homeric cento, cf. Quintilian 6.3.96 on Ovid's now lost cento of the poet Macer. I use the term 'patchwork' in an etymologically literal way, despite the arguments against its use in Harich-Schwarzbauer (2009: 332–3).

[4] Pollmann (2004: 89) and Formisano and Sogno (2010: 376–8).

Accordingly, centos, as refashioned hypotext into a new hypertext, are best understood as a poetic technique, not a literary genre.[5] While they occasionally follow epic conventions, such as invoking divine poetic inspiration, when most cento poets provide paratextual comments, they tend to focus on their method of composition and their poem's generic features.[6] Apart from these paratextual comments, modern readers are forced to rely on each cento's unique form and content in order to identify its genre. For instance, Hosidius Geta's *Medea* corresponds to an ancient genre (tragedy) despite its Vergilian (epic) hypotext, making it somewhat of a hybrid 'tragic epic'. Most other extant centos are more complicated still.[7] The process of stitching together Vergilian or Homeric lines, therefore, is simply the creative means to compose multiple, hybrid genres.[8] Said differently, one identifies the generic range of Geta's cento through engaging its form and content; the simple fact that it was composed out of repurposed Vergilian lines provides only some information. This is the case for nearly all extant Greek and Latin centos and possibly accounts for the explanatory prefaces appended to so many of the longer ones. It also explains why the scholarly perspective that views ancient centos as a literary genre depends so heavily on authorial intent, not on active readers.[9]

It would be impossible to address the Greek and Latin cento traditions comprehensively within a single chapter. Their plurality and complexity in content, technique, and literary agenda are truly astounding. Rather than cast its net too widely and risk oversimplification or generalisation, this chapter focusses on literary values shared by late antique cento poets and critics from the Latin west and Greek east.[10] Of particular interest are paratextual moments, usually prefaces and criticisms, from the Greek and Latin cento traditions, which reveal shared conventions and metapoetic

---

[5] Pollmann (2004: 79) following Genette (1982: 11–15). See the other chapters in this volume that touch upon late antique generic conventions, in particular those of Kaufmann (Chapter 5) and Verhelst (Chapter 7).

[6] This focus on poetic composition is reflected in the scholarship. Usher (1998) provides a representative example.

[7] McGill (2005: 36–7).

[8] Sandnes (2011: 107–8) calls centos a genre but does not address the multitudinous array of centos, some of which coincide with other generic categories.

[9] This is best exemplified in Glei's (2006) response to Hoch (1997). Hoch and Glei use the same terminology differently and disagree about the generic intentions behind centos, some of which are anonymous. Rondholz (2012: 27–30) recognises the difficulty arising from this approach, but she also attempts to answer the question of a cento's genre beginning with the intention of its author.

[10] Sandnes (2011) discusses the Greek and Latin Christian cento traditions.

conversations.[11] At times these conversations are direct, as later authors allude to earlier ones; other conversations are oblique and indirect. Following Marco Formisano, I adopt a model for late antique literature, of which the cento is the ideal type, marked by its (pervasive) textuality and literariness, its 'relationship with the written word'.[12] For the sake of structure and clarity, this chapter is limited to three cento authors and their wider poetic traditions: Faltonia Betitia Proba's (Vergilian) Christian Cento, Decimus Magnus Ausonius' (Vergilian) *Cento Nuptialis*, and Aelia Eudocia's (Homeric) Christian Cento. The benefit of this approach is that it clarifies the pan-Mediterranean quality of cento poetics, which over time became a technical koine, as it were, used by vastly disparate authors with equally distinctive literary agendas but one within which each cento poet self-consciously situated themselves. This chapter draws attention to the contours of late antique cento literature shared by authors and critics chronologically, geographically, ideologically, and linguistically (dis) connected.

6.1 Proba's Preface

Little is known about Faltonia Betitia Proba and her poetry beyond her Vergilian cento, a 694-line paraphrase of the opening of Hebrew Bible (creation and the fall) and the Gospel (Jesus' birth, ministry, execution, and resurrection).[13] Proba's overall literary agenda has been reconstructed piecemeal from comments she makes in her cento, especially its preface (*Cento* 1–23) where she deplores her previous epics and their content: leaders violating treaties, men driven by power, murder, war, battles, bloody weapons, triumphs, and decimated cities.[14] Her confession is

---

[11] I am indebted here to Aaron Pelttari's model of late antique paratextuality. Cf. Pelttari (2014: especially 45–72).

[12] Formisano (2007). Cf. Formisano and Sogno (2010: 379–80) for how this model applies specifically to centos.

[13] Clark and Hatch (1981: 97–102), Matthews (1992), Margoni-Kögler (2001: 121–4), Stevenson (2005: 64–71 and 532–5), Green (2008), and Cameron (2011: 327–37), among others, attribute the authorship of the Vergilian Christian cento to Faltonia Betitia Proba and not her granddaughter. Shanzer (1986), Shanzer (1994), and Barnes (2006) argue that Proba the cento poet is the granddaughter of Faltonia Betitia Proba, thus moving the date of the cento's composition back some forty years. The confusion between the two dates at least back to the fifteenth century. For a summary of the argument, cf. Schottenius Cullhed (2014: 206) and Schottenius Cullhed (2015: 20–3).

[14] Unfortunately, Proba's other works do not survive. There is a parallel here between Proba and Aelia Eudocia, who is said to have composed historical/military epics earlier in her literary career. According to historians in Theodosius' court, Eudocia turned from these secular topics to exclusively Christian ones.

succinct: *confiteor, scripsi: satis est meminisse malorum* ('I confess, I wrote
these things. Remembering such evils is too much'). This comment serves
as a *captatio benevolentiae*, which simultaneously situates her cento within a
broader epic tradition and, through her allusions to Lucan, rhetorically
distances it from Roman civil war epic.[15] But these critiques also apply to
heroic epics, which contain their fair share of power-hungry men, murder,
war, and battles. At the outset, Proba marks for her audience that her epic will
eschew violence and war and will, instead, embrace peace (*Cento* 9–12).[16]

> Nunc, deus omnipotens, sacrum, precor, accipe carmen
> aeternique tui septemplicis ora resolve   10
> spiritus atque mei resera penetralia cordis,
> arcana ut possim vatis Proba cuncta referre.

> Almighty God, I pray now, accept this holy song,
> Open the mouths of your sevenfold, eternal
> Spirit, and lay bare the recesses of my heart,
> So that I, Proba, may prophetically reveal all mysteries.

To further distinguish her poem as definitely Christian, Proba invokes
God and asks him to receive (*accipe*) her divine poem (*sacrum carmen*).[17]
Not only is God the addressee of the cento, he is also Proba's Muse: the
Holy Spirit speaks and reveals the depths of her heart. She goes even
further (*Cento*, 13–22) by renouncing inspiration from the classical
Muses.[18] Hers is a song marked by God's presence (*praesens, deus*), an
upright mind (*erige mentem*), and the pious feats of Christ (*pia munera
Christi*). In this, Proba follows an emerging Christian epic tradition begun
by Juvencus.[19] This rhetorical and ideological position is undermined by
Proba's overt textual dependence on Vergil, a fact that would not have
escaped her learned readership/audience.[20]

Despite her attempts to distance herself from secular Latin epic, Proba
also recognises that her cento fuses Vergil with new, biblical content.[21] On
the one hand, she performs the cento in the prophetic (*vatis*) tradition and
relates (*referre*) mysteries (*arcana*); on the other hand, Vergil also actively
participates as a performer of her Gospel (*vergilium cecinisse loquar pia*

[15] Green (1997: 550) and Hinds (2014: 186–7). Bažil (2009: 121–2) suggests the echo (Lucan, *Civ.*
1.225) is also in conversation with early Christian epic.
[16] Sandnes (2011: 149–50).   [17] Formisano and Sogno (2010: 380) and Pollmann (2004: 80).
[18] Schottenius Cullhed (2010: 45).
[19] Bažil (2009: 121–3). For the ways Proba deviates from Juvencus, cf. Pollmann (2004: 89–90).
[20] Allusion and intertextuality are intrinsic and unavoidable features of cento poetics. Cf. McGill
(2005: 25), Bažil (2009), and Formisano and Sogno (2010).
[21] Pollmann (2004: 80, 87–90) situates Proba as an example of an 'exegetical' cento poet.

munera Christi). The *vatis*, usually interpreted as Proba, could equally be a reference to Vergil.[22] If we allow for this ambiguity, the cento, along with its message, becomes a duet sung, albeit centuries removed, by both Proba and Vergil.[23] But Proba and Vergil receive unequal airtime. Over the rest of the preface (*Cento* 24–55) the proliferation of first-person singulars situates Proba in the foreground and relegates Vergil as a backup singer, whereas her increased use of Vergilian lines over the course of the preface gives Vergil the loudest voice. Proba's explicit connection between her cento and Vergil, however, reflects an appreciation for the intersection between cento and source text regardless of content. Said differently, in Proba's view cento poetics is not intertextually neutral. Source text and original poet are inextricably bound to the new product.[24]

6.2 Ausonius' Preface to the *Cento Nuptialis*

Ausonius' preface to the *Cento Nuptialis* (*Cent. nupt.*), written a few years after Proba's cento, is the most widely discussed paratextual treatment of cento poetry.[25] As early as Erasmus, the preface to the *Cento Nuptialis* was read as a fairly straightforward handbook for writing centos, the rule by which all ancient centos are measured.[26] Despite my doubts that this approach is the best way to read Ausonius' writings, especially the preface to the *Cento Nuptialis*, much scholarly discussion on centos still begins with or is largely based on the *Cento Nuptialis*.[27] As an alternative, by contextualising the *Cento Nuptialis* within Ausonius' broader literary habits, his highly crafted and affected means of communicating with his literary circle overshadows any attempt to provide a handbook for

---

[22] The *vates* in manuscript P (Paris, Bibliothèque Nationale, Lat. 7701) is more explicitly in reference to Proba. Schottenius Cullhed (2015: 192–3) takes the *vatis* as Vergil.

[23] By Late Antiquity, Vergil and his poetry had already been appropriated within a definitively Christian context. Pollmann (2004: 89) and Hinds (2014: 177 and 187).

[24] Compare Genette (1982: 14–15). Hinds (2014: 184) asserts that late antique literary consciousness is marked primarily by literary appropriation.

[25] The traditional date for the cento hinges on its relationship to the marriage of Gratian around 374 CE. Cf. Green (1997: 518) and McGill (2005: 92–4). For my purposes here, the exact date of the *Cento Nuptialis* and its relationship to Gratian's wedding do not matter, although dating Ausonius' cento after Proba's does.

[26] Erasmus, *Adages* 2.4.58 (Mynors 1991: 221–2). For the *Cento Nuptialis* as a guide to centos, cf. McGill (2005: 1–30), Sandnes (2011: 108–13), Schottenius Cullhed (2015: 94, 137–8), Formisano and Sogno (2010: 380, 386–9), Malamud (2011: 162, 175), Hinds (2014: 171, 176, 185, 188–90), and Pelttari (2014: 64, 96–112). Pollmann (2004: 83) summarises the approach perfectly: 'All in all, Ausonius' theory of a cento does not present rigid guidelines, but is rather to be understood as an ideal programme.'

[27] For more on my approach to Ausonius and his corpus, cf. Sowers (2016).

writing centos.[28] What follows is such a reading of the preface to the *Cento Nuptialis* (praef. 1–3).

> Perlege hoc etiam, si operae est, frivolum et nullius pretii opusculum, quod nec labor excudit nec cura limavit, sine ingenii acumine et morae maturitate.[29]

> If it is worthwhile, also read this frivolous little work, a worthless piece, which neither labour composed nor attention revised and which lacks intellectual penetration and the perfection that comes from taking one's time.

When circulating poetry among his friends, Ausonius routinely describes himself and his writings in a self-deprecating manner.[30] This emerges at the very opening of the preface to the *Cento Nuptialis* when Ausonius confides to his addressee and friend, Paulus, that his cento is frivolous (*frivolum*), worthless (*nullius pretii*), a diminutive poem (*opusculum*), which lacks any of the merit found in a more serious work. His repeated use of ludic (*luserunt*) and jocular (*ioculari*) imagery gives the impression – which Ausonius later insists – that his cento should be mocked rather than praised (*quod ridere magis quam laudare possis*). He goes further by claiming that his jocular content debases the value of Vergil's original poem (*Vergiliani carminis dignitatem tam ioculari dehonestasse materia*).[31] As a ludic poet, Ausonius routinely describes himself as a swindler, peddling worthless poems to friends whom he requires to invest in his bankrupt verses.[32] Within the preface to the *Cento Nuptialis* Ausonius seems to be playing multiple games at once. On the one hand, by asking Paulus to read and evaluate his cento, which he has already admitted is worthless, Ausonius wrong-foots Paulus. On the other hand, he also wrong-foots Vergil by tarnishing his *gravitas*. Ausonius himself is also tripped up when the emperor Valentinian performs a nuptial cento (*nuptias quondam eiusmodi ludo descripserat*) and orders (*iussum, praecepit*) him to compose a similar poem. Here Ausonius plays the unwilling poet, compelled to compose in order to preserve imperial favour, a recurring motif whenever he describes his relationship with members of the imperial family (*Cent. nupt.* praef. 29–34).[33]

[28] For a discussion on Ausonius' language when writing to literary friends, cf. McGill (2007, 2009, 2014), Pelttari (2011, 2014), and Sowers (2016).
[29] Green (1999: 145–6).   [30] Cf. also Verhelst (Chapter 7).
[31] Formisano and Sogno (2010: 380) treat this motif as a feature of cento poetics, not of Ausonius' literary habit.
[32] O'Daly (2004: 141–2). Ausonius situates himself within a tradition dating back to Catullus whose poetic persona served as a model for his own. Cf. McGill (2005: 1–30) and Sowers (2016).
[33] Sowers (2016).

Et si pateris, ut doceam docendus ipse, cento quid sit absolvam. Variis de locis sensibusque diversis quaedam carminis structura solidatur, in unum versum ut coeant aut caesi duo aut unus et sequens cum medio, nam duos iunctim locare ineptum est et tres una serie merae nugae.[34]

If you will suffer me, who ought to be the student, to instruct what a cento is, then I will do so. The poem's particular structure is fashioned from various places and from diverse contexts, such that either two half-lines or one line plus a half-line immediately following join into one verse. It is unsuitable to place two (whole) lines side by side; three (whole) lines in a single series are pure silliness.

Ausonius also underhandedly mocks his ability to compose a cento when he describes cento aesthetics, specifically how the use of half-lines, whole lines, and one and a half lines in sequence is allowed, but two or three sequential lines, respectively, are amateurish and ridiculous (*nugae*). This section – frequently treated as the standard by which ancient centos are to be measured – can be read as part of a running joke between Ausonius and Paulus. Most obviously, Ausonius opens by insisting that he is an amateur, a student requiring instruction and not an accomplished teacher, only to proceed to teach Paulus about cento rules and aesthetics. More subtly, despite Ausonius' insistence that sequential lines distinguish amateur from adept cento poets, his own cento contains multiple sequential lines, a glaring deficiency. Considering he later entrusts Paulus with the task of unstitching the cento (if it fails to pass inspection) and returning the lines to Vergil, Ausonius' standard for cento aesthetics, one he himself fails to meet, must be ironic. If we treat Ausonius' failed cento aesthetics as another example of his light-hearted banter with friends, whom he wrong-foots at every turn, the depths of his paratextual jokes with Paulus come into sharper focus.[35]

External evidence suggests, however, that cento poets generally avoided two or more sequential lines. With some exceptions, the extant Latin centos follow this pattern, and Eudocia, as I argue below, apologises for her use of double lines.[36] In my view, however, when Ausonius breaks his own rules, he does so to underscore his own poetic (and ludic) persona of an incompetent poet peddling inferior verse. Modern readers can only guess how Paulus reacted when he noticed Ausonius' double lines, but,

---

[34] Green (1999: 146–7).
[35] This final section of the *Cento Nuptialis* has been read variously. For example, Formisano and Sogno (2010: 389–90) use this section to argue that Ausonius' cento (and that of Proba) simultaneous evokes (through its use of) Vergil but also rejects it.
[36] Bright (1984).

based on the survival of the *Cento Nuptialis*, he apparently did not dismantle the cento as Ausonius requested. As we will see in Eudocia's paratextual remarks, even when cento poets are aware of aesthetics about sequential lines, they break these 'rules' with impunity.

Ausonius does not limit his irony and self-deprecation to friends; his literary interaction with other cento poets, Proba in particular, is also playful and jocular. His most clever allusion to Proba comes at the end of the *Cento Nuptialis*, possibly referencing a pun she makes in her preface. After the well-known ending of the *Cento Nuptialis*, arguably one of the most graphic sexual assault scenes in Latin literature, Ausonius apologises for his sexually explicit (and lascivious) content. With a gesture to Juvenal, he asks Paulus to defend him against charges that his cento is a reflection of his life (*ne fortasse mores meos spectent de carmine*) and insists on his chastity by quoting Martial: *lasciva est nobis pagina, vita proba, ut Martialis dicit.* Paola Moretti and Stephen Hinds each independently see a gesture to Proba and her cento in Ausonius' insistence that his life is *proba*.[37] To take this one step further, through this reference to Proba, Ausonius undermines her poetic program by intertextually associating her rejection of violent and impious poetry in order to sing Vergil's Gospel with his inferior poem, marked by substandard goals and expectations. Ever the peddler of worthless rubbish, Ausonius links his life to Proba's at that moment when his poetry is pure improbity, a claim that further underscores his self-deprecating and ironic persona.[38]

6.3   The Dedication to Proba's Cento

Written shortly after Ausonius' *Cento Nuptialis* and appended to Proba's cento, a fifteen-line anonymous verse dedication, surviving in two manuscript traditions, reveals how at least one fourth-century reader interpreted her poem.[39] This section engages the dedication by focussing on three interrelated observations. First, by the end of the fourth century, Proba's cento had been appropriated within the wider literary agenda of the imperial family.[40] Second, despite Proba's emphasis on orality and performance, the dedication treats the cento primarily as a textual object, to be

---

[37] Moretti (2008: 341–3) and Hinds (2014: 195).   [38] Compare Pollmann (2004: 91).

[39] McGill (2007: 174) dates the dedication to the end of the fourth century, roughly one generation after Proba wrote the cento. On the authorship of the dedication, cf. Clark and Hatch (1981: 106), Shanzer (1986: 233), Sivan (1993: 144–5), Green (1997: 548–9), Mastrandrea (2001), and McGill (2007: 173–4).

[40] Sivan (1993) discusses the difficulty identifying the two Arcadii in this poem.

read and transmitted to future generations. Third, the dedication reacts to Ausonius' ludic approach to cento poetics by insisting that Proba's Christian content has improved Vergil (*Dedication to Proba's Cento* 3–5, 13–15).[41]

> Dignare Maronem
> mutatum in melius divino agnoscere sensu,
> scribendum famulo quem iusseras . . .   5
> haec relegas servesque diu tradasque minori
> Arcadio, haec ille suo semini; haec tua semper
> accipiat doceatque suos augusta propago.   15

> Consider it appropriate
> To re-familiarise yourself with an improved Maro, updated with a divine sense,
> which you ordered your servant to compose . . .
> Reread these (verses), preserve them well, and pass them on to the younger
> Arcadius. Let him treat these (verses) likewise for his children.
> May your eminent offspring always receive these (verses) and teach them to
> their offspring.

Over the course of the dedication, its poetic narrator addresses the emperor Arcadius as the idealised recipient of Proba's cento. Not only is Arcadius directed to consider how Proba improved Vergil's poetry by giving it a divine sense (*divino sensu*), he is also described as the commissioner (*iusseras*) of the cento. Whereas Proba attributes her inspiration to the triune godhead, rather than the traditional Muses, the dedication, in contrast, rhetorically conflates Proba's poetic inspiration with imperial patronage. For instance, in her preface, Proba asks God to receive (*accipe*) her divine poem (*sacrum carmen*); in the dedication, Arcadius and the imperial family receive (*accipiat*) the text. In this regard, the dedication updates Proba's preface by refashioning it within the context of literary patronage. This language of imperial support also opens an intertextual dialogue with Ausonius who was compelled to compose his cento for an imperial audience. Traces of Ausonius' *iussum erat, quodque est potentissimum imperandi genus, rogabat qui iubere poterat* can be seen in the dedication's *scribendum famulo quem iusseras*.

At the end of the prescript, the narrator bids Arcadius to reread the cento (*haec relegas*), to preserve it (*serves*) for the next generation, and to teach it to the younger Arcadius, who will in turn teach it to his children.[42]

---

[41] Schottenius Cullhed (2010: 43).

[42] Sandnes (2011: 146) attributes to Proba's cento a didactic function, in particular in response to Julian's famous edict limiting Christian involvement in traditional, Greco-Roman education (*Codex*

This suggests that, by the end of the fourth century, Proba's cento was primarily viewed as a textual object, to be read and studied, not sung or performed. In this regard, the dedication reflects an evolution from Proba's oral performance (*carmen, ora, canere*) and situates the cento as a bookish object (*scribendum*).[43] Its emphasis on reading (*relegas*) also intertextually points to Ausonius' request that Paulus thoroughly read (*perlege*) his cento and decide if the cento is worthy of payment. If not, he is to unstitch the lines and return them to their original Vergilian context, a detail that might be reworked in the dedication into a request of Arcadius to preserve the cento and pass it on to future generations. In other words, while Ausonius opens the possibility of the undoing of his cento, the dedicator argues for the eternal preservation of Proba's. If the dedication partially responds to Ausonius' engagement with Proba, then it here gets the final word by transforming Ausonius' claim that his cento debases Vergil's dignity into a superior claim that Proba has improved upon Vergil and, as a result, deserves to be read and reread.

6.4   Jerome, *Epistle* 53

Whereas Proba's dedicator rhetorically distances her cento from the ironic and self-deprecating claims made by Ausonius and argues, instead, that it is a holy product, above criticism or reproach, the church father Jerome, writing at approximately the same time as the dedicator, takes an explicitly critical approach to cento poetics. Jerome's condemnation of Christian centos – situated within a polemical epistle on 'irresponsible' exegesis – reveals an awareness of the wider cento tradition and an engagement with both Proba and Ausonius. Jerome's engagement with Proba is well attested, but his allusions to Ausonius have not received much attention. By drawing attention to the full extent to which Jerome has read Greek and Latin centos, this section clarifies how he uses cento poetics in specific ways for a precise audience.

In Epistle 53, Jerome outlines for Paulinus, bishop of Nola, proper Christian education, including a warning about the dangers inherent in

---

Theodosianus 13.3.5). One has to wonder about the long-term effects of Julian's edict of 362 CE on the literary imaginations of subsequent fourth-century elite. While later authors were aware of some immediate reactions to Julian, it is not clear, in my view, whether Julian's edict had any lasting effect after his death. Presumably, most Christian educators returned to business as usual in teaching Homer and Vergil.

[43] Formisano and Sogno (2010: 388) and McGill (2007: 175–7), also see a difference between how Proba presents herself and how she is depicted in the dedication.

'secular' learning. Advancing an elitist view of biblical exegesis, Jerome argues that everyone from a gabby granny (*garrula anus*), a senile senior (*delirius senex*), and a loquacious linguist (*soloecista verbosus*) claims to be an expert in interpreting scriptures (*sola scripturarum ars est, quam sibi omnes passim vindicent*). In their role as biblical experts, however, such ill-trained (and non-elite/male) exegetes invariably remove passages from their original contexts and interpret them in ways their authors never intended. Jerome here follows a long-standing tradition of church fathers discrediting rival exegetes (including cento poets) for violating authorial intent and teaching (*docent*) rather than learning (*discant*).[44] As an illustration, Jerome compares irresponsible and untrained biblical analysts to authors of Homeric and Vergilian centos (Jer. *Ep.*. 53.7):

> Quasi non legerimus, Homerocentonas, et Virgiliocentonas: ac non sic etiam Maronem sine Christo possimus dicere Christianum, qui scripserit:
> 'Iam redit et virgo, redeunt Saturnia regna.
> Iam nova progenies coelo demittitur alto.'
> Et patrem loquentem ad filium:
> 'Nate, meae vires, mea magna potentia solus.'
> Et post verba Salvatoris in cruce:
> 'Talia perstabat memorans, fixusque manebat.'
> Puerlia sunt haec, et circulatorum ludo similia, docere quod ignores: imo, ut cum stomacho loquar, ne hoc quidem scire quod nescias...

> As if we have not read the Homeric and Vergilian centos, yet we dare not call the Christ-less Maro a Christian because he wrote:
> Now returns the Virgin and Saturn's reign.
> Now the newborn child is sent from the highest heaven.
> And (in another line) the father speaking to the son:
> Son, you alone are my might, my great power.
> And (in another line) after the Savior's words on the cross:
> Saying such, he stood still and remained transfixed.
> These things are childish and similar to the game frauds play, namely, to
>   teach that which you do not know, or rather,
> and I speak with displeasure, to not even know what you do not know.

Because Jerome's example of cento poetics contains three Vergilian lines (*Ecl.* 4.6–7; *Aen.* 1.664; and *Aen.*, 2.650) used by Proba in nearly identical biblical contexts (*Cento*, 34, 403, 624, respectively), scholars have justifiably seen Jerome's criticism of centos as directed against or, at least, emerging from his reading of her cento. It naturally follows that Proba

---

[44] Compare similar critiques made by Tertullian (*De praescr. haeret.* 39) and Irenaeus (*Adversus haereses* 1.8.1).

must be the *garrula anus* Jerome mentions earlier in the epistle.[45] Challenging this view, Schottenius Cullhed takes Jerome's *garrula anus* as a rhetorical trope and points out that his other two incompetent exegetes, the senile senior (*delirius senex*) and loquacious linguist (*soloecista verbosus*), do not correspond as easily to contemporary rivals.[46] While not fully addressing the connection between Jerome's Vergilian quotations and Proba's cento, Schottenius Cullhed's argument opens the possibility that Jerome might be up to more than simply criticising Proba.

The case can be made that, in addition to reacting to Proba, Jerome is himself playfully engaged with the wider cento tradition, Ausonius' *Cento Nuptialis* in particular. There are three reasons to support this. First, Jerome's addressee in Epistle 53 is Paulinus of Nola, a literary friend of Ausonius, who was familiar with Ausonius' poetry and with whom Ausonius engages in playful literary banter.[47] When Jerome claims that 'we' have read centos (plural), he might be including Paulinus within this part of the argument and making a veiled reference to Ausonius' cento.

Second, Jerome's language in Epistle 53 goes beyond veiled allusions and explicitly mirrors Ausonius. His claim that fraudulent exegetes adapt conflicting passages to suit their own meaning (*sed ad sensum suum incongrua aptant testimonia*) parallels Ausonius' description of cento aesthetics as divergent meanings made to agree (*sensus diversi ut congruant*). By comparing centos to a game (*ludo similia*), Jerome adapts key language from the *Cento Nuptialis* (*simile ut dicas ludicro, ut ille ludus*) and one of Ausonius' favourite metapoetic images. Jerome's overarching claim that fraudulent exegetes teach before they learn or teach material they know nothing about mirrors Ausonius' self-deprecating claim: 'If you will suffer me, who ought to be the student, to instruct what a cento is, then I will do so' (*Et si pateris, ut doceam docendus ipse, cento quid sit*). Even Jerome's claim to be speaking in anger (*cum stomacho*) could be read as a veiled allusion to Ausonius' comparison of centos to a children's game, the ostomachia, which some manuscripts print as *stomachion*.[48]

Finally, in Epistle 53 Jerome builds his argument on a litany of biblical quotations, stitched together citations from Hebrew Bible and Christian

---

[45] For more on Proba within Jerome's letter, cf. Wiesen (1971), Clark and Hatch (1981: 104–5), Sandnes (2011: 134–6), and Rondholz (2012: 23–4).
[46] Schottenius Cullhed (2014: 200–1).
[47] Ausonius, *Preface to Technopaegnion*; *Epistle* 24.83; 21.31, Roberts (1985b), Knight (2005), and Sowers (2016).
[48] Jerome's *stomacho* has been interpreted variously and unsatisfactorily. Cf. Pavlovskis (1989: 80) and, more recently, Sandnes (2011: 137).

scriptures. It is an impressive feat of biblical memorisation and proof-texting, that is, removing a passage from its original context and using it for one's own purposes. In this way, Jerome's epistle is similar to his own description of a cento and can be read as a metaliterary game that ultimately undermines his own criticisms. The force of this intertextual 'ludism' only makes sense when Jerome's epistle is read as a response to Ausonius' *Cento Nuptialis* rather than to the Christian cento tradition associated with Proba. By writing Paulinus a letter teeming with so many complex and polyvalent allusions, Jerome situates himself as a suitable mentor for his addressee and a Christian replacement for Ausonius.

6.5   Eudocia's Homeric Cento

Eudocia composed her Homeric cento sometime during the middle of the fifth century either in Constantinople or after her exile from the imperial court when she resided in Jerusalem.[49] Because the Homeric centos underwent four recensions, each of which is at least partially represented in the manuscript tradition(s), it is impossible to guess how long Eudocia's cento was or what biblical episodes she paraphrased.[50] Equally uncertain is Eudocia's literary engagement with previous cento poets and critics. While she might have had access to and was influenced by Proba's cento, Eudocia probably did not closely follow her. For example, it is unlikely that she gave equal treatment to Genesis and the Gospels. Similar to Proba and Ausonius, however, Eudocia opens with a thirty-four- or thirty-eight-line paratextual preface situating her cento within a wider metapoetic conversation.[51] To date very little scholarly attention has been given to comparing Eudocia's preface with those of Proba and Ausonius. Because Eudocia's style, vocabulary, and language differ significantly from her Latin predecessors, making it difficult to draw direct connections between Eudocia and Proba or Ausonius, what follows is a literary reading of the intersections, however oblique, between the Greek and Latin cento traditions (Eudocia, *Preface* 1–4):

> ἥδε μὲν ἱστορίη θεοτερπέος ἐστὶν ἀοιδῆς.
> Πατρίκιος δ᾽, ὃς τήνδε σοφῶς ἀνεγράψατο βίβλον,
> ἔστι μὲν ἀενάοιο διαμπερὲς ἄξιος αἴνου,
> οὕνεκα δὴ πάμπρωτος ἐμήσατο κύδιμον ἔργον.

---

[49] Cf. Whitby (2007: 207–8), Sowers (2020).
[50] The attempt to identify specific recensions out of various manuscript traditions has been led by Usher (1998 and 1999), Rey (1998), and Schembra (2006, 2007a, and 2007b).
[51] Usher (1997), Rey (1998: 518–21), Usher (1999: IX–X), and Schembra (2007b: 518–21).

This is the account of a poem pleasing to God.
Patricius, who sagaciously authored this book,
Is eternally worthy of ever-flowing praise,
Especially since he was the very first to plan the glorious work.

Eudocia credits the initial inspiration for writing a biblical, Homeric cento to Patricius, the first (πάμπρωτος) to undertake the project, which he carried out intelligently (σοφῶς).[52] Similar to Proba's dedication, which describes her cento as a lasting (*diu, semper*) possession, Eudocia ascribes to Patricius forever (διαμπερές) and eternal (ἀενάοιο) praise for his 'God-honoring' (θεοτερπέος) song. By introducing her cento in this way, Eudocia echoes Proba's preface and dedication.

As encomiast, Eudocia commends Patricius; as redactor, she criticises his deficiencies, which, she says, were threefold: his cento was not truthful (ἐτήτυμα), it lacked harmony (ἁρμονίην), and it included non-Homeric lines. In this regard, Eudocia has a more complex approach to cento poetics than Proba and her dedicator, who describe centos in categorically positive terms. With her candid assessment and critical engagement with Patricius' content, Eudocia writes more in the style of Jerome and Ausonius as she justifies her revision. But, unlike Jerome and Ausonius, Eudocia avoids exclusively ideological readings or a reliance on dissimulation and self-deprecation, making her generally earnest and practical critique indispensable for reconstructing late antique cento poetics.

That does not mean that her assessment of Patricius is clear or straightforward. For example, her assertion that Patricius' cento was untruthful is frustratingly vague, and her active editorial hand, which has made recovering Patricius' 'erroneous' cento impossible, only further complicates matters. In condemning Patricius' truthfulness, is Eudocia implying that his poem had a heresiological quality? Or did it contain Gospel episodes not found in the prose Gospels available to her? Additionally, her ἐτήτυμα πάντ' ἀγόρευεν echoes *Odyssey* 1.174 (cf. *Od.* 1.179), where Telemachos asks Athena, disguised as Mentes, to identify herself and to tell him how she knows Odysseus. By criticising Patricius' falsehood with a nod to a Homeric passage where a goddess openly practices deception, Eudocia subtly undermines her own assessment and might be playing with her reader, who presumably knows the Homeric epics as well as she.

Eudocia's criticism of Patricius' cento anticipates, perhaps even models, the critical engagement she expects of her readers and invokes parallel

---

[52] What follows agrees with Whitby (2007: 208–9).

sentiments expressed by Ausonius to Paulus.[53] For instance, Eudocia's concern with cento harmony underscores how similar her role as poet-reader is to Ausonius. Aristotle defines harmony as a combination and composition of opposites (κρᾶσιν καὶ σύνθεσιν ἐναντίων).[54] Ausonius expresses a similar idea when he says that cento hemistiches should be so seamless that their joints are undetectable (*sensus diversi ut congruant, adoptiva quae sunt ut cognata videantur . . .*).[55] Despite her later admission that she was unable to resolve this deficiency, Eudocia expresses a comparable aesthetic.

Finally, Patricius had apparently inserted some original, that is, non-Homeric, verses into the cento, likely to smooth over those periphrases, inevitable when one uses Homer to paraphrase the Gospel. After all, Homer never mentioned Jesus or the twelve disciples. Eudocia removed these lines, which suggests an awareness that centos were limited to Homeric lines or hemistiches. If we adopt Ausonius' ludic language, Eudocia here follows the 'rules' of the 'game' (*Preface* 9–14).

> ἀλλ' ἐγὼ ἡμιτέλεστον ἀγακλεὲς ὡς ἴδον ἔργον
> Πατρικίου, σελίδας ἱερὰς μετὰ χεῖρα λαβοῦσα,   10
> ὅσσα μὲν ἐν βίβλοισιν ἔπη πέλεν οὐ κατὰ κόσμον,
> πάντ' ἄμυδις κείνοιο σοφῆς ἐξείρυσα βίβλου·
> ὅσσα δ' ἐκεῖνος ἔλειπεν, ἐγὼ πάλιν ἐν σελίδεσσι
> γράψα καὶ ἁρμονίην ἱεροῖς ἐπέεσσιν ἔδωκα.

> But when I beheld Patricius' glorious, half-completed project
> And took the holy pages in hand,
> Whatever verses were not in order
> I ripped out of that man's clever book,
> And whatever he neglected, I wrote back into the text
> And I gave harmony to the holy verses.

After identifying Patricius' deficiencies, Eudocia expunges (ἐξείρυσα) the inferior materials (οὐ κατὰ κόσμον) and adds whatever was needed. Despite her active hand in redacting his cento and calling it half-finished (ἡμιτέλεστον), Eudocia emphasises its sanctity, making it nearly indistinguishable from the Bible. Unlike the Bible, however, Eudocia, as active reader/critic, is free to expunge and supplement Patricius' poem, perhaps because the content she adds comes directly from the Bible, via Homer. In this way, Eudocia focusses her reader's gaze squarely on Patricius' biblical paraphrase, not on the Homeric epics, which recede into the background

---

[53] Sowers (2016).   [54] *De Anima* 407b30–2.
[55] Ausonius, *Cent. nupt.* 53–5 (Green 1999: 147).

of hypertext. Here Eudocia differs from Proba and her dedicator, who rhetorically emphasise Vergil. Read alongside Ausonius' preface, Eudocia's active engagement with Patricius' text also situates her as a member of his literary coterie responsible for critical feedback and emendations. Like Paulus in the *Cento Nuptialis,* Eudocia evaluates Patricius' poetry and emends his shortcomings (*Preface* 15–18):

εἰ δέ τις αἰτιόῳτο καὶ ἡμέας ἐς ψόγον ἕλκοι,   15
δοιάδες οὕνεκα πολλαὶ ἀρίζηλον κατὰ βίβλον
εἰσὶν Ὁμηρείων τ' ἐπέων πόλλ' οὐ θέμις ἐστίν,
ἴστω τοῦθ', ὅτι πάντες ὑποδρηστῆρες ἀνάγκης.

But if someone casts aspersions and drags us into censure
Because in the remarkable book there are many double lines
And many Homeric verses in succession are not customary,
Let him know this – all men are the slaves of constraint.

Despite these emendations, Eudocia's cento contains consecutive Homeric lines (δοιάδες), a violation of Ausonius' 'rules', which, Eudocia assumes, will elicit criticism.[56] As an excuse, she argues that necessity (ἀνάγκης) compelled her to use double lines, unlike Tatian, a popular and well-received (τέρψειεν ἀκουήν) poet whose cento assiduously avoided them. According to Eudocia, Tatian had the advantage of writing an epic that followed the Trojan war cycle, whereas Patricius and, by association, Eudocia herself tell a new story, that of the Hebrew people (γένος Ἑβραίων) and the son of god (υἱέα καὶ γενετῆρα). Eudocia reveals an awareness of the same compositional aesthetic expressed by Ausonius, although she dismisses her (mis)use of the Homeric hypertext as a product of her biblical hypotext. If Eudocia's invocation of Tatian supports her case, her possible awareness of Proba, who avoids sequential lines, does not.

Over the course of her preface, Eudocia blends oral and textual language, which echoes parallel language in Proba's preface and dedication, and Ausonius' *Cento Nuptialis.* At times she implies that Patricius' cento was sung (ἀοιδῆς, ἀγόρευεν, ἐπέων, εἶπεν); elsewhere she emphasises the physical and textual features of the text (ἀνεγράψατο, ἔργον, σελίδας ἱερὰς μετὰ χεῖρα λαβοῦσα, βίβλου, ἐν σελίδεσσι γράψα). Even her apologetic use of Tatian weaves orality and textuality. According to Eudocia, her imagined reader/critic experiences pleasure when hearing Tatian (τέρψειεν

---

[56] Sandnes (2011: 186–9) conspicuously omits this section from his translation and discussion of Eudocia's cento and her understanding of cento aesthetics.

ἀκουήν), whereas her product with Patricius is decidedly bookish (τῆνδε σοφὴν ἀνεγράψατο δέλτον). It is tempting to suggest that, similar to Valentinian in Ausonius' *Cento Nuptialis*, centos were first performed and only later circulated as written poetry.

6.6 Conclusion

Over the course of the fourth and fifth centuries, Greek and Latin cento poets and cento readers composed, critiqued, emended, and circulated a number of centos on various subjects. This chapter has traced the paratextual comments made by and about Proba, Ausonius, and Eudocia. Proba opens the conversation by situating her work as a prophetic fulfillment of Vergil's own Christianised message, a theme which her dedicator builds on and develops further by suggesting that Proba improved Vergil. Ausonius, in contrast, focalises his cento through the lens of his broader literary agenda, with its typical self-deprecations and dissimulations. Ever difficult to pin down, Ausonius insists that centos are ludic pieces that debase Vergil, and as self-described novice, he proceeds to explain to his literary friend, Paulus, the 'rules' for composing a cento which he himself breaks. Finally, Ausonius playfully invokes Proba at the precise moment in his cento when he debases Vergil the most. Assumed to have been written with Proba in mind, Jerome's letter to Paulinus is more about irresponsible biblical exegesis. In my reading, his criticism of centos echoes Ausonius' ludic language, his aesthetics for centos, and perhaps even his reference to the bone game known as an ostomachion. That Jerome uses Ausonian language in a letter to a former friend of Ausonius underscores his own intertextual playfulness, despite the epistle's serious content. Chronologically last, Eudocia blends various themes seen in the Latin tradition. Similar to Proba and her dedicator, Eudocia describes the Homeric Christian cento as a sacred project. Similar to Ausonius and Jerome, Eudocia has very specific criticisms of the cento she receives and redacts, and her aesthetics are similar to Ausonius', which suggests that, even if Ausonius' *Cento Nuptialis* was not written as a guide to writing centos, it does contain poetic theories adopted by subsequent cento poets. For that reason, only by reading Eudocia's Greek preface alongside the Latin cento tradition can we appreciate the interrelatedness and interdependence of late antique cento poetics.

CHAPTER 7

A 'Revival' of the 'Epyllion' as a 'Genre'?
Genre Awareness in Short Epic Narrative from Late Antiquity

Berenice Verhelst

Whether the so-called epyllion can be called a genre depends more on the definition of 'genre' and the definition of 'epyllion' than on the interpretation of the poems which are sometimes given this label. The current scepticism regarding the term 'epyllion' has to be understood in light of the scholarly history of this term (eighteenth to twenty-first century) and the difficulty to reach a consensus definition for a genre that was never defined as such by the ancients and which – depending on the definition – consists either of a very small or a very heterogeneous group of poems.[1] 'Revival', furthermore, implies a gap between a first and second period of bloom, since, unlike the other genres discussed in this section, the epyllion is not considered a late antique phenomenon, but is usually regarded as a Hellenistic invention. Specifically for Late Antiquity, Severin Koster suggested 'Kleinepos' or 'miniature epic' as an alternative generic category and as a way of distinguishing the shorter late antique hexameter poems both from the Hellenistic epyllion and the grand epic genre, but this, again, implies a clear and well-defined idea of the Hellenistic epyllion – which brings the discussion back to its starting point.[2]

---

[1] After the introduction of the term in eighteenth-century scholarship (by Ilgen in 1796 referring to the *Homeric Hymn to Hermes* and by Wolf referring to the pseudo-Hesiodic *Shield*: posthumously published in 1840), 'epyllion' was in the nineteenth century more and more specifically defined as referring to certain Greek Hellenistic and Latin neoteric poems, especially Catullus' *Poem 64* (Tilg 2012; Trimble 2012). In the twentieth century, the epyllion genre was further established by Crump (1931), who situated its 'invention' in the context of the rivalry between Apollonius and Callimachus as a clear rejection of grand epic. She also defined an influential set of genre characteristics. Notwithstanding Allen's vehement opposition (1940 and 1958) against treating this 'non-genre' as a generic category, Crump's definition of the genre remains omnipresent in literary histories as well as in scholarship specifically discussing epyllia (Gutzwiller 1981: 2–9, Fantuzzi 1998/2004, Merriam 2001: 1–24, Bartels 2004: 3–4, and Dummler 2012). For a critical overview, cf. Bär (2015).
[2] The distinction made by Koster between the Hellenistic epyllion and the late antique 'miniature epic' is primarily based on two, for him, indispensable characteristics of the Hellenistic epyllion: epyllia have to have a love story as subject matter ('ein ἐρωτικὸν πάθημα') and a complex narrative structure with an embedded narrative (Koster 2002: 40). He claims that late antique shorter hexameter poems are, indeed, formally not modelled on the 'Großform' of Vergil's *Aeneid* but,

This final chapter in the section on genre focusses on shorter narrative hexameter poems from Late Antiquity. All the examples under consideration would be categorised as miniature epic by Koster.[3] In scholarship some poems receive the label 'epyllion' more often than others, but I will refrain from arguing either in favour or against such a denomination. I rather choose to follow the definition of Charles Segal of genre as a 'medium of literary communication'.[4] My basic assumption hereby is that in order for a poem to be understood by its audience, the information readers need to set and adjust their (generic) expectations has to be present in the poems themselves. These do not need a generic label to be understandable to their readers and can reflect genre awareness regardless of whether contemporary *literati* thought of shorter epic as a distinct genre or not. What certainly remains a significant factor for the way these poems present themselves to their contemporary audience is the idea of epic. The choice of the hexameter already suggests epic as an important framework within (or against) which to interpret every new piece of information that is revealed in the poem.[5]

My analysis is based on a selection of eight poems. Four are in Latin: Ausonius' *Cupid Crucified* (fourth century, Trier), Dracontius' *Tragedy of Orestes* (late fifth century, Vandal Africa), Reposianus' *Intrigue of Mars with Venus* (contemporary to Dracontius?), and the anonymous *Illness of Perdica* (same circle as Dracontius?). The remaining four are in Greek: Triphiodorus' *Sack of Troy* (probably third century, Egypt), Musaeus' *Hero and Leander* (late fifth century, Egypt?), Colluthus' *Abduction of Helen* (late fifth or early sixth century, Egypt?), and the anonymous *Orphic*

---

because of their altogether simple narrative structure, neither on the epyllion (ead.: 47). In Fantuzzi's (1998/2004) *DNP* lemma 'epyllion', Musaeus is the only late antique example mentioned without any restrictions. Triphiodorus and Colluthus are both mentioned as 'examples not fitting the pattern', because of their traditional epic theme and 'deficient unity of action'. Latin examples are missing altogether from Fantuzzi's overview.

[3] Quite a few of them also meet at least one of his criteria for being called epyllion: that of the ἐρωτικὸν πάθημα.

[4] In his foreword to Conte (1994), Segal points out that generic concepts should be understood (1994: xiii) 'not as something external to the work or as a category that modern critics impose for their convenience, but rather as the ancient poet's instrument for reaching the reader. ... Genre is a medium of literary communication ... in cultures like the Greco-Roman that have strongly defined literary traditions and therefore literary competences to connect author and audience in a common frame of reference.' Cf. also Depew and Obbink's (2000: 6) working definition of genre as a 'conceptual orienting device' that suggests to a hearer the sort of receptorial conditions in which a fictive discourse might have been delivered.

[5] Although hardly any traditional epic is written in this period, the idea of epic remains crucial to later hexameter poets for defining their own poetry (cf. also Chapter 5 by Kaufmann). Compare also n. 8 on Ovid's generic play but stereotyped conception of genres.

Argonautica (probably early fifth century).[6] They were written in very different times and contexts, ranging from the third to the sixth century CE, from Trier and Carthage to Egypt. What they do have in common is their mythological subject matter, which excludes other types of narrative hexameter poetry (Bible epic, panegyric epic, . . .) from the present survey. These would shed yet further and indeed interesting light on this discussion, but it would be quite impossible to treat in any depth the large and even more heterogeneous corpus that would result from their inclusion within the limits of one chapter. The poems in the present selection are between 103 (*Cupid Crucified*) and 1,376 (*Orphic Argonautica*) lines long. Their topics vary from traditional epic material, over tragic subjects and lesser-known legends, to a highly original underworld tableau.[7] In this chapter, I focus on a number of (potentially) meta-generic passages: prefaces, prologues, invocations to the Muses, and *mise-en-abymes*. They are meta-generic in the sense that they stand out as the passages that most explicitly communicate about genre and poetics, but of course they do not tell the whole story. The reader's expectations are constantly adjusted.

7.1 Generic Transformations

Very explicit reflection on the genre of the poem within the poem itself can be found in the prologues of Dracontius' *Tragedy of Orestes* and the *Orphic Argonautica*. Both narrators in these poems announce what could be called a generic transformation. Similar to what Helen Kaufmann has already pointed out for Dracontius' *Medea* (cf. Section 5.3.2), also in the *Tragedy of Orestes* Dracontius' narrator explicitly connects specific subject matters with specific poetic genres, which, in turn, are defined by their metre (13–14).[8]

---

[6] I quote from the following editions: for Ausonius, Green (1991; translation Evelyn White 1919); for Dracontius, Bouquet and Wolff (1995; my own translation); for Reposianus, Cristante (1999; translation Duff and Duff 1934); for the *Aegritudo Perdicae*, Grillo (2010²; my own translation), for Triphiodorus, Gerlaud (1982; translation Mair 1928); for Musaeus, Gelzer (1975); for Colluthus, Livrea (1968; translation Mair 1928); for the *Orphic Argonautica*, Vian (2002; my own translation). Existing translations have been adapted and modernised when necessary.

[7] The selection aims to be representative but not exhaustive. I am here taking into account only one of Dracontius' 'epyllia' (his *Abduction of Helen, Hylas* or *Medea* would also be obvious candidates) and I also leave aside the short (though multi-book) *Abduction of Proserpina* of Claudian and his fragmentary *Gigantomachies*.

[8] Dracontius' traditional way of defining the genres he plays with (both here and in his *Medea*) is in line with what has been observed regarding Ovid and other Roman poets who use 'stereotyped definitions' (Hinds 2000: 225) but simultaneously disregard them and play with genre conventions. Barchiesi (2001: 157): 'Often Roman texts are projecting a hyped, exaggerated alias, which includes memories and imaginings of how genres had been in their pure, uncompromised origins.'

Te rogo, Melpomene, tragicis descende cothurnis
Et pede dactylico resonante quiescat iambus:

I ask you, Melpomene, descend from your tragic cothurns. Let the iambic
metre be silent while the dactylic foot resounds.

Melpomene, the Muse traditionally responsible for tragedy, is asked to
leave the tragic scene and to support the poet while he rewrites the
Aeschylean *Oresteia* trilogy into a dactylic poem.[9] Later on, in the poem's
epilogue, the story of Orestes is once more explicitly referred to as a
tragedy, an 'onstage Mycenaean trilogy' (972: *Ecce Mycenaea triplex iam
scaena*). The deictic *ecce* in this line is self-referential:[10] Dracontius' hexameter narrative, thus, is still regarded as Orestes' 'tragedy', which might
be an argument in favour of *Orestis Tragoedia* as the poem's original title.[11]
But, as a tragedy, it has been translated into epic poetry. By highlighting
this tragic aspect, both at the beginning and at the end of his poem,
Dracontius also emphasises his own feat of transforming tragic iambics
into 'resonant' (14) dactylic poetry. In this way he invites the reader to pay
attention to the shifts that go with a generic transformation from tragic
dialogue to epic narrative, and to see Dracontius' own hand in, for
example, the introduction of narratorial comments (270–90), similes
(224–6, 242–4, 265–9, 302–4, 622–5, 631–8, 711–12 and 846–8)[12]
and descriptive details (e.g. 254–69: the gruesome murder of
Agamemnon), alien to the tragic genre.[13] Not coincidentally, I think, the
narrative proper starts with a description (30–40) of Agamemnon's private
thoughts (30: *corde silenti*) as a first demonstration of the omniscient epic
narrator's privileges, thus confirming its genre-belonging after the already
epic prologue.

Other aspects may also recall the generic conventions of the ultimately
'tragic' story. David Bright emphasised the tripartite structure of the poem
(following the structure of Aeschylus' trilogy) and saw a further division of

---

[9] Cf. also Wasyl (2011: 92). As a third 'genre', judicial oratory is also important in the *Tragedy of
Orestes*. Immediately after the cited address to Melpomene, she is asked to help the narrator to
acquit Orestes (16: *purgare*; 151 and 945: *purgandus Orestes*) from any charges against him. The
poem ends (898–962) with his trial and acquittal. Wasyl (2011: 96–7) also points out the novelistic
elements in this final episode.
[10] Cf. Bright (1987: 199).
[11] Cf. Bouquet and Wolff (1995: 161–2) and Wasyl (2011: 43) for a summary of the discussion.
[12] Often with pronouncedly 'epic' subject matter as *comparans*: the Gigantomachy, Pyrrhus visited by
the ghost of Achilles, Diomedes accompanying Odysseus, Ajax approaching Hector in battle, and
the madness of Hercules, Ajax, and Lycurgus.
[13] There is also a second Muse invocation with a question for information (350–2) that jumpstarts the
second part of the poem. Cf. also Wasyl (2011: 92–3) on the role of the narrator.

each tragedy in five (Senecan) 'acts'.[14] Also the high percentage of speech
in the *Tragedy of Orestes* has been connected with its tragic roots.[15] The
poem has a 51 per cent speech ratio, which is exceptionally high for epic
poetry after Homer,[16] but can be regarded as a typical characteristic of
Dracontius' rhetorical 'epyllia'.[17] A small, but distinctively tragic feature is
the arrival of an anonymous messenger (807: *nuntius ... venit*) to introduce a new plot twist. Interestingly, this brief messenger scene – the only
messenger scene in the poem – has no immediate tragic antecedent. The
glimpse of tragedy one might think to see here is actually a clever
Dracontian mirage.[18]

In the *Orphic Argonautica*, there is a different process of transformation
at work. Because of its narrator, none other than the legendary Orpheus,
the *Orphic Argonautica* offers a singular perspective on its own poetic
composition. Orpheus is very present as a narrator and figures as an
important character in his own story. Whereas the *Argonautica* can be
regarded as a genuinely epic subject, Orpheus is not a typical epic bard. He
is the ultimate mythical singer, but also a mystic, a priest, and a teacher,
and the contrast between his usual repertoire and his current endeavour is
thematised throughout the poem, but foregrounded most explicitly in the
prologue (7–11).

> Νῦν γάρ σοι, λυροεργέ, φίλον μέλος ἀείδοντι
> θυμὸς ἐποτρύνει λέξαι τά περ οὔ ποτε πρόσθεν
> ἔφρασ', ὅταν Βάκχοιο καὶ Ἀπόλλωνος ἄνακτος
> κέντρῳ ἐλαυνόμενος, φρικώδεα κῆλ' ἐπίφασκον,   10
> θνητοῖς ἀνθρώποισιν ἄκη· μεγάλ' ὄργια μύσταις·

Because now, my lyre player and singer of dear songs, my mind incites me
to tell you what I have never told before, when my words were still guided

---

[14] Bright (1987: 139–40).

[15] Bright (1987: 202). Wasyl (2011: 91–7) nuances Bright's conclusions by drawing attention to the
important interventions of the narrator's, which should indeed not be depreciated as mere 'stage
directions' to move the reader 'from the one speech to the next' (Bright 1987: 202). Wasyl (2011:
44–5), however, agrees with Bright (1987: 153) that some of the narrator's own pathetical
interventions (e.g. in 271–83, cf. infra) recall the lamentations of a tragic chorus.

[16] Homer's famous balance of speech and narrator text (*Iliad* 45% speech, *Odyssey* 68%) remained
unparalleled in the later (grand) epic tradition, both in Greek (Apollonius Rhodius 29%, Quintus
of Smyrna 24%, Nonnus 36%) and in Latin (Vergil 38%, Lucan 32%, Valerius Flaccus 34%,
Statius 37%, Silius Italicus 31%, Claudian 30%). Colluthus with his 37% has the highest speech
ratio of the Greek poems under consideration here. Cf. Elderkin (1906: 5–6), Lipscomb (1909: 15),
and Verhelst (2017: 17–18).

[17] According to my calculations the *Hylas* has 58% speech, *Medea* 43%, and the *Abduction* 42%.

[18] A Greek point of comparison for Dracontius' translation of tragedy into epic is Nonnus' 'Pentheid'
(*Dion.* 44–46). Nonnus, however, nowhere explicitly refers to the topic as tragic.

by the spur of Bacchus and Apollo, and I sung about their terrible shafts, about remedies for mortal men, and about the noble mysteries for initiates.

After a brief invocation to Apollo, Orpheus in this passage announces to his narratee Musaeus that he will tell what he has never told before (8),[19] which then serves as the preamble for an elaborate catalogue of his previous work (10–46), all examples of Orphic poetry. These he interestingly claims to have composed 'driven by the sting' (10: κέντρῳ ἐλαυνόμενος) of Dionysus and Apollo,[20] and with a didactic purpose (46: δεδάηκας, cf. earlier 33: ἐδάης). Now that the gadfly (47: οἶστρος; presumably referring back to 10: κέντρῳ) has left his body and freed him from its frenzy, Orpheus will broach a new subject. The story of Jason and the Argonauts starts immediately afterwards (50) with Jason's invitation to Orpheus to join his heroic quest. Orpheus, now as a character, accepts but also tells Jason how he used to travel around revealing divine decrees (102: θέσφατα φαίνων) to the people, but then was relieved of the gadfly by his mother (103–4: ἐξ οἴστρου ἐσάωσε | μήτηρ ἡμετέρη) – the epic Muse Calliope – so that he might spend a calm old age at home. Both Orpheus' participation in the heroic quest and his report of this quest to Musaeus are thus presented as a new phase in Orpheus' life. The gadfly appears to be the symbol of his mystic inspiration, and its absence allows him to live quietly, participate in a heroic quest, and, ultimately, write heroic epic.[21]

Not the narrative – as in the *Tragedy of Orestes* – but the narrator undergoes a transformation in order to conform himself to a new genre.[22] In both cases the new genre, explicitly announced as the transformation's product, is heroic epic narrative. Neither poem alludes to a further distinction between grand epic and 'epyllionic' shorter epic. Whereas for Dracontius the shift in metre (iambics to hexameters) symbolises a fundamental transformation between two distinct genres, the difference is much subtler in the case of the *Orphic Argonautica*, where the shift has to be

[19] Cf. Ov. *Met.* 1.1: *In nova fert animus mutatas dicere formas*, as pointed out in Hunter (2005: 152). Hunter also compares this passage with Ov. *Met* 10.148–54, where Orpheus prepares to sing a song on the, for him, unusually light topic of Jupiter's love for Ganymede and includes a similar *recusatio*.

[20] Cf. Cassandra's maddened state of mind (connected with both Apollo and Dionysus) when she pronounces her inspired prophecies in Triphiodorus 358–416.

[21] Hunter (2005: 151): 'In very loose generic terms, we might say that the shift which Orpheus marks is that from didactic to epic.' Cf. also Luiselli (1993: 299–301), who interprets the motif of the gadfly as emphasis on the poet's own literary merit as a way of dissociating from other so-called Orphic poetry. Schelske (2011: 108–12) interprets the same motif primarily in a Neoplatonic sense. Cf. Juvenalis 4.123–4 and *Sibylline Oracles* 11.323 for parallel references to οἶστρος/oestrus as the source of prophetic speech.

[22] Cf. the transformation of Nonnus' narrator into a Bacchant to match his subject in *Dion.* 1.1–44.

situated within the domain of hexameter poetry (orphic/didactic to heroic) and where the state of mind of the narrator (under the influence of a maddening gadfly or not) is foregrounded as decisive.

The process of transformation, moreover, seems to work in two directions in the *Orphic Argonautica*. Whereas the prologue explicitly mentions Orpheus' intention to write in a – for him – new genre, for the reader, the *Argonautica* is a familiar epic story, now told from a new Orphic perspective, with ample attention for rituals and incantations and disinterestedly summarizing the episodes of the Lemnian women and Medea's infatuation for Jason (476, 858–9 and 1347–50), which – only of human psychological interest – are not considered worth elaborating on from Orpheus' 'Orphic' perspective.[23] The gadfly does not really seem to have left Orpheus after all.

7.2   Cross-Media Translation

A third example of very explicit reflection on genre is Ausonius' *Cupid Crucified*. Two important differences can be noted. First, this reflection is not found in the poem itself, but in the letter that serves as its preface. As a paratext, this letter has a different status than the prologues of the previous two poems. It accompanies the poem and comments on it, but is not part of it. Depending on the perspective one takes, this gives the preface more authority (the author speaks in his own voice, not through the persona of an epic narrator) or less (it does not necessarily affect the interpretation of the poem as an independent whole).[24] And second, although also in this case a transformation is announced, this is a transformation of a different nature – not between literary genres, but between media: from painting to poem. The poem's narrative character and the almost complete absence of references to the described object as an object makes it an interesting example of the 'genre' of the poetical ekphrasis.[25]

---

[23] Cf. also Hunter (2005: 157).

[24] Pelttari (2014: 10): 'Because a paratext stands apart from the work, it allows the author a space in which to read his own poem. In this way, prefaces allow poets to enact for their readers one possible approach to the text.' Cf. also Pelttari (Chapter 4).

[25] Ekphrasis can here be understood in the narrow (modern) sense as a description of a work of art. In poetry, such ekphrases appear as parts of larger poems (cf. Homer's shield of Achilles) but by Late Antiquity also as independent poems (e.g. Christodorus' *Statues of the Baths of Zeuxippus*). In ancient rhetorical handbooks ekphrasis is described in a much broader sense as 'vividly bringing the [i.e. any] subject matter before the eyes' (Ps.-Hermogenes *Prog.* 10.1, cf. Webb 2009: 1). Although the description of a work of art is nowhere treated as a separate category of rhetorical ekphrasis, it probably would have been recognised by ancient writers and readers as such, and, arguably, even 'as a paradigmatic example of ekphrasis' (Elsner 2002: 2). In this case, however, the work of art itself is

The preface of Ausonius' *Cupid Crucified* starts by specifying the object described. The location of the painting (Trier, dining room of Zoïlus) is specified as an authentication strategy.

> Hanc ego imaginem specie et argumento miratus sum. denique mirandi stuporem transtuli ad ineptiam poetandi. mihi praeter lemma nihil placet; sed commendo tibi errorem meum; naevos nostros et cicatrices amamus, nec soli nostro vitio peccasse contenti, affectamus ut amentur. verum quid huic eclogae studiose patrocinor?

> I was greatly struck by the art and the subject of this picture. Finally I translated my amazed admiration into insipid versification. Nothing in it satisfies me except the title; nevertheless I commit my failure to your care: we love our own warts and scars, and, not satisfied with erring by ourselves through our folly, seek to make others love them also. But why am I at such pains to plead the cause of this eclogue?

It is, however, not the painting itself, but the poet's own *stuporem mirandi* which he claims to have 'translated' into poetry. His admiration for both the artistic realisation (*specie*) and the subject represented (*argumento*) suggests a clear ambition to vie with the painting in a battle between the arts regarding both aspects.[26] He immediately claims that he dislikes the result, but his ironical comments on the natural pride of the poet also contextualise this claim as one of false modesty within the social conventions of literary circles.[27] Finally, he refers to the poem as *ecloga*, which should not be interpreted as a generic label in itself, but interestingly distinguishes it from longer poetic genres. It originally means 'excerpt' but has become a rather general term for a relatively short poem, and is, for example, also used in this meaning in the prefaces of Statius' *Silvae* and by several late antique authors in reference to the poems of Horace.[28]

With these premises, it does not surprise that the poem starts in a descriptive mood, with a description of the underworld scenery and a catalogue of heroines, identified by means of their deadly attributes (4: *leti argumenti*, cf. preface: *specie et argumento*). The painting still shimmers

---

not described, only its narrative subject is, which allows for my interpretation of the poem as an 'epyllion' (cf. Longus' *Daphnis and Chloe,* which is also presented as an elaborate ekphrasis but takes the form of a novel).

[26] Also this is an aspect which Ausonius' poem and the novel *Daphnis and Chloe* have in common (cf. n. 25): admiration for a painting (*Daphnis and Chloe,* pref. 3: θαυμάσαντα) and the ambition to 'rival the depiction in words' (ead.: ἀντιγράψαι τῇ γραφῇ). On ekphrasis as a 'battle of the arts', cf. Newby (2002).

[27] On Ausonius' ironical self-depreciation in letters and prefaces, cf. Sowers (2016 as well as Chapter 6 of this volume).

[28] Cf. Green (1991: 528), Franzoi (2002: 44), and Combeaud (2010: 755).

through, and the idea that this is a description of a work of art is once also
explicitly confirmed in this first section of the poem (28–9: 'Here also the
whole story of Minos and aëry Crete glimmers like some faint-limned
pictured scene').

Gradually, however, more narrative elements are introduced: the arrival
of Cupid (45–6), his crucifixion (56–62), the arrival of Venus (78–9), her
accusatory words (82–6), and subsequent flogging of Cupid (87–91).
Finally, the heroines take pity on Cupid (94–5), after which also his
mother forgives him (96–7). The single scene in the painting (preface:
Cupidinem cruci adfigunt mulieres amatrices) has thus been transformed
into a narrative poem in which at least eight different actions follow one
another at an increasing pace. Some scholars have suggested that also the
painting itself probably consisted of multiple tableaus, but I do not think
this is necessary to explain the narrativity of the poem.[29] It is the cross-
media translation itself that explains the shift from visual *enargeia* to
narrative *enargeia*. Only by adding time and movement can the poet truly
vie with the painting's illusion of reality (99–103).

> Talia nocturnis olim simulacra figuris
> exercent trepidam casso terrore quietem.
> quae postquam multa perpessus nocte
> Cupido effugit, pulsa tandem caligine somni
> evolat ad superos portaque evadit eburna.

> Such visions with their night-born shapes sometimes disturb his rest,
> disquieting it with idle fears. When he has endured these through a great
> part of the night, Cupid flees forth, banishing sleep's gloom at last, flies to
> the gods above, and escapes through the gate of ivory.

In the epilogue of the poem, with the mentioning of *simulacra* in line 99,
this very illusion of reality is, finally, deliberately shattered.[30] The reader is
drawn back from the world of the story, but not to find himself looking at
a painting once again, as he might have expected. Instead, the reader's
perspective has moved to another 'literary' instead of 'painted' reality,
where the underworld scene is revealed to be a nightmare of Cupid. Like

---

[29] Cf. Fauth (1974). Green (1991: 526): 'There is no need to doubt that Ausonius describes an actual
picture. ... There are four scenes, perhaps corresponding to three or four pictures on the walls of
Zoilus' *triclinium*.' I, however, agree with Franzoi (2002: 9–10), who argues that the painting in
Trier will probably have been Ausonius' source of inspiration, but that his poem is also more than a
mere description, and therefore could expand the narrative beyond what was represented in the
painting ('in uno spirito di emulazione').

[30] Cf. the young rowers in Ausonius' *Mosella* (227: *simulacra*) who hit the water with their oars, thus
manipulate their own reflection and enjoy the game of illusions.

the painting, Ausonius' poem is a work of art that creates a strong illusion of reality. In the case of a painting, however, the material form prevents the viewer from losing himself in it and points his attention, again, at the skill of the painter. The poem's illusion of reality, on the other hand, has the quality of a vision or a dream.[31] By deliberately pulling his reader back from this illusionary world, Ausonius invites him to resume his earlier reflections on the poem as a cross-media translation, which has now become a fully independent work of art.

7.3   Poets and Their Muses

Thus far, I have been focussing on generic transformations that are explicitly announced as such in the text and/or paratext. I will now take a closer look at an element which by convention is present in the prologue of an epic poem: the invocation to the Muses. Conspicuously absent from the Hellenistic epyllia,[32] the Muse invocation, in fact, is one of the few features shared by all eight poems. Only in the case of the anonymous *Illness of Perdica* is there no Muse present in the opening section of the poem. A Muse invocation near the end of the poem compensates for her absence at the start (246–9).

> Nunc, o Calliope, nostro succure labori:
> Non possum tantam maciem describere solus
> Nec nisi das animos viresque in carmina fundis
> Quae mihi mandasti iam possum expromere, Musa
>
> Now, o Calliope, help us with our work, for I cannot describe such thinness on my own, nor can I, unless you give me the mind for it and pour your power into my song, give expression to what you have entrusted me to tell.

This invocation is presented as a conventional call for help, but for an unconventional reason: the narrator claims he cannot describe 'such thinness' on his own, which is an ironical reversal of the grand epic

---

[31] Galand-Hallyn (1994: 341) similarly reconnects the dream and the painting in her interpretation of the preface's opening sentence *En umquam vidisti nebulam pictam in pariete?* which by Evelyn White (1919), Green (1991), and others is corrected as *tabulam pictam*. Galand-Hallyn chooses to keep the manuscript reading (which is also defended in Franzoi 2002 and Combeaud 2010) because of the possible associations of *nebula* (cloud) with 'le clair-obscur de la peinture, les brumes du songe et l'irréalité de la fiction littéraire.'

[32] Hunter (2012: 100): 'We may note that there is no role for the Muses in Callimachus' *Hecale*, Theocritus 24 and 25, Moschus' *Europa* or Catullus 64, [. . .]. If there is anything to this, we may at least wonder whether the small-scale hexameter narrative has no need of the apparatus of "tradition".'

convention of asking for help whenever the subject is too big for a human mind to grasp.[33]

The variety in the form of the invocations shows that the presence of the Muse is not merely a traditional feature that marks the poems as essentially 'epic'. The invocation is also often used as a vehicle for defining the poem's position within the broad field of epic poetry, between tradition and innovation.[34] Ausonius' use of this vehicle is probably the most provocatively un-traditional (1).

> Aeris in campis, memorat quos Musa Maronis

> In the aerial fields, which Maro's Muse brings to memory.

The mentioning of *Musa* creates the illusion of a traditional invocation. From afar it looks like one, carefully positioned at the beginning of the poem, but in fact there is no real invocation, merely an elegant reference to Ausonius' most important literary example, Vergil.[35] The Muse is only referred to as Vergil's source of information (*memorat*), but even this does not have to be taken literally. *Musa Maronis* could also be read as a metaphor for Vergil's.[36] Ausonius, thus, pays tribute to Vergil, but simultaneously indicates that what will follow will by no means be a traditional epic poem. On the other side of the spectre stands Musaeus' *Hero and Leander* (1).

> Εἰπέ, θεά, κρυφίων ἐπιμάρτυρα λύχνον ἐρώτων

> Tell of the lamp, o goddess, the witness of hidden loves

By opening his poem with the same two words that also open Nonnus' *Dionysiaca*, Musaeus raises certain expectations, especially since Εἰπέ, θεά can also be read as a reference to the first lines of both the *Odyssey* (Ἄνδρα μοι ἔννεπε) and the *Iliad* (Μῆνιν ἄειδε, θεά). This grandiose epic opening, however, is immediately contrasted with the unepic subject matter of the poem: a lamp, or rather a tragic love story as it is witnessed and facilitated by lamplight.[37] Not much later, moreover, the traditional role of the Muse is undermined by the reference to another source of information, a local

---

[33] Cf. *Il.* 2.484–93 before the catalogue of ships, or Verg. *Aen.* 9.525–9 before enumerating Turnus' victims. Also Triphiodorus 664–5, cf. infra.

[34] Cf. Shorrock (2011: 21) and Maciver (2012a: 27).

[35] Franzoi (2002: 46) moreover points out that the phrase *memorat quos musa Maronis* echoes the invocation to the Muse in the Aeneid (1.8: *Musa, mihi causas **memora quo** numine laeso*) (Franzoi's emphasis).

[36] Cf. the parallel expression in Ausonius' own prose preface: *Quarum partem in lugentibus campis Maro noster enumerate.*

[37] See Goldhill (2020: 64).

legend perhaps, which is enclosed in the word ἀκούω (5): the narrator hears the story being told – but not by the Muse.[38] By the time the prologue comes to its conclusion and opens the narrative proper with – again following traditional epic conventions – a question asking for the first cause of Hero and Leander's love (28–29),[39] it is no longer clear whether the narrator asks the question to the Muse or whether it is the narratee who asks the narrator. The first option may be suggested by genre conventions, the second is more logical within the immediate communicative context of this question. The narrator has only just addressed the narratee, and exhorted him to go and search (24 and 26: δίζεο) for Hero's lonely tower by the sea. Before embarking on such a quest, the narratee now logically will want to know how the couple fell in love.

Whereas in Ausonius the playful allusion to a Muse invocation (which actually is no invocation at all) could be read as a strong claim of not being bound by traditions, Musaeus and the anonymous author of the *Illness of Perdica* instead highlight the epic conventions they use, but position themselves within the tradition by subtly changing its premises from within. The Muses not only figure as a symbols of the poem's own position within the epic genre, but also as vehicles for important programmatic statements.

In the prologue of Triphiodorus' *Sack of Troy*, the poem defines itself as a short and swift epic poem (1–5). An 'epyllion'?[40]

Τέρμα πολυκμήτοιο μεταχρόνιον πολέμοιο
καὶ λόχον, Ἀργείης ἱππήλατον ἔργον Ἀθήνης,
ὑτίκα μοι σπεύδοντι πολὺν διὰ μῦθον ἀνεῖσα
ἔννεπε, Καλλιόπεια, καὶ ἀρχαίην ἔριν ἀνδρῶν
κεκριμένου πολέμοιο ταχείη λῦσον ἀοιδῇ.

About the long-delayed end of the hardship of war and about the ambush, the horseman's work of Argive Athena, tell straightaway to me in my haste, O Calliopeia, and remit a more copious speech. Resolve the ancient strife of men, in that war now decided, with a speedy song.

---

[38] Cf. Kost (1971: 138). Cf. Nonn. *Dion.* 25.18: Ἀονίης ἀΐω κιθάρης κτύπον ('I hear the twang of the Aonian lyre'), from the second prologue of his epic poem, in a reference to Pindar's poetry. A similar reference to the poem's subject matter as something legendary that is 'being told' among people can be found in Reposianus, where the narrative proper opens with (23) *namque ferunt Paphien* ... ('because they say that the Paphian goddess ...'). Cf. Cristante (1999: 10).

[39] Cf. *Il.* 1.8 and Verg. *Aen.* 1.8–11.

[40] Of the other poems under consideration Reposianus offers the closest parallel for the hurry of the narrator in the *Sack of Troy*. His narratorial comment in lines 51–2: *quid Gratia cessat, | quid Charites?* shows a certain impatience towards the otherwise slow pace of the story. It is also mentioned twice how Venus becomes impatient because of Mars' delay. Shortness is also reflected upon in Ausonius' reference to his poem as an *ecloga* (cf. supra).

The Muse Calliope is the active subject of three of the four verbs that syntactically structure this prologue. They are all commands: she has to (a) tell about the end of the war and the Trojan horse, (b) to make sure she does so without too many detours/without becoming too loquacious (3: πολὺν μῦθον) and, finally, (c) she has to solve with a quick song the ancient strife itself. It is presented as if by telling about the end, she can also truly make the war stop, and as if by speeding up the narrative, she can also make the fighting stop sooner in order to reduce the suffering of that toilsome (1: πολυκμήτοιο) war. Also the narrator himself is in a hurry (3: σπεύδοντι). His instructions to the Muse to avoid loquaciousness can be read as a meta-generic statement, positioning his 'swift poem' against the tradition of grand epic poetry dealing with the Trojan War.[41]

The theme of an exceedingly long war echoes throughout the narrative: in the weary and decaying armour (8–13), the impatience of the Achaeans (40–42), and the regular announcements of the approaching end (50, 124–38, 245–6). The horse, on the other hand, is swift as an arrow (333), the Trojans hurry towards their own destruction (377–8, 377: σπεύδετε), and the Achaeans later hurry back on swift ships from their hiding position (522–9, 524: σπεύδοντες). The same pervasive theme also returns in Triphiodorus' second reference to the Muses (now plural) near the end of the poem, but this time with a different division of tasks between narrator and Muses (664–7).

> Πᾶσαν δ' οὐκ ἂν ἔγωγε μόθου χύσιν ἀείσαιμι
> κρινάμενος τὰ ἕκαστα καὶ ἄλγεα νυκτὸς ἐκείνης· 665
> Μουσάων ὅδε μόχθος, ἐγὼ δ' ἅ περ ἵππον ἐλάσσω
> τέρματος ἀμφιέλισσαν ἐπιψαύουσαν ἀοιδήν.

All the multitude of strife and the sorrows of that night I could not sing, distinguishing each event. This is the Muses' task; and I shall drive, as if it were a horse, a song which, wheeling about, grazes the turning-post.

The narrator himself is responsible for the swiftness now: he is portrayed as a jockey on a racehorse, who can and will not stop to dally on all the details of the sack. That would be the Muses' task (Μουσάων ὅδε μόχθος), whose help, according to this division of tasks, seems necessary only for writing long, 'grand' epic poems, whereas Triphiodorus' narrator/jockey manages

---

[41] On this proem and the Hellenistic poetics of Triphiodorus cf. Maciver (Section 3.2) in this volume. See also Miguélez-Cavero (2013b: 62 and 120–30); Goldhill (2020); Maciver (2020).

this shorter poem on his own. The τέρμα (end, culmination, or turning point), which in the very first line of the poem was foregrounded as the poem's topic, is now used in its original meaning as the turning point in a horse race,[42] thus explicitly connecting the swiftness of the narrative with the image of a horse – and thus also the poet's craft with its subject: the eager[43] but also carefully crafted and beautifully adorned (esp. 66–70 and 95–8) Trojan horse which is the poem's true protagonist.[44]

Reposianus and Triphiodorus may at first sight not have much in common, but the stratagems used to foreground both poems' poetical programs are strikingly similar: also in Reposianus, the Muse is given an active role, and in the invocation a metaphor is introduced which is afterwards frequently alluded to in order to remind the reader of the poem's poetical premises (17–22).

> Ite, precor, Musae: dum Mars, dum blanda Cythere
> imis ducta trahunt suspiria crebra medullis
> dumque intermixti captatur spiritus oris,
> carmine doctiloquo Vulcani vincla parate,
> quae Martem nectant Veneris nec bracchia laedant
> inter delicias roseo prope livida serto
>
> Pray, come, Muses: while Mars and alluring Cythere draw fast-following sighs from the depth of their being, and while they catch the breath of intermingled kisses, do you make ready Vulcan's bonds with your learned song, so that they twine round Mars and yet do no hurt to Venus' arms that amid their dalliance are half-discoloured with the pressure of even a garland of roses.

The Muse is asked to come, not to tell about Mars and Venus' lovemaking, but to prepare (as a fellow-goldsmith?) the chains of Vulcan 'with her learned song' (20: *carmine doctiloquo*).[45] The metaphor is quite clear. The chains, as a work of art, are foregrounded as a symbol of the delicateness and learnedness of the poem. But also the second stipulation is important. The bonds have to be so extremely fine and light that they do not bruise Venus' arms, which are so tender that even garlands of roses leave a mark. This strong image can be connected with a whole range of images throughout the poem. The idea that Venus' arms should not be hurt by the bonds of Vulcan is repeated in 30–2 and 174. Indeed, even flowers can

---

[42] Cf. Miguélez-Cavero (2013b: 131).
[43] 79: αἰὲν ἑτοῖμα and 85: ὥσ περ ἔμελλον ἐπὶ δρόμον ὁπλίζεσθαι.
[44] The ekphrasis of the horse (57–107) occupies a central position in the first part of the poem. Cf. Maciver (Section 3.2) in this volume.
[45] Cf. also Häußler (1998: 85–6).

damage a tender skin (58 and 99) and garlands can be used as a lash to threaten a lover with (82).

The ideal that is foregrounded is that of *tenuitas*, refinement. Also the choice of the poem's subject as a victory of love over war, then, seems connected to its poetics of tenderness and refinement. Mars' martial weapons clearly do not belong in the poem's refined setting and are replaced by (78–9 and 94–5) and wreathed with roses and other flowers (126–9). Like Triphiodorus, Reposianus quite explicitly rejects grand epic poetry. They both do so along different lines, but both Reposianus' tender refinement and Triphiodorus' hurried brevity (and also the incredible thinness of the protagonist of the *Illness of Perdica*) recall Callimachean poetic ideals.[46]

7.4   Generic Inlay Techniques

Besides explicit statements in prologues and prefaces, a common way to invite the reader to metapoetic reflection is the figure of the *mise-en-abyme*. The inclusion of a performance of poetry, music, or dance or the description of a work of art invites comparison between (a) the described work/performance and the text-internal reactions on it, and (b) the poem itself and the reader's appreciation of it. A straightforward example is the epigram in the final line of the *Illness of Perdica*. Perdica's wish that his epitaph will make his story 'read throughout long ages' (289: *ut tumulo scriptum per saecula longa legatur*) can easily be read as the anonymous author's wish that his poem will also know a long readership. Similarly, I interpreted Ausonius' admiration (*stuporem mirandi*, cf. Section 7.2 above) for the painting as the ambition to generate similar amazement in the readers of his poem.

In several cases, a *mise-en-abyme* also bears relevance to the question of the poem's generic self-presentation. The most obvious example is that of the *Orphic Argonautica*. It will not surprise that the character Orpheus, as a foil of the narrator Orpheus, also performs a number of songs in the course of his travels[47] and even enters into a singing competition with the centaur

---

[46] Cf. Maciver (Chapter 3). For the ideal of brevity, cf. Callim. *Aetia* 1.5: ἔπος [...] τυτθόν; of refinement and slenderness: cf. 1.17: τέχνη and 1.24: λεπταλέην; of the delicateness (of sound), cf. 1.29–30: τεττίγω]ν [...] λιγὺν ἦχον |θ]όρυβον δ' οὐκ [...] ὄνων.

[47] A few examples: 251–65, 575, 592–3, 704–7, 1001–3 and 1274–83. In the two longer passages, which contain a more elaborate direct or indirect rendering of the songs themselves, it is mentioned that the song is inspired by Orpheus' mother Calliope.

Chiron.[48] These performances further underline the differences between Orpheus' usual repertoire and the epic story which he simultaneously is relating (cf. Section 7.1 above).

Orpheus is, however, certainly not the only protagonist with musical skills. When Colluthus' Paris and Reposianus' Venus are introduced into their respective stories, they are passing their time a-singing and a-dancing. Indeed, to some extent, Colluthus' *Abduction of Helen* presents yet another kind of generic transformation: the transformation of the bucolic herdsman Paris into a Homeric (anti-)hero.

Paris' paradoxical nature is already highlighted in the prologue of the poem: he is both herdsman and judge (5: θεμιστοπόλοιο [. . .] μηλοβοτῆρος), he has business both on land and – although unaccustomed to sailing – at sea (9: πόντον ὁμοῦ καὶ γαῖαν). When the reader first meets Paris again in the narrative, this paradoxical situation has not yet become reality. He is introduced with a full bucolic portrait as a musical shepherd (101–20). His 'accustomed ways' (110: ἤθεα βαιόν) recall the 'unaccustomed sea' (7: ἀήθεα πόντον) from the prologue, but what is of interest here is his portrait as a musician, and thus as a potential foil for the poet himself. He plays the rustic reed pipe during his wanderings through the hills (111: ἀγροτέρων καλάμων), is presented as a regular singer (112: πολλάκι [. . .] ἀείδων), and when he plays the syrinx (114: σύριγγα) his music has the Orpheus-like quality of silencing the beasts, or at least the pastoral animals: dogs and bulls (116, cf. *Orphic Argonautica* 436–7). His song, however, cannot last. As soon as he sees Hermes approaching from afar, he is struck with fear, sets his instruments aside, and stops singing (125–6):

καὶ χορὸν εὐχελάδων δονάκων ἐπὶ φηγὸν ἐρείσας
μήπω πολλὰ καμοῦσαν ἑὴν ἀνέκοπτεν ἀοιδήν.

He leaned against an oak his choir of musical reeds and checked his lay that had not yet laboured much.

A metaliterary reading seems to be suggested by these lines. If the singer Paris is a foil for the poet, the end of his bucolic song also marks a generic transition within the poem, which at that point is also not yet very long

---

[48] 406–42. The subjects both singers choose are appropriate to their characters: Chiron, as a Centaur, but also as the tutor of the epic war-hero-to-be Achilles, sings about battle between Centaurs and Lapiths, while Orpheus sings a cosmogony. After Chiron's performance no reaction follows, but already during Orpheus' performance the reaction of nature is described (plants, stones, animals – all are enchanted by his song). Chiron is the only one of the other characters to react: he claps his hands and afterwards (448–9) hands Orpheus a prize. Cf. also Hunter (2005: 154): 'In generic terms, the contest of Orpheus and Cheiron matches narrative epic against theogonic didactic.'

(126: μήπω πολλὰ καμοῦσαν) and which, indeed, with the Trojan
Nymphs taking the place of the Muses in the very first line, kicked off
with the generic premises of a bucolic song.[49] The setting changes from
now on, and the reader will not hear about Paris' cows and sheep again.
For Paris, in any case, the end of his bucolic song is the starting point of a
process of transformation. The arrival of Hermes is the prelude to the
judgement. Athena promises him a heroic future (142: σαόπτολιν), which
for a reader versed in Homer will recall the Iliadic Hector, protector of the
city (Il. 6.403: οἶος γὰρ ἐρύετο Ἴλιον Ἕκτωρ). Paris' eventual choice for
the offer of Aphrodite, however, requires him to start travelling: the fate of
an Odysseus-like hero. Δύσπαρις (193) seems not to be used as a reproach
(cf. Il. 3.39 and 13.769), but rather expresses the narrator's pity for Paris
who now has to change his comfortable bucolic lifestyle dramatically.
Easily impressed by a not so very long sea voyage and a not so very
dangerous storm (205: πολυτλήτων [...] μόχθων) and more concerned
with his own looks than anything else (230–3), the adventurer Paris leaves
a very poor impression on the reader, but this does not prevent him from
bragging about his heroic descent (278–9, esp. 282: ἀριστεύων) and ditto
voyage (esp. 295: ἧς ἕνεκεν τέτληκα καὶ οἴδματα τόσσα περῆσαι) to the
infatuated Helen. From a bucolic shepherd he has become a character of
heroic epic, but the transformation (into both an anti-Hector and an anti-
Odysseus) has not been particularly successful.[50] Instead of becoming
Troy's protector he will be the cause of its destruction (392 = final line:
ἀρχέκακον πολιήτην).[51]

Reposianus' *Intrigue of Mars with Venus* also has a musical protagonist.
After a long prologue (1–32), the narrative proper starts with a description of
the *locus amoenus* of Venus and Mars' lovemaking (33–63). Mars has not yet
arrived, and Venus plays, sings, and dances with the girls of Byblos (67–71).

> Nunc varios cantu divum referebat amores
> inque modum vocis nunc motus forte decentes
> corpore laeta dabat, nunc miscens denique plantas,
> nunc alterna movens suspenso pollice crura,   70
> molliter inflexo subnitens poplite sidit;

---

[49] Cf. Harries (2006), Prauscello (2008), and Cadau (2015: 37–82) for more on the strong (sometimes
also contradictory or ironical) presence of bucolic elements in Colluthus' epyllion, especially in the
first part of the poem. On the interpretation of καμοῦσαν (125) in the context of the Hellenistic
debate about whether bucolic poetry flows spontaneously (Philetas) or rather is the elaborate
product of the poet's efforts (Theocritus), cf. Giangrande (1969: 151).

[50] In another contribution (Verhelst 2019), I discuss the characterisation of Paris as an anti-Odysseus
in more detail. The topic is briefly touched upon in Magnelli (2008: 157) and Cadau (2015: 253).

[51] See also Goldhill (2020: 59).

Now she would rehearse in song the chequered amours of the gods and to the vocal measure now joyously, as it befell, make seemly movements with her body; now in turn plying intricate steps, now on light fantastic toe moving alternate feet, she sinks down resting upon her gracefully bended haunch.

Her musical activities have two features of interest. As is appropriate for the goddess of love, the subjects of her song are the *varios* [. . .] *divum* [. . .] *amores* (67), which implies that she (at least as regards content) sings the same type of song as that of which she is part herself, which strengthens the idea of a *mise-en-abyme*. The second point of interest is the combination of song and dance, with an elaborate and probably mimetic choreography, which may be a reference to the pantomime genre. It is well known that stories of adultery (including the loves of the gods, and more specifically the story of Venus and Mars) were popular subjects for the mime and pantomime genre.[52] The dancing performance of Venus more probably refers to a pantomime, rather than to the more vulgar mime.

The question then arises whether the short passage of Venus' performance was intended to recall a random pantomime performance or whether it was meant as a tribute to a specific pantomime of Venus and Mars' story, which may have served as Reposianus' source of inspiration.[53] In the latter case the passage could be read, in a meta-generic sense, in line with Lucio Cristante's suggestion to interpret the poem as a literary transformation of a pantomime play.[54] In this case, however, the absence of more explicit metapoetic statements makes it very difficult to substantiate this hypothesis. Our limited knowledge of the pantomime genre remains an impediment for further assumptions.[55]

---

[52] As attested in Lucian, *Salt.* 63.

[53] Smolak (1989) remains sceptical about this idea and suggests that Venus' dance may just as well be a spring motif.

[54] Cristante (1999: 9). 'Sembra la trasposizione letteraria (almeno in parte) di una *fabula saltica*.' An intriguing parallel for such a potential 'trasposizione' can be found in Dracontius' *Medea*, where the narrator explicitly announces that he will sing an epic version of a pantomime play (16–18: *Nos illa canemus,* | *quae solet Polyhymnia docta theatro* | *muta loqui*). Especially with Dracontius in mind, it is certainly tempting to interpret Venus' dance in Reposianus along similar lines. Pieri (1979: 213–16) already suggested that the influence of the pantomime genre may explain the sensuality and the many descriptions of movement in the poem.

[55] Over the past decades there has also been some discussion about another short hexameter poem, the *Alcestis Barcinonensis* (papyrus discovered in 1979, probably late fourth century CE, 122 hexameters, mostly dialogue), which according to some is a pantomime libretto (hypothesis raised in Gianotti 1991). If this is indeed the case, it would at least provide a tangible point of comparison in this discussion.

7.5 Conclusion

The most general conclusion that can be drawn from the passages discussed in this chapter is that these late antique shorter hexameter poems indeed show a high degree of genre awareness. Genre conventions are, however, in most cases not evoked to conform to a genre, but rather to negotiate the poem's own singular place within or in between genres. Attempts to categorise these poems as examples of a well-defined genre – the 'late antique epyllion' – would not do them justice. Instead, several of them emphatically present themselves as the result of a generic transformation. All in some way or another define their own position within or *vis-à-vis* the (grand) epic genre, which remains an important framework for the reader's interpretation of these poems. The outcome is for each poem very different. The common ground between these poems is not in *what* they say about genre but in *how* they say it. The grand epic feature of the Muse invocation is turned into a vehicle for many different programmatic messages, but the essence of her function and where she appears remains unchanged. Without such recognisable vehicles the message would not be conveyed. Genre conventions are needed to talk about genres.

In line with the general topic of this book, the question should also be asked how the Greek and Latin poems that are discussed relate to one another and what advantages the effect of studying them together brings. I deliberately ordered my observations in this chapter to show similarities and contrasts between individual poems from different periods and regions, not between two languages or two traditions. The comparison shows the strong common ground of classical *paideia* throughout Late Antiquity. The classical tradition is kept alive through constant *aemulatio* (cf. the challenges posed by a battle between arts and between genres) and by a search for novelty (as expressed emphatically in *Illness of Perdica* 50: *nunc nova visenda est*). Self-conscious poets like Ausonius quite openly reflect on this practice. With a sense of irony he states that, no matter what, we love our birthmarks and our scars (preface: *naevos nostros et cicatrices amamus*). Birthmarks are, I would suggest, the talents we are born with, but we also love our scars – the marks left by education, the heritage of one's own, but also of one's culture's past.

PART 3

The Context of Late Antiquity

CHAPTER 8

Saying the Other
The Poetics of Personification in Late Antique Epic

Emma Greensmith

> Whichever path personification chooses, it is on a collision course with itself.
>
> Whitman (1987: 7)

Personification epic is traditionally considered to have begun in the fifth century CE with Prudentius' *Psychomachia*, an influential Christian Latin poem depicting an allegorical battle of virtues and vices for the human soul. Personification, however, has its roots in much earlier poetry – the abstract forms on Achilles' shield and those which populate Hesiod's genealogies[1] – and also features markedly in the Greek epics written during the Roman empire. In this chapter, I explore the significance of personification in late antique epic by taking as a centre-point a work widely deemed the most traditional imperial Greek poem: the *Posthomerica* of Quintus Smyrnaeus (ca. third century CE), a fourteen-book Iliadic sequel and Odyssean prequel with a strongly Homerising style.

I begin by considering late antique treatments of personification as a literary trope, drawing first on evidence from the Latin rhetorical handbooks, and then the figuration techniques in the *Psychomachia*, which most self-consciously displays the device in epic form. I focus on the increasingly reflexive emphasis on sight and sound in these texts, developed through corporeal physicality and character speech. I then examine the complex ways in which Quintus explores these same elements in his poem: in *Arete* on Achilles' shield, the war abstractions and the pointed absence of the personification device in the speeches of characters. Through these readings, I argue that Quintus uses personification to centralise ideas of visuality, and its limitations, in his poem, highlighting the paradoxes inherent to his project of writing Homeric song. This analysis will ultimately suggest the role of personification in expounding the conflicting components of epic poetics as perceived by its late antique inheritors.

---

[1] Brief history in Feeney (1991: 241–9).

8.1 Posthomeric Personification

In *Posthomerica* 5, Thetis presents the arms of Achilles. The central prize is the shield, unfolded in a new ekphrastic vision (Quint. Smyrn. 5.16–101). Upon this new-old shield, amidst images of cosmos (5.6–16), war (17–24), peace and labour (44–65), divinities (67–96), banquets and dancing (66–8)[2] are a number of personifications. Winged Desire appears smiling (71). *Dike* watches over everything (46). In the scenes of war, an elaborate army of abstractions joins in the fighting (Quint. Smyrn. 5.25–37):[3]

Ἐν δ᾽ ἄρα καὶ πόλεμοι φθισήνορες, ἐν δὲ κυδοιμοί   25
ἀργαλέοι ἐνέκειντο. Περικτείνοντο δὲ λαοί
μίγδα θοοῖς ἵπποισι· πέδον δ᾽ ἅπαν αἵματι πολλῷ
δευομένῳ ἤικτο κατ᾽ ἀσπίδος ἀκαμάτοιο.
Ἐν δὲ Φόβος καὶ Δεῖμος ἔσαν στονόεσσά τ᾽ Ἐνυώ,
αἵματι λευγαλέῳ πεπαλαγμένοι ἅψεα πάντα·   30
ἐν δ᾽ Ἔρις οὐλομένη καὶ Ἐριννύες ὀβριμόθυμοι,
ἣ μὲν ἐποτρύνουσα ποτὶ κλόνον ἄσχετον ἄνδρας
ἐλθέμεν, αἳ δ᾽ ὀλοοῖο πυρὸς πνείουσαι αὐτμήν.
Ἀμφὶ δὲ Κῆρες ἔθυνον ἀμείλιχοι, ἐν δ᾽ ἄρα τῆσι
φοίτα λευγαλέου Θανάτου μένος· ἀμφὶ δ᾽ ἄρ᾽ αὐτῷ   35
Ὑσμῖναι ἐνέκειντο δυσηχέες, ὧν περὶ πάντων
ἐκ μελέων εἰς οὖδας ἀπέρρεεν αἷμα καὶ ἱδρώς.

Then there were scenes of devastating warfare and horrible fighting, with people killed on every side together with their horses. All the ground appeared to be drenched with copious blood upon that solid shield. There were Panic and Fear and the ghastly Enyo, their limbs all hideously bespattered with blood. There too was deadly Strife and the fierce avenging spirits,[4] Strife spurring men to engage in combat without restraint, the avenging spirit breathing blasts of destructive fire. Rushing all around were the pitiless Fates and with them roamed the force of dismal Death, while close to that were seen the deafening spirits of battle. From the limbs of all these, blood and sweat were streaming onto the ground.

These images reflect a prominent feature of the poem: the large number of warfare personifications, far more than are found in Homeric epic. Ares,[5]

---

[2] On these scenes cf. Köchly (1850: 258), Byre (1982: 184), and James and Lee (2000: 33).
[3] This passage is analysed in Section 8.3.
[4] Translations of Quintus throughout are adapted from James (2004). For the purposes of clarity, I shall follow James' (2004) practice of using 'avenging spirits' for the Erinyes but will re-substitute 'Enyo' where he opts for 'war goddess'.
[5] Quint.Smyrn. 1.55, 141, 187, 291, 318, 461, 513, 561, 641, 667, 676, 803; 2.213, 484; 6.40, 55, 294, 453; 7.98, 197, 359, 620, 669; 8.239, 258, 263, 276, 485; 9.102, 218; 10.10, 170; 11.12, 139, 152, 198, 269, 297, 301, 360, 413, 500; 12.223, 301; 13.80, 85, 99.

Enyo,[6] Eris,[7] the Erinyes,[8] Battle,[9] Death,[10] Doom,[11] and Fear[12] all feature prominently. Also personified are elemental concepts such as Fire,[13] Earth[14], Wind[15], and, to a pronounced extent, various manifestations of Fate.[16] These instances range from unembellished metonymy,[17] where war is called by the name of Ares, or fire Hephaestus, to more embellished descriptive scenes, 'capable of allegorical interpretation'.[18]

The shield, however, does not stop at these images. In the middle of the ekphrasis, we encounter a remarkably un-Homeric portrait of *Arete* in allegorical form (Quint. Smyrn. 5.49–56):

Αἰπύτατον δ' ἐτέτυκτο θεοκμήτῳ ἐπὶ ἔργῳ
καὶ τρηχὺ ζαθέης Ἀρετῆς ὄρος· ἐν δὲ καὶ αὐτή   50
εἰστήκει φοίνικος ἐπεμβεβαυῖα κατ' ἄκρης
ὑψηλὴ ψαύουσα πρὸς οὐρανόν. Ἀμφὶ δὲ πάντη
ἀτραπιτοὶ θαμέεσσι διειργόμεναι σκολόπεσσιν
ἀνθρώπων ἀπέρυκον ἐὺν πάτον, οὕνεκα πολλοὶ
εἰσοπίσω χάζοντο τεθηπότες αἰπὰ κέλευθα,   55
παῦροι δ' ἱερὸν οἶμον ἀνήιον ἱδρώοντες.

Also wrought on that god's creation was the steep and rugged mountain of sacred Virtue, with Virtue herself standing with her feet on the top of a palm tree, so high that she touched the sky above. On every side pathways interrupted by crowding bramble bushes impeded the approach of men's feet, for many there were who turned back overawed by the steep ascent and few who persisted, sweating up the sacred way.

---

[6] Quint. Smyrn. 1.365; 2.525; 5.29; 8.186, 286, 425; 11.8, 152, 237; 12.437; 13.85.

[7] Quint. Smyrn. 1.159, 180, 366; 2.540; 5.31–2; 6.359; 7.165; 8.68, 192, 325; 9.146, 324; 10.53; 11.8, 161; 13.563.

[8] Quint. Smyrn. 1.29; 3.169; 5.31, 33, 454, 471; 8.243; 10.303; 11.9; 12.547; 13.382.

[9] Quint. Smyrn. 5.36; 8.426.   [10] Quint. Smyrn. 1.310; 2.486; 5.35; 6.14; 12.543; 13.218, 362.

[11] Quint. Smyrn. 8.325; 10.101, 449; 11.306.   [12] Quint. Smyrn. 5.29; 10.57; 11.13.

[13] Quint. Smyrn. 1.793; 3.711, 729; 5.380; 7.570, 550, 329, 446, 492, 501.

[14] Quint. Smyrn. 1.346; 3.396.   [15] Quint. Smyrn. 2.550, 567, 574, 581, 585; 4.6.

[16] Cf. Gärtner (2007).   [17] Most recently Matzner (2016).

[18] James (2004: xxviii). My reasons for not discussing the subject of divine metonymy in any detail in this analysis are in line with Whitman (1987: 271–2), worth quoting in full: 'It is necessary to distinguish two meanings of the term "personification". One refers to the practice of giving an *actual* personality to an abstraction. This practice has its origins in animism and ancient religion. The other is the historical sense of *prosopopoiia*. This refers to giving a consciously *fictional* personality to an abstraction, "impersonating" it. This rhetorical practice requires a separation between the literary pretence of a personality, and an actual state of affairs.' To illuminate this second sense, I shall not focus on the 'religious' background to the abstractions in the poem: on which cf. Wenglinsky (2002: 144–65; with Feeney 1991 and Burkert 1985: especially 185). On Fate: Gärtner (2007 and 2014).

This passage has attracted significant scholarly attention.[19] Commentators have focussed on identifying the sources behind the allegory:[20] the Hesiodic road to *Arete* (*Op.* 287–92), Prodicus' 'Choice of Heracles' (Xenophon *Mem.* 2.1.22–3), and Cebes' *Tabula* (16–18) – an important imperial educational work, dated to the first or second century CE, which professes to be an interpretation of a picture on which the multiple temptations of human life are symbolically represented.[21] Maciver has also demonstrated the scene's Stoic connections: as is suggested by three excerpts from Lucian (*Ver. Hist.* 2.18.11–2, *Vit. auct.* 23, and *Hermot.* 2), the Mountain of *Arete* had by Quintus' era become a stereotypical image associated with the philosophy. Reading the shield as a *mise-en-abyme* for the poem, he thus argues that the *Arete* allegory thematises the Stoic tenor of the epic beyond its superficial Homeric inheritance.[22]

Such readings, however, leave uninterrogated a central aspect of *Arete*'s portrayal on the shield: the fact that Quintus' Virtue is personified. This point of the scene has received less attention than any other structural or compositional feature.[23] And yet it departs both from the primary Hesiodic model and the Stoic mountain as preserved by Lucian. It also presents a very different type of personification from the figures in Prodicus or Cebes, who are described in terms of their physical feminine appearance,[24] clearly participate in the action, and, in the case of Xenophon's Prodicus, deliver speeches extolling the characteristics after which they are named (*Mem.* 1.2.23). Quintus removes any separation between allegorical mountain and personified figure,[25] declines to describe her bodily appearance, and, in contrast to Prodicus, his Virtue never speaks.

The ekphrastic setting of the image is even more striking. If ekphrasis, on a fundamental level, aims to render vivid and visible that being described,[26] then Quintus' scene is punctuated with reminders of this

---

[19] Maciver (2007: 259 n. 1) provides an overview of scholarship.
[20] For possible influences behind the palm tree, cf. Vian (1966: 204–5) and Byre (1982: 192–3).
[21] For further introduction to the *Tabula*, cf. Fitzgerald and White (1983) and Trapp (1997) with comprehensive bibliography.
[22] Maciver (2007 and 2012a).
[23] Maciver (2012a: 73 n. 129) notes that the personification is an 'immediate difference' from Hesiod, but does not pursue the topic. Cf. also a later example of this Mountain, in Nonn. *Dion.* 20.91–6, which, despite the many abstract personifications elsewhere in that poem, does not include a personified figure.
[24] Cf. Cebes *Tabula* 16.1 and Xen. *Mem.* 2.1.22.
[25] James and Lee (2000: 53) doubt, without reason, connectivity between Cebes and Quintus.
[26] Cf. the definitions in the *progymnasmata*: 'descriptive language, bringing what is portrayed clearly before the sight' (Aelius Theon *Progymnasmata*. 18, similar at Hermogenes *Progymmnasmata*. 22;

illusive game. The repeated ἐν, the starkly concessive note that the galloping horses are 'only silver' (καὶ ἀργύρεοί περ ἐόντες, 96), ὡς ἐτεόν περ, repeated like a mantra: we are reminded time and again that this shield is a manufactured object, and the images carved upon it *seem* to come to life only through the power of poetic description.[27] With *Arete*, however, this transparent quality breaks down, as the unprecedented inclusion of an allegory upon an ekphrasis,[28] on the very shield which itself was steeped in a vast tradition of allegorical interpretation,[29] creates an opacity at odds with the vivid ideals of *enargeia*, jarring against the pointed artificiality of the other scenes.[30]

The shield's intertextuality further suggests a preoccupation with the visualisation of concepts. The presence of Hesiod, via the personified *Dike*, encourages associations with the poet whose œuvre provides the archetypes of personified abstractions: in addition to the Theogonic forces, *Aidos* and *Nemesis* (*Op.* 197–200) became the *loci classici* for the lively participation of abstract forms.[31] The dialogue of the *Tabula* is similarly centred on interpreting painted figures of obscure and elusive meaning, thematising the gap between the visual and the abstract inherent to the act of viewing.[32]

The emphasis on 'textual visuality'[33] in late antique literature has been widely explored. Through ekphrastic texts on a range of subjects,[34] and other works in which the act of looking plays an important role (tragedy and comedy, as well as para-theatrical texts like epic and the novel), there has been detected a penchant for presenting the visual in written form – what Elsner neatly terms 'the rhetoricisation of the visual'.[35] Such tendencies have been identified as indicative of the close interaction between the written and performed word in the later imperial period, the synesthetic connections between the modes of reading and viewing.[36] Poetic personification formed part of this matrix: widely pursued, for instance, in the

---

Aphthonius *Progymnasmata* 36; Nicolaus *Progymnasmata* 68). Bibliography on this and other aspects of ekphrasis is gargantuan. On these points especially cogent are Webb (1999), Elsner (2007b), and Zeitlin (2013).

[27] For more on Quintan ekphrasis, cf. Baumbach (2007).   [28] Cf. Kakridis (1962: 54–6).

[29] Buffière (1956) and Most (2010). Further discussion in Section 8.4.

[30] Cf. Maciver (2012a: 66): 'A mountain is something easy enough to visualise, but a mountain of a personified abstraction is something altogether different.' Further discussion in Section 8.3.

[31] On Hesiodic personifications, cf. particularly Burkert (2005).

[32] Elsner (1995: 39–46) is a fascinating attempt to use the *Tabula* to recover ancient modes of viewing.

[33] For the term, cf. e.g. Cadau (2015: 140).

[34] Artworks, paintings, buildings, cities, churches, natural features. Cf. Bartsch and Elsner (2007b), Goldhill (2007), and Webb (2009).

[35] Elsner (1995).   [36] Cf. e.g. Elsner (1995) and Agosti (2006).

cosmological and terrestrial imagery in Nonnus' *Dionysiaca*[37] and the personifications of Night, Sleep, and Anger in Colluthus' epyllion.[38]

Quintus' numerous personifications, however, have not been considered as part of this visual turn. Scholars have tended instead to see them as little more than an exaggeration of the techniques in Homer: as Gärtner summarises, they are mute, their physical appearance is scarcely described, and their interventions in the narrative rare.[39] In what follows, I contend that personification in the *Posthomerica* does fundamentally differ from that in Homer, and that this difference offers a revealing commentary on the nature and function of visuality as a literary process. This commentary is all the more significant given that, on one level, Quintus' poem presents itself as a continuation of the *Iliad* – the work of Homer himself.[40] This claim means that Quintus' personifications offer interpretative opportunities distinct from those of his poetic siblings. First, any change in emphasis from the Homeric picture will be subtle, due to the text's commitment to its conceit, constructed so as to *almost* – but never quite – escape the notice of the reader. Second, any questions raised by such changes also become questions about Homeric epic and its reception as a text to be read, spoken, or 'viewed'.

In order to address such questions, I shall argue that the *Posthomerica* should also be placed within a broader picture of personification in the later imperial period, and particularly considered against Latin works which are most explicit about their literary uses of the figure.[41] This consideration necessarily involves breaking down barriers which have proven particularly durable for Quintus' epic, whose relationship to Latin sources remains contentious and difficult to prove.[42] My reading aims to circumvent the historicist parameters of this so-called Latin question. Moving sideways in space and forwards as well as backwards in time, highlighting shared practices without positing direct borrowing, I shall suggest that the *Posthomerica* has much in common with 'personification epic'[43] in its later, fuller forms, and explores how far new ideas about the device can – and cannot – be reincorporated into Homeric epic itself.

[37] Miguélez-Cavero (2013c).   [38] Cadau (2015: 215–17).   [39] Gärtner (2007).
[40] The lack of opening proem, in-proem (Quint. Smyrn. 12.306–13), and presence of the shield itself all encourage a reading of Quintus as still Homer. See most recently Greensmith (2020: 1–7) with further bibliography on this central aspect of Quintus' poetics.
[41] For further discussion of what is meant by 'literary' in this sense, cf. Section 8.2.
[42] For the Latin question in relation to Quintus, cf. Gärtner (2005), James (2007), Maciver (2011), and Greensmith (2020: especially 36–41).
[43] Cf. Whitman (1987: 4), Paxson (1994), and Copeland and Struck (2010: 6).

8.2 Trope, Poetics, and Practice

By the time Quintus came to compose his poem, personification as an interpretative and compositional tool had been adopted, challenged, and renegotiated in a variety of ways. The aim of this section is not to provide a general survey of these developments, but to trace a particular strand of development. Post-classical criticism has applied the term 'allegory' to a range of practices. The term itself has Greek origins: *allos* (other) and *agoreuein* (to speak in public): 'other-speaking'.[44] In its most common usage it refers to two related procedures: interpretation, the older practice,[45] and composition. Whilst the relationship between allegory and personification is notoriously complex, personification, understood as a *mode* of allegorical expression, also took interpretative and creative forms.[46] As a means of interpreting myth, personified deities or other figures were taken to represent cosmological forces or abstract values. As an act of composition, personification, also an ancient device of poetry, in the Hellenistic period entered the rhetorical handbooks as a trope, taught as part of the classroom *progymnasmata* and practised by orators, where it was handled under the term *prosopopoiia* – making a mask or face.

A crucial component of these various forms is the sheer self-consciousness of expression, manifested in the strain between the oblique and direct, divergence and correspondence. In his seminal account of ancient allegory, Whitman shows how personification offers a particularly intense space for exploring these dilemmas. To create personification, authors have to depart from a perfect system of correspondence – such as wisdom as wisdom – to give a fictional character a body, action, or speech. And the more personal attributes a concept gets, the more it is turned into a character type, and finally an individual, not the concept at all.[47]

---

[44] This chapter will follow Brown's succinct definition of allegory (2007: 5): 'a mode of representation which renders the supernatural visible'. For historical definitions of allegory, Whitman (1987) remains the best starting point.

[45] The noun *allegoria* did not emerge until the Roman period: Plutarch in the first century CE still considers it a 'new term'.

[46] The connection between allegory and personification is as contentious as it is complex. Paxson (1994: 1–7) supports the arguments that personification should be removed from the purview of allegory altogether. And yet the connections between allegory and personification, both in their ancient conceptions and their interpretative effects, are strong, as even Paxson admits (1994: 7): 'In some cases there is a direct and sometimes *necessary* connection between personification and allegory.' The texts discussed in this chapter seem to recognise and even play on this connection. I shall thus adopt a definition of personification in line with that of Copeland and Struck (2010: 5): 'an outgrowth of the literary dimension of allegory, the transference of the reading process into the compositional process'.

[47] Whitman (1987).

Once personification entered into the rhetorical handbooks as a distinct
procedure of composing fictions, the potential to discuss these difficulties
increased. Quintilian's *Institutio Oratoria* contains the most thorough
description of personification in the surviving treatises. Quintilian defines
his trope carefully, delineating the features considered crucial to its success.
The first such feature is speech, central to achieving this technique in the
courtroom (9.2.29). He also muses on the role of physical form, either its
presence or absence (9.2.37):

> Est et iactus sine persona sermo: 'Hic Dolopum manus, hic saeuus tendebat
> Achilles.'[48]

> One can even have speech without any person: 'Here camped Dolopes,
> fierce Achilles here.'

The same double emphasis is found in imperial school manuals. Theon
gives the name *prosopopoiia* to the exercise of creating a speech in the words
of a character in a certain situation – called *ethopoiia* by other writers –
whereas Ps. Hermogenes (*Prog.* 20.9–14) reserves the term for a passage
where words are attributed to inanimate objects.

The impact of such discussions on the poetic uses of personification is
significant. Whilst of course there are cases throughout the poetic tradition
where passages of allegorical intent were inserted into larger heroic narratives, when the device of personification as a discrete literary figure was
transported *back* into poetry, and particularly into epic – a mode so
centred on the traditional portrayals of gods and the deeds of fleshly
human characters, but which itself had been subject to copious allegorical
interpretation[49] – real potential for a clash between the traditional and
tropological emerged. Although there is some suggestion that earlier
works began to activate such tensions,[50] it is generally considered that
the first epic to provide a full, reflexive portrait of this clash comes from
Prudentius.

---

[48] = *Aen.* 2.29.   [49] Cf. e.g. Most (2010) with bibliography.

[50] Statius' *Virtus* (*Theb.* 10.632–82) and *Pietas* (11.452–81), which influenced Prudentius, may seem
particularly relevant: more detailed than Vergilian and Ovidian personifications, but still tentative,
as *Virtus* must undergo a metamorphosis (to Manto) before she can be embodied in speech and
action. I have forgone any expansive discussion of such intervening poets to suggest the
methodological benefits of comparing apparent extremes of personification in epic: one hyper-
traditional, the other the archetype of innovation. For a succinct overview of allegory in Hellenistic
poetry (through philosophy, via the classroom), cf. Most (2010). On personification allegory in
imperial Latin poetry, cf. Hardie (2002) and Lowe (2008) on Vergil and Ovid; Feeney (1991) and
Coleman (1999) on Statius; Cameron (1970a: 271–8) and Roberts (2001) on Claudian.

Personification-as-trope, exported from rhetoric, is expansively thema-tised in Prudentius' *Psychomachia*, becoming the poem's main character and a means of commenting on its practice of writing extended personi-fication into epic. The physical body and the act of speech are central to this process, as Prudentius both centralises and diminishes these aspects of his allegorical figures. Thus, to consider as an illustration the most dra-matic example, during the final fight, the denouement of the poem's moral excursus, the graphic demolition of the Vices as warriors, at the hands of the Virtues is a striking and elaborate feature of the narration (*Psychomachia* 629–725). Such grisly descriptions have clear epic prece-dents, particularly in Vergilian battle descriptions.[51] However, even as versions of such *topoi*, Prudentius' macabre visions seem jarringly excessive and conflict ironically with the ideational properties of characters that are supposedly abstract universals.[52] Yet this gory excess is the *only* expressly physical detail with which Prudentius invests his characters: their corporeal traits are otherwise eerily insubstantial. The narrative provides some gen-eral descriptions of the warriors' clothing and hair – the iron chain mail protecting Concord's body (673–80); the olive wreath crowning Discord's locks (687) – but nothing as sustained in its 'realism' as the carnage which they inflict and suffer. Concord's battle outfit is described only through its functional purpose as a 'covering', illuminating not so much her appear-ance as her experience of the wound which she receives (*Psychomachia* 670–80):

> Inter confertos cuneos Concordia forte   670
> dum stipata pedem iam tutis moenibus infert,
> excipit occultum Vitii latitantis ab ictu
> mucronem laevo in latere, squalentia quamvis
> texta catenato ferri subtegmine corpus
> ambirent sutis et acumen vulneris hamis   675
> respuerent, rigidis nec fila tenacia nodis
> inpactum sinerent penetrare in viscera telum.
> rara tamen chalybem tenui transmittere puncto
> commissura dedit, qua sese extrema politae
> squama ligat tunicae sinus et sibi conserit oras.   680

Concord, thronged in the press of close-packed companies, just as she is setting foot within the safety of the ramparts, receives a treacherous thrust in her left side from the stroke of a lurking Vice, albeit the stiff fabric of iron chain-mail covered her body and with its links repelled the deadly point, and

---

[51] See Eagan (1965: 82–3). Malamud (1989: 48–54) suggests martyrological contexts.
[52] Cf. Paxson (1994: 66–7).

the firm, hard-knotted strands did not suffer the weight of the blow to reach the flesh; yet an open joint let the steel pass through with a slight prick, just where the last scale is fastened to the bright cuirass and the breast-piece connected with the skirt.

The awkwardness and partiality of the personification trope is thus centralised in the scene, as the physicality of *prosopopoiia* becomes at once overwhelming and wilfully insufficient.

Prudentius also uses recurrent images of faces and throats, upon which he concentrates his violent depictions (*Psychomachia* 49–52; 419–24; 715–18):

> Tunc exarmatae iugulum meretricis adacto
> transfigit gladio; calidos vomit illa vapores   50
> sanguine concretos caenoso; spiritus inde
> sordidus exhalans vicinas polluit auras.

Then with a sword-thrust she pierces the disarmed harlot's throat, and she spews out hot fumes with clots of foul blood, and the unclean breath defiles the air nearby.

~

> Hunc vexilliferae quoniam Fors obtulit ictum
> spicula nulla manu sed belli insigne gerenti,   420
> casus agit saxum, medii spiramen ut oris
> frangeret, et recavo misceret labra palato.
> dentibus introrsum resolutis lingua resectam
> dilaniata gulam frustis cum sanguinis inplet.

As Chance has put this weapon in the standard-bearer's way (for she carries no javelins in her hand, but only the emblem of her warfare), chance drives the stone to smash the breath-passage in the midst of the face and beat the lips into the arched mouth. The teeth within are loosened, the gullet cut, and the mangled tongue fills it with bloody fragments.

~

> Non tulit ulterius capti blasphemia monstri   715
> Virtutum regina Fides, sed verba loquentis
> inpedit et vocis claudit spiramina pilo,
> pollutam rigida transfigens cuspide linguam.

No further did Faith, the Virtues' queen, bear with the outrageous prisoner's blasphemies, but stopped her speech and blocked the passage of her voice with a javelin, driving its hard point through the foul tongue.

These images also echo traditional epic battle narratives, where faces are commonly smashed and throats slit. But the specific parts that Prudentius destroys – *oculi, dentis, linguae,* and breath – also correspond to the internal components for making speech. In his vociferous warriors and their lengthy diatribes throughout the poem, Prudentius highlights speech as a critical component of personification. But in this ultimate destruction of vocal faculties specifically, he also revels in showing how this component can be broken down.

As a final stage of this dismemberment, Discordia's[53] corpse is torn apart and divided up (*Psychomachia* 719–25):

> Carpitur innumeris feralis bestia dextris;
> frustatim sibi quisque rapit quod spargat in auras,   720
> quod canibus donet, corvis quod edacibus ultro
> offerat, inmundis caeno exhalante cloacis
> quod trudat, monstris quod mandet habere marinis.
> discissum foedis animalibus omne cadaver
> dividitur, ruptis Heresis perit horrida membris.   725

Countless hands tear the deadly beast in pieces, each seizing bits to scatter to the breezes, or throw to the dogs, or proffer to the devouring carrion crows, or thrust into the foul, stinking sewers, or give to the sea-monsters for their own. The whole corpse is torn asunder and parcelled out to unclean creatures; so perishes frightful Heresy, torn limb from limb.

By shattering this 'corpus', Prudentius eliminates physical formation as the other essential building block of his trope, removing and, in so doing, reflecting the two criteria for personification from the handbooks.

Whereas some earlier allegorical narratives such as Prodicus' also make use of the physical body and the human voice, it is this literary reflexivity that, it is argued, makes Prudentius' poem such a turning point in personification literature:[54] these features are foregrounded *as* figurative agents, which make their own poetic text and rewrite the traditional epic medium in which they are placed. Now, compared to this tropological *tour de force,* the personifications of the *Posthomerica* may indeed seem exactly as Gärtner describes them: traditional, limited, not much changed from Homer. And yet Quintus, who would have received a full education in rhetoric,[55] and who in his very endeavour shows an interest in closely renegotiating epic of the past, also centralises personification in his poem, and closer examination of his personified episodes undermines their

---

[53] Also known as *Heresy,* a double-name which she explains when surrounded by the Virtues before her assassination: . . . *Discordia dicor | cognomento Heresis* ('I am called Discord, and my other name is Heresy', *Psychomachia* 715–25).
[54] Cf. Paxson (1994: 70).   [55] Cf. Baumbach and Bär (2007: 1–26) and Maciver (2012a: 17–18).

straightforwardly Homeric complexion. In light of this wider perspective, I thus want to return to the Quintan shield of Achilles, to consider what role personification can play in its own reflexive poetics.

8.3   Returning to the Mountain of *Arete*

The tentative way in which *Arete* is personified on the shield in the *Posthomerica* can in fact be perceived as also displaying the difficulties of its own description; difficulties similarly organised around matters of physical form and sound. There is a provocative physicality to Quintus' Virtue. First a 'location' (the jagged ὄρος) in the genitive, she then becomes the subject (αὐτή 5.50), and this status continues in the subsequent verbs. ἐπεμβεβαυῖα (51) suggests an active process of ascent:[56] like the men approaching her, she has had to climb to get to the top. In ὑψηλή, ψαύουσα πρὸς οὐρανόν (52) it is *Arete*, not the mountain or the palm, who is stretching (her arms?) to the heavens.

Yet this physicality is also pointedly provisional. The active verbs are carefully chosen so as to undercut, as much as suggest, a reading of agency. ψαύουσα can have either physical or metaphorical connotations of touching. Εἱστήκει (51), grammatically active but intransitive in meaning, can indicate *Arete* sitting upon the palm tree or an object placed on top of it. The epithet ζάθεος (50), in keeping with Homeric practice, is almost always used for places in the *Posthomerica*,[57] occurring personally on only one occasion, for Achilles after he appears in deified form to his son (Quint. Smyrn. 14.304).[58] Its application to *Arete* thus works within the gap created by ὄρος and αὐτή: a personified person, divinity, or place – what *is* this? *Arete* is made to play multiple roles at the same time in this description, and it is difficult to hold on to which is which.

The scene is equally flirtatious with sound. Whilst the Homeric shield at times 'disobediently' breaks the illusionistic barriers of ekphrasis by pointing to the audibility of the images described,[59] Quintus expands the realm of the sonorous into his opaque allegorical scene. Ἐπεμβεβαυῖα in battle contexts can have noisy connotations of 'trampling.'[60] The seemingly innocuous verb χάζοντο (55), describing the men turning back, in almost

---

[56] Liddell–Scott–Jones [LSJ] s.v. ἐπεμβαίνω.
[57] Quint. Smyrn. 2.444, 3.88, 3.545, 4.575, 5.50, 6.146, 8.295, 10.127, 11.42, 12. 482, 13.276, 13.435, 14.87, and 14.304. Cf. James and Lee (2000: 54) and Maciver (2007: 262).
[58] I return to this meeting in Section 8.5.
[59] *Il.* 18.493, 495, 502, 530, 539–71, 575, and 586. Cf. Laird (1993) with Maciver (2012a: 45).
[60] LSJ s.v. ἐπεμβαίνω (II).

all other occurrences in the *Posthomerica* describes a clamorous retreat from fighting[61] – a militaristic tone further intimated by εἰσοπίσω.[62] An intra-text also suggests the verb's connection with battle *speech*. In the deadly confrontation between Apollo and Achilles, the god warns the hero to turn back, and his threat is hubristically ventriloquised (Quint. Smyrn. 3.40 and 51–2):

'χάζεο, Πηλείδη, Τρώων ἑκάς ...'

'Back off, son of Peleus, away from the Trojans.'

~

'ἀλλ' ἀναχάζεο τῆλε καὶ ἐς μακάρων ἕδος ἄλλων
ἔρχεο ...'

'Back off now, far away, and go to join the rest of the gods at home ...'

Arete may be silent, but the readerly act of interpreting her seems to require engagement with sound as well as sight.

We have seen that in addition to the image of *Arete*, the shield also contains the most concentrated series of abstract war personifications (5.25–37). To James, these images cannot be compared: there is 'a difference between the personifications of warfare and the ... personified Virtue'; however, he offers no indication of what exactly he perceives this difference to be.[63] In fact, Quintus connects all of the abstractions on his shield, creating a series of linguistic associations which build to a centre-point in *Arete*. The recurring πάντα/πάντη – first in the war scene (5.30), then for the objects under the eyes of *Dike* (46), and then for the pathways leading to *Arete* (52) – links each personification by a note of non-specificity: the reader is not permitted to picture how many limbs are involved in the massacre, what exactly *Dike* is watching over,[64] or how many paths stand in the way of the virtuous one. The sweat (ἱδρώς) pouring from the war creatures (5.37) is also echoed by the sweating (ἱδρώοντες) of those struggling up the sacred way (56), perversely linking the bloody toil of the battling abstractions to the noble struggle of the few. Quintus' *Arete*, therefore, does not stand in figurative isolation. In its overt novelty, it can function as an interpretative hinge for the surrounding personified images. Within the emblematic shield, it offers us an allegory of allegories – a commentary on how to 'do' and read personification in this poem.

---

[61] Cf. Quint. Smyrn. 1.319 and 11.228, where the noise of the soldiers' retreat is compared to waves and wind.
[62] Cf. ὀπίσω χάζοντο Quint. Smyrn.1.319 and 11.299.   [63] James (2004: xxviii).
[64] This is a further contrast to the Hesiodic model: cf. *Op.* 225–37.

This series of warfare personifications itself closely echoes *Iliad* 18.535–40 and the Pseudo-Hesiodic *Shield of Heracles* (154–60).[65] Any close imitation of a Homeric passage, however, particularly on *this* shield, of course heightens the interpretative significance of differences that occur. Whereas in both the Iliadic and Pseudo-Hesiodic scenes the figures are stressed as being 'like' men (ὥς τε ζωοὶ βροτοί *Il.* 18.539), their ontological difference from humans remains clear: both passages include a contrast with the 'real' men whom the figures are attacking (ἄλλον ζωὸν ἔχουσα νεούτατον, *Il.* 18.536 = [Sc.] 157). The Pseudo-Hesiodic shield even specifies the human origin of the blood which soaks Fate's clothing (αἵματι φωτῶν, [Sc.] 159). In Quintus' expanded description there is no such separation: the personifications dominate the scene, and their mortal victims become implicit.

Quintus' version also heightens the emphasis on blood and gore. In the Iliadic and Pseudo-Hesiodic models, the bloodshed is described through its impact on the victims, transferred onto the clothing of *Ker* (Κήρ). The blood of the Posthomeric scene is set up in the opening panorama, where the whole ground (not just a robe) is drenched with blood (5.27). It is re-emphasised three verses later (5.30), and it occurs again at the scene's close (5.38), where it is the *limbs* of the abstractions that are bespattered with blood: a physical detail not found in the earlier versions, and a transferral of anatomy from victim to figure.

Another notable departure is Quintus' suggestion of breath and sound. Unlike Homer's mute entities, these Erinyes breathe out their fiery breath (πνείουσαι ἀυτμήν), and Eris goads men into battle (ἐποτρύνουσα) and the Battle Spirits ἐνέκειντο δυσηχέες (36). Δυσηχής is frequently applied to un-personified πόλεμος, where it has a general meaning 'bringer of great woe'. When applied to more solid entities, however, it refers to something more audible: 'ill-sounding', 'giving a dull sound', or 'clanging'.[66] Quintus' Ὑσμῖναι allow for both meanings, shown by the different translations of the phrase. Way renders it 'battle incarnate onward pressed | yelling'.[67] Vian suggests 'avec sa suite de Combats hurlants'.[68] Hopkinson opts for the epithetical 'ill-sounding',[69] and James is more vociferous still: 'the deafening spirits of battle'.[70] Like the subtle soundings of *Arete*, we do not hear these figures speak, but their acts of speaking are almost described,

---

[65] Further on this intertextuality in Baumbach (2007). For the Iliadic passage as a possible interpolation from the Pseudo-Hesiodic shield, cf. James (2004: 295). My reading, like Baumbach's, allows for intertextual interactions with both 'source' texts.

[66] Cf. LSJ s.v. δυσηχής.   [67] Way (1913: 213).   [68] Vian (1966: 19).

[69] Hopkinson (2018: 245).   [70] James (2004: 80–1).

interpreted for us by the primary narrator. If we were in his position, we would hear their cries.

Prudentius' extended display of *prosopopoiia* clearly points to the compositional mechanisms underpinning the device: the descriptive process of creating the body and adding sound to mute concepts. This extreme and elaborate example helps to illuminate ideas embedded in Quintus' *Arete*, and the personified images which it conditions. Within this opaque version of epic's most famous visual/conceptual object – an actual shield which also contains the cosmos – Quintus' abstractions pose an interpretative problem which they engage the reader in solving. The same terms are made to straddle the conceptual, natural, and corporeal, and written words are exposed as both able and inadequate to signify sound. Quintus creates an image which *insists* upon a confrontation of the challenges involved in picturing this mental-metal scene, bringing into focus the conflicting imaginative efforts required to visualise descriptions ὡς ἐτεόν περ.

8.4 Narrative Personifications: Broken Collisions

As we move away from the illusionistic world of ekphrasis and encounter personification in scenes of direct action, further questions are raised about the function of abstract concepts in epic narration and readerly methods of interpreting them.

The longest scene of combined personifications outside the shield occurs during the final battle before the sack of Troy (Quint. Smyrn. 11.4–19):

νωλεμέως πονέοντο, μάχη δ' οὐ λῆγε φόνοιο,
καί περ Ἀλεξάνδροιο δεδουπότος, οὕνεκ' Ἀχαιοί   5
Τρωσὶν ἐπεσσεύοντο ποτὶ πτόλιν, οἳ δὲ καὶ αὐτοί
τείχεος ἤιον ἐκτός· ἐπεί σφεας ἦγεν ἀνάγκη.
Ἐν γὰρ δὴ μέσσοισιν Ἔρις στονόεσσά τ' Ἐνυώ
στρωφῶντ', ἀργαλέῃσιν Ἐρινύσιν εἴκελαι ἄντην,
ἄμφω ἀπὸ στομάτων ὀλοὸν πνείουσαι ὄλεθρον·   10
ἀμφ' αὐτοῖσι δὲ Κῆρες ἀναιδέα θυμὸν ἔχουσαι
ἀργαλέως μαίνοντο. Φόβος δ' ἑτέρωθε καὶ Ἄρης
λαοὺς ὀτρύνεσκον· ἐφέσπετο δέ σφισι Δεῖμος
φοινήεντι λύθρῳ πεπαλαγμένος, ὄφρά ἑ φῶτες
οἳ μὲν καρτύνωνται ὁρώμενοι, οἳ δὲ φέβωνται.   15
Πάντη δ' αἰγανέαι τε καὶ ἔγχεα καὶ βέλε' ἀνδρῶν
ἄλλυδις ἄλλα χέοντο κακοῦ μεμαῶτα φόνοιο·
ἀμφὶ δ' ἄρά σφισι δοῦπος ἐρειδομένοισιν ὀρώρει,
μαρναμένων ἑκάτερθε κατὰ φθισήνορα χάρμην.

They kept on toiling without a break in the battle's slaughter, even with Alexander fallen, for the Achaeans were attacking right up to the city and the Trojans ventured outside their walls by force of necessity. There among them Strife and the ghastly Enyo were moving, looking like the grievous spirits of vengeance, both of them breathing death and destruction from their mouths. Close to them the Fates that have no shame or respect were fiercely raging. Elsewhere Panic and the war god were stirring up the armies accompanied by Fear, whose appearance, all spattered with crimson gore, made some men stronger while others were filled with fright. Everywhere the warriors' javelins, spears and arrows were streaming in all directions intent on making a kill. A constant clatter of colliding arms enveloped those who fought on either side in that murderous battle.

This passage has strong verbal ties to the figures on the shield: Ἔρις στονόεσσα ~ Ἔρις ... ἐποτρύνουσα; ὀλοὸν πνείουσαι ~ ὀλοοῖο πυρὸς πνείουσαι. This description also has its own Iliadic analogue: the exceptional passage in Homer's poem where personified battle abstractions appear in the main narrative (*Il.* 4.439–45):

> ὄρσε δὲ τοὺς μὲν Ἄρης, τοὺς δὲ γλαυκῶπις Ἀθήνη
> Δεῖμός τ' ἠδὲ Φόβος καὶ Ἔρις ἄμοτον μεμαυῖα,   440
> Ἄρεος ἀνδροφόνοιο κασιγνήτη ἑτάρη τε,
> ἥ τ' ὀλίγη μὲν πρῶτα κορύσσεται, αὐτὰρ ἔπειτα
> οὐρανῷ ἐστήριξε κάρη καὶ ἐπὶ χθονὶ βαίνει·
> ἥ σφιν καὶ τότε νεῖκος ὁμοίϊον ἔμβαλε μέσσῳ
> ἐρχομένη καθ' ὅμιλον ὀφέλλουσα στόνον ἀνδρῶν.   445

And the Trojans were urged on by Ares, and the Achaeans by flashing-eyed Athene, and Terror, and Rout, and Strife who rages incessantly, sister and comrade of man-slaying Ares; she first rears her crest only a little, but then her head is fixed in the heavens while her feet tread on earth. She it was who now cast evil strife into their midst as she went through the throng, making the groanings of men to increase.

Whereas Homer presents these warfare concepts in the same series as the 'real' gods Ares and Athena, Quintus' version is more alert to their slippery status as figures. His Eris and Enyo breathe ἀπὸ στομάτων (11.10), with στόμα often denoting the mouth as the specific organ of speech.[71] What they are breathing, however, is harder to picture: ὀλοὸν ὄλεθρον, a tautological (un-personified) death. Here again the notion of speech is suggested but ultimately withdrawn, as instead of a battle cry, Quintus' abstractions breathe out another abstraction.

---

[71] Cf. LSJ s.v. στόμα (2).

In contrast to the shield, in this episode the Erinyes are not depicted as present on the battlefield. Instead, they are the object of a comparison: Eris and Enyo were *like the Erinyes* as they charged (11.9). This presents an interesting hierarchy of physicality. The Erinyes had by Quintus' era enjoyed a long tradition of artistic representation: as well as on the tragic stage, they feature on pots, sculptures, and statues from the archaic to the Roman periods.[72] Quintus nods to this tradition elsewhere in his poem. When introducing the Amazon Queen Penthesilea, he describes the Erinyes pursuing her, unseen, and the accompanying gnome (κεῖναι γὰρ ἀεὶ περὶ ποσσὶν ἀλιτρῶν | στρωφῶντ᾽, οὐδέ τιν᾽ ἐστὶ θεὰς ἀλιτόνθ᾽ ὑπαλύξαι: 'for constantly on the heels of the wicked they move, no sinner can escape those powers', 1.31–2) confirms that this role is widely recognised. By contrast, artistic representations of Enyo and Eris are few[73] and earlier literary references to them shadowy, with the two figures often treated as synonyms.[74] Unlike later Greek poets such as Nonnus and Colluthus who increase the corporeal features of Enyo and Eris,[75] Quintus retains their traditional, limited physical presentation. But through their comparison to the Erinyes, he also suggests the exegetical significance of these restrictions. Although all three sets of figures occupy similar roles in the personification scenes, operating as synonyms for war, the range of mental images that can be brought to bear for the Erinyes means that they are granted a greater share of descriptive imagery: able to be drawn upon as material for *comparanda*, they are used to bring into sharper focus that which might otherwise remain opaque. In this merging of poetic devices, turning the Erinyes *into* a simile *for* a personification, Quintus deftly highlights the fundamental fact that some of these abstractions are easier to picture than others.

Quintus also problematises these figures as works of description by contrasting their literal presentation with their 'capability for allegorical interpretation'.[76] With γάρ[77] (8) he cites the involvement of the abstractions as the cause of the continued fighting. Then at 15–16, after the only

---

[72] LIMC (III. 2 p. 595–606) records fifty-six depictions of the figure, with birds' wings, a female face, and bare breasts, often hovering over mortal victims.

[73] LIMC (III.2. p. 562) records just one, archaic, image of Enyo: a coin depicting her face on the obverse and temple on the reverse (*RecGén* I pl. K, 9; K, 11 and 12, 4); and three vase paintings of Eris (III. 2. p. 608–9).

[74] Cf. Eustathius 944. Cf. Wilcock (1976: 58).

[75] Cf. Colluthus 41–5 and 46–63; and Nonnus *Dion.* 5.41 and 20.35–98; although both figures still play limited roles in the poems' narratives (cf. Hopkinson 1994a: 5–6 on Eris in Nonnus).

[76] To re-evoke James' remark (James and Lee 2000: xxviii).

[77] Curiously left untranslated by both Vian (1969: 48) and James (2004: 176).

physical detail in this description (14), the purpose clause and participle ὁρώμενοι suggest a literal 'sighting', with Fear becoming both concept in verse 13 and effect two lines later. Quintus then describes various celestial reactions to the fighting (Quint. Smyrn. 11.150–3):

ὡς ἄρα Τρώιοι υἷες ἐϋπτολέμοισιν Ἀχαιοῖς 150
ἔνθορον ἐσσυμένως. Κεχάροντο δὲ Κῆρες ἐρεμναί
μαρναμένων, ἐγέλασσε δ' Ἄρης, ἰάχησε δ' Ἐνυώ
σμερδαλέον· μέγα δέ σφιν ἐπέβραχεν αἰόλα τεύχη.

Such was the speed with which the sons of Troy leapt onto the warlike Achaeans. The black Fates were delighted with the fighting, the war god laughed, and Enyo shrieked horribly and loud was the clash of flashing armour.

Here the Fates, Ares, and Enyo seem to behave not as extensions of the conflict but as independent characters watching and responding to it. Ares' glee is mirrored in Enyo's later response to Troy's destruction, where she is joined in her merriment by Athena and Hera (Quint. Smyrn. 12.436–9):

αὐτοὶ δ' ἐστέψαντο κάρη· μέγα δ' ἦπυε λαός
ἀλλήλοις ἐπικεκλομένων. Ἐγέλασσε δ' Ἐνυώ
δερκομένη πολέμοιο κακὸν τέλος· ὑψόθι δ' Ἥρη
τέρπετ', Ἀθηναίη δ' ἐπεγήθεεν. . . .

They crowned their own heads likewise. Great were the cries of the people encouraging one another. Enyo laughed to see that war's bad outcome, while on high Athena and Hera were both delighted.

It is one thing for Hera and Athena – Olympians, frequently anthropo-morphised[78] – to rejoice at a scene of battle. For abstractions of the very concept of war to do the same is more problematic: war cannot laugh at itself. But no sooner does Enyo assert herself as a participatory character in the narrative than this status is stripped away again: in the Book 11 scene, her shouting merges back into the clang of the weapons (11.154) and the figures retreat into the explanatory fabric of the battle, no longer agents interpreting it for us.

---

[78] Hera appears at Quint. Smyrn. 3.128, 137; 4.48; 5.397; 10.334; 12.373;439; 13.417. Athena, the most frequently featured Olympian in the poem aside from Zeus, is present directly or indirectly at Quint. Smyrn. 1.124–37, 289; 3.533–9; 5.360–4, 451–2; 7.556–64; 8.341–68; 9.404–5, 437; 11.285; 12.106–16, 396–480;14.420–57, 630–4.

8.5 Readers and Interpreters: The Poet's Trope

I have shown that Quintus' personification episodes update their Homeric models by foregrounding and fragmenting the physical and audible components of their descriptive strategies, advertising their status as literary figures, and thereby problematising the Homeric textuality of the poem. The final passage to discuss in this respect returns us to *Arete* once more. As this emblematic figure is pursued beyond the confines of the shield, Quintus most provocatively presents his personifications as Posthomeric (re)writings of the Homeric mode.

In the final book, the ghost of Achilles appears to Neoptolemus, advising him on how to conduct himself (Quint. Smyrn. 14.195–200):

Κεῖνος δ' οὔ ποτ' ἀνὴρ Ἀρετῆς ἐπὶ τέρμαθ' ἵκανεν   195
ᾧ τινι μὴ νόος ἐστὶν ἐναίσιμος· οὕνεκ' ἄρ' αὐτῆς
πρέμνον δύσβατόν ἐστι, μακροὶ δέ οἱ ἄχρις ἐπ' αἴθρῃ
ὄζοι ἀνηέξη<ν>θ'· ὁπόσοισι δὲ κάρτος ὀπηδεῖ
καὶ πόνος, ἐκ καμάτου πολυγηθέα καρπὸν ἀμῶνται
εἰς Ἀρετῆς ἀναβάντες ἐυστεφάνου κλυτὸν ἔρνος.   200

The goal of Virtue is never attained by the man whose thinking is not honourable, because her trunk is difficult to climb and high up in the air her branches extend. But those whose strength is combined with toil will reap delightful fruit from their work when they have scaled the famous tree of fair-crowned Virtue.

The connection with the shield imagery has long been noted. Byre takes the two scenes as 'allegorical cognates', suggesting that the details which Achilles adds – for instance, what awaits the climbers after their struggle – show what must have been presupposed in the earlier scene by the imperial reader.[79] For Maciver, 'Achilles expounds, with modification, what was narrated to us in *Posthomerica* 5'.[80] But if Achilles acts as reader and interpreter of the allegory on his shield, there is a significant aspect which his lesson has missed. As Byre also notes, '*Arete* here is not presented as a concrete personage but rather seems to be identified with the tree itself'.[81] Achilles removes *Arete*'s personification: any suggestion of her physical or vocal nature is gone.

Ἀρετῆς (195) corresponds to the structure of 5.49, where *Arete* is in the genitive, referring to the ὄρος. But instead of the syntax of 5.50, Achilles' virtue remains confined to this genitive state (οὕνεκ' ἄρ' αὐτῆς, 196), never

[79] Byre (1982: 191).   [80] Maciver (2012a: 79).   [81] Byre (1982: 191).

promoted to the performer of her own actions.[82] Removed too is the epithet ζάθεα, with its divine and humanising connotations. That Achilles is exceptionally given the epithet himself (14.304) serves as a reminder of its previous application to *Arete*, drawing attention to its absence now. The substitute in Achilles' formulation can even function as an un-reading of ζαθέης Ἀρετῆς (14.50). Εὐστέφανος (14.200) is commonly used both of cities and goddesses,[83] and in all other instances in the *Posthomerica* occurs as the epithet for Aphrodite.[84] In its final appearance here, this people-place term provides a hint of the personified potential of *Arete*, but this time our internal narrator falls short of fulfilling it.

Achilles successfully reads the *Arete* allegory from his shield, capturing its complexity and expanding its moral significations; but he fails to read the personification used to create it. Despite his divine status, like his Iliadic counterpart (*Il.* 19.16–19),[85] his reaction to the wonders of his armour remains partial and incomplete. In this scene of character didacticism, filial instruction, and character-speech narration, any conflation between Achilles' voice and Quintus'[86] is forcefully disrupted by this deficiency in the art of figurative presentation. The personification of *Arete* in fact remains unique to the Book 5 ekphrasis: for all of its echoes elsewhere, Virtue does not take embodied form again.[87] As a character in epic – stuck in the mythological space and time of the *Iliad* – Achilles is unable to grasp the Posthomeric potential of personification: he and the other Homeric characters remain blind to its figurative capabilities. As it is misread by internal narrators, the trope is revealed as the privileged device of the poet and his readership, inscribing their shared participation in the act of poetic description and interpretation.

[82] Maciver (2016) suggests that Virtue's gesture of stretching up to the heavens has connections with Achilles' 'Posthomeric' afterlife. This interpretation, whilst plausible, still does not account for the figurative differences between *Arete*'s portrayal in this speech and her depiction on the shield.

[83] LSJ s.v. εὐστέφανος.   [84] Quint. Smyrn. 1.667, 5.71 and 10.318.

[85] Achilles here (*Il.* 19.16–19) is famously enlivened by his shield (his eyes flash), but it is a belligerent excitement, fuelled by his anger and desire for revenge: the singer of κλέα ἀνδρῶν cannot at this point in the story be finely tuned to the nuances of artistic creation.

[86] Cf. Greensmith (2020: 264–73) on the role of this scene in Quintus' filial metapoetics.

[87] *Arete* un-personified occurs seven times in the poem, all in the words of secondary narrators (Quint. Smyrn. 1.732; 3.124; 5.592; 7.651, 668; 14.195, 200). Some characters use warfare abstractions in their speech, most frequently Ares (Quint. Smyrn. 6.55; 7.669; 10.10); and they certainly discuss Fate, personified and un-personified (cf. Gärtner 2014). They are not, however, granted the ability to personify Virtue, this emblematic example of the trope.

8.6 Coda: Personifying Impersonation

In its pointedly partial personifications, the *Posthomerica* should be recognised as an important participant in late antique musings on literary visuality. Rather than straightforwardly enlivening his abstract figures, making them easy to picture and understand, Quintus foregrounds the difficulties in the process of drawing these poetic images, allowing the seams of allegorical creation and the strains of its interpretation to show through. Reflexivity, however, can never be the whole answer, and Quintus' techniques do more than highlight tensions 'for their own sake': rather, they strike at the core of the distinct agenda of the epic. In the specific identity poetics of the *Posthomerica*, which in its very claim to be 'still Homer' must persistently confront the conflicting demands of imitation and innovation, and gives voice to (dare we say it, 'personifies') the ancient figure of the bard, personification provides a fertile means for displaying the stylistic and conceptual dilemmas at stake in creating an imperial Homer. In this poem, a written continuation of an oral song, at pains to emphasise both its literary inheritance and performative connotations, aspects of physical form and audibility take on constant double meaning, helping the text to exploit the gap between full and false embodiment of the Homeric voice.

I end with a final word on the 'Latin question'. By reassessing Quintus' personifications using parallels from intentionally unusual examples – later Latin texts against which imperial Greek epics are rarely ever set – I hope to have shown what can be gained if we move away from hunting for safe sources and certain intertexts. The *Psychomachia* provides the most profound illustration of the rhetorical capabilities of personification and the uses to which it could be put by those wishing to reconfigure traditional poetics. The extent to which it can elucidate hints in Quintus' ever-evasive poem suggests that it is productive to think less of a direct flow of influence than of conceptual nodes of interaction: diverse, but related, teaching, experiments, and concerns. As a Posthomeric practitioner of personification, Quintus is best understood not only if we allow him access to a range of models and *comparanda*, but if we allow ourselves access to them too.

CHAPTER 9

Internal Audiences in the New Testament Epics of Juvencus and Nonnus

Laura Miguélez-Cavero

Christian epic became a popular (sub-)genre in Late Antiquity in both the western[1] and eastern[2] halves of the Mediterranean. While only those in possession of a detailed knowledge of the Bible – that is, learned Christians – could fully appreciate the combination of Christian detail and classical form, the programmatic passages of these poems often address non-Christian audiences. For instance, the *protheoria* of the *Metaphrasis Psalmorum* mentions as the aim of the poem 'that the others too will know that every language proclaims Christ King':[3] 'others' (ἄλλοι) has been taken to refer to the pagans, who would be the target readers of the poem together with the Christians.[4] In the preface to his *Carmen Paschale* Sedulius addresses a dinner guest whose religion is not mentioned (*Praef.* 1 *Paschales quicumque dapes conviva requires*) and then he invites those with an obsession with (pagan) philosophy to abandon it for Christian belief (1.38–42). Sedulius' initial statement could be a form of traditional posturing for the benefit of a broader audience, perhaps to be related to specific Gospel calls to make disciples of all nations,[5] because his poem then seems to be pitched at the level of an informed Christian and ridicules pagan worship (1.242–81).[6]

---

[1] In the fourth century CE, Juvencus composed his *Evangeliorum libri quattuor*, and Proba her *Cento vergilianus de laudibus Christi*. Sedulius wrote his *Carmen Paschale* under Valentinian III (425–55) and Theodosius II (408–50). Arator's *Historia Apostolica* was recited in public in Rome in 544. Paulinus of Nola *Carm.* 6 (*Laus sancti Iohannis*) is essentially a paraphrase of Luke 1. Overviews in Green (2006) and Roberts (1985a).

[2] Empress Eudocia (ca. 400–60) is responsible for *The Martyrdom of St. Cyprian* (a paraphrase in verse of a prose hagiography) and the *Homeric centos*. Extant paraphrases of books of the Bible: the *Paraphrase of the Psalms* attributed to Apollinaris, and the *Paraphrase of the Gospel of John* by Nonnus of Panopolis.

[3] *Metaphrasis Psalmorum* Protheoria. 32–3 ἵνα γνώωσι καὶ ἄλλοι | γλῶσσ᾽ ὅτι παντοίη Χριστὸν βασιλῆα βοήσει.

[4] Agosti (2001a: 89).

[5] E.g. the 'Great Call' to make disciples of all nations and baptise and instruct them (Mt 28.19–20).

[6] Springer (1988: 31) and Green (2006: 245–6).

174

This chapter proposes a new take on the question of the intended audience and possible proselytising aim of two Christian epics, the *Evangeliorum Libri Quattuor* [ELQ] by Juvencus and the *Paraphrase of the Gospel of John* [*P.*] by Nonnus of Panopolis.

Gaius Vettius Aquilinus Juvencus was, according to Jerome (*De viris illustribus* chapter 84), an aristocrat and priest from Hispania, under Constantine.[7] Juvencus began his *Evangeliorum Libri Quattuor* with a preface:[8] classical poets such as Vergil have enjoyed ample readership and fame for their singing of *sublimia facta* despite their lies, but their works will perish in the final conflagration (Praef. 6–16), whereas Juvencus' song will bestow on him eternal glory (17–18). The subject of his work, Christ's deeds, is a source of life (19 *Christi vitalia gesta*), a divine gift to all peoples (20 *divinum populis . . . donum*), and has the added advantage of being free from the charge of falsehood (20 *falsi sine crimine*).[9] This initial call to a broad readership ties in with the final verses of the poem, a paraphrase of Matthew's Great Call (4.784–801) and has a visible impact on the main narrative: Juvencus reformulates Gospel passages with a specific Jewish orientation (e.g. geographical details, cultural references) to give them a universal scope that makes them suitable for a broader (Roman or romanised) audience.[10]

Nonnus hailed from the Egyptian town of Panopolis and is dated to the fifth century CE. He composed first a *Paraphrase of the Gospel of John*, in 21 books, one per chapter of the Gospel, and then the *Dionysiaca*, a poetic account on Dionysus, from his ancestors to his accession to the Olympus.[11] Nonnus' *Paraphrase* lacks a proem and any other programmatic space in which its author could address his audience.[12] We have no

---

[7] Constantine is addressed in the epilogue of the ELQ (4.806–12), published probably after 324: McGill (2016: 3–5) and Green (2006: 1–14).

[8] To be read with Green (2004a). For the difference in Late Antiquity between a preface (paratext commenting upon the text) and a proem (introductory material incorporated into the poem), cf. Pelttari (2014: 45–8). He notes (p. 48, n. 9) that Juvencus' preface, despite its name, functions more like a proem.

[9] Green (2004a: 214–16), Green (2006: 18), and McGill (2016: 5–11).

[10] McGill (2016: 20–1, 24) and Herzog (1975: 111–15).

[11] The use of formulae specifically developed for the *P.* in the *Dion.* confirms that the *P.* was composed first and that Nonnus was always a Christian: Vian (1997). Dating of Nonnus: Vian (1976: ix–xviii) and Accorinti (2016: 28–37). Nonnus' religion cf. also Shorrock (2011), Chuvin (2014), and Accorinti (ed. 2016: 37–46, 68–9, 75–88, 91–110).

[12] There is no marked programmatic space except for a certain authorial self-awareness in the final lines of the poem (21.139–43). Agosti (2001a, 95–6) reads Nonnus *P.* 21.142 βίβλους . . . νεοτευχέας as self-referential to the composition of the poem in the 'new style'. Faulkner (2014: 107–8) is sceptical.

concrete information about the contemporary reception of the poem,[13] but the choice of the Gospel of John as a text base for the *Paraphrase of the Gospel of John* has been said to be at least partially motivated by the interest it had aroused in Neoplatonic circles, especially the initial Hymn to the Logos.[14] Nonnus could well be targeting the educated elites of Alexandria, which in the fifth century CE included Christians, Jews, and polytheists,[15] but how exactly he approached them is more difficult to ascertain. A good point of comparison is the preface of the *Commentary on the Gospel of John* by Cyril of Alexandria, Nonnus' main theological source:[16] Cyril says that as a priest he is under the obligation 'to announce to the people what they need to learn',[17] effectively subjecting his broad approach to the usual Christian paraenetic intent.[18] He clearly advertises that the commentary will have a dogmatic focus, aimed at the correction of heretical doctrines.[19]

I will read the reactions to Jesus and his Gospel in both poems as paradigms for how these poets related to their audiences, with a special focus on (1) symbolic images of the audience (Matthew's parable of the sower, John's initial Hymn of the logos), (2) introductions of choral characters as they interact with Jesus, and (3) divisions of the audience. Juvencus paraphrases mainly the Gospel of Matthew,[20] but he includes a number of Joannine episodes which come across as useful terms of comparison with Nonnus. I will pay special attention to their points of contact

[13] Though we can see that it was cited early and widely: overview in Tissoni (2016: 691–701).
[14] According to Eusebius *Praeparatio Evangelica* 11.18.26–19.2, Amelius, a disciple of Plotinus, composed a commentary on John's Prologue. Cf. Dörrie (1972), Agosti (2001a: 97–9), De Stefani (2002: 19), Franchi (2016: 243), and Spanoudakis (2016: 604).
[15] On Alexandria in Late Antiquity, cf. Haas (1997) and Watts (2010).
[16] For an overview of Nonnus' exegetical sources, cf. Simelidis (2016).
[17] Cyril *Comm. in Jo.* Praef. (Pusey 1.2): 'The statutes of the law stress this even more [the need to speak up] when they command those who have been called to the divine priesthood to use trumpet blasts to announce to the people what they need to learn.' Translation Maxwell and Elowsky (2013–15).
[18] In general, ancient commentators of the Bible produced a paraenetic reading of Scripture: overview in Young (1997: 203–5, 209–10, 219, 235–7, 285–99).
[19] Cyril *Comm. in Jo.* Praef. (Pusey 1.7) 'I will muster my discourse for battle, as well as I can, against the false opinions of those who teach wrongly [ταῖς τῶν ἑτεροδιδασκαλούντων ψευδοδοξίαις]. I will direct the discussion at every point to a doctrinal explanation [εἰς δογματικωτέραν ... ἐξήγησιν]'. Also, the Praef. to book 1: while the synoptic Gospels provide a precise narrative account, John reaches out for subjects that are beyond human comprehension, as a response against false shepherds and teachers who had thrown the people into confusion with their impious and ignorant teachings. Cyril begins his commentary explaining the orthodox faith and criticises all deviations from it, including references to the Arians (*Comm. in Jo.* 1.1, Pusey 1.31–44), the Eunomians (1.2, Pusey 1.45–64), and Origen (1.9, Pusey 108–26 – Cyril does not name Origen, but criticises in this chapter one of the core tenets of Origenism, the pre-existence of the soul).
[20] Juvencus follows a preconceived plan, combining the Gospel of Matthew with sections of Luke and John. On Juvencus' selection of the Gospel narrative, cf. Green (2006: 23–50).

and divergences, which I will relate to the specific context of creation of both poems: the Constantinian Latin-speaking West for Juvencus and 430–60 Alexandria, dominated by the figure of Cyril (bishop 412–44), for Nonnus.

9.1   Images of the Audience

9.1.1   Juvencus' Parable of the Sower

The parable of the sower (Mt 13.4–9, 18–23; Mk 4.3–9, 14–20; Lk 8.5–8, 11–12) could easily become a programmatic image for a broad audience, as it describes different forms of listening to Jesus' preaching and presents faith as a consequence of attentive listening and understanding. Jesus preaches the word of the kingdom to everyone, just as the sower sows everywhere; some listeners do not understand (the seed sown on the edge of the path, which never germinates), others listen superficially and defect when trials come (the seed sown on patches of rock), others listen but their faith is choked by their daily worries (the seed sown in thorns, choked by them), and finally some listen to the word, understand it, and live according to it to the best of their means (the seed sown in rich soil yields a harvest with different degrees of fertility).

In Juvencus' paraphrase of this passage, the only valid type of listening to Jesus is the spiritual one, as hinted by his rendering of Jesus' concluding statement (Mt 13.9; ELQ 2.754):

Qui habet aures audiendi audiat.
Let anyone with ears listen!

~

Audiat haec, aures mentis qui gestat apertas.
Let him hear this, whose ears of the soul are open![21]

The metaphoric interpretation of the ears and the listening may go back to Origen or a vaguer exegetic tradition on this passage,[22] but this conclusion to Jesus' speech 'authorises' a spiritual reading of the passage, emphasised

---

[21] Juvencus used a pre-Vulgate translation of the Bible, probably one of the versions of the Old Itala: here Jülicher (1938) for Matthew; Jülicher and Aland (1963) for John. Translation of the Gospels are taken from the New Revised Standard Version (NRSV) (adapted). The translation of the ELQ is taken from McGill (2016).

[22] McGill (2016: 193, n. to 754) 'Origen states that these are not ears of the body, but of the soul (*anima*). Juvencus need not have relied on Origen directly, however, since his interpretation of *aures audiendi* in Mt 13.9 appears more widely, including in the homiletic and commentary traditions.'

in line 761 (of those who do not understand Jesus' parables) (Mt 13.11; ELQ 2.761):

> Illis autem non est datum [nosse mysterium regni].
> But to them it has not been given [to know the mystery of the kingdom of heaven].

~

> Illis pro merito clauduntur lumina mentis.
> The eyes within their souls are rightly sealed,

Juvencus also rephrases the link between knowledge and faith, and fosters a moral reading of the parable. In the Gospel, knowledge is God's gift, whereas in Juvencus faith is a prerequisite to it: the disciples can know the mysteries of the kingdom because they have a robust faith (Mt 13.11; ELQ 2.758–60).[23]

> Quia vobis datum est nosse mysterium regni.
> Because to you it has been given to know the mystery of the kingdom.

~

> Vobis, qui firmo robustam pectore mentem
> ad capienda Dei penetralia constabilistis,
> concessum est aditis penitus consistere regni.
> You who have strengthened your unshaken souls
> within firm breasts to grasp God's mysteries
> can settle in the kingdom's inmost depths.

Matthew (13.12–16) then specifies that the gap between those who understand and those who do not will get broader, in fulfilment of Isaiah (6.9–10), according to whom the people have hardened their hearts and shut their ears and eyes, lest they convert because of what they hear and see. In Juvencus the division between those who know and those who do not know is redressed in moral terms: the knowledgeable are just (762 dignus, 772 beati), the ignorant are drawn by sin (763 errant,[24] 771 noxia plebes), even after conversion (2.762–4; 2.770–2):

---

[23] Noted by McGill (2016: 193, n. to 758–9). Similarly, for Jo 3.10–11 (Jesus and Nicodemus: Jesus answered him, 'Are you a teacher of Israel, and yet you do not understand these things? Very truly, I tell you, we speak of what we know and testify to what we have seen; yet you do not receive our testimony'), Juvencus has 2.208–12 Nec potes obtunso comprendere talia sensu? | Ecce fides nulla est, tantum terrestria dixi! ('Can your dull sense not understand such words? | Behold – no faith: I spoke of earthly things!'). In his take on these particular verses, Nonnus makes no reference to faith as a prerequisite to knowledge (Nonnus P. 3.50–7), although unshakeable faith (3.84 πίστιν ἐς ἀστυφέλικτον) and correct faith (3.92 ὀρθὴν πίστιν) will be later the requisites to eternal life.

[24] For sin Juvencus uses error, peccatum, and scelus: cf. Green (2006: 97).

Si quis habet **dignus**, capiet potiora redundans;
qui vero expertes caelestis muneris **errant**,
amittent etiam, proprium quodcumque retentant.

Whoever justly has shall gain much more;
but those who stray, not knowing heaven's gift,
will even lose what little they possess.

~

Auribus adsistunt clausis oculis que gravatis,
ne conversa bono sanetur **noxia plebes**.
Quam vestrae nunc sunt aures oculi que **beati**!

Their ears and eyes are sealed, so that the crowd
will not be cured of guilt once turned to good.
But now how blessed are your ears and eyes.

Again, in the explanation of the parable of the sower, Juvencus' version
transforms the Matthaean lack of understanding into the opposite of a
sensible and stable reception of the precepts (777), that of faith (Mt 13.19;
ELQ 2.776–80):[25]

Omnis qui audit verbum regni et non intellegit, venit malus et rapit quod
seminatum est in corde illius.

When anyone hears the word of the kingdom and does not understand it the
evil one comes and snatches away what is sown in the heart.

~

Quisque meum verbum summas dimittit in aures,
nec sensus recipit stabili praecepta vigore,
eripit illius totum de pectore daemon.

Whoever skims the surface of my words
but does not hear commands with steadfast firmness –
the devil snatches all of them from him.

---

[25] The description of the man who hears the word and understands it (the rich soil) is built along
similar lines: 790–4 *Pinguia sic itidem paribus stant viribus arva | illis, qui clarae capiunt praecepta
salutis, | quae penetrant animum* **sensu** *tractante* **tenaci** *| centiplicem que ferunt* **virtutis robore** *frugem*
('Likewise, rich fields are as robust as those, | who grasp the teachings of salvation's light, | which
penetrate the mind with steadfast thought | and yield a hundredfold through strength of virtue').
Note Green (2006: 97): 'His normal word is the biblical *fides*, sometimes replaced by or combined
with *constantia* (2.80, 395) or *robur*, as in 3. 191 and 4. 383.'

Furthermore, Juvencus upgrades the Gospel's 'evil one' (*malus*) to the devil (778 *daemon*), the one waiting to punish those who lack faith on the Last Day.[26]

The main innovation in Juvencus' paraphrase of the parable of the sower is the notion that faith engenders knowledge and fairness, whereas lack of it goes hand in hand with imperfect listening and understanding and *error*/*errare*, a combination of sin and unstable wandering. Juvencus reaches out to his audience both in intellectual and moral terms: his narrative reminds the learned that the knowledge they have of the world is only sound if grounded in faith; otherwise they only hold an appearance of knowledge. Ignoring this point has enduring consequences, not only in terms of lack of direction in life but also subjecting oneself to the tyranny of the devil in this life and beyond.

The admonition to consider knowledge inspired by God as superior to knowledge founded on human experience occurs in other New Testament writings[27] and was to become one of Augustine's main lines of thought later in the fourth century.[28] In the *Evangeliorum Libri Quattuor*, it does not seem to have a particular theological connection, and could target both Christian and non-Christian members of Juvencus' learned audience: no matter what their faith, they are called to acknowledge that the classical *paideia* they acquired through a painful educational process is secondary to the knowledge derived from God. This accommodation of learning has also been considered a defence against sectarian Christians who relied on their own philosophical schooling.[29] We can tie this in with the preface of the poem in which Juvencus proclaims that his poem is relevant and called to achieve eternal glory because of its subject matter, Christ himself (Praef. 17–20), not because it is an expression of Vergilian *paideia*, since Vergil's works are doomed to perish (6–16).

9.1.2   Nonnus' Hymn of the Logos

The Gospel of John begins with the so-called Hymn of the Logos, describing the figure of Jesus (He is the Word, God's son, the light of the world) and his incarnation. The first affirmation of Jesus' divine power (1.10 'He is in the world from the beginning and everything comes to being through him') comes into contrast with the anticipation of the

---

[26] Mt 25.41 *discedite a me maledicti in ignem aeternum qui paratus est diabolo et angelis eius* (after which ELQ 4.287 *Daemonis horrendi sociis*). Cf. McGill (2016: 194, n. on 778).
[27] E.g. Ro 1.18–22; 1 Cor 1.17–31.   [28] Ayres (2010: 142–70).   [29] Rubenson (2000: 112).

negative reception the Incarnate Word will experience: the world does not recognise him, those closest to him do not receive him (Jo 1.10–12).

ἐν τῷ κόσμῳ ἦν, καὶ ὁ κόσμος δι' αὐτοῦ ἐγένετο, καὶ ὁ κόσμος αὐτὸν οὐκ ἔγνω. 11 εἰς τὰ ἴδια ἦλθεν, καὶ οἱ ἴδιοι αὐτὸν οὐ παρέλαβον. 12 ὅσοι δὲ ἔλαβον αὐτόν, ἔδωκεν αὐτοῖς ἐξουσίαν τέκνα θεοῦ γενέσθαι, τοῖς πιστεύουσιν εἰς τὸ ὄνομα αὐτοῦ.

He was in the world, and the world came into being through him; yet the world did not know him. He came to what was his own, and his own people did not accept him. But to all who received him, who believed in his name, he gave power to become children of God.[30]

Jesus' identity is revealed in the opening chapter of the Gospel and reactions to this revelation are presented as polar opposites, marked by faith and lack of it. The main body of the narrative of the Gospel is then constructed out of a series of encounters of Jesus with characters who either reject or accept the revelation of his identity (in the latter case sometimes their faith and commitment prove frail).[31] These characters are thus defined by their (in)ability to grasp who Jesus is, enforcing a sharp distinction between insiders and outsiders, those who understand Jesus and those who do not.[32] This means that the Hymn of the Logos provides a more divisive model of treatment of the audience than the parable of the sower.

The *Paraphrase* follows faithfully the narrative of the Gospel[33] and derives from it what has been called antithetical characterisation or technique of dual polarity, that is, the setting up of agents of action one against the other,[34] but while this opposition can be ascribed to the base text of the paraphrase, Nonnus' elaboration adds an additional layer of meaning worth exploring (Nonnus *P.* 1.27b–34):

ἔην δ' ἐν ἀπειθέι κόσμῳ
ἀπροϊδής, καὶ κόσμος ἀπείριτος ἔσκε δι' αὐτοῦ,
καὶ λόγον οὐ γίνωσκεν ἐπήλυδα κόσμος ἀλήτης.
ἐγγὺς ἔην ἰδίων, ἴδιοι δέ μιν ἄφρονι λύσσῃ   30
ὡς ξένον οὐκ ἐγέραιρον· ὅσοι δέ μιν ἔμφρονι θυμῷ

---

[30] The Greek text is that of Nestle-Aland 28th ed.; English translation NRSV.

[31] Culpepper (1983: 3–33, 88–9, 103–4, 145–6) and Thatcher (2008: 25–6, 28).

[32] Thatcher (2008: 25–6) and Moore (1989: 49–50). John's plot is 'ironic' in that the characters are continually striving to learn what the reader already knows: Culpepper (1983: 89).

[33] On Nonnus' paraphrastic technique, see the introductions of the modern editions of the *P.*: Agosti (2003: 149–74), Livrea (1989: 54–7), Accorinti (1996: 45–55), Livrea (2000: 92–105), Greco (2004: 28–35), Caprara (2005: 59–64), and Spanoudakis (2014a: 68–87).

[34] Spanoudakis (2014a: 78–81).

ἀπλανέες δέξαντο καὶ οὐ νόον εἶχον ἀλήτην,
οὐρανίην πάντεσσι μίαν δωρήσατο τιμήν
τέκνα θεοῦ γενετῆρος ἀειζώοντος ἀκούειν.

He was unforeseen in the faithless world, and the infinite world became through him, and the erring world did not recognise the visiting Logos. Near was He to his own people, but his own people in senseless frenzy would not honour him as a guest-friend. But all who with sensible mind without error received him and did not have an erring mind, to all of them he granted a heavenly honour, to be called children of God.[35]

In the *Evangeliorum Libri Quattuor*, faith is a pre-requisite of knowledge. In the *Paraphrase of the Gospel of John*, disbelief (27 ἀπειθέι), unstability (29 ἀλήτης), and madness (30 ἄφρονι λύσσῃ) lead to lack of recognition of the Incarnate Logos (29 λόγον οὐ γίνωσκεν) and the opposite qualities (31–2) enable listeners of Jesus to accept him (32 δέξαντο), that is, to know who He is and receive him, and to be recompensed with God's gift of adoption (33–4).

Behind Nonnus' lines is the analysis of the Gospel passage in the *Commentary* by Cyril of Alexandria. Cyril elaborates mainly the characterisation of the creatures who reject the word, and contends that the Jewish people and some gentiles reject the Son of God (the Logos) out of ignorance and unbelief (Cyril, *Comm. in Jo.* 1.11; 1.130 Pusey):

> The Evangelist expands his defense that the world did not know the one who enlightens it, that is, the Only Begotten. From the worse sin of the Israelites [τῶν ἐξ Ἰσραὴλ ἁμαρτίας], he presses on to strengthen the charge against the Gentiles as well, pointing out the disease of ignorance [δυσμαθείας] and unbelief [ἀπειθείας] that was imposed on the whole world.

Cyril here refers to 'his own people' as the Israelites and earlier in the commentary to 'the world' as the Gentiles.[36] What Cyril reads in the Gospel is that the appropriate reaction to the Son of God is that of faith, which guarantees the true knowledge of the divine. The alternative is lack of faith and ignorance, and is defined in moral terms as a sin and in judicial

---

[35] Greek text from De Stefani (2002; for the modern editions of the *P.*, cf. n. 33; otherwise, Scheindler 1881). Translation adapted from Sherry (1991).

[36] Cyril *Comm. in Jo.* 1.11 (1.131 Pusey) 'The world, or the Gentiles [ὁ μὲν γὰρ κόσμος, ἤτοι τὰ ἔθνη], lost their relation to God through the fall into evil, and along with it they lost their knowledge of the one who enlightens them. But those who greatly expanded their knowledge [τὴν γνῶσιν] through the law and who were called back to a delightful citizenship with God later fell willingly because they did not receive the Word of God, whom they already knew and who had come to dwell with them as with his.'

terms as worth punishing. As we will see, these notions surface regularly in the *Paraphrase of the Gospel of John*, but already in 1.27–34 Nonnus introduces the lines of division of the audience in these terms: he already makes the connection between lack of faith and lack of knowledge (29 λόγον οὐ γίνωσκεν), and the instability he attributes to the unbelieving world and the Jewish people is a characteristic of the mad, whose erratic wanderings replicate their mental disorientation, but is also a way of describing sin. Where Juvencus insisted in the chronological frame (first faith, then knowledge), Nonnus statically lumps together on the one hand faith, recognition of Jesus, and a series of positive character traits, and on the other lack of faith, rejection of Jesus, and a series of negative character traits.

The connection between faith and understanding appeared frequently in earlier Greek authors[37] and had a particular relevance in the work of Cyril. He stands out for the frequency of his usage, the clarity with which he emphasises the priority of faith over understanding,[38] and for his differentiation between two levels of illumination (instead of a progressive post-baptismal enlightenment):[39] the general illumination given to all humans when they are created (basic human rationality),[40] and a deeper form consubstantial with the reception of the Holy Spirit at baptism. The latter form is necessarily grounded in faith and enables the reader of the Scripture to grow in virtue and understanding by beholding the mystery of Christ. Following Cyril's line of reasoning, those who reject Christ (especially the Jews, among which especially the Pharisees) do so blinded by unbelief[41] and passions so excessive that they can be called madness.[42]

---

[37] Irenaeus *Dem* 3, Clem. Al. *Strom.* 2.2.8.2, 4.21.134.4, Origen *Comm. in Mt* 16.9, Eusebius of Caesarea *D.E.* 7.1.26–8, and Cyril of Jerusalem *Cat.* 5.4.

[38] Crawford (2014: 226–7).

[39] Crawford (2014: 182–232). I will refer only to the *Commentary on the Gospel of John*, but the two levels of illumination are recurrent in Cyril's works. Cf. for instance *Comm. in Is.* 30.25–6 (PG 70.685–8).

[40] Cyril *Comm. in Jo.* 8.55 (Pusey 2.128) 'The *logos* of a human being (that is, the definition of humanity's essence) is: a rational animal, mortal and receptive of intellect and knowledge [ζῷον λογικόν, θνητόν, νοῦ καὶ ἐπιστήμης δεκτικόν].'

[41] Cyril often cites Is 7.9 (in his version 'If you will not believe, neither will you understand'): *Comm. in Jo.* 6.53 (Pusey 1.529), 6.69 (1.576), 17.3 (2.668), 18.37–8 (3.56).

[42] E.g. Cyril *Comm. in Jo.* 9.34 (Pusey 2.196) 'Most people find the wounds of rebuke and correction hard to take. ... These wounds are bitter ... for those who love sin [τοῖς φιλαμαρτήμοσι] ... because they have set their mind on debasing pleasures [ταῖς εἰς τὸ φαῦλον ἡδοναῖς], and so they reject as vexing any admonition that would cut them off from those pleasures ... so the wretched Pharisees are upset. They shriek like animals at him who presents to them the noblest of ideas. They welcome the beginnings of anger [ἐπὶ τὰ τῆς ὀργῆς χαίρουσι προοίμια]. As the extreme madness comes gushing out of them [μανίας ἀπρόσιτον ἀπαρχὴν ἀναβλύζοντες], they heap abuse on him contrary to the law.'

Whereas in the *Evangeliorum Libri Quattuor* Juvencus does not seem to refer to any particular theological source, any reader of Nonnus who was familiar with Cyril's theology would have made a connection between the exegete and the poet, the latter deriving his claim to orthodoxy from the standing of the former. The same reader would have noticed that Nonnus' take on Cyril was selective: there is no trace in the *Paraphrase of the Gospel of John* of the two types of illumination and no emphasis on the priority of faith over knowledge, the most complicated part of the theological argument. On the contrary, Nonnus' systematic characterisation of believers and disbelievers is a poetic elaboration of Cyril's colourful descriptions of the characters of the Gospel. Nonnus' stand before his readers is theological, *ma non troppo*.

9.1.3 *Juvencus and Nonnus*

Despite living in different centuries and areas of the Mediterranean and writing in different languages, Juvencus and Nonnus agree in rephrasing their base texts to remind their readers that the appropriate reception of Jesus and his Gospel is faith and expand on the consequences of not believing: ignorance, sin, instability (madness in Nonnus). Morals come to the forefront in both cases. Their poetic version of the Gospels offers no doubts to their audiences: lack of faith should not be an option. It is not a matter of seducing the unbeliever, but of making them see their moral wretchedness and ignorance. Non-Christian members of the audience of both the *Evangeliorum Libri Quattuor* and the *Paraphrase of the Gospel of John* are treated with a certain harshness, but the Gospel descriptions of the appropriate (faithful) reaction to Jesus' revelation do not become self-congratulatory back-slapping of contemporary Christians. In other words, the gap between the haves and the have-nots of faith is not enlarged with an encomium of the former.

Although having a common paraenetic intent, Juvencus and Nonnus have different stylistic approaches to it. Juvencus favours a fluid narrative, a poetically dignified version of the Gospel, with a few adjectives and explanatory periphrases, and prioritises the visibility of a number of key concepts (faith is preliminary to knowledge and virtue). Nonnus' lines are loaded with adjectives and periphrases that give poetic shape not so much to the Gospel narrative, but to the theological elaboration which his contemporaries could relate to Cyril, bishop of Alexandria and champion of Christian orthodoxy. The *Evangeliorum Libri Quattuor* would have been more accessible to a non-Christian reader than the *Paraphrase of the Gospel of John*, but Juvencus composed it in the times of Constantine, when

Christianity had spread, but was still in the process of creating its own poetic voice. Juvencus' plain narrative would not have seduced the members of the fifth-century Alexandrian cultural élites, accustomed to the convoluted argumentation of the Alexandrian philosophical schools, in the same way as the elaborate narrative of the *Paraphrase of the Gospel of John*.

9.2 Choral Reactions to Jesus and His Gospel

9.2.1 Juvencus

Juvencus elaborates on and intensifies the emotions of the crowds as they react to Jesus' speeches, mostly with adjectives, a form of poetic elevation that has long been noted.[43] What is not so frequently emphasised is that, at least in the comments to the reactions of the crowd, Juvencus seems to be following a predetermined plan, escalating in his elaboration.

Thus, in the first part of the narrative, where the crowds of the Gospel simply react with admiration (Mt 7.28 *admirabantur turbae*), Juvencus underlines their response (ELQ 1.728–9):

> Talia dicentem fixa admiratio plebis
> inmensum stupuit.

> In total awe, the crowd was greatly stunned
> at what he said.

As the narrative advances, passions intensify in the *Evangeliorum Libri Quattuor*, not in the Gospel: when Jesus comes down from the mountain great crowds follow him in the Gospel (Mt 8.1 *secutae sunt eum turbae multae*, emphasis on number), which in the *Evangeliorum Libri Quattuor* (1.731–2) read as follows, with an emphasis on number and a passionate reaction for the readers of the poem to mirror:[44]

> Denique linquentem celsi fastigia montis
> Stipabat gaudens populorum turba sequentum.

> And then great throngs of joyous followers
> swarmed him when he descended from the mount.

---

[43] Kirsch (1989: 113–14) talks of 'Psychologisierung' and Thraede (2001: 902) of 'Emotionalisierung'.

[44] Also Mt 8.18 *Videns autem Iesus turbas multas circum se* ('now when Jesus saw great crowds around him') becomes ELQ 2.9–10 *Ecce sed exorta maior cum luce tumultus | gratantis populi cum turbis* ('Behold – at dawn, a greater uproar rose | from the rejoicing, thankful crowds').

Then, to the elaboration and intensification of the passions Juvencus adds
the division of the listeners between those who stand in awe and the hostile
Pharisees. For instance, when Jesus heals the man with a withered hand
(Mt 12.9–13), the Gospel only mentions the reaction of the Pharisees,
who start plotting against Jesus (12.14 *exeuntes autem Pharisaei consilium
faciebant adversus eum quomodo eum perderent*), whereas in the
Evangeliorum Libri Quattuor the Pharisees stand in opposition to the
people who witness the sign (ELQ 2.596–8):[45]

> His tum pro signis, quae vix ueneratio posset
> mirantis digno populi sustollere cultu,
> conciliis trucibus conclamant decipiendum.

> Faced with this sign, which the people's awed respect
> found hard to honour with befitting praise,
> they cried in savage meetings Christ must die.

As the scribes and Pharisees gain more narrative space in the Gospel, the
neutral introductions to their reactions become in the *Evangeliorum Libri
Quattuor* accusations of dishonesty, cunning, mendacity, and madness.
Compare Mt 15.1 to ELQ 3.133–4:

> Tunc accesserunt ad eum scribae et Pharisaei ab Hierosolymis dicentes ...

> Then Pharisees and scribes came to Jesus from Jerusalem and said ...

> ∼

> Ecce Pharisaei scribae que hinc inde dolosi
> captantes Christum promunt fallacia dicta.

> Look – Pharisees and cunning scribes now swarmed;
> trying to snare Christ, they spoke lying words.

Mt 16.1–2 to ELQ 3.221–3:

> Et accesserunt ad eum Pharisaei et Sadducaei temptantes et rogaverunt eum
> ut signum de caelo ostenderet illis. At ille respondens ait illis ...

> The Pharisees and Sadducees came, and to test Jesus they asked im to show
> them a sign from heaven. He answered them ...

> ∼

> Ecce Pharisaei Sadducaeique **dolosi**
> poscere temptantes instant caelestia signa.

---

[45] In a similar way, after the healing of a blind and dumb man, the blind faction of the Pharisees (ELQ
2.605 *Caeca Pharisaeae ... factio gentis*) comes into contrast with the man who was blind and now
can see.

Sed Christus cernens **fallacia pectora** fatur . . .

Look – Pharisees and cunning Sadducees,
testing him, urged that he seek signs from heaven.
But Christ observed their lying hearts and said . . .

And Mt 22.15 to ELQ 4.1–2:

Tunc abierunt Pharisaei et consilium acceperunt ut caperent eum in sermone.

The Pharisees went and plotted to entrap him in what he said.

~

Talia dicentem confestim **factio frendens**
temptare adgreditur **verbis cum fraude malignis.**

As he said this, the frenzied faction rushed
to test him with malign, deceitful words.

The descriptions of madness become more elaborate in the narrative of the passion. Compare Mt 26.62 to ELQ 4.549–50:

Et surgens princeps sacerdotum ait illi . . .

The high priest stood up and said . . .

~

Ipse sacerdotum princeps urgere tacentem
insistit **frendens furiis** ac talia fatur . . .

The high priest, gnashing teeth in frothing fury,
Continued pressing silent Christ and said . . .

Mt 26.65 to ELQ 560–1:

Tunc princeps sacerdotum scidit vestimenta sua . . .

Then the high priest tore up his clothes and said . . .

~

Talibus auditis scindit de pectore vestem
exsultans furiis et **caeco corde** sacerdos

When he heard this, the priest, awash in rage
and blind emotion, tore his clothes from his breast[46]

and Mt 27.41 to ELQ 4.674–7:

---

[46] Also, Mt 27.39 *praetereuntes autem blasphemabant eum* becomes ELQ 4.668–9 *sed caeca furentis* | *insultat plebis fixo vaesania Christo* ('Yet the enraged | people's blind frenzy jeered the hanging Christ'); Mt 28.12 *Congregati cum senioribus* becomes ELQ 4.777b–82 *Sed manus amens* | *iam semel insano penitus devota furore* ('Yet the mad band, | now wholly doomed to their demented rage').

Similiter et principes sacerdotum deludentes cum scribis et Pharisaeis
dicebant . . .

In the same way the chief priests also, along with the scribes and Pharisees
were mocking him and said . . .

~

Haec **vulgi** proceres **vaecordis** dicta sequuntur;
atque Pharisaei scribae que et **factio demens**
inludunt motu que caput linguas que loquellis
insanis quatiunt aeternae ad vincula poenae.

The leaders echoed the demented crowd;
the Pharisees and scribes and maddened faction
mocked him, insanely wagging heads and tongues,
while heading for the bonds of endless torment.

ELQ 4.674–7 is the longest elaboration of an introduction to a speech.
Juvencus resorts to the amplification of internal elements: 674 *Haec vulgi
proceres vaecordis dicta sequuntur* develops Mt 27.41 *similiter*, replicating
the behaviour of the crowds in the previous verse; 676–7 *motu que caput
linguas que loquellis | insanis* builds on Mt 27.30 *moventes capita sua*. He
adds the usual intensified passionate reaction and a one-off moral judgement: this behaviour sends the unwitting Jews to eternal punishment, as
described in Mt 25.46 *in supplicium aeternum*, which in Juvencus' hands
becomes 4.304 *Aeternum miseri poena fodientur iniqui* ('Eternal pains will
pierce the wicked wretches').

According to Green (2006: 42), adjectives aim at endowing the
narrative with an emotional and moral intensity unknown to the Gospel:
'They guide and intensify the emotions and reactions of the reader; while
by presenting strongly delineated events, objects, and characters they act as
an incentive to meditation.'[47] If we add the careful stages in the descriptions of the audience's reactions, we realise that Juvencus took the 'guid-
ance' of his own audience towards faith and understanding in earnest, and
that he assumed that his poem could be read in a continuous form (as
opposed to episodic reading) as a means to personal and/or community
edification. He seems to expect gaining the trust of his audience before
introducing a more aggressive elaboration of the Gospel text, one that
perhaps would shock his audience if introduced earlier.[48]

---

[47] According to Herzog (1975: 148), epic emotions contribute to the edification of the reader.
[48] Admittedly the polarisation of the good and the evil is inaugurated in the first lines of the poem,
contraposing the cruel Herod (1.1 *Herodes . . . cruentus*) and the just Zechariah (1.2 *servator iusti
templique sacerdos*).

9.2.2 Nonnus

On the contrary, Nonnus introduces from the beginning to the end of the poem a whole array of regular expressions to divide Jesus' audience clearly into two opposing halves, usually elaborating longer on the negative aspects: unbelief, lack of sense (or madness), and ignorance are central to the characterisation of those who reject Jesus in the *Paraphrase*.

Negative: 5.57 Ἑβραῖοι μανιώδεες ἄφρονι θυμῷ ('the Hebrews, frantic with senseless anger'); 8.43–4 καὶ θρασὺς Ἑβραίων κυμαίνετο λαὸς ἀκούων, | ἄφρονα λωβητῆρι χέων ῥόον ἀνθερεῶνι ('And while listening the bold Hebrew people seethed, pouring forth a senseless flow with their slandering throat'); 8.141–2 καὶ θρασὺς Ἑβραίων ἐπεπάφλασε λαὸς ἀκούων | ἄφρονι λωβητῆρι χέων ἔπος ἀνθερεῶνι ('And while listening the bold Hebrew people blustered, pouring forth a senseless speech with their slandering throat'); 15.93–4 νῦν δὲ μαθόντες | οὐ πρόφασιν μεθέπουσιν ἐλεύθερον ἄφρονος ἄτης ('But now having learned, they do attend the liberating pretext of senseless delusion').

Positive: 7.53 Ἰουδαίων ... ἑσμὸς ἐχέφρων ('the sensible swarm of Jews'); 7.174–5 καὶ ἔννεπον ἔμφρονι μύθῳ | ἀπλανέες δασπλῆτος ὑποδρηστῆρες ἀνάγκης (the servants of the priests refuse to hold Jesus prisoner after listening to him: 'And the unerring ministers of a horrible necessity said with sensible expression').

The negative characterisation is emphasised when the narrator introduces the powerful Jewish groups (Pharisees and priests) in their encounters with Jesus. Again and again, they are judged as mentally unstable or outright mad:

1.88=7.121 ἁμαρτινόων Φαρισαίων; 3.1 νοοπλανέων Φαρισαίων; 4.10 λύσσαν ... Φαρισαίων; 9.126 ζηλομανεῖς ... ἀρχιερῆες; 11.188 ἄφρονες ἀρχιερῆες; 12.43 ζαμενὴς Φαρισαῖος ὅλος χορός; 18.13 πολὺν οἰστρήεντα ... Φαρισαίων; 19.33 μεμηνότες ἀρχιερῆες; 19.161 ζαμενεῖς ἱερῆες.

and presented in moral terms as crooked, deceptive, perverse, and arrogant:

7.122 φθονεροὶ ... ἀρχιερῆες; 7.177 θρασὺς ... ὅμιλος ... Φαρισαίων; 9.78 φθονεροί τινες ... Φαρισαίων; 11.214 ἀναιδέες ἀρχιερῆες; 11.215 χορὸς ἀγκυλόμητις ... Φαρισαίων; 11.234 χορὸς ἀγκυλόμητις ὑπερφιάλων Φαρισαίων; 11.236 δολορραφέων Φαρισαίων; 12.42 φθονεροὶ ... ἀναιδέες ἀρχιερῆες; 18.13 ἀρχεκάκων Φαρισαίων; 18.146 φθονεροῖς στομάτεσσιν ἀνίαχον ἀρχιερῆες; 19.26 ἀθέσμιοι ἀρχιερῆες; 19.78 καὶ δολίοις στομάτεσσιν ἀνέκραγον ἀρχιερῆες; 19.84 ἀναιδέες ἀρχιερῆες.

This comes together with the constant reference to their incredulity and faithlessness, when they are qualified with the adjectives ἄπιστος 'incredulous' (1.88, 4.10, 7.121, 9.73, 9.92, 11.187, 11.215), ἀπειθής 'unbelieving' (11.233), and even ἀντίθεος 'contrary to God' (7.172; 9.69; 11.186).

Again, Nonnus gives poetic expression to the characterisation broadly effected in Cyril's commentary:

> Stability/unstability: Cyril *Comm. in Jo.* 7.12 (Pusey 1.596) 'But those who did not hesitate to call him a deceiver, though he guides us on the unerring path of righteousness, are swimming in the most absurd opinions and have left the truth far behind' [ἀλογωτάταις δὲ λίαν ἐπινήχονται δόξαις, καὶ τῆς ἀληθείας ἀφεστᾶσι μακρὰν, οἱ **πλάνον** ἀποκαλεῖν οὐκ ὀκνήσαντες τὸν εἰς **ἀπλανῆ** τῆς δικαιοσύνης κατευθύνοντα τρίβον]; 9.37 (Pusey 2.199) when Jesus speaks he gives 'aids to faith that are free from error and aberration' [τὰ εἰς πίστιν βοηθήματα τὴν **ἀπλανῆ** τε καὶ ἀδιάστροφον]; 14.5–6 (Pusey 2.409) 'He is the ruler and plumbline of an unerring understanding of God' [ὁ τῆς **ἀπλανοῦς** περὶ Θεοῦ διαλήψεως κανών τε καὶ στάθμη]; 16.7 (Pusey 2.618) [Christ as guide to] unerring conduct [**ἀπλανοῦς** πολιτείας].[49]

> Senselessness/insanity/ignorance: 8.25 (Pusey 2.22) 'But they go on to the wildest unbridled madness [πρὸς ἐκτοπωτάτην καὶ ἀχάλινον χωροῦσι μανίαν], and from limitless arrogance [ἐξ ἀμέτρου τῆς ὑπεροψίας] they practically cut off the Savior's statement before he is finished'; 8.57 (Pusey 2.132) 'Pitiful, then, is the senseless Jew [παράφρων Ἰουδαῖος], ever the friend of deep ignorance [ἀπαιδευσία], raised with his wild companion insanity [μανίαν]'; 13.37 (Pusey 2.395) 'At one time Christ was sojourning in Galilee to avoid the senselessness of the Jews, their sheer anger and their unbridled tongue [τὰς τῶν Ἰουδαίων ἀποπληξίας, καὶ τὸ ἀκρατὲς τοῦ θυμοῦ, καὶ τὸ τῆς γλώττης ἐξήνιον].'

The difference between Nonnus and Cyril is that Cyril's characterisation of the Jews does not respond to a predetermined plan, whereas Nonnus builds on his initial division of the audience in the paraphrase of the Hymn of the Logos (cf. Section 9.1.2) and exploits it systematically throughout the poem via a number of repeated formulae.

9.2.3   *Juvencus and Nonnus Compared*

Juvencus and Nonnus, then, agree in describing the negative reactions of the Jewish people to Jesus and his Gospel as a consequence of the

---

[49] In the background is the notion that the one who does not have a complete focus on Christ has his mind split into two and is therefore unstable: e.g. Cyril *Comm. in Jo.* 9.6–7 (Pusey 2.158–9) 'Faith [ἡ πίστις], therefore, is noble and strengthens the God-given grace in us, while double-mindedness [τὸ διψυχεῖν] is harmful. For [159] the double-minded man is unstable in all his ways [Jas 1.8].'

dishonesty, cunning, mendacity, and madness that they attribute to them as character traits. Juvencus develops this characterisation slowly as the narrative advances and does not seem to rely on a particular theological source, whereas Nonnus seems to work on a character template based on Cyril's *Commentary* from the beginning of the poem. In both cases the abuse on the Jewish people rules out that either of the two poets thought of contemporary Jews as potential readers, and perhaps has a secondary implication in terms of readership: presenting the Jews as the 'real' enemies of Jesus and the Christian faith leaves room for non-Christian audiences to side with the Christians. The Jews would become the common enemy of readers supporting reason, self-restraint, and moral uprightness, all of them values cherished by the educated elites, both Christian and polytheistic. This means that the negative portrait of the Jews, itself a reflection of contemporary prejudices, could be designed to attract both a Christian and a non-Christian audience.

The episode of the cleansing of the temple (Jo 2.13–25)[50] which both poets paraphrase allows us to make a closer comparison of how they treat the audiences of the Gospel. Compare Jo 2.18 in Latin to ELQ 2.163–4:

> Responderunt ei Iudaei et dixerunt 'quod signum ostendis nobis, quod haec facis?'

> The Jews then said to him: 'What sign can you show us for doing this?'

~

> Tum poscens signum plebes Iudaea fremebat,
> Quo fidens animos in talia facta levaret.

> The roaring crowd of Jews pressed him to know
> what sign he trusted in for such a deed.

and Jo 2.18 in Greek to Nonn *P*. 2.91–4:

> ἀπεκρίθησαν οὖν οἱ Ἰουδαῖοι καὶ εἶπαν αὐτῷ, Τί σημεῖον δεικνύεις ἡμῖν, ὅτι ταῦτα ποιεῖς;

~

> καί οἱ ἀπειλήτειραν ἀνήρυγε λαὸς ἰωήν ·
> ποῖα παρ' Ἑβραίοις ἑτερότροπα σήματα δείξεις,
> ὅττι σὺ ταῦτα τέλεσσας; ἀμιλλητῆρι δὲ λαῷ
> θαμβαλέην ἄγνωστον ἄναξ ἠρεύγετο φωνήν

---

[50] The two passages are compared by Hilhorst (1993).

> The people roared a threatening voice at him, 'What sort of diverse signs among the Hebrews will you show us why you did these things?' And to the contentious people the king roared a stupendous unrecognisable voice.

Both Juvencus and Nonnus add a hostile touch to the intervention of the Jews (ELQ 2.163 *fremebat*;[51] Nonnus 2.91 ἀπειλήτειραν ... ἰωήν, 93 ἀμιλλητῆρι δὲ λαῷ), but Juvencus summarises the intervention of the Jews in indirect speech, whereas Nonnus slightly expands the direct speech. Nonnus' Jews no longer ask for a sign (Jo 2.18 σημεῖον), but for a number of them, and of different sorts (94 ἑτερότροπα σήματα), and the introduction of their speech is built in contrast with the introduction of Jesus' reply: unjustified menacing (91 ἀπειλήτειραν ... ἰωήν) against words that cause amazement (94 θαμβαλέην) and which the people will not be able to understand because of their ignorance (94 ἄγνωστον). The verbs chosen (91 ἀνήρυγε, 94 ἠρεύγετο) intensify the contrast:[52] ἐρεύγομαι and ἀνερεύγω have a catachrestic or banalised sense (emphatic speech) used here for the Jews,[53] and a prophetic or oracular one, for which they often designate Jesus' words.[54] Not that Juvencus avoids a polar expression, as immediately afterwards in Jesus' speech he contrasts the money changers' 'polluted hands' (*pollutis manibus*) and his Father's 'venerable temple' (2.166 *venerabile templum*). In Nonnus the contrast comes from confronting the passions of the Jewish assailants and Jesus' capacity to cause marvel with a knowledge they cannot understand, whereas Juvencus' contrast is done in moral terms[55] and more concisely.

A few verses later John closes the episode with a final reference to the numbers of people who come to believe in Christ upon witnessing his signs. Compare Jo 2.23 in Latin to ELQ 2.175–6:

> Multi crediderunt in nomine eius videntes signa, quae faciebat.

> Many believed in his name because they saw the signs that he was doing.

---

[51] Also 2.169 *murmure caeco*.   [52] Cf. Lightfoot (2016: 635).

[53] And in the *Dion.* for the vain menaces of the impious Indian king Deriades: 21.240, 27.21. Cf. Livrea (2000: 276–7, on Nonnus *P.* 2.91).

[54] Besides *P.* 2.94, cf. 7.58, 13.97, 14.40. In Nonn. *Dion.* Dionysus' words (12.206, 40.411) and other prophetic utterances by Cadmus (1.485), Astraeus (6.89), a Naiad (7.227), Atropos (12.141), Idmon (38.57), Heracles Astrochiton (40.442, 40.501).

[55] All the more emphasised by calling the disciples *digni ... uiri* (173–4), with 'dignus' as Juvencus' regular transposition of 'fair', 'just'.

~
               Sed signa videntes
Tum multi cepere fidem santumque seviti.

But many people, witnessing these signs,
discovered faith and followed the divine.

and Jo. 2.23 in Greek to Nonn. *P.* 2.114–15:

πολλοὶ **ἐπίστευσαν** εἰς τὸ ὄνομα αὐτοῦ, θεωροῦντες αὐτοῦ τὰ σημεῖα ἃ ἐποίει.

~
πολλοὶ λύσσαν ἄπιστον ἐπετρέψαντο θυέλλαις
Χριστοῦ πίστιν ἔχοντες ἐς οὔνομα.

Many turned their faithless madness over to the tempests and had faith in the name of Christ.

Juvencus glosses over the movement of conversion: not only did they grasp faith (175 *cepere fidem*), but as a consequence of it they became followers of Christ (175 *santumque seviti*). Nonnus chooses a closer transposition of the conversion (115 Χριστοῦ πίστιν ἔχοντες ἐς οὔνομα, for Jo ἐπίστευσαν εἰς τὸ ὄνομα αὐτοῦ) and introduces a contrast between the new belief and the old state of unbelief (114 ἄπιστον) and madness (114 λύσσαν). He describes the transition between the two states as a violent movement (114 ἐπετρέψαντο θυέλλαις). In this case Juvencus elaborates the neutral narrative of the Gospel, whereas Nonnus introduces a confrontation between the life of faith and the life of faithlessness that cannot be simply deduced from the Gospel.

A similar situation is described after the resurrection of Lazarus, also paraphrased by both poets. In this case the Gospel mentions two reactions to the witnessing of signs: many believe and some tell the Pharisees what Jesus has done. Compare Jo 11.45–6 in Latin to ELQ 4.398–402:

Multi ergo ex Iudaeis, qui venerant ad Mariam, videntes quae fecit, crediderunt in eum. Quidam vero ex ipsis abierunt ad Pharisaeos et dixerunt eis, quod fecit Iesus.

Many of the Jews therefore, who had come with Mary and had seen what Jesus did, believed in him. But some of them went to the Pharisees and told them what he had done.

~
Iudaei postquam factum venerabile cernunt,
qui tanti Mariam fuerant Martham que secuti,
pars credens sequitur tantae virtutis honorem;   400
ast alii repetunt urbem procerum que superbis
cuncta Pharisaeis rerum miracula narrant.

After the many Jews who went with Mary
and Martha saw the deed deserving awe,
some followed the glory of so great a work;
others went back to town and told the haughty
Pharisees all about the miracle.

and Jo. 11.45–6 in Greek to Nonn. *P.* 11.180b–8:

Πολλοὶ οὖν ἐκ τῶν Ἰουδαίων, οἱ ἐλθόντες πρὸς τὴν Μαριὰμ καὶ θεασάμενοι ἃ
ἐποίησεν, ἐπίστευσαν εἰς αὐτόν· τινὲς δὲ ἐξ αὐτῶν ἀπῆλθον πρὸς τοὺς
Φαρισαίους καὶ εἶπαν αὐτοῖς ἃ ἐποίησεν Ἰησοῦς.

~

Ἰουδαίων δ' ἄρα πολλοί
Μάρθης καὶ Μαρίης ἐπὶ πένθιμον οἶκον ἰόντες
παιδὶ θεοῦ πίστευον ἐσαθρήσαντες ὀπωπαῖς,
κοίρανος ἔργον ἄπιστον ὅπερ κάμε, νεκρὸν ἐγείρας
Λάζαρον ἀχλυόεντος ἀναθρώσκοντα βερέθρου   185
νόστιμον ἐκ νεκύων ταχινῷ ποδί. καί τινες αὐτῶν
εἰς πόλιν ἴχνος ἔκαμψαν ἐς ἀντιθέους ἱερῆας
πληθύι κηρύσσοντες ἀπιστοτάτων Φαρισαίων
ἔργα θεοῦ Χριστοῖο.

Then many of the Jews, after going to the grieving house of Martha and
Mary, upon observing with their eyes the unbelievable deed that the lord did
by having raised the corpse, Lazarus, who sprung up from the misty pit
returning from the dead with a speedy foot, believed in the child of god. And
some of them bent a track to the city to the anti-god priests, heralding to the
multitude of the most faithless Pharisees the deeds of Christ the god.

Juvencus upgrades the Gospel's terse *quae fecit* so that Jesus' action
becomes worthy of veneration and honour (398 *factum venerabile*, 400
tantae virtutis honorem) and a miracle (402 *miracula*). Nonnus achieves a
similar effect with a summary of the actual miracle (182b–5a), and his
expansion of the narrative can be read as an added opportunity for
contemplation, so that the audience can find out what an effect the
previous passage has had on them. Juvencus notes the diverse reaction of
the audience to the miracle (400–1 *Pars . . . ast alii . . .*) and describes the
Pharisees in the negative (401–2 *superbis . . . Pharisaeis*). As in the episode
of the cleansing of the temple, Juvencus elaborates on the movement of
conversion: the witnesses believe and become followers of Christ (400
credens sequitur tantae virtutis honorem). Nonnus' intervention is more
aggressive: he elaborates further on the presentation of the Pharisees (186
ἐς ἀντιθέους ἱερῆας, 187 πληθύι κηρύσσοντες ἀπιστοτάτων Φαρισαίων)

and introduces an opposition absent in the Gospel text between belief (182 παιδὶ θεοῦ πίστευον, of what would sound unbelievable 183 ἔργον ἄπιστον) and unbelief (187 ἀπιστοτάτων Φαρισαίων), which converts its subjects into *theomachoi* (186 ἀντιθέους ἱερῆας).

Juvencus is more interested in exploring the notion of conversion, whereas Nonnus takes every possible opportunity to confront belief and unbelief, and aggressively criticises not only those who do not believe, but also those whose reaction towards Christ is not immediate belief but a different one, such as telling the Pharisees what has happened. One can conclude that in this Juvencus talks about the fourth-century world, in which Christianity was still regularly welcoming converts (hence the emphasis on the how-to of conversion) and already demonises the Jews, whereas Nonnus relates a society that sees itself as less mobile, with religious groups somehow stabilised in their numbers, and again clear prejudices against the Jews.

9.3 Division of the Audience

9.3.1 Juvencus

The Matthaean passage in which a division of the audience is most visible is the Last Judgement (Mt 25.31–46): when the Son of Man comes in his glory, all the nations will be assembled before him (32 *congregabuntur ante eum omnes gentes*) and he will divide them like a shepherd separating sheep on the right and goats on the left. Those on the right, blessed by the father (34 *benedicti patris mei*), will receive a kingdom for the fairness they have shown in helping those in need (37 *iusti*). Those on the left are *maledicti* (41) because they failed to succour those in need and will go to the eternal fire prepared for the devil and his angels (41 *in ignem aeternum, quem paravit pater meus diabolo et angelis eius*). The parable concludes sending the latter to eternal fire and the just to eternal life (46 *ibunt hi in ignem aeternum, iusti autem in vitam aeternam*).

Juvencus underlines the opposition between the good and the evil by introducing the parable in moral terms from the beginning (4.261–4; first passage) and reinforcing the contrast with opposing clusters and anaphora in the closing lines (4.304–5; second passage):[56]

---

[56] Compare Sedulius on Jesus' teaching on the two paths (Mt 7.13–14): *Carmen Paschale* 2.294–7 *Sed dextra bonorum | semita conspicuos vocat in sua gaudia iustos | inque tuos, patriarca, sinus. At laeva malorum | exercet poenas et ad impia Tartara ittit* ('But the right path of those who are good | calls the righteous in their glory into its joys | and into your bosom, O patriarch! But the left path of those who are bad | exacts punishments and sends them to wicked Tartarus').

Tum gentes cunctae diversis partibus orbis
convenient iustos que omnes de labe malorum
secernet dextra que libens in parte locabit,
at prauos laeua despectos parte relinquet

All nations through the world will then convene:
he will remove the just from evil men's
ruin and gladly place them at his right
but leave the wicked ones scorned at his left.

~

Aeternum miseri poena fodientur iniqui,
aeternum que salus iustis concessa manebit.

Eternal pains will pierce the wicked wretches;
the righteous will receive eternal life.

For the Matthaean *benedicti* (Mt 25.34) Juvencus has *sancti* (4.268) and
iustis (270), while the *maledicti* (Mt 25.41) receive longer, moral elaboration (cf. ELQ 4.284–7 and 4.300–2):

At vos, iniusti, iustis succedite flammis
et poenis semper mentem torrete malignam.

But you, the unjust, go down to just flames
and ever sear your wicked souls with pains.

~

His rerum dicet Dominus: 'Cum vestra superbo
angustis rebus feritas sub corde tumebat
calcavit que humiles minimos, me sprevit in illis.'

The Lord will answer, 'When your cruelty toward
the straightened swelled in haughty hearts and trod
upon the least, it spurned me in those ones.'

In the Gospel the wicked ones are punished for a crime of negligence
against those in need. Juvencus duly reproduces their (temporary) lack of
action when paraphrasing the speeches of Jesus and the wicked
(4.288–99), but their punishment is not done solely on these grounds.
Juvencus adds a moral judgement, a condemnation of their perverse
nature: they are unjust (284 *iniusti*), malign (285 *mentem ... malignam*),
harsh (300–1 *vestra ... feritas*), and haughty (300–1 *superbo ... sub corde*).
Furthermore, *calcavit ... humiles minimos* (302 '[your cruelty] trod upon
the humble little ones') reveals that not only did they passively spurn the
weak by not offering help when needed, but actively harmed them. In
Juvencus' narrative the division of the peoples is more extreme than in the

Gospel, with a particular emphasis on the description of the evil ones, punished for their wickedness in all areas.

The polarisation of the internal audience and focus on the evil ones recur in other passages of the *Evangeliorum Libri Quattuor*, such as the mission of the twelve (Mt 10). In the Gospel, Jesus simply tells the disciples not to pay attention to the gentiles and the Samaritans, and to focus 'on the lost sheep of Israel'. Compare Mt 10.5–6 to ELQ 2.433–5:

> In viam gentium ne abieritis et in civitates Samaritanorum ne intraveritis. Sed potius ite ad oves, quae perierunt, domus Istrahel.

> Go nowhere among the Gentiles, and enter no town of the Samaritans, but go rather to the lost sheep of the house of Israel.

~

> Devitate itiner, quod gentes perfidiosae
> et Samaritarum fraudis vestigia calcant.
> Pergite, qua patrii pecoris custodia labat.

> Avoid the road where faithless Gentiles go
> And where Samaritans tread their false path.
> Go where care of the paternal flock is weak.

Juvencus' gentiles lack faith (2.433 *gentes perfidiosae*), the Samaritans walk on the wrong path, the path of lies (434 *Samaritarum fraudis vestigia calcant*), and the disciples no longer focus on Israel, but follow a broader call to assist the Father's children (435 *patrii pecoris*)[57] who lack a shepherd (435 *custodia labat*), with the parable of the lost sheep in mind (Mt 18.12–14). Further down, in the Gospel Jesus advises his disciples to stay in houses that are respectable and worthy of their peace (with the adjective *dignus*).[58] In Juvencus' version (2.445–54) the disciples should lodge where it is fitting for the just (2.446 *Hospitio quorum par sit succedere iustis*): a house worthy of their peace will be still (448 *tranquilla*) and unworthy the one inhabited by unjust tenants with terrible morals (449 *Sin erit indignis habitantum moribus horrens*). The disciples of the Gospel should shake the dust of their feet if nobody receives them and listens to

---

[57] As noted by McGill (2016: 178–9, n. to 435). McGill (*ibid.*) notes the different approach of Sedulius who limits the mission to Israel, but explains that this is so because Jesus had not yet elevated all nations with this title: *Carmen Paschale* 3.160–2 *et tristes morborum excludite pestes,* | *sed domus Israhel (quia necdum nomine gentes* | *auxerat hoc omnes).*

[58] Mt 10.11–14 *in quamcumque civitatem aut castellum intraveritis interrogate quis in ea **dignus** sit et ibi manete donec exeatis. Intrantes autem in domum salutate eam et siquidem fuerit **domus digna** veniat pax vestra super eam si autem **non fuerit digna** pax vestra ad vos revertatur. Et quicumque non receperit vos neque audierit sermones vestros exeuntes foras de domo vel de civitate excutite pulverem de pedibus vestris.*

them (Mt 10.14): Juvencus' disciples do so when they come across a host whose behaviour does not adjust to the law (451 *ferus*), to ensure that no injustice adheres to them (454 *haereat iniustae ne vobis portio vitae*).

Juvencus insists on dividing the audience of Jesus and his Gospel in terms of justice: those who believe are just, those who do not are unjust and perpetrators of a number of punishable offences, starting with their reprehensible immoral nature. Rather than assuming that Juvencus is automatically characterising all Christians as just because of their faith, we should read here an incitement to his contemporary readers to honour the irreproachable model of those communities who first believed in Christ. This moral invitation would work primarily for a Christian audience.

9.3.2 Nonnus

The Gospel of John does not include a description of the Final Judgement (save for 5.28–9, analysed below in Section 9.3.3), or clear images of division of the audience (save for the Hymn of the Logos, discussed earlier in Section 9.1.2). The opposition between the believers and the unbelievers is done differently: John alternates episodes in which Jesus gains a positive reaction (e.g. chapter 4, Jesus among the Samaritans and cure of a royal official's son) and others in which the opposition of the Jewish people to the revelation is emphasised (e.g. chapter 5, cure of a sick man at the pool of Bethesda).

Nonnus, however, introduces a clear division of Jesus' audiences with a number of systematic strategies. The first of them is exaggerating the contrasts of the Gospel between the two groups. This is visible in Nonnus' rendering of choral reactions to Jesus' figure and speeches, as we can see in some examples in book 7.

> At the feast of the shelters, the Jews are on the look-out for him (Jo 7.10–11), some thinking he is a good man (7.12 Ἀγαθός ἐστιν), others thinking he is leading the people astray (7.12 Οὔ, ἀλλὰ πλανᾷ τὸν ὄχλον). In the *Paraphrase of the Gospel of John* they consider Jesus either wise (7.42a ὅττι σοφὸς τελέθει) or not wise at all (7.44 οὐ σοφός, οὐ σοφὸς οὗτος ἐτήτυμον).

> The crowds display different reactions on hearing Jesus speak: some say he is the prophet (Jo 7.40 Οὗτός ἐστιν ἀληθῶς ὁ προφήτης), some say he is the Christ (7.41 Οὗτός ἐστιν ὁ Χριστός), and others note that according to the Scriptures, the Christ must come from Bethlehem, not from Galilee (7.41–2). The evangelist concludes that the people could not agree about

him (7.43 σχίσμα οὖν ἐγένετο ἐν τῷ ὄχλῳ δι᾽ αὐτόν). Nonnus renders these three opinions (7.154–66a) and then splits the audience into two groups: 166b–7a μεριζομένοιο δὲ λαοῦ | ἀμφιλαφὴς **διχόμητις** ἔην ἔρις ('With the people becoming divided there was a vast dispute of double counsel').

A second means of polarisation is to contrast Jesus (knowledgeable, sensible, a figure of faith) with the completely negative response of his Jewish audience. For instance, in Jo 3.11–12 Jesus complains that his listeners do not accept even his testimony on earthly things, and they cannot possibly believe in him when he talks about heavenly things.[59] In his rendition of this passage (*P.* 3.53–64), Nonnus' Jesus contraposes his own testimony which should lead his audience to faith (3.59 πιστὴν μαρτυρίην) and his unerring knowledge of deeds on earth (59–60 ἀπλανέων . . . ἐπιχθονίων. . . ἔργων), with the lack of knowledge of his audience (58 ἀδίδακτος . . . νόος), that makes them uncharmable (58 ἀκηλήτων . . . ἀνδρῶν) and slow in developing faith (61 βαρυπειθέες . . . ἀκουαί; Nonnus *P.* 3.58–61):[60]

ἡμετέρην δ᾽ ἀδίδακτος ἀκηλήτων νόος ἀνδρῶν
πιστὴν μαρτυρίην οὐ δέχνυται· ἀπλανέων δὲ
εἴ τινα μῦθον ἔειπον ἐπιχθονίων χάριν ἔργων,   60
καὶ τόσον ὑμείων βαρυπειθέες εἰσὶν ἀκουαί . . .

The untaught mind of uncharmable men does not receive our trustworthy testimony. If I had said an expression about the unerring worldly deeds, and your listening is so slow to believe . . .

A third means of polarisation is to present opposing descriptions of those who believe and those who do not. We have seen how Nonnus treats slow believers. At the other end of the scale of reception of Jesus' words is the royal officer, a pagan (Jo 4.46–54): in the Gospel, he is told that his child has healed and matches the hour of his recovery with the moment when Jesus said, 'Your son will live' and he and his household believe.[61] In his

---

[59] Jo 3.11–12 ἀμὴν ἀμὴν λέγω σοι ὅτι ὃ οἴδαμεν λαλοῦμεν καὶ ὃ ἑωράκαμεν μαρτυροῦμεν, καὶ τὴν μαρτυρίαν ἡμῶν οὐ λαμβάνετε. εἰ τὰ ἐπίγεια εἶπον ὑμῖν καὶ οὐ πιστεύετε, πῶς ἐὰν εἴπω ὑμῖν τὰ ἐπουράνια πιστεύσετε.

[60] Nonnus was probably adapting Cyril *Comm. in Jo.* 3.11 [1.222 Pusey] 'He finds the man uninterested in learning, exceedingly uneducated [Ἀφιλομαθῆ καὶ λίαν ἀπαίδευτον εὑρίσκει τὸν ἄνθρωπον], and, because of the extreme dullness of his mind [διὰ πολλὴν παχύτητα νοῦ], still unable to be led to the understanding of divine teachings, even after expending a long explanation with various examples on him.'

[61] Jo 4.53 ἔγνω οὖν ὁ πατὴρ ὅτι ἐν ἐκείνῃ τῇ ὥρᾳ ἐν ᾗ εἶπεν αὐτῷ ὁ Ἰησοῦς, Ὁ υἱός σου ζῇ. καὶ ἐπίστευσεν αὐτὸς καὶ ἡ οἰκία αὐτοῦ ὅλη.

paraphrase of this episode Nonnus emphasises the speed with which the officer believes in Jesus' words (4.228–9):

κραιπνὸς ἀνὴρ ἐπεπείθετο μύθῳ,
Ἰησοῦς ὃν ἔειπε, καὶ ἔστιχεν ἐλπίδι πειθοῦς

... The man rapidly trusted in the expression that Jesus had said, and he marched off in the hope of faith.[62]

It shows that the realisation of what has happened dawns on him without exterior help, so that belief implies an automatic gain of knowledge (Nonn. 4.242–4):[63]

ἔγνω δ' αὐτοδίδακτος ἀνὴρ ὀδυνήφατον ὥρην,
τῇ ἔνι θέσκελος εἶπεν ἄναξ ζωαρκέι φωνῇ·
ἔρχεο σὸν ποτὶ δῶμα, τεὸς πάις ἐστὶν ἀπήμων.

Self-taught the man recognised the pain-killing hour in which the divine king spoke in a life-preserving voice, 'Go to your house, your son is without pain.'

Αὐτοδίδακτος here establishes a connection between him and Jesus, who is also self-taught.[64]

Finally, the fourth strategy is to modify the reactions of individuals or groups who do not fully fit a clear-cut audience division (e.g. not all Pharisees fit the negative description of unbelief, ignorance, and passionate reactions): Nonnus reformulates the narrative so that they do not appear to be exceptions at all. For instance, in the case of those who, despite being Pharisees, believe in Jesus (Jo 12.42), Nonnus' rendition introduces the usual qualities of those who have faith: they are unerring (12.167 ἀπλανέες) and knowledgeable (167 ἴδμονι σιγῇ), they have shame (170

---

[62] Similar emphasis in Juvencus' take on the same episode: 2.339–40 *His verbis fructum mox perceptura salutis | pulchra fides animum laetanti in pectore firmat* ('At this, the man's great faith, now soon to reap | salvation's fruit, encouraged his glad heart').

[63] Cf. also Jesus's words: 8.135b–8 καὶ εἰ νημερτὲς ἐνίψω, | τίπτε μοι οὐ πείθεσθε σαόφρονι; πᾶς σοφὸς ἀνήρ | εἰς θεὸν αὐτογένεθλον ἔχων νόον ἠδέι θυμῷ | μύθους οὐρανίοιο θεοῦ ζώοντος ἀκούει ('And if I speak unerringly, why do you not believe me who am prudent. Every wise man, who with pleasing heart has his mind on the self-begotten father, hears the expressions of the living god in heaven'), after Jo 8.46–47 εἰ ἀλήθειαν λέγω, διὰ τί ὑμεῖς οὐ πιστεύετέ μοι; ὁ ὢν ἐκ τοῦ θεοῦ τὰ ῥήματα τοῦ θεοῦ ἀκούει ('If I speak the truth, why do you not believe me? Whoever comes from God listens to the words of God'). The characterisation of himself as sensible (136 μοι ... σαόφρονι) and of his listeners as wise (136 πᾶς σοφὸς ἀνήρ) does not occur in the Gospel narrative.

[64] Αὐτοδίδακτος as Jesus: 2.118b–20 ἔργα δὲ φωτῶν | ᾔδεεν αὐτοδίδακτος, ὅσα φρενὸς ἔνδοθεν ἀνὴρ | εἶχεν ἀκηρύκτῳ κεκαλυμμένα φάρεϊ σιγῆς ('But self-taught he knew men's deeds, all those that within his heart a man has veiled in the unheralded cloak of silence' – after Jo 2.25 αὐτὸς γὰρ ἐγίνωσκεν τί ἦν ἐν τῷ ἀνθρώπῳ); 6.58 εἰδὼς δ' αὐτοδίδακτος ἄναξ ὑποκάρδιον ὀμφήν ('Knowing self-taught the prophetic voice in his heart' – after Jo 6.15 Ἰησοῦς οὖν γνοὺς ὅτι ...).

αἰδομένου – unlike the shameless priests: 11.214 ἀναιδέες ἀρχιερῆες) – all of which stands in contrast with the fear and jealousy of the standard Pharisees (12.170 φόβον καὶ ζῆλον ... Φαρισαίων; Nonn. *P.* 12.167–73):

ἔμπης **ἀπλανέες** τινὲς ἀνέρες **ἴδμονι** σιγῇ
ἀρχοὶ Ἰουδαίων, ὑψαύχενος ὄμματα βουλῆς,
παιδὶ θεοῦ πείθοντο θεηγενέων χάριν ἔργων·
ἀλλὰ **φόβον καὶ ζῆλον** ἀλυσκάζων **Φαρισαίων**   170
ἀμφαδὸν οὔτις ἔφηνεν ἑὸν νόον· **αἰδομένου** δέ
ἐνδόμυχος τότε πίστις ὑπὸ φρένα φωτὸς ἑκάστου
ἀπροϊδής, ἀβόητος ἐκεύθετο φωλάδι σιγῇ·

Nevertheless, some unerring men with knowledgeable silence, leaders of the Jews, eyes of haughty counsel, believed in the child of god because of his god-born works. But avoiding the fear and jealousy of the Pharisees, no one openly revealed his mind. The current inmost faith of each reverencing man was hidden in his mind by a lurking silence to be unseen, unexpressed.

That is to say, the Pharisees if they believe are treated as believers, in confrontation with the typical Pharisees, characterised by moral debauchery and disbelief.

Along the same lines of argument, in some Gospel passages the disciples do not immediately understand the meaning of Jesus' words and actions, which would be at odds with the combination of faith and knowledge in the *Paraphrase of the Gospel of John*. For instance, in chapter 2, Jesus claims that he can destroy the Temple and rebuild it in three days (2.19) and the evangelist notes that he was speaking of the Temple of his body (2.21), but that the disciples only understood this after his resurrection. Compare Jo 2.22 to Nonnus *P.* 2.104–10a:

ὅτε οὖν ἠγέρθη ἐκ νεκρῶν, ἐμνήσθησαν οἱ μαθηταὶ αὐτοῦ ὅτι τοῦτο ἔλεγεν,
καὶ ἐπίστευσαν τῇ γραφῇ καὶ τῷ λόγῳ ὃν εἶπεν ὁ Ἰησοῦς.

After he was raised from the dead, his disciples remembered that he had said this; and they believed the scripture and the word that Jesus had spoken.

~

ἀλλ᾽ ὅτε δὴ μετὰ κόλπον ἀνοστήτοιο βερέθρου
νόστιμος ἐξ Ἀίδαο παλινζώῳ τινὶ πότμῳ   105
ἀρχαίην παλίνορσος ἑὴν ἀνεδύσατο τιμὴν
οὐρανίην, τότε μῦθον ἀνεμνήσαντο μαθηταί,
ὅττι δόμον δέμας εἶπε· θεογλώσσοιο δὲ βίβλου
θεῖον ἐπιστώσαντο λόγον πείθοντό τε μύθῳ,
Ἰησοῦς ὃν ἔειπε.   110

> Now when Jesus, after the gulf of the unreturnable pit, returned from Hades with a revivified fate, and was clothed again in his honour of old, only then did the disciples recall that by 'temple' he meant 'bodily temple'. They trusted the divine word of the god-tongued book and they believed the expression which Jesus said.

Nonnus follows the narrative of the Gospel and does not make a reference to the ignorance of the disciples, nor does he call them slow to listen, believe, or understand (compare e.g. 3.61 βαρυπειθέες … ἀκουαί, 3.95 βραδυπειθέι θυμῷ, 20.108 βραδυδινέι θυμῷ). The only temporal note is that of the ἀλλ' ὅτε … τότε, meaning that they only understood Jesus' words after the resurrection. And then he emphasises that their faith is complete with the two verbs of the conclusion (109 ἐπιστώσαντο … πείθοντό).[65]

9.3.3   Comparison of Juvencus and Nonnus

The comparison of how Juvencus and Nonnus divide the Gospel audiences reveals a common strategy of polarisation, and the different terms used for the division. We have seen that Juvencus highlights moral terms and focusses on justice, whereas Nonnus, in the wake of Cyril, calls attention to the coupling faith-knowledge. For a more detailed analysis we can compare how both authors paraphrase Jo 5.29, a brief reference to the end of the world, with the dead being sent to the resurrection or to the final judgement depending on their deeds in life. Compare Jo 5.29 to ELQ 2.660–1:

> Et prodient, qui bona gesserunt, in resurrectionem vitae, qui iniqua gesserunt, in resurrectionem iudicii.

> And they will come out – those who have done good, to the resurrection of life, and those who have done evil, to the resurrection of condemnation.

> ~

> Iustorum que animas redivivo corpore necti,
> iudicio que gravi miseros exsurgere pravos.

---

[65] Juvencus paraphrases the same Gospel passage: 2.173–5a *Hoc verbum quondam post tempora debita digni | cognovere viri, proprio de corpore Christum | delubrum dixisse Dei* ('In due time, worthy men perceived that Christ | referred to his own body as God's temple'). Juvencus does not report the late realisation of the disciples and turns them into 'worthy men' (*digni … viri*). He compresses the reference to the resurrection into 'in due time' (*tempora debita*), which when read against the paraphrased text adds a cosmic resonance: they realised that Christ referred to his own body at the right time, after Christ's body had experienced the resurrection. Cf. McGill (2016: 164, n. to 173–4): 'As elsewhere (cf. on 1.307–8 and 1.352–3), the events of Jesus' life are predetermined and invested with cosmic significance in the unfolding of Christian history.'

And that just souls are joined to reborn flesh,
while wicked wretches rise to grievous judgement.

Juvencus transforms the division of deeds in the Gospel into his usual moral division, between the just and the wicked. Nonnus reproduces virtually *verbatim* the second part of the sentences, adding only two 'cosmetic' adjectives (Jo 29 εἰς ἀνάστασιν ζωῆς ≈ Nonn. 114 ζωῆς ἀθανάτης ἐς ἀνάστασιν; Jo 29 εἰς ἀνάστασιν κρίσεως ≈ Nonn. 116 κρίσιος ἐσσομένης ἐς ἀνάστασιν), but elaborates notably the first half. Compare Jo 5.29 to Nonn. *P.* 5.113–16:

καὶ ἐκπορεύσονται, οἱ τὰ ἀγαθὰ ποιήσαντες εἰς ἀνάστασιν ζωῆς, οἱ δὲ τὰ
φαῦλα πράξαντες εἰς ἀνάστασιν κρίσεως.

~

οἱ μὲν ἀεθλεύσαντες ἀμεμφέα πιστὸν ἀγῶνα
ζωῆς ἀθανάτης ἐς ἀνάστασιν, οἱ δὲ καμόντες
ἔργα πολυπλανέος βιοτῆς ἑτερόφρονι λύσσῃ   115
κρίσιος ἐσσομένης ἐς ἀνάστασιν·

Some have competed in a blameless faithful contest unto the resurrection of eternal life, but others have done deeds of a much-erring life because of versiminded madness unto the resurrection of the judgement about to be.

Where Juvencus has two moral labels (*iustorum* vs *miseros ... gravos*), Nonnus has two loaded paraphrases. The good have voluntarily undertaken a contest of faith (113 ἀεθλεύσαντες ... πιστὸν ἀγῶνα) that leads to eternal life: the image is clearly of Pauline ascendance,[66] but this should not obscure the fact that reaching eternal life no longer depends on deeds, but on faith. Also, although the notion of a contest could suggest evolution or a progressive enhancement in the quality of faith, the adjective ἀμεμφέα (113 'blameless', 'without reproach') suggests perfection from beginning to end: faith grants perfection and a clear trajectory towards eternal life. At the opposite end of the scale are those who lead a life without a clear trajectory (115 πολυπλανέος βιοτῆς), because they are out of their minds (ἑτερόφρονι), virtually insane (λύσσῃ).

One of the possible explanations to why Juvencus emphasises moral propriety and justice and Nonnus knowledge could be that each of them chose the notion that would relate best to his audience. In Juvencus' (and Constantine's) time, when law and justice were not universally formulated in Christian terms, Christian claims of superiority could be grounded in

---

[66] 1 Tim 6.12 (ἀγωνίζου τὸν καλὸν ἀγῶνα τῆς πίστεως, ἐπιλαβοῦ τῆς αἰωνίου ζωῆς); 2 Tim 4.7 (τὸν καλὸν ἀγῶνα ἠγώνισμαι, τὸν δρόμον τετέλεκα, τὴν πίστιν τετήρηκα). The metaphor is elaborated in 1 Cor 9.24–7. Cf. Agosti (2003: 479–82).

moral superiority. On the contrary, in Nonnus' (and Cyril's) time, Christians had long occupied important positions in the political spheres from which laws and policies emerged, but there were still different forms of authority to be achieved: Christianity needed to be seen as an intellectually defensible system of thought to overtake the authority of classical philosophy. This explains why markedly Christian texts, such us hagiographies, often claim that the knowledge derived from God is stronger than the superficial knowledge of pagan philosophers, in spite of their complicated syllogisms.[67] Hence Cyril's emphasis on knowledge, and hence Nonnus' emphasis on a poetic version of the same knowledge.[68]

---

[67] Clearly visible in one of the most influential early Christian hagiographies: in Athanasius' *Life of Antony*, Antony is unschooled and illiterate and defeats philosophical reasoning in three encounters with philosophers; Antony's simplicity and natural wisdom, inspired by God, is contrasted with the futile cunning of the philosophers and their acquired letters. Cf. Rubenson (2000), an analysis of how the authors of early Christian biographies presented the education of the saint.

[68] Gregory of Nazianzus motivates his election of poetry among other reasons to make Christian doctrine more agreeable and easier to remember to the young and to provide a Christian counterpart to traditional Greek poetry (*In suos versus* 2.1.39).

CHAPTER 10

Colluthus and Dracontius
Mythical Traditions and Innovations
Marcelina Gilka

Around 500 CE, two poets each composed an epyllion entitled *The Abduction of Helen.* One was written in Greek by the Egyptian Colluthus of Lycopolis, while a Latin poem came from the pen of Blossius Aemilius Dracontius in Vandal Africa. It has not been established which of the two came first and there is no compelling indication that either one depended on the other.[1] Although they have a common theme, the two works are interested in very different aspects of the myth in question and they are so dissimilar in content that a direct comparison of the motifs can only be achieved to a limited extent.[2] In the present chapter, I shall use them as examples of how the Antehomeric myth was adapted respectively in the east and the west. In doing so, I endeavour to shed light on late antique engagements with the epic tradition through the lenses of society, politics, and religion.

The two works are the results of contrasting techniques and reveal divergent aims. Colluthus' mode of adaptation can be described as constructive, Dracontius' as destructive. The former preserves the most common tradition of Helen's disappearance and puts his own stamp on it by enriching it with details and novel perspectives. The latter, in turn, bases his narrative on a less well-known model and uses it to subvert the classical literary heritage.

10.1 Colluthus

Colluthus' epyllion, the *Harpage Helenes* (Coll.), consists of 392 verses which generally tell a very conservative story of the abduction. The

---

[1] The suggestion by De Prisco (1977: 298) that Dracontius has used Colluthus as a model is not based on solid arguments and has rightly been refuted by Simons (2005: 283 n. 200).

[2] Most recently, however, Morales has made a case for considering the two poems alongside each other, despite their differences (2016: 74). See also Stoehr-Monjou (2014: 97–8).

narrative is linear and creates a domino-effect from one event to the next: it begins with the wedding of Peleus and Thetis, which leads to the Judgement of Paris, his consequent journey to Sparta and meeting and elopement with Helen. Up to this point the plot is remarkably congruent with that of the *Cypria* summary offered by Proclus (except for the minor detail of Menelaus' absence from the very start). In fact, no other author we know of between the Epic Cycle and Colluthus includes all these events in one coherent account. Scholars seem to be in agreement that by the time of Colluthus the entire cyclic poems were lost and existed only as synopses.[3] It is most likely that the poet himself knew only about as much of the *Cypria* as we do nowadays, and thus his aim was possibly to write a new version of its subject matter, since none was available.[4] This signifies a silent approval of and compliance with the old literary canon, which is adapted and perpetuated over a millennium later. Such an alignment would be particularly apt if Colluthus operated as a court poet under Anastasius I, harnessing the power of earlier epic to benefit his own poetry and praise the emperor.[5]

The last part of Colluthus' *Harpage*, however, shifts the focus in a most interesting way and presents an innovation which I will attempt to explain against the context of its time. After Helen has left, we are presented with an extended scene in which her little daughter Hermione laments for her mother. She is involved in a dialogue with her attendants and asks them where Helen may be. They console her half-heartedly and say that she will certainly come back soon. Thereupon the girl makes foreboding but educated guesses as to what may have happened and says that she has already looked everywhere. She then cries herself to sleep and, in a dream, is visited by Helen, who tells her that she has been abducted. Finally, Hermione starts up and sends birds to fly to Menelaus and report to him that a stranger has destroyed the household. The figure of Hermione is frequently mentioned by previous authors as having been left by Helen either in order to aggravate the latter's guilt or to make a point about the overwhelming power of love,[6] and the adult Hermione appears in

---

[3] West (2013: 8–10 and 56); Bär and Baumbach (2015: 621–2).

[4] De Lorenzi (1928: 40) even theorises that the epyllion is only part of an entire *Antehomerica* which Colluthus wrote as a counterpart to Quintus Smyrnaeus' *Posthomerica*. Cf. Magnelli (2008: 171 n. 79).

[5] Colluthus is reported by the *Suda* to have produced *Encomia*, probably glorifying Anastasius, during whose reign he flourished, according to the encyclopaedia. See Jeffreys (2006: 129). Cameron (1982: 237 n. 82) suggests that Colluthus' *Persica*, also mentioned in the *Suda*, dealt with Anastasius' recapture of Amida in 505. Cadau (2015: 7) agrees.

[6] Cf. Triphiodorus 493–4 and Sappho fr. 16.10–11.

tragedy.[7] The first time her desperate response to Helen's abduction is briefly sketched is in Ovid's *Heroides* 8.73–81 where a grown-up Hermione recalls the situation, and it is possible that the passage has influenced Colluthus' epyllion.[8] Yet Colluthus' portrayal of the girl goes even further and includes lengthy speeches by her. It is unprecedented not only because of the original treatment of the character, but also because it is the very first meaningful representation of a human female child in a fictive work.[9] I strongly suspect the reason for this to be that ancient Greek and Roman literature up to that point is not interested in children or their thoughts.[10] The overall view emerges across a multitude of sources that they are considered irrational creatures and 'unfinished' humans.[11]

Fictive children in antiquity are generally silent, weak, or inept. They are often present in the text beside their parents, because they are necessary for the plot, but either do not get a voice at all or their utterances are limited to helpless cries. This can be observed well in tragedy: in Sophocles' *Oedipus Rex* the young Antigone and Ismene are *personae mutae*, but when they become older in *Oedipus at Colonus* they do speak and actively take part in the play as their father's messengers and sensible advisors; in the *Antigone* the entire plot is of course driven by them. In Euripides' *Medea*, the heroine's children do not even have names, but are referred to as 'child A' and 'child B'. They are only significant as vehicles of Medea's atrocity, and by definition they do not survive to reach adulthood; thus, inventing names for them would be a superfluous exercise. The few lines they get in the play are words of despair as they are being murdered by their mother (Eur. *Med.* 1270a–79). In Seneca's version of the tragedy they remain mute altogether. In the same way, Itys in Ovid's *Metamorphoses* greets and beguiles his mother Procne in reported speech (Ov. *Met.* 6.624–6), but his only real words are *'mater! mater!'* (Ov. *Met.* 6.640) when he realises that he is about to die. Another quality of children in ancient literature is stupidity. For example, in Seneca's *Thyestes*, the protagonist converses with his son Tantalus who is used to illustrate utter naïvety and a deficiency of *ratio* as a contrast to his father who at that time

---

[7] For example in Euripides' *Andromache* and a lost *Hermione* by Sophocles.

[8] For the debate, see Zöllner (1892: 55–115), De Lorenzi (1928: 42–58), and Livrea (1968: xiv–xxiii). For parallels between Ovid and Nonnus, see Carvounis and Papaioannou in this volume (Chapter 1).

[9] By this I mean a girl who has not reached puberty and is not yet ready for marriage.

[10] See Dixon (1992: 100).

[11] See Bakke (2005: 16). Cicero says that the only good thing about children is their potential to grow up (*De Republica* 137.3).

is still a good cautious Stoic (Sen. *Thyestes* 421–90). The other two children are mute, and one of them is also unnamed.

Furthermore, children in the *Iliad* have been identified as the opposite of the ideal hero on account of both physical and mental inferiority.[12] One example of comparable perceptions about mortal children that springs to mind is the little Astyanax who is frightened by his father's helmet, to the hilarity of his parents (*Il.* 6.466–74). However, the scene could also be interpreted as highlighting the silliness of infants, and arguably its main function is to evoke *pathos* in conjunction with Astyanax' subsequent death. Again, it is not so much the toddler who is the object of pity, but his mother whose hope for the son's future shall remain unfulfilled.

Whenever childhood is depicted in a positive light or is given prominence, it is always with a view to the child's future as an adult. For instance, the existence of Ascanius, whom we see growing up throughout the *Aeneid*, is teleological like the epic itself: he receives much attention in the poem as a boy, because he will become the great founder of Alba Longa when he comes of age.[13] An interesting case is that of Gorgo, daughter of Cleomenes, who is said by Herodotus to have advised her father on politics at the age of eight or nine with a witty comment (Hdt. 5.51). While this passage is concerned with a real person, the account is nevertheless fictitious. The brief story is unique and delightful in that it grants power and wisdom to a female child of about the same age as that of little Hermione (according to Apollodorus, she was nine when Helen left Sparta). However, Gorgo's childhood anecdote is hardly significant for its own sake, but rather is intended as a flattery of the figure who later becomes queen, to show that she had been very capable early on.

The same is true for the interesting case of aetiological episodes from the childhood of deities, where amusement is created by pairing the expectation of helplessness in a child with supernatural powers. This begins with the *Homeric Hymn to Hermes* that tells how the one-day-old Hermes, already able to speak and walk, steals Apollo's kine as his very first trick and ultimately earns respect for himself. The theme was mainly taken over and elaborated in the Hellenistic period:[14] Theocritus' *Idyll* 24 presents us

---

[12] Cf. Ingalls (1998: 17–18). Notwithstanding, the poem also displays the devotion of parents to their children: see Pratt (2007).

[13] Feldmann (1953: 304–5).

[14] Ambühl (2007) states on the first page of her chapter that '[t]he Hellenistic age is said to have discovered childhood as a subject in its own right' (373), but adds on the last page: 'the children in Callimachus's poetry are always set into a relationship with adult figures' (383). Thus, here too childhood is only a pre-stage of what really matters, but is not important in itself.

with the story of baby Heracles strangling the snakes in his cradle and an account of his upbringing. Young Artemis in her Callimachean hymn sits on Zeus' lap, and asks to be allowed to keep her maidenhood forever and to receive a bow and arrows and all the other emblems associated with her; however, she is too small to reach his beard with her arm. A sibling rivalry with her twin brother Apollo can also be detected. Meanwhile, in Apollonius Rhodius 3.112–57 Eros cheats Ganymede at a game of dice, but is subsequently bribed by Aphrodite with the promise of a new toy. All these instances of childish gods capture and promote the delightful charms of their age, which means that this cuteness was at least appreciated by authors and readers alike.

The only instance I have been able to identify as a kind of predecessor to Colluthus' episode is the παῖς of Alcestis in Euripides' eponymous tragedy who delivers a dirge after his mother has died (Eur. *Alc.* 396–415). Despite its brevity, the passage contains a number of parallels with the speeches of Hermione. Importantly, the topics are strikingly similar: the boy grieves for his dead mother, while Hermione cannot explain the loss of her parent except with death, and her reaction is accordingly one very close to mourning. The process of dealing with the situation is also almost identical in both cases. It consists of three stages. Both speakers begin with addressing others who are present (Admetus and Hermione's handmaids, respectively) and state what has happened. Next, they switch to a direct apostrophe to the mother herself, as though to ascertain whether she will hear it. Finally, they resign and once again turn to the interlocutors before them (the boy to his father and sister; Hermione to the birds). The children each open their lament by saying that the mother has left them and gone away (βέβακεν [. . .] προλιποῦσα δ᾽ ἐμὸν βίον: Eur. *Alc.* 395–6; με λιποῦσα [. . .] ᾤχετο: Coll. 330, and later με [. . .] φυγοῦσα | κάλλιπες: Coll. 372–3). There is a note of blame detectable in the words, and rightly so, since both Alcestis and Helen have left of their own choice – though the former has done it for virtue, the latter for vice. The boy also applies to Alcestis the adjective τλάμων, which, just like the English 'wretched', can mean 'miserable' in a compassionate sense, but it can also be translated in a rebuking manner as 'reckless'. Hermione, too, complains to her mother with embittered questions at Coll. 372–5. Another shared feature is the mention of heavenly bodies in conjunction with the loss which gives it a cosmic dimension: Alcestis does no longer walk under the sun (Eur. *Alc.* 395), while Helen has not returned despite the fact that the stars have awoken (Coll. 349–50). The boy also draws attention to the features of his mother's lifeless body lying before him (Eur. *Alc.* 397–8; 404), whereas

Hermione imagines finding Helen's corpse in the woods (Coll. 355; 358). While Hermione proceeds from worry towards blame, the πάις starts with blame, but then addresses his mother almost apologetically and desperately implores her to listen to 'her chicklet', as she perhaps used to call him endearingly, and kisses her lips (Eur. *Alc.* 399–403). Remarkably, both Alcestis' son and Hermione come to the same conclusion at the very end of their speeches. They claim that through the absence of the mother their home has been ruined (οἰχομένας δὲ σοῦ, | μᾶτερ, ὄλωλεν οἶκος, 'With you gone, mother, the house is ruined': Eur. *Alc.* 414–5; χθιζὸν ἐπὶ Σπάρτην τις ἀνὴρ ἀθεμίστιος ἐλθών | ἀγλαΐην ξύμπασαν ἐμῶν ἀλάπαξε μελάθρων, 'yesterday some lawless man came to Sparta and destroyed the entire splendour of my palace': Coll. 383–4).[15] This very much chimes with a modern child's (stereo-)typical primary worries about their family life: Euripides and Colluthus created very realistic figures of children by making them voice the most deeply ingrained wish for an ideal household with their mum and dad, and their sense of the whole world collapsing when a parent is no longer there.

The above survey reveals that if we do encounter fictitious children in ancient texts they are, unsurprisingly, almost exclusively male. It is indeed a challenge to find in them a female mortal prepubescent individual, yet Colluthus' Hermione occupies a non-negligible proportion of his poem in which we gain an insight into her thoughts and feelings. Moreover, far from being a foolish child, she shows herself remarkably sensible, for example, when she berates her handmaids for telling her implausible things (Coll. 346–7). She is indeed more sensible even than her mother who agrees to elope with a man she has only just met. But why does Colluthus venture into taking children seriously? I suggest that his extensive treatment of Hermione's feelings reflects the society within which he wrote. O. M. Bakke has traced ancient perceptions about children from a cultural-historical angle, and, as the title of his monograph suggests, has found that they changed radically with the rise of Christianity. There is evidence that Christian parents may have spent more time with their children than pagans and were closer to them emotionally as a result.[16] We see this played out in the *Harpage* through Helen's and Hermione's bedtime ritual (Coll. 331–3, 372–4). The church began to value children for their own sake: St. Cyprian, bishop of Carthage in the mid-third century, regards them as complete human beings from birth, because they are made by God, and as equal to adults (Cypr. *Epist.* 64.2–3). Clement of

---

[15] All translations are my own.   [16] Bakke (2005: 285).

Alexandria praises children for the very fact that they are truthful and innocent and for their lack of sexual desires, and therefore even poses them as examples for adults (*Paedagogus* 1.5–6). Ambrose states that Christ does not discriminate between ages, but even as a child one is as answerable and mature as an adult; he says that even small children bear witness to Christ when faced with persecutors (Ambr. *Epist.* 72.15).

Colluthus, too, portrays Hermione as a much better person than Helen. He even pointedly de-sexualises the girl:[17] the dream scene inverts the literary topos of the maiden who has a dream which involves her parents and a future husband, demonstrating her readiness for marriage. An early version of this can be observed with Nausicaa, who is told by Athena that she will not remain a virgin for much longer (*Od.* 6.25–40). Prenuptial dreams are then developed into more vivid and disturbing nocturnal phantasies: Medea fights with bulls and chooses to abandon her parents for a stranger (Ap. Rhod. *Argon.* 3.616–33), while Ilia is abducted by a beautiful man and errs about an unknown place, but is reassured by her father's voice (Enn. *Ann.* I, fr. 28 in Cic. *Div.* 1.40–41).[18] The theme is also somewhat subverted in Nonnus' *Dionysiaca* where Erigone is visited in her sleep by the ghost of her father who tells her that because of his murder she is never to be married (Nonn. *Dion.* 161–86).[19] In contrast to those examples, Hermione's nightmare focusses on her puellile attachment to her mother and her birth-family, rather than a willingness to be carried off from home by a husband. As in the cases of Medea and Ilia, the vision does also feature a stranger who separates her from her parent, but with the difference that he snatches away the latter. The child does not dream about her own love-life, but about her mother's erotic escapade, and seems not even to grasp it fully. The *topos* is thus skewed on two levels: firstly, the intertextual associations enhance the distorted image of Helen, a reckless adulteress playing the part of a passive, bashful maiden. Second, as

---

[17] Morales (2016: 72–3) presents the opposite view: she suggests that Hermione can be eroticised as a substitute for her mother, since she sleeps in Menelaus' bed (Coll. 373), which suggests father-daughter incest scenarios during the mother's absence. However, I disagree, since she sleeps there not with Menelaus while Helen is away, but precisely with Helen while Menelaus is away and thus she is rather a replacement for him (as Morales herself concedes: 72 n. 23). See also Paschalis (2008: 140). Apart from nothing in the text pointing to child sexual exploitation, it rather makes sense for Menelaus to be concerned with finding a husband for his only daughter – as he is in the mythical tradition – and to preserve her virginity. If anything, this notion would have only intensified with a Christian society.

[18] See Krevans (1993: esp. 261–2).

[19] Nonnus' Erigone has been cited as an inspiration for Colluthus' Hermione by Orsini (1972: xxiii–xxiv) and Cuartero i Iborra (1992: 50–1).

opposed to the typical scenario that points to the dreamer's sexual maturity, here the child's innocence is highlighted.

Church Fathers give guidelines on educating children: it is the parents' responsibility to care for their well-being in both body and soul, which is the way to salvation.[20] John Chrysostom, *Adversus Oppugnatores Vitae Monasticae* 3.3, considers neglect of one's child to be the height of sin. The exception is godly women who desert their children for their faith.[21] Hermit practice had sprung from Egypt with St Anthony of the Desert in the third century and continued to flourish there with ascetic communities of 'Desert Fathers' and 'Desert Mothers' into Colluthus' time. St. Jerome tells of Melanium and Paula who belonged to the group of Desert Women in the fourth century and left their children behind to become missionaries (*Epist.* 45.4). In *Epist.* 108.6 he comments that Paula's love for Christ was even greater than her love for her children. As a contrast, Helen leaves her daughter behind not only not for God, but for sinful lust.[22] She would therefore be doubly condemned in the eyes of a Christian audience for being both promiscuous and a bad mother. Thus, a Christian dimension may be added to Colluthus' epyllion, which both complements and competes with the pagan tradition.[23]

Finally, I would like to attempt another sociocultural interpretation regarding Hermione's age. Apollodorus' *Epitome* 3.3 informs us that she was nine years old at the time of Helen's departure and this age could easily fit Colluthus' character. However, the matter is slightly complicated by the mention of a veil upon Hermione's head, which she throws off when we first encounter her in line 326. Lloyd Llewellyn-Jones, who has investigated veiling from the archaic period up to the second century CE, asserts in the conclusion of his eighth chapter that Greek females, just like women of modern-day veil-societies, were '[n]o doubt first veiled at menarche'.[24] It would follow from this that for Colluthus' Hermione to be veiled she must have reached sexual maturity, and thus it is questionable whether she is still a child. I contend nevertheless that Hermione should be classified as a child. First, veiling practices could have significantly changed by 500 CE (perhaps with the onset of Christianity) and girls could have been veiled

---

[20] See, for example, the exhortation to teach children about god in the *Epistle of Barnabas* 19.5.

[21] Bakke (2005: 263) mentions Perpetua, Felicitas, and Agathonice who suffered martyrdom despite being mothers.

[22] For this argument see Gilka (2014: 18) and, independently, Morales (2016: 70 n. 20).

[23] Goldhill (2020: 61), too, discusses the influence of Christian morality on the way Colluthus chooses to tell the myth of the abduction.

[24] Llewellyn-Jones (2003: 247).

pre-emptively from a certain age, before they became fertile. Furthermore, at nine years an early-blooming girl could conceivably be menstruating, but still very much be a child mentally, which is true of Hermione's concerns and the way she speaks. At any rate, there is nothing else in the text that would point to the fact that she is marriageable. An even more convincing explanation is that Hermione's veil is an expression of mourning.[25] She does not wear it on a daily basis, but temporarily dons it in her moment of distress, which is most similar to grieving a death.[26] Second, Hermione's veil, which is crucially inspired by and dependent on the representations of females in the *Iliad* and the *Odyssey*, serves as a way of linking Colluthus' text to Homeric epic.[27] As Llewellyn-Jones states, the veils of Homer's female characters are signifiers of high status;[28] thus veiling may be appropriate for a royal of any age. The headgear is exploited here as a literary commonplace, rather than a realistic representation.

In conclusion, Colluthus aims to situate his epyllion in a line-up of poetry dealing with the Trojan War and makes the text stand out with the lengthy depiction of Hermione. The fact that the work lends such a prominent voice to a little girl is compelling and possibly due to a growing interest in the role of children in sixth-century society. The episode also vilifies the character of Helen by adding to her well-known vice of being a bad wife also that of being a bad mother, a trait which would have been perceived as particularly abominable by a Christian audience.

10.2 Dracontius

In comparison with Colluthus' *Abduction*, Dracontius' epyllion (*De Raptu Helenae* = *Romulea* 8) is significantly longer (655 lines) and much more complex in plot, and it also implies many events that lie outside of its narrative frame. Apparently using the avant-garde version of Dares Phrygius as a model, it offers first a background story of Paris' youth as a shepherd (he had been exposed following a prophecy) and his restoration into the royal family. Since he wants to prove himself, Priam lets him go on a journey to Salamis to recover his aunt Hesione, who had been taken by Telamon in the aftermath of Heracles' attack on Troy. The Trojans are dissuaded from taking Hesione back, but on the return journey they are

---

[25] Llewellyn-Jones (2003: 302–3).   [26] See also Goldhill (2020: 56–7).
[27] For a detailed discussion of the headgear trope and its function within Colluthus' poem, see Gilka (2020: 194–6).
[28] Llewellyn-Jones (2003: 121–30).

caught in a storm and Paris lands on Cyprus, where he meets Helen. They quickly agree to flee and are persecuted by a mob and Menelaus on horseback. They then return to Phrygia, where Paris has been presumed dead, and celebrate their nuptials. The relationship of the *De Raptu Helenae* (*De Raptu*) with epic predecessors is also more complicated than that of the *Harpage,* and rather hostile.

Given the subject matter of *Romulea* 8, it is tempting to interpret the piece in a political way. This has been done most prominently by Díaz de Bustamente, in whose view the poem's message is the glorification of Rome as the eternal city which is to rise from the ashes of Troy.[29] I would agree with this if the author of the *De Raptu* were Publius Vergilius Maro. However, by the time of Dracontius the reality looked somewhat different: the city of Rome ceased to be the *caput mundi*, except nominally, and in 410 it was, *horribile dictu*, pillaged by Alaric's Goths. In 455, around the time of Dracontius' birth, it was sacked for the second time by the Vandals. Yet Carthage, which the Vandals had conquered some 15 years earlier, remained the capital of their new kingdom. Thus, one may see in this a repetition of the ancient rivalry between the two cities that started with the Punic Wars, with the scales tipped in favour of Carthage this time.[30] While poets like Dracontius would have been sentimental about Rome's fall, they must have been pleased that their own city, the former periphery, was now in the spotlight. The Vandals were striving to establish themselves in Carthage as the new superpower, not only militarily but also culturally, albeit with mixed success.[31] Literary activity flourished among individuals who had received a thorough education based on the Latin Classics, with Dracontius himself perhaps being the most eminent example. It would thus have made sense for writers to adapt tales of Africans and Latians and to re-interpret Roman founding myths to suit the current situation. Vergil's *Aeneid*, as the national epic, stands out as an obvious target,[32] and even more so since its proto-Roman protagonist tellingly abandons a Carthaginian queen in order to find his promised land and receives divine prophecies about its everlasting success. While an African poet could not simply rewrite the story of Dido and

---

[29] Díaz de Bustamente (1978: 124), building on Morelli (1912: 104).

[30] This parallel was, in fact, drawn by contemporaries and the events were described as a 'fourth Punic War' by Sidonius Apollinaris (*Carm.* 7.444–6). For a detailed discussion, see Miles (2017).

[31] See the discussion by Merrills and Miles (2010: 204–27), which gives examples of both decline and continuity of classical culture within the Vandal kingdom.

[32] For example, Fulgentius, another North-African poet, wrote a Christianising allegorical interpretation of the *Aeneid,* the *Expositio Virgilianae Contentiae.*

Aeneas, he could certainly subvert the message of the *Aeneid* at its root, at a mythologically prior point. At the same time, this provided an opportunity to reinforce a Christian worldview against a narrative dictated by pagan gods.

I do not wish to discuss in detail Dracontius' biography or his potential personal motivations; it will suffice to say a few words. There can be no doubt as to Dracontius' Christian belief, as evidenced by his great work *De Laudibus Dei* alone. As an advocate in Carthage, he seems to have been a patriot, too, though we know that his attitude towards the Vandal rulers was problematic. They probably deprived him of his land, which caused him to write a praise of a foreign ruler. This offended Gunthamund and ended in a prison sentence for the poet. Although after his liberation from prison Dracontius supposedly wrote a panegyric on Thrasamund,[33] this does not necessarily mean a sincere change of heart and true admiration of the king. Though brought up in Carthage, the poet enjoyed a traditional Roman aristocratic education and must have felt himself a Roman,[34] as opposed to the barbarian rulers. This may have caused an even greater accentuation of those differences, and an increased pride in the Roman heritage as a means of contrast with the Vandals. Rome was no more, but if any remnants of its cultural spirit still existed, they could be found in Carthage. On the one hand, the preservation of 'Romanness' is a covert rebellion against the Vandal rule;[35] on the other hand, the usurpation of the throne of 'the Roman poet' must inevitably lead to a literary struggle with Vergil. Dracontius' awareness of this is also reflected in the hybridity of his piece, which follows Vergil in metre and general subject matter, but then chooses to present it contrarily to expectations by playing with the genre and the message, in a fashion reminiscent of Ovid's *Metamorphoses*. I propose that in his *De Raptu* Dracontius defines himself against the past in this way, in particular undermining Vergilian and Augustan Rome.

Despite Dracontius' claim in the prologue that the choice of narrative content for his poem is based on a process of elimination of material covered by Vergil and Homer, there is also another intention. The work is set in a mythical time before the Trojan War, which is a significant prerequisite to the plot of the *Aeneid*. Thus Dracontius' epyllion purports

---

[33] Conant (2012: 147).

[34] Miles (2017: 403–5) draws attention to Dracontius' positive sentiment towards Rome in one of his early works, *Rom.* 5. Cf. the allegiance expressed by Ausonius to both Rome and his native Bordeaux, as discussed by Ward-Perkins (1997: 381).

[35] This was also voiced by Díaz de Bustamente (1978: 132) after Morelli (1912: 104), Romano (1959: 20), and Bouquet (1995: 56 and 58).

to precede Vergil's great work, although it is composed almost half a millennium later. It discredits the *Aeneid* by revealing the dark past of Rome's ancestry at Troy. While Vergil mostly strove to show the hardships and sacrifices bravely endured by a Trojan for the future of a glorious empire, Dracontius' aim is to demonstrate the futility of the venture. As emphasised in both the opening lines and in the invocation (*De Raptu* 1–2, 11–12, 29–30), the central point of *Romulea* 8 is the vice of Paris as the main trigger for the war and the Fall of Troy.[36] In his short work, Dracontius treats a relatively vast mythological scope, with many pro- and analepses, which allows him to air as much dirty Trojan laundry as possible. There are continuous references to both the first defeat of Ilium by the Greeks under Heracles and to the even worse calamity which is to follow. Both are attributed to Trojan cheating. Apart from his chief crime of breaking the seventh Commandment, Paris also proves himself dishonourable by being a partial judge, becoming haughty because of the office, and deserting Oenone and his country life, but then turning out to be a coward during the shipwreck and wishing he were a shepherd again (*De Raptu* 35, 61–8, 398–424).

At the end of the initial terrible exposition of future events we find a *sententia* from the narrator concerning the fates (*De Raptu* 57–60):

> Compellunt audere uirum fata, impia fata,
> Quae flecti quandoque negant, quibus obuia nunquam
> Res quaecumque uenit, quis semita nulla tenetur
> Obuia dum ueniunt, quibus omnia clausa patescunt.

> The fates drive a man to be bold, impious fates
> which at any time refuse to be turned, whom nothing ever
> attacks, for whom no path is held fast
> when they attack, for whom everything shut opens up.

Though the above is very general, the *vir* could also be specifically understood as Paris whose actions are determined by those wretched *fata*, while he himself has no choice in the matter. The tone comes across as mockingly ironic. The lament about the power of the fates is demonstratively excessive, as it is in fact an invective against those who refuse to take the responsibility for their own actions. On the one hand, this is aimed at the guilt of Paris and Helen; on the other hand, it also ridicules the *Aeneid* in which the fates are a constant presence and the highest motivation of

---

[36] See also Simons (2005: 228); *contra*, Bretzigheimer (2010), who thinks that this is only one of three factors, the other two being the fates and the wrath of the gods.

pius Aeneas. To call them *impia* is a blunt jibe at both Vergil and pagan thought as a whole. Moreover, it reflects Christian ideology, since according to Augustine of Hippo, *De civ. D.* 5 there is no fate in the sense of a horoscope inscribed in the stars, only God's providence. The theologian also goes to great lengths defending its existence alongside free will. Furthermore, Augustine cites Cicero's reasoning against the Stoic belief in a fatalistic necessity which would cancel free will (which leads Cicero to deny *fata*). I suggest that Dracontius is trying to refute classical Roman mentality from within. Since the poem's action is set in a pagan world, he can point to the flaws of those convictions in a sophisticated manner.

First and foremost, Dracontius represents the traditional deities as base, implicitly opposing them with the true God of the New Testament. In lines 37–9, though briefly, Minerva is painted as a revengeful character who is going to make Paris pay for judging her a loser in the beauty contest. She and Jove are also said to be *ingrati* in response to the annual propitiations offered by Priam (80–2). Cassandra explains that Paris enraged 'the Thunderer' *cuius postponens Vulcani laudat amorem* ('whose love he disregarded and praised that of Vulcan': 168). Here *amor* may refer to both Juno as Jupiter's wife and Minerva as his daughter, as indeed the two are mentioned together two verses before. Like Helenus before her, Cassandra foresees Troy's grim future, but unlike Helenus who gives up his prophetic speech because he accepts that the *fata* and *fortuna* are fixed and that there is nothing to be done (*De Raptu* 131–33) she actually rails against them.

She insistently tries to persuade her parents and brothers to kill Paris. This is of course a continuation of the myth of Paris' birth and childhood also mentioned within the poem (*De Raptu* 95–102, 122): Priam and Hecuba received the omen that Paris will grow up to become a torch that burns down the city, and according to other sources they were advised by seers to murder him as a baby, but he was exposed instead. We are not told what exactly happened in Dracontius' version, but it is safe to assume that the two had no heart to kill the boy, since their kindness and love towards him is evidenced by their affectionate behaviour (*De Raptu* 104–15): they blush, embarrassed about their former deed, and cry tears of joy and kiss him eagerly. However, this human reaction also reveals the inconsistency of their decisions. They are too good-natured to take radical steps, but also foolish enough to think that there will be no consequences. Thus Cassandra, despite her vicious demand and the harshness with which she blames her parents, is actually the only sensible one, trusting that the *fata* can be turned around. Unfortunately, the family's reaction to her chants is not revealed, but it is quite possible that Cassandra would have eventually persuaded them, were it not for an Apollo *ex machina* appearing at that very moment to give the fates a helping hand.

Apollo and Cassandra have a history that perhaps also plays a role here. She traditionally refused the god's sexual advances, whereupon he cursed her to the effect that nobody would believe her true prophecies.[37] Whether or not Dracontius had in mind those previous events, Apollo here goes so far as to prevent the Trojans from listening to Cassandra in person. Before he begins his speech, we are informed that he has come with an evil intent. The memory of the wall building is evoked, which was the cause of the first sack of Troy (*De Raptu* 184–7). Priam's father Laomedon had promised to reward Apollo and Poseidon for encircling the city with a wall, but later denied them their rightful reward. Traditionally Apollo then sent a plague and Poseidon a sea monster. Nevertheless, Apollo still seeks to take revenge on Laomedon's descendants. This malice, so unlike the Christian God's mercifulness, was meant by Dracontius to arouse contempt for the pagan idol.

Thymbraean Apollo directly denies the statements of the priests by adducing the argument that the fates ordered by the gods do not allow Paris to be expelled (*De Raptu* 190–2). Simons has rightly remarked that the fates are used as part of a manipulative rhetoric.[38] They are of course the ultimate explanation for everything, and consequently defy any form of disagreement. However, judging from the untrustworthiness of the divinity, we are led to understand this as a trick. While Apollo claims that Paris' destiny has already been immovably decided, in reality it is nothing other than the god's very words that produce this destiny as he speaks. Since he also predicts a state of perpetual bliss after an episode of hardship – though this part is elegantly passed by – the fates can be said to function as a kind of *Opium des Volkes*.

Lines 193–9 are most sensational. The promise of a never-ending rule for the Trojan race by decree of Jove echoes the passage in Book 1 of the *Aeneid* in which the highest god communicates to Venus the fate of her son. Line 198 (*fata manent*) appears to derive from *Aen.* 1.257–8. Tellingly, the wording of 199, *imperium sine fine dabit*, is identical with *Aen.* 1.279 (*imperium sine fine dedi*), and it is therefore put in quotation marks by editors to signal that Apollo here cites exactly what was foretold. Just as Vergil had used the benefit of hindsight to make prophecies in his epic match already historical facts (and well-established fiction),

---

[37] Apollod. *Bibl.* 3.12.5.   [38] Simons (2005: 290–9).

Dracontius uses the same technique to cancel their validity. While Jupiter's promise would have been true for Vergil's times and Augustus' Golden Age, Dracontius already knows that it has turned out to be false. Thus, by repeating the same prophecy despite the awareness of Rome's doom, he completely reverses the message and exposes Apollo, the very patron god of Augustus, as a shameless liar, again in contrast with the omniscient God of Christendom.

Another way in which the *De Raptu* antagonises the *Aeneid* is through the polarity of their male protagonists. Simons has drawn attention to the fact that Paris is an anti-Aeneas. Traditionally, there is a notable familial tie between the two characters, as they are both second cousins and brothers-in-law.[39] Dracontius tellingly also involves Aeneas in his narrative as one of Paris' companions on his journey, which becomes a kind of distorted prototype of the Aeneiadic voyage.[40] The figure of Aeneas has, in my opinion, a symbolic, or even metaliterary, function within the poem. He has been chosen by Priam to go with Paris for his divine descent and good reputation (*De Raptu* 238–41). In his few appearances he shows himself to be quite the type of pious hero we know from Vergil: he converses with Ajax (*De Raptu* 364–5) and praises his war prowess in the farewell address to Telamon, the only speech he delivers (*De Raptu* 372–8). Of course, this is an ironic detail, given that the same Ajax is later to destroy his city, but it also furthers the disparity between Aeneas and Paris: the former tries to maintain friendly terms, which are subsequently thwarted by the latter's folly. Aeneas wishes the family well and, as we might expect from his famous care for multiple generations, he speaks of a happy old age for Telamon and a blooming youth for Ajax. Paris then presents a stark contrast, since his actions are to rend the family bliss.

And sure enough, once Aeneas' good influence is removed from the scene through the shipwreck, Paris is free to wreak havoc and he seduces Helen. Parallels have been drawn between the meeting scene of Paris and Helen and that of Aeneas and Dido in Vergil.[41] However, this only alerts us further to how different the outcomes are: with Aeneas, reason ulti-mately wins over passion, but the opposite is true of Paris. The two heroes reflect unfavourably on each other: it is easy to see that on the one hand Paris' negative characterisation is to a large extent based on his role as a

---

[39] Their common great-grandfather is Ilus, and Aeneas' wife Creusa is commonly known as Paris' sister (cf. Ps.-Apollod. *Bibl.* 3.12.5 and Hyg. *Fab.* 90).

[40] Interestingly, in Dares Phrygius 44, when Aeneas escapes from Troy he takes the 22 ships which Paris used to sail to Greece.

[41] Edwards (2004: 155) and Wasyl (2011: 83–4).

counterpart to Aeneas. On the other hand, this does not make Aeneas better, but rather taints his image, since he is part of a clan of Trojans who are all adulterers and cheaters. In fact, Aeneidic characters hostile to Aeneas refer to him as another Paris.[42] This undermines the very foundation of the *Aeneid* and Roman founding myth: in the new Christian era the descendants of the lustful, egoistic Phrygians do not deserve to rule the world, but to meet a ruinous end – which they indeed did with the Vandal invasions.

10.3   Conclusions

Apart from date, genre, and title, the two *Abduction* poems have very little in common: Colluthus polishes up an old tradition which had almost certainly been lost and continues it into his own age, but adds the novel perspective of little Hermione, which is a product of Christian influence. Meanwhile, Dracontius' epyllion rails against both established mythology and the pagan worldview in which it is set and covertly disseminates Christian attitudes. This corroborates the finding made elsewhere that later Greek poetry is more conservative compared to its somewhat experimental Latin counterparts.[43] Whereas the *Harpage* makes no references to the Trojan War as such (although it is demonstrably designed as a prequel to the *Iliad*), the *De Raptu* is all-encompassing, and its judgemental narrator constantly shows awareness of the events before and after his *fabula*, as well as his relationship with past epicists. Despite their vastly different renditions of the same material, each of the two works reflects the time and the society in which it was written. An important common factor in the two texts is the application of Christian standards of morality and faith to pagan myth, albeit with different results.

Both poets also seem to presuppose educated audiences, able to appreciate subtleties and to supplement their reading of these texts with a good knowledge of classical lore. Colluthus' appropriation of a classical storyline aligns him with distant literary predecessors. He generally harmonises his narrative and characters with the dominant mythical tradition, so that the resulting poem easily 'slots in' alongside well-known mythology. The reinvention of Hermione, however, gives it a fresh nuance. This previously neglected facet of Greek legend makes for exciting subject matter, reflects

---

[42] King Iarbas, one of Dido's spurned suitors, voices this as an insult at *Aen.* 4.215, and Juno compares the two as she summons the Fury Allecto at *Aen.* 7.321.
[43] See Maciver in this volume (Chapter 3).

an interest in the emotions of children, and offers plenty of scope for showing off learnedness through intertextual parallels. Colluthus thus casts Greek *paideia* in a distinctly late-antique mould. Meanwhile, Dracontius uses the story to the opposite end: the African explicitly disassociates himself from Rome in favour of his own cultural and religious identity. Old, mistaken concepts are completely uprooted and replaced by new, enlightened ones. In sum, Colluthus' treatment of the abduction hints at his ambition to join the literary canon and steer it gently in a new direction. In contrast, Dracontius' tactic is to infiltrate the epic establishment and overthrow it by exposing its flaws.

CHAPTER 11

Objects of the Lusting Gaze
Viewing Women as Works of Art in Late Antique Poetry

A. Sophie Schoess

> Quas inter Cereris proles, nunc gloria matris,
> mox dolor, aequali tendit per gramina passu
> nec membris nec honore minor potuitque videri
> Pallas, si clipeum ferret, si spicula, Phoebe.

> Between the two, Ceres' child, now her mother's pride, so soon to
> be her sorrow, treads the grass with equal pace, no less than they in
> stature and majesty; Pallas you may think her, were she carrying a
> shield, Diana, if arrows.
>> Claudian, *De Raptu Proserpinae* 2.36–9.[1]

Claudian's description of the young Proserpina is in many ways evocative
of descriptions of literary characters from earlier poetry.[2] Throughout
Greco-Roman epic, young women are likened to goddesses to emphasise
their outstanding beauty,[3] just as stout fighters preparing for and entering
battle are compared to fierce Ares/Mars to underscore their virile strength.[4]
The divine comparison affords the poet the opportunity to create an epic
scene, stressing the almost divine character of his heroic protagonist. The
emphasis of such comparisons is on character traits or physical attributes
that mark the figure not only as a hero or heroine, but also as a being

---

[1] The Latin text follows Hall (1969); the translation is adapted from Platnauer (1922). I wish to thank
Berenice Verhelst and Tine Scheijnen for organising a stimulating workshop and the audience for
their helpful questions and comments.
[2] Claudian's *De Raptu Proserpinae* is dated to between 395 and 397 CE, shortly after his move from his
native Alexandria to Italy; see Hall (1969: 92–111) on the context and sources of the *De Raptu
Proserpinae*.
[3] E.g. Hom. *Il.* 19.282 on Briseis, *Od.* 6.145–61 on Nausicaa, and *Od.* 17.37 on Penelope. Compare
Hymn. Hom. Ven. 93–8 and Verg. *Aen.* 1.325–34, discussed below (Section 11.1). Compare also the
emphasis on Helen's divine heritage e.g. *Il.* 3.418 (Διὸς ἐκγεγαυῖα) and 3.426 (κούρη Διὸς
αἰγιόχοιο).
[4] E.g. *Il.* 2.477–9 on Agamemnon, 11.292–5 on Hector, and 11.602–4 on Patroclus. This epic
tradition continues throughout Late Antiquity. Quintus Smyrnaeus' *Posthomerica*, for instance,
features many such comparisons e.g. 1.18–19 and 1.190–1 on Penthesileia, 2.212–13 on
Memnon, and 7.98–100 on Eurypylus.

beyond human measure.[5] They are not, however, intended to highlight the attributes the figure lacks in comparison with the divinity, nor the difference between man and god, but rather the difference between hero and mere mortal. It is in this respect that Claudian's description is strikingly different.

Proserpina is a goddess in her own right, but in the lines cited above she is defined entirely in terms of those attributes, those powers, she does not possess, Minerva's shield, symbolic of her dominion over war, and Diana's arrows, symbolic of her dominion over the hunt. Her divine appearance, in turn, is validated through its comparison with that of two other virginal goddesses.[6] The reader might expect Proserpina's beauty to be self-evident precisely because of her status as a young, virginal goddess. Why, then, should Claudian choose such a manner of description? The answer to this question lies, I argue, in a growing fascination and engagement with visual culture in the literature and in the rhetorical schools of Late Antiquity.[7] While such overtly artistic comparisons go back at least as far as two instances in Ovid's *Metamorphoses*,[8] it is in the works of late antique authors such as Claudian, Nonnus, and Colluthus that they gain additional literary and cultural meaning. A period that saw the rise of Christianity and was shaped by the cultural changes resulting from it, Late Antiquity witnessed many and varied responses to the pagan culture of Classical Antiquity, especially to its artistic and architectural heritage.[9] Laws recorded in the *Codex Theodosianus*, a compilation of laws established

---

[5] Comparisons with works of art have a similar effect e.g. *Od.* 6.229–37 and *Aen.* 1.588–93. On these and similar passages, see Lovatt (2013: 273–83).

[6] Compare Stat. *Achil.* 1.293–300, where Deidamia's beauty is compared to that of Venus and Diana, as well as to Minerva's, should only that goddess set aside her powerful attributes, *si pectoris angues | ponat … exempta…casside.*

[7] See e.g. Roberts (1989: 66–121); cf. Elsner (2002).

[8] Ov. *Met.* 1.694–8 and 10.515–18. Here, Ovid's comparison, while similar in form to Claudian's, still performs the classical function of highlighting the figures' beauty, marking them as superior beings. Unlike Claudian's Proserpina, Ovid's Syrinx does not lack her own attribute, but the attribute differs only in certain details from Artemis', causing actual confusion regarding her identity. Ovid here playfully introduces the idea that while attributes can be defining features in the visual arts, they are not necessarily restricted to one figure. Similarly, the nudity of the newborn Adonis is seen as mirroring that of little cupids in the visual arts. As in Syrinx' case, the artistic comparison is designed to underscore the beauty of Adonis by drawing a direct link to a specific type of depiction. Ovid's comparison may be seen as more playful than Claudian's, highlighting the difficulty of accurately visualising literary figures and of accurately identifying visual ones. On the influence of Ovid's works on late antique writers, see e.g. Carvounis and Papaioannou (Chapter 1) and Hardie (Chapter 12) in this volume.

[9] See e.g. Agosti (2014: 163–4, with bibliography) on Nonn. *Dion.* 48.689–98. See also n. 12 below.

under Christian emperors,[10] for instance, sought to preserve ancient temples and statues as works of art, cleansed of their religious – their pagan – associations.[11] In this process, statues were to be stripped of their original religious reference, in order that they might be appreciated as beautiful objects *per se*,[12] iconographically recast to delight the viewer. The literary comparisons studied here follow a pattern similar to this Christian treatment of statues, stripping the images of their attributes and recasting them as reminders of an ancient beauty.

In what follows, I examine as case studies three such descriptions in order to explore their function and meaning within their narrative context. In each, I explore poetic references to the visual arts, drawing attention to the types of artwork highlighted, and draw connections between these late antique descriptions and comparisons and those found in earlier Greek and Latin literature. The discussion will show that while such comparisons are in many ways grounded in earlier literary traditions, they differ from these in their cultural signification and in their effect. I argue that the use of this form of comparison, that of literary characters to works of art, is restricted to very specific scenes in Late Antiquity, scenes designed not only to objectify but also to present the characters in their most vulnerable state.

11.1   Objectifying Goddesses

In the passage cited above, Claudian's comparison of Proserpina to her companions, Minerva and Diana, is markedly visual. The reader is tasked not only with picturing a young woman of divine stature, but also with conjuring up a specific visual *type*. The Diana and Minerva invoked by Claudian are not simply beautiful virginal goddesses, but qualified images

---

[10] Though the *Codex Theodosianus* was first published in 438 CE, it contains laws dating back as far as 312 CE.

[11] On the treatment of pagan statues, see e.g. *Cod. Theod.* 16.10.19: *[s]imulacra, . . . quae alicubi ritum vel acceperunt vel accipiunt paganorum, suis sedibus evellantur . . .* ('The images, . . . which either have received or still receive religious observance by the pagans, have to be torn out of their seats/ removed from their seats.'). The temples, in turn, were to be appropriated for public uses (*Cod. Theod.* 16.10.19); see e.g. *Cod. Theod.* 16.10.15: *sicut sacrificia prohibemus, ita volumus publicorum operum ornamenta servari* ('Though we forbid sacrifices [to pagan gods], we still wish to save the decorations of the public structures.'); *Cod. Theod.* 16.10.8: *. . . artis pretio quam divinitate metienda.* In *Contra Symmachum* 1, Prudentius relates to some of these laws, e.g. *C. Symm.* 1.502–5; cf. *Cod. Theod.* 16.10.8. Compare the practice of melting down classical sculpture for practical usage as wistfully described in e.g. *Anthologia Palatina* 9.773.

[12] Compare, for instance, the ambiguity inherent in the representations of Saint Hippolytus, whose sufferings closely resemble those of his classical namesake (Prudentius, *Peristephanon* 11); see O'Hogan (2016: 133–64) and Hershkowitz (2017: 205–13).

of them, works of art characterised by their visual attributes, Diana by her arrows and Minerva by her shield.[13] The comparison is neither generic nor purely literary, but specific and visually meaningful. Both goddesses exercise authority over a number of domains, and their specific roles in literary scenes are expressed through the use of epithets, or else are to be inferred from the narrative context. Their quintessential attributes in Greco-Roman art, Minerva/Athena's helmet, shield, spear, and aegis and Diana/Artemis' quiver and bow, fulfil a similar function, symbolising the various roles the goddesses hold. The image of an armed female figure, especially one whose breastplate depicts the Gorgon, is easily identified as Minerva/Athena, irrespective of the presence or absence of labels, just as the epithet γλαυκῶπις is sufficient for the reader to identify the character as Athena, whether or not her name is actually mentioned. Epithets and visual attributes do at times agree, as, for instance, in the case of Artemis' epithet ἰοχέαιρα and her visual attributes of quiver and bow,[14] highlighting their importance in the creation of (divine) identities in literature and the visual arts.[15] Since their visual attributes are very much linked with the goddesses' roles, they are often essential elements of literary narratives as well. Athena/Minerva, for instance, is often seen arming herself for battle in epic narrative, allowing the poet to highlight her involvement in the fight and her relationships with the heroes she supports.[16] Likewise, we hear of Diana/Artemis' reaching for her arrows whenever the narrative demands it.[17]

Similarly, we encounter scenes of partial or complete undress, as in Callimachus' *Hymn to Athena* (*Hymn* 5) and in other treatments of the Actaeon myth.[18] In Colluthus' description of the wedding of Peleus and Thetis, too, Athena and Artemis, along with Ares, set aside their attributes (*Abduction of Helen* 32–9).[19] It is the narrative context here that demands such a change of dress and the removal of attributes. By shedding their armour and weapons, Colluthus' Ares, Athena, and Artemis divest themselves of clues vital to their visual identity; they become, much like Claudian's young Proserpina, visually equivocal. Colluthus here plays with

---

[13] The Latin *spicula* is better translated as 'arrows' than 'javelin', as Platnauer's translation has it, to reflect more accurately the visual depictions of Diana/Artemis invoked here.

[14] E.g. *Il.* 5.53, 21.480 and *Od.* 11.198.

[15] Some attributes and epithets are, of course, not unique to individual figures. In such cases, further details are required for disambiguation; see n. 8 above.

[16] E.g. *Il.* 5.733–47; cf. Lissarrague (1989: 45–8).   [17] E.g. *Met.* 3.188.

[18] See e.g. Platt (2002: 99–100) and Liveley (2010: 46).

[19] Colluthus, from Lycopolis in the Egyptian Thebaid, flourished under Anastasius I (491–518 CE); see Cadau (2015: 5–35) for a detailed discussion of Colluthus' life, work, and context.

the reader-cum-viewer's expectations as he initially invokes the images of the fully-armed Athena and Ares and of the wild huntress Artemis, but subsequently strips them of their defining attributes. Rather than maintaining visual prominence as individual gods, they become iconographically meaningful as part of the wedding procession and celebration. Depictions of this wedding, as for instance on the François Vase (ca. 570–560 BCE), typically show the gods with their usual attributes, enabling the viewer to identify the individuals within a large group of figures.[20] Colluthus plays with this idea of a visual aid for the viewer as he reminds his readers of the attributes his characters choose to doff for the occasion. At the same time, however, he suggests that his presentation is in a way more realistic than that of the visual artist; his gods dress in ways evocative of real characters rather than of stock figures.

Claudian, too, plays with the donning and doffing of Minerva's armour and with the adjustment of Diana's attributes (*D.R.P.* 2.141–50 and 2.205–8). Though Minerva is first seen relinquishing her spear and adorning her helm with flowers as she joins Proserpina, she is later portrayed as seizing her arms in a vain attempt to defend Proserpina against her fated husband. Diana, too, takes up her bow and arrows in the fight against Pluto, she after having left her mountain hunt and joined in the flower gathering. Both goddesses doff and don their visual characteristics according to the narrative's demands. Their domains are defined and visualised through attributes that also perform narrative functions. In this, these two goddesses differ profoundly from the main protagonist of the poem, the young Proserpina. At this stage in her narrative, the goddess is still defined exclusively through her relationship with her mother; as Ceres' child, she is associated with harvest and agriculture, but her main role is that of the young, unmarried daughter. Iconographically, too, the young Proserpina/Persephone is rarely depicted in her own right, as her visual identification depends on her association with Ceres/Demeter. As a consequence of this lack of iconographic identity, the few free-standing statues of Proserpina/Persephone still extant today have been identified as such either without certainty, on the basis of votive inscriptions, or through comparison with known depictions of the goddess surrounded by other figures, as, for instance, in vase paintings or on reliefs.[21] By playing the visually ambiguous figure of Proserpina against the highly recognisable types of Minerva

---

[20] See Shapiro et al. (2013) for recent studies on the vase; cf. Morwood (1999) on the relationship between Catullus 64 and the François Vase.

[21] E.g. *LIMC* s.v. 'Persephone', numbers 1, 2, 4–6, 10–15, 18, 25–38.

and Diana, Claudian highlights the young Proserpina's lack of her own visual identity and of her own divine domain. He presents the reader with a young goddess who has assumed neither her unique place among the gods nor her distinctive iconography within the visual arts.

In many ways, this young Proserpina is similar to the young Dionysus in Nonnus' *Dionysiaca*, who, as Miguélez-Cavero shows, has yet to adopt his full visual array of attributes.[22] Both the *Dionysiaca* and the *De Raptu Proserpinae* tell the story of a young divinity's path to a destined station in the cosmos – Dionysus through his ascent to Olympus and Proserpina through her descent to the underworld.[23] The rape of Proserpina/ Persephone, epitomising her future struggle to balance her life on earth with that in the underworld, is a popular motif in Greco-Roman art, and it is the central narrative moment of Claudian's work.[24] While the focus of the abduction scene, both in the visual arts and in literature, is naturally on Pluto/Hades and Proserpina/Persephone, the figures surrounding them add narrative depth. In paintings, such as the one in the Tomb of Persephone at Vergina, her companions' preoccupation with gathering flowers highlights the innocence of the scene disrupted by Hades' appearance.[25] In the *De Raptu Proserpinae*, too, the events leading up to the rape are described in great detail, and great emphasis is placed on the peacefulness of the flower gathering, as exemplified in the disarming of Minerva and Diana (*D.R.P.* 2.56–150). Claudian's scene as a whole, then, corresponds quite well to known visual treatments, but his focus on Proserpina's figure highlights that her surroundings, in addition to being key to the literary narrative, are essential to her visual identity. The reader witnesses Proserpina's coming of age and her attempts to find a place in this world. Their knowledge of related motifs in the visual arts enables them to create a more vivid picture to follow the narrative train by linking it with a visual one.

Claudian offers almost whimsical insights into Proserpina's attempts to shape her own identity, an identity that is, unbeknownst to her, already fixed by Jupiter's decree (*D.R.P.* 1.216–19; cf. 2.4–8). After the abduction,

---

[22] Miguélez-Cavero (2009: 558–60).

[23] Interestingly, even in her role as queen of the underworld, Proserpina/Persephone is still frequently compared to other divinities or, as in Statius, linked to her mother by means of epithets such as *Iuno inferna | stygia* (e.g. *Aen.* 6.138 and Stat. *Theb.* 4.526–7, respectively) or *inferna | profunda Ceres* (*Theb.* 5.156 and 4.459–60, respectively); cf. Ζεύς καταχθόνιος as an epithet for Hades (e.g. *Il.* 9.457).

[24] *LIMC* s.v. 'Persephone', numbers 193–248.

[25] On the excavations of the royal tombs at Aigai in general and on the Tomb of Persephone in particular, see Andronikos (1984 and 1994).

the reader, alongside Ceres, learns from Proserpina's nurse that the young goddess had tried on Minerva's armour and Diana's dress for size before leaving to gather flowers (*D.R.P.* 3.216–19):

> nunc arma habitumque Dianae
> induitur digitisque attemptat mollibus arcum,
> nunc crinita iubis galeam laudante Minerva
> inplet et ingentem clipeum gestare laborat.

> Now she dons Diana's arms and dress and tries her bow with her soft fingers. Now crowned with horse-hair plumes she puts on the helmet, Minerva commending her, and endeavours to carry her huge shield.

Proserpina's attempts to match Minerva and Diana are presented as those of a younger sister playing dress-up with her older sisters' clothes. Her soft fingers are by no means suited to Diana's bow, and she struggles to lift Minerva's armour;[26] her innocent attempts, however, are endearing both to the reader and to the other goddesses. Proserpina is portrayed as identifying with the other two virgin goddesses and they as identifying with her,[27] as can be seen not only from their enjoying her play with their attributes, but also from their rush to arms to protect her virginity when Pluto threatens it (*D.R.P.* 2.204–8). In this moment, the importance of these visual attributes for Diana's and Minerva's roles as strong female figures ready to fight becomes apparent and the contrast with the vulnerable and unarmed Proserpina is highlighted. Yet, the reference to the visual arts is nowhere more pronounced than in Claudian's direct comparison of Proserpina to Minerva and Diana, with which this chapter began. The reader's imagination is stimulated by the many visual clues Claudian provides as they draw on a shared cultural framework and visual tradition to create their own images of the narrative.[28] Though these visual clues do not in themselves constitute ekphrases of works of art, they do create ekphrastic *enargeia* through their reliance on known visual representations, as the reader is able to transform these clues into coherent images based on known artistic types and compositions.[29]

---

[26] The motif of disorder in the divine domains being linked with an inappropriate distribution of attributes is explored both in Ovid (*Am.* 1.1.5–16) and in Nonnus (*Dion.* 24.279–91), though there in much more serious, even negative, contexts.

[27] Compare *Met.* 5.375–7.

[28] See e.g. Quint. *Inst.* 6.2.29–32, 8.3.64, and 8.3.71; cf. Webb (1999: 13–14).

[29] For extensive studies of visual culture, ekphrasis, and *enargeia*, see e.g. duBois (1982), Elsner (1995 and 1998), Benediktson (2000), Small (2003), Bartsch and Elsner (2007), Squire (2009), and Webb (2009).

These references to artistic representations, scattered throughout the poem, reflect a late antique interest in the visual arts and in the ways in which they express narrative and adapt classical material. While the references seem few and far between, their effect is nonetheless pronounced, as they function as appeals to the reader's visual knowledge, inviting them to engage with their surroundings and to connect their experiences of the same narrative in different media. The comparison of divine beauties, while obviously not new in poetry, is presented here with clear reference to the visual arts. Where earlier comparisons are designed to highlight a general sense of beauty, Claudian's comparison draws on a specific type of beauty, that of works of art. The reader's reception of the comparisons, too, is markedly different, as they are left to visualise their own idea of divine beauty in the former but are asked to draw on existing images in the latter.

Two examples, one from the *Homeric Hymn to Aphrodite* and one from the *Aeneid*, may help to illustrate this difference. In both poems, Aphrodite/Venus takes on mortal form to face a mortal man – Anchises in the hymn and Aeneas in the epic. The mortal, in turn, recognises the supernatural beauty and appears to feel the presence of a divinity, addressing the disguised goddess with reverential language. Both men attempt to identify the goddess and offer possible divine identities: Anchises suggests that she might be Artemis, Leto, Aphrodite, Themis, Athena, one of the Graces, or a nymph (*Hymn. Hom. Ven.* 93–8), while Aeneas wonders whether she might be Diana or a nymph (*Aen.* 1.325–34). These guesses could be misconstrued as flattery,[30] but the narrators' insistence that the men truly believe themselves to be facing a goddess discourages such a reading. The emphasis is on the divine beauty of the unfamiliar figure, and the list of possible identities serves only to provide a general framework; there is no attempt to identify Aphrodite/Venus based on her similarity to the other goddesses and no emphasis on elements that mark her out as being one or another. Aphrodite/Venus' beauty, her very presence, appears to overwhelm both men, whose words express pious awe, appealing to the divine spirit for protection and prosperity in return for offerings. Especially in the *Hymn to Aphrodite*, the reader is constantly reminded of the presence of the divinity and of their own role as worshipper, always cautious not to overstep boundaries of propriety, just as Anchises tries to balance his responses. It is important to note that Anchises' case is more

---

[30] Compare *Od.* 6.145–6 and *Dion.* 10.196–216; Lucian, *Essays in Portraiture Defended* 21–5. Compare below, n. 54.

complex than Aeneas', and that some aspects of his response to Aphrodite's presence do, in fact, foreshadow Claudian's treatment of Proserpina. Aphrodite's beauty is described as causing Anchises to feel both θαῦμα and ἔρος (*Hymn. Hom. Ven.* 90–1).[31] Aphrodite, of course, appears to Anchises for the sole purpose of seducing him, so it seems only appropriate for him to respond to her with a sense of longing; he does, nonetheless, temper his address to Aphrodite, recognising the problematic nature of desiring a goddess.[32] While Anchises' sexual experience of Aphrodite's divine beauty can be explained by the demands of its narrative context, it also sets a precedent for the kind of comparison we encountered in the passage from Claudian's *De Raptu Proserpinae*.

Indeed, in his treatment of the young Proserpina, Claudian proffers her as an object of the reader's gaze, a vulnerable creature, stripped of all power, as her lack of attributes underscores. Both her vulnerability and Pluto's lack of restraint in his response to her demonstrate how differently, in comparison with Aphrodite in the above passages, Proserpina is to be viewed by the reader. In a period when pagan statues and temples are coming to be stripped of their religious associations in order to be appreciated as purely aesthetic *objets d'art*,[33] Claudian presents his young goddess as visually meaningless beyond her appeal to the viewer's aesthetic sense. Claudian's reader joins Pluto in treating Proserpina as a beautiful object to be ravished; she is by no means presented as a goddess to be treated with respect or awe, analogously, perhaps, to how statues of pagan divinities are rendered profane under the Christian influence of Late Antiquity.

11.2 Objectifying Women

Though Claudian's objectifying description of Proserpina presents one of the most striking examples of the kind studied here, the most common subjects of such comparisons in Late Antiquity are not gods but mortal women. Nonnus' ekphrasis of the sleeping Ariadne offers a particularly

---

[31] Compare below (Section 11.2) on Dionysus' response to the sleeping Ariadne in Nonnus' *Dionysiaca.*

[32] Compare, for instance, Athena's reminder of Cronus' divine law regarding the protection of divine bodies from the uninvited gaze in Callimachus' *Hymn* 5.100–2.

[33] See the laws in *Cod. Theod.* cited above (n. 10).

rich example (*Dion.* 47.271–94), developing further the model previously
encountered in the works of Ovid and Claudian:[34]

Ὑπναλέην δέ
ἀθρήσας Διόνυσος ἐρημαίην Ἀριάδνην
θαύματι μῖξεν ἔρωτα· . . .
‘ . . .   ἐάσατε Κύπριν ἰαύειν·—
Ἀλλ’ οὐ κεστὸν ἔχει σημάντορα Κυπρογενείης.
Πείθομαι ὡς δολόεντι Χάρις νυμφεύεται Ὕπνῳ·
ἀλλ’ ἐπεὶ ὄρθρος ἔλαμψε καὶ ἐγγύθι φαίνεται Ἠώς,
Πασιθέην εὔδουσαν ἐγείρατε. Τίς παρὰ Νάξῳ,   280
τίς Χάριν ἐχλαίνωσεν ἀνείμονα;— Μὴ πέλεν Ἥβη;
ἀλλὰ δέπας μακάρων τίνι κάλλιπε;— Μὴ παρὰ πόντῳ
κέκλιται αἰγλήεσσα βοῶν ἐλάτειρα Σελήνη;
Καὶ πόθεν Ἐνδυμίωνος ἐθήμονος ἐκτὸς ἰαύει;—
Μὴ Θέτιν ἀργυρόπεζαν ἐπ’ αἰγιαλοῖσι δοκεύω;   285
Ἀλλ’ οὐ γυμνὸν ἔχει ῥοδόεν δέμας.— Εἰ θέμις εἰπεῖν,
Ναξιὰς Ἰοχέαιρα πόνων ἀμπαύεται ἄγρης,
θηροφόνους ἱδρῶτας ἀποσμήξασα θαλάσσῃ·
τίκτει γὰρ γλυκὺν ὕπνον ἀεὶ πόνος. Ἀλλ’ ἐνὶ λόχμῃ
Ἄρτεμιν ἑλκεχίτωνα τίς ἔδρακε;— Μίμνετε, Βάκχαι.   290
στῆθι, Μάρων· μὴ δεῦρο χορεύσατε· λῆγε λιγαίνων,
Πὰν φίλε, μὴ σκεδάσειας ἑῶιον ὕπνον Ἀθήνης.
Καὶ τίνι Παλλὰς ἔλειπεν ἑὸν δόρυ; Καὶ τίς ἀείρει
χαλκείην τρυφάλειαν ἢ αἰγίδα Τριτογενείης;’

When Dionysos beheld the deserted Ariadne sleeping, he mingled love with
wonder . . . : ' . . . Let Cypris sleep! – But she does not have the cestus, the
attribute (symbol) of the Cyprus-born. I believe it is the Grace who was
given in marriage to wily Hypnos. But since dawn is bright and morning
seems near, awaken sleeping Pasithea. But who has covered up the naked
Grace in Naxos, who? Is it Hebe? But to whom has she left the goblet of the
Blessed? Can this be Selene, that bright driver of cattle, lying on the
seashore? Then how can she be sleeping apart from her inseparable
Endymion? Is it silverfoot Thetis I see on the strand? No, it is not naked,
that rosy form. If I may dare to say so, it is the Archeress resting here in
Naxos from her labours of the hunt, now she has wiped off in the sea the
sweat of hunting and slaying. For hard work always brings sweet sleep. But
who has seen Artemis in the woods in a long chiton? Stay, Bacchants; stand

---

[34] Egyptian by birth like Claudian and Colluthus, Nonnus was from the city of Panopolis. His
Dionysiaca, likely written in Claudian's birth-city of Alexandria, is dated to 450–70 CE; see
Accorinti (2016) for a detailed study of Nonnus' biography, including his familiarity with
Claudian's poetry. On the history of the question of whether Nonnus knew and engaged with
Latin works such as those of Ovid, see the Introduction to this volume, esp. n. 6, and Carvounis
and Pappaioannou (Chapter 1) in this volume.

still, Maron; dance not this way; stop singing, dear Pan, that you may not disturb the morning sleep of Athena. No – with whom did Pallas leave her spear? And who takes up the bronze helmet or aegis of Tritogeneia?'[35]

Here, Dionysus encounters the sleeping Ariadne for the first time, as yet unable to recognise her figure. That Dionysus does not recognise Ariadne here, especially while accompanied by Eros, jars with the preceding narrative; Eros had already promised Ariadne to Dionysus as consolation for a lost contest with Poseidon (*Dion.* 43.422–36). Dionysus' apparent forgetfulness does not serve a narrative purpose but rather disrupts the narrative flow. It does, however, offer the narrator the opportunity to create a detailed image of the sleeping beauty, allowing the reader's gaze to linger on Ariadne's body, before resuming the narrative thread.[36] Similar to the viewer of a solitary statue, Nonnus' Dionysus here attempts to identify the sleeping figure, taking in every detail and allowing his gaze to linger on her body. Much as in Claudian, Dionysus' analysis of the unknown figure here depends on his knowledge of different visual types, marked by their attributes.[37] Unlike Claudian's Proserpina, however, Nonnus' Ariadne is not presented as a familiar figure who might be mistaken for another were it not for a lack of attributes,[38] but rather as an unfamiliar one whose actual identity depends on the recognition of relevant attributes. Yet, Ariadne's visual identity is closely linked with her narrative – for instance, with her role in Theseus' fight with the Minotaur and her abandonment on Naxos. Visual representations of the heroine therefore require the presence of other figures to act as narrative attributes necessary for the decoding of the scene, just as the young Proserpina/Persephone needs to be accompanied by Ceres/Demeter and her older self by Pluto/Hades to be recognised. Nonnus' Dionysus here fails to see what the reader knows from the very beginning, that his presence offers the visual clue required to understand the scene and therefore to identify Ariadne.[39] The poet plays with his reader's familiarity with the visual type to enable them to visualise

---

[35] The Greek text quoted throughout this chapter follows the *Belles Lettres* editions (Chuvin 1992 and Vian 2003); the translation is adapted from Rouse (1940).

[36] See Verhelst (2017: 253–62) for further discussion.

[37] Compare Panofsky's detailed analysis of iconological approaches to images (Panofsky 1939: 3–31). On the art historical aspects of this episode, see e.g. Shorrock (2014: 318–22).

[38] Compare this also to the Ovidian examples (*Met.* 1.694–8 and 10.515–18), and see above n. 8. In its emphasis on the figure's novelty, Nonnus' treatment of Ariadne resembles much more closely that of Colluthus' presentation of Paris (*Abduction of Helen* 251–67) discussed below (Section 11.3).

[39] See Haskell and Penny (1981: 184–7) on the process of identifying the statue of the sleeping Ariadne in the Vatican. See McNally (1985) on the visual history of Ariadne's abandonment; compare Elsner (2007a).

the scene, but he then refocusses the internal and external audiences' attention on the sleeping figure alone, stripping her of her attributes and reducing her to a solitary work of art, an object of Dionysus' and, by extension, the reader's lusting gaze.

As known visual types of beautiful goddesses and nymphs are invoked in Dionysus' study of Ariadne's sleeping figure, their common beauty and their appeal to the male viewer are emphasised as they are stripped of their defining features. Ariadne, in turn, is characterised by her explicit lack of attributes, connecting her to the other figures through beauty and sexual allure alone. Moreover, not only are typical attributes, such as Athena's spear and helmet, invoked here, but emphasis is put on Ariadne's attire and on the question of the kind and amount of clothing appropriate to each divinity listed. Artemis is characterised not by her quiver and bow, but by the length of her dress, while Pasithea and Thetis are reduced to their naked bodies, their identities otherwise dependent on context. As the viewer's gaze lingers on Ariadne's body, she is slowly stripped of her clothing, not in fact by the figures in the narrative, but visually in the imagination of the reader as they draw on known visual types of nymphs, graces, and goddesses in various states of *déshabillé*. That the reading of Ariadne's body is to be highly sexualised can already be seen from Dionysus' first possible identification, Aphrodite. The naked form of the goddess of love is a favoured motif in Greco-Roman art, enticing the viewer with erotic lure and sensuality.[40] By invoking such images, Nonnus ensures that Ariadne's body is presented to the reader's gaze as an erotic object, enabling them to create their own image of the scene and to relate to Dionysus' desire, his feelings of θαῦμα and ἔρος.[41] That Ariadne is viewed without inhibition, but rather with a burning desire, already subjects her to the reader's unconstrained gaze; that she is treated like an *objet d'art* only underscores this objectification of her figure.

It is worth exploring further the literary tradition behind these explicit comparisons of women with works of art. Much like the comparisons with divinities, comparisons with works of art are often introduced in order to highlight a woman's beauty, especially the whiteness of her skin or the flawlessness of her features.[42] Ovid's Perseus, for instance, is so taken with the quiet beauty of Andromeda and overwhelmed by a sense of θαῦμα that

---

[40] Praxitiles' Aphrodite of Knidos especially is famed for its effect on viewers; see e.g. Plin. *HN* 36.20; Pseudo-Lucian, *Amores* 11–16. For modern studies, see e.g. Kraus (1957) and Havelock (1995).
[41] On Nonnus' use of θαῦμα and ἔρος here, see Shorrock (2014: 318–22).
[42] Cf. Lovatt (2013: 277–8).

he initially mistakes her for a statue, a *marmoreum opus* that almost causes him to forget to beat his wings mid-flight (*Met.* 4.672–7). Andromeda is literally being objectified in this moment, as Ovid immortalises her statuesque pose and Perseus' confused response in his poetry. As Elsner has shown, the figure of Andromeda chained to the rock is tremendously popular in Greco-Roman art; indeed, some Campanian wall paintings even depict her in such a way as to suggest to the viewer that she is really a statue.[43] Ovid's Andromeda is the object of Perseus' and, by extension, the reader's gaze, while simultaneously negotiating through her tears her personhood against this objectifying gaze. Nonnus' Ariadne similarly regains her personhood upon waking by taking on her literary attribute, her lament (*Dion.* 47.295–418),[44] while Claudian's Proserpina is afforded no such opportunity; her identity continues to be negotiated by others.

What the women and goddesses compared to works of art have in common, then, is that they are exploited by the male gaze and are objectified like works of art. While the works of art evoked in the comparisons vary, the women are all framed in the same way, as the type of the beautiful young girl whose purpose it is to please a male onlooker. Their fates, their stories, are driven by male characters and, at the moment of objectification, the women seem almost interchangeable. Their lack of defining attributes visually characterises them as the kind of woman who is inevitably targeted and raped in classical myth. Nonnus makes this clear in his description of Zeus' first encounter with Semele (*Dion.* 7.205–9):

Καὶ Σεμέλην ὁρόων ἀνεπάλλετο, μὴ σχεδὸν ὄχθης
Εὐρώπην ἐνόησε τὸ δεύτερον· ἐν κραδίῃ δέ
κάμνε πάλιν Φοίνικα φέρων πόθον· ἀγλαΐης γάρ
τῆς αὐτῆς τύπον εἶχεν, ἀεὶ δέ οἱ ἀμφὶ προσώπῳ
πατροκασιγνήτης ἀμαρύσσετο σύγγονος αἴγλη.

At the sight of Semele, he leapt up, in wonder if it were Europa whom he saw on that bank a second time, his heart was troubled as if he felt again his Phoenician passion; for she was of the same beautifully shaped type, and on her face gleamed the inborn brightness she shared with her father's sister.

Semele is compared to Europa, Zeus' past lover, with an emphasis both on her beauty and on Zeus' almost violent physical response to it. The two women share an outstanding beauty and an innocence that marks them as potential victims of Zeus' lust, but on their own they are

---

[43] Elsner (2007b: 3–11).
[44] On Ariadne's lament in the *Dionysiaca*, see e.g. Shorrock (2014: 322–8) and Verhelst (2017: 256).

indistinguishable.[45] Visually, they depend on the full depiction of their rape narratives, including Zeus in his distinct disguises. Late antique poets explore these motifs of innocence and vulnerability, and add to the physical violation of the girls an act of visual violation committed not only by the literary characters but also by the readers themselves. The intrusion in such a scene of a Peeping Tom, an internal viewer directing the external viewer's gaze and making them conscious of their own act of voyeurism, is linked directly to the visual arts, where it is a common motif in Greco-Roman antiquity.[46]

11.3 Objectifying Men

Thus far, the discussion has focussed on female objects of the male gaze, in large part because the female body is more frequently and straightforwardly objectified in ancient art and literature. In his *Abduction of Helen*, however, Colluthus describes Helen's first encounter with Paris in striking terms, presenting him as the object of her desiring gaze.[47] Helen is seen marvelling at the beauty of the stranger, wondering whether he might be Eros or Dionysus before dismissing both possibilities, as Paris lacks their traditional attributes, the quiver and vine, respectively (*Abduction* 251–67):

οὐ Διὶ τοῖον ἔτικτεν ἐπήρατον υἶα Θυώνη·
ἱλήκοις, Διόνυσε· καὶ εἰ Διός ἐσσι γενέθλης,
καλὸς ἔην καὶ κεῖνος ἐπ' ἀγλαΐησι προσώπων.
ἡ δὲ φιλοξείνων θαλάμων κληῖδας ἀνεῖσα
ἐξαπίνης Ἑλένη μετεκίαθε δώματος αὐλήν   255
καὶ θαλερῶν προπάροιθεν ὀπιπεύουσα θυράων
ὡς ἴδεν, ὡς ἐκάλεσσε καὶ ἐς μυχὸν ἤγαγεν οἴκου
καὶ μιν ἐφεδρήσσειν νεοπηγέος ὑψόθεν ἕρδης
ἀργυρέης ἐπέτελλε· κόρον δ' οὐκ εἶχεν ὀπωπῆς·
ἄλλοτε δὴ χρύσειον ὀισαμένη Κυθερείης   260
κοῦρον ὀπιπεύειν θαλαμηπόλον – ὀψὲ δ' ἀνέγνω,
ὡς οὐκ ἔστιν Ἔρως· βελέων δ' οὐκ εἶδε φαρέτρην –

---

[45] Compare Moschus' treatment of Europa's basket, which depicts her ancestor Io's rape, foreshadowing her own (*Europa* 37–62).

[46] On Pentheus and Acteon as Peeping Toms in art, in literature, and on stage, see Gregory (1985) and Platt (2002), respectively; cf. Bal (1991: 156–71) and Squire (2011a: 75–114). On the integration of the viewer into the scene, see Zanker (2004: 103–23); cf. Elsner (2007a) on the directing gaze.

[47] Another striking example is Nonnus' treatment of Ampelus (*Dion.* 10.175–11.351, especially 10.196–216), though Ampelus is here the object of the male, not the female, gaze; see e.g. Verhelst (2017). For a detailed analysis of the Ampelus episode, see Kröll (2016). On the visuality of Colluthus' work, see Cadau (2015: 135–221).

πολλάκι δ᾽ ἀγλαΐῃσιν ἐϋγλήνοισι προσώπων
παπταίνειν ἐδόκευε τὸν ἡμερίδων βασιλῆα·
ἀλλ᾽ οὐχ ἡμερίδων θαλερὴν ἐδόκευεν ὀπώρην   265
πεπταμένην χαρίεντος ἐπὶ ξυνοχῇσι καρήνου.
ὀψὲ δὲ θαμβήσασα τόσην ἀνενείκατο φωνήν·

Not so fair was the lovely son whom Thyone bore to Zeus: forgive me,
Dionysus! even if you are an offspring of Zeus, he, too, was beautiful and his
face charming. And Helen unbarred the bolts of her hospitable chamber and
suddenly went to the court of the house, and, looking in front of the goodly
doors, as soon as she saw him, she called him and led him inside the house,
and bade him sit on a newly-wrought chair of silver. And she could not
satisfy her eyes with gazing, now thinking she was seeing the golden youth
that attends Cythereia – and late she recognised that it was not Eros; she saw
no quiver of arrows – and often in the beauty of his face and his bright eyes
she looked to see the king of the vine: but no blooming fruit of the vine did
she behold spread upon the meeting of his gracious brows. And after a long
time, amazed, she uttered her voice and said: . . .[48]

Colluthus introduces his scene by comparing Paris' beauty to that of
Dionysus, stressing that the Trojan prince's surpasses that of the god.[49]
He then describes Helen's response to Paris, which echoes his earlier
description. Helen, much like her male counterparts in the passages
discussed above, marvels at the figure of Paris, gazing at him unceasingly
and uninhibitedly. Colluthus offers the reader an insight into Helen's
mind, into her process of iconographic analysis, just as Nonnus relates
Dionysus' attempt at identifying Ariadne. Paris on his own, much like
Proserpina/Persephone or Ariadne, is a visually ambiguous figure; the few
free-standing statues and statuettes of Paris listed in the *Lexicon
Iconographicum Mythologiae Classicae* are identified only tentatively, as his
most prominent attribute, the Phrygian cap, is also worn by other figures,
such as Ganymede and Ascanius.[50] Paris' most prominent visual moment,
his most easily recognisable portrayal, is his Judgement,[51] a scene which

---

[48] The Greek text follows Mair's edition; the translation is adapted from the same (Mair 1928).
[49] See Cadau (2015: 188–91) and Paschalis (2008: 141). We find strikingly similar language in the
chorus' description of Hippolytus in Seneca, *Phaedra* 753–7. It is worth noting that, as with
Artemis, Athena, and Aphrodite for women, Eros, Apollo, and Dionysus are the most commonly
offered figures of comparison for men in this context. The three youthful and somewhat effeminate
gods are drawn on for expressions of male beauty, where Ares provides a *comparandum* for
warlike masculinity.
[50] *LIMC* s.v. 'Alexandros', 1–4.
[51] The *Iudicum Paridis* is so prominent in the visual arts of Classical Antiquity that it has a separate
entry in *LIMC*.

requires the presence of other characters to convey meaning, much as Ariadne's abandonment or Persephone's rape does.[52]

Colluthus' Paris, then, while striking in his beauty, is visually ambiguous, just like the female figures discussed above. Though the reader is aware of the stranger's identity, Helen has nothing but his appearance to go on in her visual analysis of Paris' figure. She must gather visual clues in order to arrive at that same point, for, unlike the audience, she cannot see that her presence offers a vital visual clue to Paris' identity.[53] Interestingly, Helen's address to Paris, while following the general paradigm introduced by the narrator, does not propose any divine identities; instead, she lists famous Argive men and dismisses them on the basis that she knows their appearances (*Abduction* 268–77). Though we learn from Colluthus that Helen at first considers Paris a divinity, she does not pursue this line further, unlike Aeneas, Anchises, or even Odysseus.[54] Paris' lack of attributes marks him as a mortal rather than immortal figure in the visual arts, and his mortal figure cannot easily be disambiguated from others. Much like Ariadne or Europa, Paris fits a generic type, that of the beautiful young man; he is a generic object to be desired or admired, a figure without narrative meaning *per se*.

In this passage, Helen takes on the role of the desirous viewer, treating Paris as an object, one to be gazed at, perhaps even to be used, for its beauty.[55] Such a reversal of generic gender roles may easily be explained by Paris' lack of masculine virtues, as is evident both in literature and in the visual arts. Paris cannot be compared to Hector or Achilles, as his primary role is very much that of the lover,[56] a role which, as Miguélez-Cavero has shown, can break even Ares, the paragon of masculinity.[57] Paris cannot be held to the same standards as other male figures; he allows himself to be subdued by women and by Aphrodite. Though presented as an object of Helen's gaze and desire at their first meeting, Colluthus' Paris still does not take on quite the same role as Claudian's Proserpina or Nonnus' Ariadne, newly objectified in the eyes of their viewers. It is Paris, after all, whose

---

[52] See above in Sections 11.1 and 11.2.

[53] Compare Dionysus' failure to recognise himself as the visual clue to identifying the sleeping Ariadne and the importance of Pluto/Hades or Ceres/Demeter in identifying images of Proserpina/Persephone, discussed above (Sections 11.1 and 11.2). See Zanker (2004: 72–80) for a discussion of reader and viewer supplementation.

[54] *Hymn. Hom. Ven.* 93–8, *Aen.* 1.325–34, and *Od.* 6.145–61, respectively.

[55] See Cadau (2015: 185–6) on Helen's gaze; cf. Lovatt (2013: 205–61) for a detailed discussion of the female gaze in ancient epic. Cf. e.g. Eck (2001 and 2003). Compare *Met.* 10.15 in contrast with *Dion.* 10.196–216, as Adonis is set up as the object of desire for a female figure, Aphrodite, and Ampelus for a male figure, Dionysus.

[56] See e.g. *Il.* 3.38–75 and 6.313–41; cf. Lovatt (2013: 268–9).

[57] Miguélez-Cavero (2009: 370–2).

choices drive the fated narrative: it is his crowning Aphrodite the winner of the contest that leads him to Helen, and it is his abduction of Helen that causes the outbreak of the Trojan War. Neither Ariadne nor Europa, Andromeda nor Persephone has a similar agency in her fate; their status as beautiful objects leads male characters to drive the narrative forward instead. Paris' beauty, on the other hand, serves his own purpose; his effect on Helen is such that she abandons her home and follows him to Troy.

Paris is nonetheless objectified in a similar way, as are other male figures, such as Adonis or Ampelus; these youthful figures are each presented as the epitome of the handsome, though effeminate, young man, a visual type to be enjoyed by the viewer. While the literary device, the visual comparison, is thus applied to both men and women, the ways in which it is employed in the narrative are subject to social conventions. The reader-cum-viewer is permitted to gaze uninhibitedly at both the beautiful women and the beautiful men so described, but the narrative's direction reminds them of the relative positions of power of male and female characters both in literature and in society. Where female beauty makes its owner more vulnerable to the lusting gaze and physical violence, male beauty holds a certain kind of power over its beholder and, by visual and social convention, provokes less uninhibited responses from the viewer.[58] Beauty thus serves to highlight and perpetuate traditional gender roles and relationships. Late antique authors use this complex web of beauty, objecthood, and power to make their narratives more dynamic and to engage the reader in a complex interplay of gazes.

This treatment of androgynous or effeminate male figures as objects and specifically as *objets d'art* is, of course, by no means new to Late Antiquity. In Plato's *Charmides* (154 b–d), for instance, we find a striking example of a young man becoming the object of the desiring gaze. To Plato's Socrates and his interlocutors, Charmides appears most marvellous, θαυμαστός, and a group of young boys throngs around him, gazing at him as if he were a statue, ὥσπερ ἄγαλμα ἐθεῶντο αὐτόν.[59] While the older men, as possible *erastai*, are, at least according to Socrates, expected to recognise and respond to Charmides' outstanding beauty, he shows himself surprised at the young boys' devotion to the beautiful young man.[60] What is of

---

[58] Cf. Miguélez-Cavero (2009: 564–9) on the mocking of Dionysus' effeminate appearance.

[59] Compare the description of Olympus and the satyrs' response to his beauty in Philostr. *Imag.* 1.20.

[60] It is beyond the scope of this chapter to discuss the complexities of the two groups of gazers, the older men surrounding Socrates and the young boys following Charmides, or to examine in detail Socrates' claim that male responses to male beauty are determined by age. For further discussion of such questions, see e.g. Dover (1978), Penwill (1978), Cohen (1991), and Larmour, Miller, and Platter (1998).

interest to the present chapter is the comparison not merely of a beautiful person to a statue but also of a group of followers to that of a devoted crowd following a (divine) image. Charmides' beauty is so overwhelming for his young audience that they treat him almost like a divinity, as an image of a god.[61] Charmides, while the object of the male gaze, the object of lust, thus wields great power over those who see him. Much like Paris, then, Charmides commands the attention of his audience, but it is his masculinity, albeit a beautiful and youthful one, that creates boundaries that protect him from the kind of violation to which the female characters discussed here are vulnerable.

11.4 Conclusion

Though the types of comparisons employed by the poets of Late Antiquity build on the models of earlier periods, the function as well as the form of many of these literary devices differ in important ways. Poets of Classical Antiquity compare extraordinarily beautiful or otherwise outstanding characters to divinities in order to emphasise their exceptional qualities. Such comparisons allow authors to explore heroic characteristics and to illustrate the majesty of their mythical figures. Similarly, comparisons to works of art serve to highlight beauty and to signify a level of extraordinary charm and grace. Both kinds of comparison ultimately not only objectify the compared figure, but also serve to create a sense of awe in the reader by appealing to their imagination.

The late antique examples discussed in this chapter diverge from this classical literary tradition, building on models first found in Ovid's *œuvre*. Where classical comparisons serve to create a general sense of awe toward the described character, the late antique comparisons invoke very specific images and scenes familiar from the visual arts. The character, envisioned as an *objet d'art*, is stripped of his or her attributes and thus left vulnerable to the penetrating gaze. As the character is reshaped as a work of art, the reader adopts the role of voyeur, taking advantage of the character's objecthood. Female characters treated in this way are presented as particularly vulnerable and as extremely passive: their lack of visual attributes serves to underscore their status as a generic type of beautiful woman, whose only purpose is the visual gratification of her male audience. Male characters, on the other hand, while also objectified, retain a sense of control over their bodies, able, to some degree, to leverage their beauty

---

[61] Compare *Aen.* 1.588–93; see Lovatt (2013: 277) on Dido's response.

to their advantage. What all of these comparisons have in common is the dismantling of known visual types: the evoked image is altered beyond the point of recognition as its defining attributes are stripped away. This literary phenomenon gains additional meaning in a cultural environment in which pagan statuary is being taken out of its original, its religious, context and redefined as *ars gratia artis*. The treatment of the classical goddesses, heroes, and heroines by the late antique authors discussed here resembles these Christian attempts to come to terms with their pagan heritage, to allow for an aesthetic appreciation of familiar but potentially dangerous or challenging objects. Both these literary figures and the pagan statues are redefined as objects of the viewer's gaze. These late antique authors, then, engage not only with the literary tradition they are building on but also with their own cultural environment, as they seek to reshape ancient figures and renegotiate their traditions.

CHAPTER 12

Metamorphosis and Mutability in Late Antique Epic

Philip Hardie

This chapter surveys some of the uses of metamorphosis in late antique poetry in both Greek and Latin. In part this is a contribution to the growing body of work on the reception of Ovid in Late Antiquity, and, as such, also a contribution to the question of how far late antique poetry is the product of a classicising culture.[1] On the Greek side I shall look at metamorphosis in Nonnus. This will be done not as an exercise in *Quellenforschung* (and the jury is still out on the question of whether Nonnus does draw directly on Ovid),[2] but rather as a comparative study, with two emphases. First, how Ovidian is Nonnus' use of metamorphosis, both as subject matter and as implicit poetics? Second, how does Nonnian metamorphosis compare with the uses of metamorphosis in late Latin texts?

This latter topic opens up another large issue, that of the comparability of the handling of metamorphosis in, on the one hand, Christian poetry and, on the other hand, poetry on non-Christian subjects, especially mythological. In Christian Latin poetry metamorphosis has a central place in the histories both of the world and of the individual: in the Old Testament, God's creation of the world and of mankind can be narrated as processes of transformation, while the New Testament story tells of metamorphoses that operate between the human and divine. Miracles, in both Old and New Testaments, are often metamorphic events (turning the sea into dry land, water into wine). In the histories of individuals, conversion, a turning to God, can also be experienced as a transformation within the self, transferring the Ovidian lexicon of metamorphosis from the physical to the spiritual level.

---

[1] On Ovid in Late Antiquity, cf. now Fielding (2017). For an important discussion of Claudian's Ovidianism, cf. Hinds (2016); on Prudentius and Ovid, cf. Salvatore (1958: chapter 2, 'Ovidio cristiano'); on ps.-Cyprian *De Sodoma*, cf. Hexter (1988).

[2] On Nonnus and Ovid, cf. Braune (1935), D'Ippolito (1962, 2007), Eller (1982), Herter (1981), Knox (1988), Schulze (1985), and West (2003). Cf. also Carvounis and Papaioannou (cf. Chapter 1).

As disputed as is the question of Nonnus' relation to Ovid, are the questions, first, of the relationship of the *Dionysiaca* to Nonnus' *Paraphrase of the Gospel of St John*, and, second, of the significance within the *Dionysiaca* of apparent parallels with events in Christian history and with Christian doctrine. Metamorphosis is one focal point in which to explore this. Are the metamorphic powers of Dionysus an analogue for Christ's often metamorphic miracle-working, is the conversion of the world of the *Dionysiaca* to a universal Dionysiac realm an analogue for the transformation of history effected by the birth of Christ, and for the subsequent mission of the conversion of the world to the Christian faith? Or is Dionysiac polymorphism more aptly compared with the shifts and delusions of another archetypal shape-shifter, the Christian devil? I shall end on a Satanic note with another comparison, this time not between Nonnus and Ovid, but between Nonnus and one of the most Ovidian of the Christian Latin poets, Prudentius.

12.1   Nonnus and Ovidian Metamorphosis

Nonnus places metamorphosis at the heart of his poetics in the proem (1.11–33).[3] After calling on the Muses to bring him the fennel-wand and thyrsus of Dionysus, he asks them to set beside him as partner in the dance Proteus πολύτροπος 'versatile, shifty'. Proteus' metamorphic ποικίλον εἶδος 'many-coloured, changeful shape' corresponds to the poet's own ποικίλος ὕμνος 'varied, ever-changing hymn', and his shape-shifting will be seen later in the poem to correspond to Dionysus' shape-shifting, although that connection is *not* made explicitly in the proem.[4] Now, Proteus does not make a major appearance in Ovid's *Metamorphoses*, although he does have a central cameo part in Achelous' account of multiple shape-shifters at *Met.* 8.730–7. There Achelous gives a rapid catalogue of some of the shapes that Proteus can take, which may be compared with the list of Proteus' disguises in the Nonnian proem.[5]

Nonnus' opening definition of his metamorphic poetics feeds into a much larger network of conceptual and linguistic figures for the characters

---

[3] On metamorphosis in Nonnus, cf. Fauth (1981), Eller (1982), Espinar Ojeda (2005), Paschalis (2014), and Buxton (2009: 143–53). Translations of the *Dionysiaca* are by W. H. D. Rouse (Loeb).

[4] On Proteus as symbol for Nonnian poetics, cf. Fauth (1981: 23–4), Hopkinson (1994b: 9–11), and Shorrock (2001: 20–2, 117–19).

[5] Achelous' list of transformations: youth, lion, boar, serpent, bull, stone, tree, water, fire. Nonnus' list: serpent, lion, leopard, boar, water, tree. Cf. also Ov. *Met.* 11.249–56: Proteus' advise to Peleus on how to deal with the shape-shifter Thetis.

and their actions in the *Dionysiaca*, a terminology that maps readily on to a vocabulary of poetic representation and imitation. Anyone who has read even short sections of the *Dionysiaca* will be familiar with the relentless repetition of words like μιμηλός 'imitative', ἰσότυπος 'of like shape', ἀντίτυπος 'of corresponding shape', νόθος 'counterfeit, fake', and a range of terms of deceit and disguise, ἀπάτη, compounds of δόλος 'ruse', ψεύδομαι 'lie', and cognates.[6] In what is still one of the best discussions of Nonnian poetics, Daria Gigli Piccardi sees Nonnus' language of imitation, copies, ἀντίτυπον μίμημα 'corresponding imitation', τύπος μιμηλός 'mimetic impression' as central to Nonnus' vision of reality, or, it might be better to say, vision of a Dionysiac reality.[7] Gigli Piccardi sees metamorphosis as part of a complex of phenomena that includes the following: imitation, dreams, mirror image, invention of an object as imitation of something already existing,[8] and metaphor.

Gigli Piccardi was preceded in her study of this complex of terminology and associated phenomena by Margarete Riemschneider, who discusses these matters under the heading of 'das Scheinbild' ('illusion').[9] Riemschneider links mirror images, masks, toy miniatures, dream, delusions of madness, metamorphosis, and ekphrasis. She also points to a commonality between Nonnus and Claudian in a liking for ekphrasis and an interest in the play on reality and appearance, material, and representation.[10] Now, Claudian's investment in these areas certainly does owe much to Ovid.

For Gigli Piccardi these various relationships of *mimesis* are expressive of a late antique world-view, a Neoplatonic and Stoic natural sympathy, for

---

[6] Newbold (2010) catalogues the vocabulary of deceit, disguise, mimicry, and shape-shifting, seen as symptomatic of a view of the world as an endless series of transformations, characterised by transience and impermanence but also capable of engendering a sense of eternal union with the divine, caught in a tension between the sensate and the ideational.

[7] Gigli Piccardi (1985). Cf. Fauth (1981: 38) for a brief checklist of the lexicon of Dionysiac shape-shifting.

[8] E.g. *Dion.* 40.506–12 ὑπερκύψας δὲ θαλάσσης | ἀντίτυπον μίμημα φέρων ἰσόζυγι μορφῇ | εἰς πλόον αὐτοδίδακτον ἐνήχετο ναυτίλος ἰχθύς· | τὸν τότε παπταίνοντες ἐοικότα νηὶ θαλάσσης | καὶ πλόον εὐποίητον ἄτερ καμάτοιο μαθόντες, | καὶ σχεδίην πήξαντες ὁμοίιον ἰχθύι πόντου | ναυτιλίης τύπον ἴσον ἐμιμήσαντο θαλάσσης ('out of the sea popped a nautilus fish, perfect image of what I meant and shaped like a ship, sailing on its voyage self-taught. Thus observing this creature so like a ship of the sea, they learnt without trouble how to make a voyage, they built a craft like to a fish of the deep and imitated its navigation of the sea'). This draws on Oppian *Halieutica* 1.343–59, but with the addition of the typical Nonnian vocabulary of imitation and likeness.

[9] Riemschneider (1957).

[10] Riemschneider (1957: 58–9). On Nonnus and Claudian, cf. Braune (1948), arguing that Nonnus' story of Beroe is based on Claudian, and that Harmonie's cosmic web, *Dion.* 41.294–302, is derived from *De Raptu Proserpinae* 1.246–72.

which she adduces parallel expressions in Plotinus and Proclus. But
whatever the importance of late antique philosophical perspectives for
Nonnus' world-view, it is hard to miss the similarity between Nonnus'
metamorphic and mimetic world and the world of Ovid's *Metamorphoses*,
which like the world of the *Dionysiaca* is an alternative world, a hetero-
cosm. If we make a combined shopping list of Riemschneider's and Gigli
Piccardi's typically Nonnian features, we find that many of them are also
typically Ovidian: the mirror image of Narcissus, Agave's maddened
delusion that Pentheus has taken the shape of a boar (cf. Ov. *Met.* 3.715
ille mihi feriendus aper), Daedalus' imitation of natural wings through
technology. Ekphrasis, a predilection for which is often seen as characteristic of late antique poetry in both Greek and Latin, is an important feature
of Ovid's *Metamorphoses*, and the connections between ekphrasis and
metamorphosis have been extensively explored in recent Ovidian criticism.

When it comes to dreams, we will think of Ovid's dream-god Morpheus
in *Met.* 11. Morpheus, rather than Ovid's Proteus, has some claim to be the
Ovidian equivalent to Nonnus' Proteus, as the major metapoetic embodiment of the shifting and delusory world of the *Meta-morphoses*.[11] Morpheus
is an artist, a technician of shape-changing, and he is a feigner, counterfeiter
of shapes (*artificem simulatoremque figurae*, 11.634); he is an imitator (*hic
solos homines imitator*, 638).[12] Thus Morpheus shares with Nonnus' metamorphic poetics the aspects of imitation (μιμηλός), of likeness (654 *exanimi
similis*: cf. ἰσότυπος, ἰσάζειν), of fraud and fakery (νόθος). Morpheus is also
a consummate actor, able to persuade Alcyone that he is the real thing when
he impersonates her dead husband Ceyx in a dream.[13] Nonnus' likenesses
and shifts often hint at the work of the artist, for example, in the striking
pantomime performance of Seilenos at *Dion.* 19.225–95, whose
πολύστρεπτος τέχνη 'much-twisting art' ends with his metamorphosis into
a river, whose spinning eddies are a natural imitation of the whirling art of
the formerly anthropomorphic dancer. The book ends, 'and all marvelled

---

[11] Cf. Hardie (2002: 276–8).   [12] On Ovidian imitation, cf. Burrow (1999).

[13] Morpheus (*Met.* 11.636–8) *exprimit incessus vultumque sonumque loquendi;* | *adicit et vestes et
consuetissima cuique* | *verba,* 'he reproduces the gait, the expression, and the sound of speech; to
which he joins the clothing and each person's most habitual vocabulary': for *exprimo* of actors, cf.
TLL 5. 2. 1790.60ff. Tissol (1997: 78–9) points out that Dryden, himself an experienced writer for
the stage, recognises that Ovid's dreams are stage-actors, in his translation of Ovid's Ceyx and
Alcyone (translating *Met.* 11.635–8, 671–3): 'Morpheus, of all his numerous train, express'd | The
shape of man, and imitated best; | The walk, the words, the gesture could supply, | The habit
mimick, and the mein bely; | Plays well, but all his action is confin'd, | Extending not beyond our
human kind.' 'Thus said the player-God; and adding art | Of voice and gesture, so perform'd his
part, | She thought (so like her love the shade appears) | That Ceyx spake the words, and Ceyx shed
the tears.'

when they saw the winding waters of the liquefied tumbler Seilenos, the much-twisting river that was his like-natured imitation (ἰσοφυὲς μίμημα)' (347–9). Nature imitates art, a very Ovidian paradox.

The pantomime and hydromime are dramatic forms whose aesthetic seems close to the verbal performances of Nonnus, as a number of scholars have noted.[14] Gigli Piccardi refers to Lucian's rationalising exegesis of Proteus as 'a dancer, an imitative (μιμητικόν) fellow, able to shape himself and change himself into anything' (*On the Dance* 19). Karl Galinsky has made a case for the newly fashionable pantomime in Augustan Rome as exhibiting strong affinities with Ovid's *Metamorphoses*. Galinsky refers to Lucian's requirement in *On the Dance* 37, that the pantomime artist 'beginning with Chaos and the primal origin of the world, must know everything down to the story of Cleopatra the Egyptian', as an analogy to the reach of Ovid's poem *primaque ab origine mundi ad mea tempora*.[15] Nonnus, like Ovid, ends his compendious and universalising epic with the assumption of a mortal to the heavens to join the gods – although, unlike Ovid, Nonnus does not draw out the metamorphic aspect of this transition.

The translated title of Gigli Piccardi's book is *Metaphor and Poetics in Nonnus*, and she speaks of the significant intertwining of metamorphosis and metaphor. For example, at *Dion.* 45.311–14 a snake hurled at a tree by a Maenad turns into ivy, winding itself round the tree, 'imitating the knot made by serpents coiling themselves round': this is described by Gigli Piccardi as 'a circular process, from reality to the metamorphosis, and from this to the metaphor which coincides with the point of departure' (235). In Ovid's *Metamorphoses* the changing of physical shapes (*formae, figurae*) is inextricably bound up with verbal figuration – metaphor, simile, metonym, personification.[16] The shape-shifting of the *Metamorphoses* can be understood as generated in large part by the shiftiness of language. This is a world in which the figurations of speech take shape in physical forms, a world in which there is no simple correspondence between phenomena and essences, a world corrupted, perhaps, by language. In this might be seen a strong contrast to the Christian message, whereby the word,

---

[14] Cf. the important pages in Gigli Piccardi (1985: 150–4) 'L'arte. La danza', linking pantomime and hydromime to Nonnus' obsession with *poikilia* and metamorphosis, and his predilection for imitated form. On the importance of pantomime in Nonnus, cf. Agosti (2008, with bibliography at 20 n. 10).

[15] Galinsky (1996: 265–6). Cf. Shorrock (2001: 110) on the 'compendious, universalizing epic[s]' of both Nonnus and Ovid.

[16] Cf. Hardie (2002: chapter 7, 'Absent Presences of Language').

Verbum, has been made flesh, a transformation that imposes an unequivocal significance on a world redeemed.

To illustrate these points I take one of the longest continuous episodes in the *Dionysiaca*, and one placed at a structurally significant point, at the end of the first quarter of the poem. This is the story of Ampelus, the beautiful boy beloved of Dionysus (10.175–12.291). This is an aetiological metamorphosis: the dying Ampelus turns into the grapevine named after him (in reality, of course, the aetiological priority is the other way round: Ampelus is always already named after the grapevine). The story is of a kind exemplified by the Ovidian tales of dying boyfriends of Apollo, Hyacinthus, and Cyparissus, or by another dying boyfriend, whose lover happens to be himself, Narcissus. The introduction of Ampelus is immediately preceded by an example of what I call 'metamorphic landscapes', of which striking examples may also be found in the Latin poetry of Claudian, Prudentius, and Paulinus of Nola:[17] the banks of the river Pactolus are transformed, sprouting roses and lilies as the young Dionysus swims in the river. The gold of the river effects a kind of metamorphosis on his hair, 10.174 'the unbound locks (βόστρυχα) of his dark hair were reddened (ἐρυθαίνετο)'. βόστρυχος of a 'curl of hair' already suggests a closeness to the vegetable world: the diminutive βοστρύχιον is used of a 'vine-tendril', and the word is close in sound to βότρυς 'bunch of grapes', which is used figuratively of Ampelus' curling locks a few lines later, χαίτης | βότρυες εἰλικόεντες (181–2). The 'reddening' of Dionysus' hair from the reflection of the Pactolus might remind us of the reddening of ripening grapes (for vegetable reddening, cf. 190: ἐκ ποδὸς ἀργυφέοιο ῥόδων ἐρυθαίνετο λειμών). The application of further figurative language of plants and flowers to Ampelus suggests that his is a body ripe for metamorphosis: ἥλικος ἠιθέοιο ῥοδώπιδι θέλγετο μορφῇ ('[Dionysus] was enchanted by the rosy form of the youth of his own age', 176), νεοτρεφὲς ἔρνος Ἐρώτων ('newly reared sprout of the Loves', 178). These linguistic features are examples of what Leonard Barkan calls 'protometamorphosis', with reference to the figurative anticipation of a physical metamorphosis in Ovid's *Metamorphoses*:[18] for example, Hecuba is transformed into a rabid dog (*Met.* 13.567–9), but some lines before the terminal metamorphosis she is compared in a simile (13.547–8) to a lioness enraged at the theft of her cubs.

---

[17] I do not have space here to discuss 'metamorphic landscapes', but hope to do so elsewhere.
[18] Barkan (1986: 20–1).

At the wrestling contest between Ampelus and Dionysus the umpire Eros, himself a winged likeness of Hermes, the more usual overseer of games, weaves a garland of narcissus and hyacinth, ominously foreshadowing both the death of Ampelus and Ampelus' own vegetable transformation. In the next book, the swimming race in the Pactolus yields more reflections and proto-metamorphoses in Dionysus' address to Ampelus. The doubling of Ampelus through reflection, as he cuts through the gold-gleaming waters with his golden palm, reflects back on the prefatory image of Dionysus swimming in the river, his hair reddened by the reflection from the water, suggesting a narcissistic quality in Dionysus' love for Ampelus, a reflection of himself, and perhaps also hinting that Dionysus himself is the incarnation of the vine.

After the swimming race, Ampelus dresses up as Dionysus, wreathing himself with a cluster of vipers, making himself an imitation of the god, wearing a 'counterfeit' version of the god's clothing (11.58–62), 'He bound his head with a cluster of vipers, an imitation (μίμημα) of Lyaios' terrible wreath of snakes. Often seeing the dappleback tunic of Bromios, he put over his limbs a counterfeit (νόθην) spotted dress in imitation, and pushed his light foot into a purple buskin.' After the boy's death, Dionysus will dress his corpse in his own νεβρίς 'fawnskin', with κόθορνοι and θύρσος (11.232–41), on which Vian comments 'il devient, après la mort, un véritable Bacchant et s'identifie à Dionysos' (2003: 11).

The ruddy gleam of the Pactolus matches the gleam of Ampelus' limbs: ἀστράπτει ῥόος οὗτος ἐρευθιόωντι μετάλλῳ | ὡς σὺ τεοῖς μελέεσσι ('both are radiant, this river with its red metal, and you with your limbs', 11.26–7); this leads inevitably to the floral image, as Dionysus says that he will shout out to the Satyrs: 'πῶς ῥόδον εἰς ῥόδον ἦλθε;' ('How did rose come to join rose?', 30). The word used for the 'cluster' of vipers that Ampelus puts on his head, κόρυμβος, is literally 'cluster of ivy-fruit'. At the 'resurrection' of Ampelus in book 12 Atropos announces to Dionysus that he will exchange his own garland of snakes for tendrils of the vine into which the boy has been metamorphosed: 'The Muses shall cry triumph for Ampelus the lovely with Lyaios of the Vine. You shall throw off the twisting coronal of snakes from your head, and entwine your hair with tendrils of the vine' (152–5). In retrospect, Ampelus' self-crowning with snakes is a kind of proto-metamorphosis through costume-disguise. Curling snakes and curling vines have a habit of turning into each other throughout the *Dionysiaca*; we have seen Gigli Piccardi taking this likeness as an example of the affinity between metamorphosis and metaphor.

By the time of the resurrection and metamorphosis of the body of
Ampelus at 12.174–87, his vegetable transformation seems inevitable,
the realisation in physical form of the linguistic games that have been
going on since the beginning of the Ampelus story. A halfway stage
between human and vegetable is found in the personifications of the
Seasons at 11.48–521, with their metamorphic, Arcimboldo-esque, bodies.
In Ovid there is a profound connection between the *enargeia* of
personification and physical metamorphosis. It is no accident that the
western tradition of personification allegory (cf. Greensmith in
Chapter 8) receives one of its most powerful impulses precisely in Ovid's
Metamorphoses. Of Nonnus' four seasons, Autumn is as yet a pale shadow
of what she will become after the creation of the vine through the
metamorphosis of Ampelus: 'For there were as yet no (οὔ πω) vine-
branches (βότρυες ἀμπελόεντες), trailing about the nymph's neck with
tangled clusters of golden curls; not yet was she drunken with purple
Maronian juice beside the wine-vat that loves neat wine' (515–18). 'Not
yet' (*nondum*) is used repeatedly by Ovid in anticipation of a metamorphosis in the future.[19] The quasi-metamorphic Seasons are privy to a
prophecy of the transformation of Ampelus into vine on the oracular
tablets of Harmonia in the House of Helios.

The metamorphosis itself (12.174–87) is described in a loving and
punning detail that reminds the reader of an Ovidian extended metamorphosis, for example, that of Daphne into laurel in *Met.* 1:

καὶ γὰρ ἀναΐξας ἐρόεις νέκυς ὡς ὄφις ἕρπων
Ἄμπελος αὐτοτέλεστος ἐὴν ἠλλάξατο μορφήν,   175
καὶ πέλε νήδυμον ἄνθος· ἀμειβομένοιο δὲ νεκροῦ
γαστὴρ θάμνος ἔην περιμήκετος, ἄκρα δὲ χειρῶν
ἀκρεμόνες βλάστησαν, ἐνερρίζωντο δὲ ταρσοί,
βόστρυχα βότρυες ἦσαν, ἐμορφώθη δὲ καὶ αὐτή
νεβρὶς ἀεξομένης πολυδαίδαλον ἄνθος ὀπώρης,   180
ἀμπελόεις δὲ κόρυμβος ἔην δολιχόσκιος αὐχήν,
ἰσοφυὴς δ' ἀγκῶνι τιταίνετο καμπύλος ὄρπηξ
οἰδαίνων σταφυλῇσιν, ἀμειβομένου δὲ καρήνου
γναμπτῆς κυρτὰ κόρυμβα τύπον μιμεῖτο κεραίης.
κεῖθι φυτῶν στίχες ἦσαν ἀπείρονες· αὐτοτελὴς δέ   185
ὄρχατος ἀμπελόεις χλοεροὺς ὄρπηκας ἑλίσσων
οἴνοπι γείτονα δένδρα νέῳ μιτρώσατο καρπῷ.

---

[19] E.g. *Met.* 1.450 *nondum laurus erat*, 7.233 *nondum mutato vulgatum corpore Glauci*, 8.372 *at gemini,
nondum caelestia sidera, fratres*, 9.17 (Hercules) *nondum erat ille deus*, and 14.157 *litora adit nondum
nutricis habentia nomen*.

For Ampelos the lovely dead rose of himself, like a creeping snake, and changed his shape, and turned into a sweet flower. As the body changed, his belly was a long long stalk, his fingers grew into top-tendril, his feet took root, the clusters of his hair became clusters of grapes, his fawnskin itself morphed into the much-variegated flower of the growing fruit, his long neck became a bunch of grapes, a bending shoot swollen with berries stretched out of like nature with his elbow, his head changed and twisted clusters imitated the shape of his bent horns. There were rows of plants without end; there self-made was an orchard of vines, twining green twigs round the neighbouring trees with the new wine-coloured fruit.

Just as Ovid's Apollo appropriates the newly created laurel as his own divine attribute, and places a laurel garland on his own head, so Dionysus covers his temples with the leaves of the vine (12.193–5; at 245–50 he vaunts his superiority over Apollo who garlands himself with the mourning petals of the hyacinth).

Rob Shorrock offers a persuasive reading of Ampelus' transformation into the vine as a climactic moment in Nonnus' metamorphic metapoetics. Shorrock writes: 'Nonnus' unique way of writing poetry, his *process* of poetic production, is symbolised by the vine. His distinctive approach to poetry, the very nature of the Dionysiac aesthetic, will be one not of active creation, but of appropriation – and most especially transformation.'[20] But we need not stop at the level of the aesthetic. Wolfgang Fauth speaks of the 'conversion' of the cosmos to a Dionysiac cosmos, 'the triumph of the powerfully and miraculously expanding Dionysiac alteration of the world'.[21] The *Dionysiaca* is the life history of a god, whose earthly career effects the transformation of the world into a Dionysiac realm, what might be called a Dionysiac conversion, accompanied by metamorphic miracles of various kinds, including the recurrent transformation of water into wine.[22] That is but one of the many parallels that have been spotted between elements in Nonnus' story of Dionysus and elements in the story of Christ; there is a high concentration of these quasi- or pseudo-Christian moments in the story of Ampelus. I shall not venture an opinion on the nature of Nonnus' own religious beliefs or on the direction of travel between the *Dionysiaca* and the *Paraphrase of the Gospel of St John*, although I have sympathy with the view that some version of a symbiosis of Christian and pagan is a more productive way forward than reading for rigid ideological and theological oppositions.[23]

---

[20] Shorrock (2001: 137).   [21] Fauth (1981: 65).
[22] Noetzel (1960) compares the miracle at Cana (John 2) and Dionysiac wine miracles.
[23] In this I follow Shorrock (2011: chapter 3, 'Christ and Dionysus: Nonnus' *Paraphrase* of St John's Gospel'; chapter 4, 'Dionysus and Christ: Nonnus' *Dionysiaca*').

12.2 Metamorphosis in Christian Latin Poetry

I turn now from Dionysiac to Christian narratives of metamorphosis, and from Greek to Latin texts. Late antique Christian Latin poets draw on the traditions of metamorphic, above all Ovidian, narrative at various points in the Judaeo-Christian story. The cosmogony at the beginning of Ovid's *Metamorphoses*, in which the primeval chaos is given order and form by *deus et melior . . . natura* ('god and a better nature', 1.21), could easily be adapted to Christian orthodoxy.[24] And, as a grand narrative of cosmic process, of cosmic change, Ovid's cosmogony is a suitable preface not just to a history of the world from its beginnings but also to a poem on metamorphosis. In the opening hymn of the *Carmen Paschale*, Sedulius (fl. 435 CE) addresses God: *qui diversa novam formasti in corpora terram, / torpentique solo viventia membra dedisti* ('who shaped the new earth into different bodies, and endowed the sluggish soil with living limbs', 1.68–9), echoing the opening of the *Metamorphoses*: *In nova fert animus mutatas dicere formas | corpora*. Dracontius' (ca. 455 – ca. 505) hexaemeron in book 1 of the *De Laudibus Dei* narrates the making of the creatures of the deep on fifth day, through a process of metamorphosis out of water: *in corpus solidantur aquae nervisque ligantur. | musculus humor erat, fluctus durescit in ossa | atque oculi gemmantur aquis humore gelato* ('the waters are solidified into body and are bound with sinews; the liquid becomes muscle, the waves harden into bones and sparkling eyes form as liquid water freezes', 1.235–7). The creation of Adam is a metamorphic process, *sed dominaturum cunctis Dominator et Auctor | plasmavit per membra virum de pulvere factum. | limus adhuc deformis erat, membratur in artus | corporeus, species hominis, caelestis imago. | conspicitur nova forma viri sine mente parumper. . . iam cutis est qui pulvis erat, iam terra medullas | ossibus includit, surgunt in messe capilli* ('But the Lord and Creator moulded the limbs of man, made from dust, destined to lord it over all things. The mud was still shapeless, and was formed into bodily limbs, in the shape of man, a heavenly likeness. There to be seen was the new shape of a man, for a while without a mind. ... Now what had been dust is skin, now the earth encloses the marrow within the bones, and a crop of hair rises up', 1.335–44). Sedulius introduces a catalogue of Old Testament miracles with more metamorphic language: *te duce difficilis non est via; subditur omnis | imperiis natura tuis, rituque soluto | transit in adversas iussu dominante figuras* ('under your guidance the way is not hard; all nature is subject to your rule, and freed from its usual path changes into contrary shapes at your lordly command', 1.85–7).

---

[24] On the *interpretatio Ovidiana* of Genesis, cf. Roberts (2002).

But it is, understandably, the transformation and innovation, or reno-
vation, of the world brought about by the Incarnation that particularly
draws the attention of Christian poets. Novelty and metamorphosis are
bound together from the second word of Ovid's *Metamorphoses*, *in nova
fert* (*Met.* 1.1). Novelty is an essential feature of both the subject matter
and the poetics of Ovid's poem. Novelty is an even more fundamental
feature of the New Testament's theology of a making new of mankind that
is at the same time a re-formation of the world and of man, amounting to a
repetition of the original creation of unfallen humanity, a doctrine developed especially by St. Paul.[25] Rob Shorrock draws attention to the surprising novelty of both wine in Nonnus and the message of Christ.[26]

Ingo Gildenhard and Andrew Zissos list the main metamorphic
moments in the story and worship of Christ: the incarnation (as the
'changing' of an immortal god into a mortal man an unparalleled inversion
of the almost routine pagan transformation in the opposite direction, from
mortal to immortal god), the transfiguration (for which the verb
μεταμορφοῦν is used in Matthew and Mark), the resurrection; and the
transubstantiation of the Eucharist.[27] The power of Christ is manifested in
miracles, which are often narrated as metamorphoses. The first of Christ's
miracles, the turning of water into wine at the wedding in Cana, is a
straightforward example of metamorphosis. Here is Sedulius' account
(*Carmen Paschale* 3.1–11):[28]

> Prima suae dominus thalamis dignatus adesse
> virtutis documenta dedit convivaque praesens
> pascere, non pasci veniens. mirabile! fusas
> in vinum convertit aquas. amittere gaudent
> pallorem latices, mutavit laeta saporem   5
> unda suum largita merum, mensasque per omnes
> dulcia non nato rubuerunt pocula musto.
> implevit sex ergo lacus hoc nectare Christus.
> quippe ferax qui vitis erat virtute colona
> omnia fructificans, cuius sub tegmine blando   10
> mitis inocciduas enutrit pampinus uvas.

---

[25] Central is Ladner (1959) on the idea of reform. The key Pauline passages are Rom 12.2, Eph
4.22–4, Col 3.10–11, 2 Cor 3.18, and 2 Cor 5.17.

[26] Shorrock (2011: 110). On novelty in late antique Latin poetry, see Hardie (2019: chapter 5).

[27] Gildenhard and Zissos (2013: 187).

[28] For comparative treatments of the less metamorphic narratives of the miracle at Juvencus 2.127–52
and Prudentius *Dittochaeon* 125–8, cf. Springer (1988: 110–27) and Herzog (1979: 52–69, at 61).
On Sedulius' use of Ovid, see also van der Laan (1993: 143–5).

The Lord deigned to attend a wedding and there gave the first evidence of his power. As a guest he came to the feast to feed, not to be fed. How amazing! He changed the dispensed water into wine. The liquids rejoiced to lose their pale colour, and the happy wave changed its own flavour, producing pure wine, and on all the tables the sweet cups blush, filled with new, unnatural, wine. So it was that Christ filled six vats with this new nectar. For he who was the fruitful vine, with his power as cultivator, was making all things to bear fruit. Under his kindly shade the supple vine brings forth never failing grapes.[29]

The miracle uses the vocabulary of metamorphosis (*convertit, mutavit*). Wonder (*mirabile*) is a recurrent reaction to the transformations in Ovid's *Metamorphoses*, and there are more specific parallels with Ovidian narratives: with *amittere gaudent pallorem latices* compare *Met.* 7.290 (rejuvenation of Aeson) *pulsa fugit macies, abeunt pallorque situsque* ('his emaciation is driven into flight, his pallor and decrepitude leave him'), and, in a reverse process, 14.754–5 (the petrifaction of Anaxarete) *calidusque e corpore sanguis | inducto pallore fugit* ('as a pallor comes over her, the warm blood flees from her body'). With *dulcia non nato rubuerunt pocula musto* compare *Met.* 10.248–9 *formamque dedit, qua femina nasci | nulla potest* ('[Pygmalion] gave [his statue] a shape/a beauty that no woman can be born with'), describing the miraculous power of Pygmalion's art to transcend nature. Compare also a metamorphic moment in Vergil's *Georgics* (the effect of grafting), *G.* 2.82 *miratastque novas frondes et non sua poma* ('[the tree] marvels at its new leaves and fruits not its own'). Sedulius also exploits the slippage from metaphor to metamorphosis: the transformation of water into wine is the work of one who is, figuratively, a vine.

St Paul calls on the individual Christian to transform himself into the new man. Gildenhard and Zissos discuss the two uses of the verb μεταμορφόω in the Letters of Paul (Rom 12.2, 2 Cor 3.18) in the light of the 'structural analogy between transformation and conversion', and conclude that 'From this point of view, conversion emerges as the Christian equivalent to pagan metamorphosis.'[30] Prudentius uses the Ovidian lexicon of metamorphosis in his narrative of the conversion to Christianity of the magician Cyprian: *iamque figura alia est quam quae fuit oris et nitoris* ('and now his face and sleek looks took on another appearance', *Peristephanon* 13.28). Later, as Cyprian prays in prison to God, and prepares himself for martyrdom, he remembers his conversion: '*iamque tuus fieri mandas, fio Cyprianus alter | et*

---

[29] Translation by Springer (2013).
[30] Gildenhard and Zissos (2013: 194–5). Conversion as metamorphosis is to be distinguished from conversion as a turning *to* God: *converto, conversio* are more usually used in this latter sense.

novus ex veteri nec iam reus aut nocens, ut ante ('and now you bid me become yours, and I become another Cyprian, a new man in place of the old, no longer the guilty sinner I was before', 59–60).

Paulinus of Nola (353/4–431 CE) draws on the language of metamorphosis to describe his own conversion and that of others, beginning with his famous exchange of letters with Ausonius in which Paulinus justifies to his former teacher his turn to a more committed and ascetic form of Christian life. Paulinus uses the full armoury of allusive poetic play at the same time as he defends himself for saying farewell to his former devotion to the classical Muses.[31]

Ausonius asks of Paulinus, reproachfully: *vertisti, Pauline, tuos, dulcissime, mores?* ('Paulinus, my dearest, have you changed your ways?' *Epistle* 21.50 Green). The answer is clear. For all that Paulinus asserts that his friendship with Ausonius is undying, he has undergone a radical change, nothing less than a conversion, which Ausonius will be unable to reverse.

The themes of novelty and transformation, implicit in the opening iambics of Paulinus *Carmen* 10, are brought fully into the open in the hexameters, at 128–53. Paulinus did not change his own behaviour, as Ausonius had stated, he is not a *per-versus* (83, 275), a word frequent in the Latin Bible and in the Fathers in the sense 'wicked, perverse'. Rather God is the agent of this metamorphosis and innovation, *cui placet aut formare meos aut vertere sensus* ('who wills to shape or change my thinking', 130); *promptius ex hoc | agnosci datur a summo genitore novari* ('from this it may be more readily recognised that I am made new by the highest father', 136–7). The themes of change and novelty reach a climax at 138–43:

> Non, arbitror, istic
> confessus dicar mutatae in prava notandum
> errorem mentis, quoniam sim sponte professus
> me non mente mea vitam mutasse priorem.
> mens nova mi, fateor, mens non mea, non mea quondam,
> sed mea nunc auctore deo . . .

I do not think that by saying this I shall be considered to have admitted the reprehensible sin of a debased mind, though willingly proclaiming that I have amended my former life through a purpose not my own. I admit that my attitude has changed. My mind is not my own – or rather, it was not mine before, but now it is mine through God's agency.[32]

---

[31] For a detailed analysis of this correspondence, see Hardie (2019: chapter 1).
[32] Translation by Walsh (1966–1967).

Horatian and Ovidian allusions are put to the service of a Christian confession of conversion: *mens nova* (142) alludes to Horace's account of his own Dionysiac possession in *Odes* 3.25 (2–3: *quos agor in specus | uelox mente nova?*), while the repetitions of the personal adjective (*non*) *meus* point to Ov. *Met.* 10.339 (Myrrha) *nunc, quia iam meus est, non est meus*, where there is a different kind of divided identity (Myrrha complains that because Cinyras is 'my' father, he cannot be 'my' sexual partner). Split identity is a recurrent phenomenon in the world of Ovidian metamorphoses, here transferred by Paulinus to a spiritual metamorphosis. The experience recorded by Paulinus in this poem is of a transition between two worlds: even if we reject Hermann Fränkel's account of Ovid himself as a poet between the two worlds of paganism and Christianity,[33] the kinds of in-betweenness repeatedly explored in the *Metamorphoses* lend themselves readily to the kind of spiritual autobiography of which we have here an example.

Metamorphosis continues to inform the poetry that Paulinus wrote after he settled at the shrine of St. Felix in Nola. Luciano Nicastri has given a subtle and detailed account of the theme of 'conversion-as-transformation' in Paulinus, whom he goes so far as to label a 'poet of Christian metamorphosis'.[34] Nicastri also emphasises the importance of novelty, innovation, in Paulinus' concept of the metamorphosis of conversion ('mutamento innovativo', 1999: 896–901). For Nicastri, Prudentius is a 'master of conversion' (ibid. 901) for the reason that conversion is at the centre of his experience, as it is for his friend and correspondent, Augustine. Paulinus ascribes the motive force in his spiritual transformation to Saint Felix, his patron saint.

12.3   The Metamorphoses of Sin

When it comes to gods and metamorphosis, there is a major difference between the pagan and the Christian. The Christian god is one and unchanging (in orthodox theology, the Incarnation in no way alters the full divinity of the second person of the Trinity). The bewildering plurality of the Greco-Roman gods is further complicated by their propensity to metamorphose their shapes.[35] This is well discussed by Richard Buxton in his *Forms of Astonishment: Greek Myths of Metamorphosis*; Buxton also looks at philosophical challenges to the metamorphic tradition of divinity, Plato's unchanging perfect god, incapable of change into πολλαὶ μορφαί, and Aristotle's unmoved mover, the source of all change but himself unchanging.

---

[33] Fränkel (1945).
[34] Nicastri (1999: 907; discussion of the metamorphic theme in Paulinus at 888–910).
[35] Buxton (2009: chapter 6, 'Shapes of the Gods').

Paulinus, Nicastri's 'poet of Christian metamorphosis', is clear as to the limits of mutability in his universe: *omnia praetereunt, sanctorum gloria durat | in Christo, qui cuncta novat, dum permanet ipse* ('All things pass, the glory of the saints endures in Christ, who makes all things new, while he himself abides', *Carm.* 16.3–4).[36] But in the Christian world-view there is a supernatural being who is notorious as a shape-shifter, and that being is Satan, together with the host of demons, identified with pagan gods by Augustine and others.

Earlier I cited a passage of Prudentius as an example of the (good) metamorphosis of Christian conversion. Prudentius (348 – after 405 CE) is also eloquent on the (bad) metamorphoses of sin. Prudentius' most spectacular tour de force of Ovid-style metamorphosis is his account of the transformation of the wife of Lot into a pillar of salt, *Hamartigenia* 723–76. Here I focus on a passage earlier in the *Hamartigenia*, which locates metamorphosis at the *prima origo* of sin, in the description of the effects of self-corruption on the body of Satan, formerly one of God's bright-shining angels, 186–205.[37]

> deterior mox sponte sua, dum decolor[38] illum
> inficit invidia stimulisque instigat amaris.[39]
> arsit enim scintilla odii de fomite zeli
> et dolor ingenium subitu conflavit iniquum.
> viderat argillam simulacrum et structile flatu   190
> concaluisse Dei, dominum quoque conditioni
> impositum, natura soli pelagique polique
> ut famulans homini locupletem fundere partum
> nosset et effusum terreno addicere regi.
> inflavit fermento animi stomachante tumorem[40]   195
> bestia deque acidis vim traxit acerba medullis;[41]
> bestia sorde carens, cui tunc sapientia longi

---

[36] Paulinus is close to Augustinian formulations: cf. August. *Conf.* 1.4 ... *inmutabilis, mutans omnia, numquam novus, numquam vetus, innovans omnia*; 9.10.24 *in se permanenti sine vetustate atque innovanti omnia*, on which O'Donnell compares Wisd. 7.27 *in se ipsa manens innovat omnia*, Aug. *Conf.* 7.9.14, 7.11.17; *Sermo* 12.10.10; *en. Ps.* 109. 12.136.7, 138.8. Cf. also Dracontius *Satisfactio* 7 *omnia permutans nullo mutabilis aevo*, on which Moussy compares Dan. 2.21 *et ipse mutat tempora et aetates*; Malach. 3.6 *Ego enim Dominus et non mutor*.

[37] Cf. Palla (1981) and Malamud (2011).

[38] Cf. *Aen.* 8.326 *deterior ... ac decolor aetas*, the Golden Age changing into an Iron Age.

[39] Cf. *Aen.* 11.336–7 (Drances) *quem gloria Turni | obliqua invidia stimulisque agitabat amaris*.

[40] Picking up Prud. *Hamartigenia* 168–9 (Satan) *nimiis dum viribus auctus | inflatur, dum grande tumens sese altius effert*: cf. *Geo.* 3.553 (Tisiphone) *inque dies avidum surgens sese altius effert* 'he is puffed up with the excessive strength to which he had grown, bearing himself too highly in his big-swelling pride': cf. *Geo.* 3.553 (Tisiphone) *inque dies avidum surgens sese altius effert* 'day by day she greedily raises her head higher'.

[41] Cf. *Geo.* 3.271 *continuoque avidis ubi subdita flamma medullis* (mares in heat).

corporis enodem servabat recta iuventam,
complicat ecce novos sinuoso pectore[42] nexus,
involvens nitidam spiris torquentibus alvum.   200
simplex lingua prius varia micat arte loquendi,
et discissa dolis resonat sermone trisulco.
hinc natale caput vitiorum,[43] principe ab illo
fluxit origo mali, qui se corrumpere[44] primum,
mox hominem didicit nullo informante magistro.   205

. . . afterwards corrupt of his own will because envy marked him with her stain,
and pricked him with bitter stings. For the spark of hate blazed up from the
kindling of jealousy, and anguish set light to his resentful heart. He had seen
how a figure fashioned of clay grew warm under the breath of God and was
also placed as lord over creation, so that earth and sea and sky had learned to
pour forth their rich produce in the service of man, and grant it lavishly to an
earthly king. He puffed up his swollen spirit with the passion/ferment of his
irritated mind, and the bitter beast drew strength from the acid in his marrow;
a beast formerly without stain, when upright wisdom kept his tall young body
free of knots. See! – with his winding breast he enfolds new/strange coils,
twisting his bright belly in curling spirals. His formerly single tongue flickers
with the art of varied speaking, and divided by guile sounds with three-forked
words. This is the original source of vices, from that author/prince [of
darkness] flowed the source of evil, who instructed by no teacher learned to
corrupt first himself, and then mankind.[45]

This is the moment of transformation in which the once-beautiful Lucifer
corrupts himself into the Satanic serpent, twisting the unknotted uprightness
of wisdom into the coils of pride and envy, a physical complication mirrored
in the discordant variety of speech issuing from the newly forked tongue, in a
self-poetics of novelty. That variety is also mirrored in the densely intricate
intertextuality of the passage, 'a mosaic of typical Vergilian phraseology on
serpents',[46] interspersed with fragments from other Latin poets (documen-
ted in the footnotes). One might speak of a metamorphic practice of allusion
that reveals the Satanic lurking in pagan descriptions of serpents and snakes.

---

[42] Cf. Persius 5.27 *ut quantum mihi te sinuoso in pectore fixi.*
[43] Palla 1981 ad loc. contrasts *Ham.* 32 (God) *virtutum sublime caput,* and sees in the opposition the
contrast between virtues and vices that is the theme of the *Psychomachia.*
[44] G. 3.480–2 *et genus omne neci pecudum dedit, omne ferarum,* | **corrupitque** *lacus, infecit pabula tabo.*
| *nec via mortis erat* **simplex,** '[the season of plague] condemned to death every kind of tame animal,
every kind of wild beasts, and tainted the bodies of water, and infected the fodder with corruption.
Nor was there only one path to death.'
[45] Translation adapted from H. J. Thomson (Loeb).
[46] Mahoney (1934: 200). The major Vergilian and Ovidian models for the description of a serpent:
Verg. *G.* 3.425–39; on which Vergil draws for the serpents at *Aen.* 2.203–19, 2.471–5; and Ov.
Met. 3.32–4, *Martius anguis erat, cristis praesignis et auro;* | *igne micant oculi, corpus tumet omne*

The principal Vergilian model for the passage is the elaborate description of the 'evil snake in Calabrian pastures' at *Georgics* 3.425–39. Lucifer's metamorphosis into that lurid enemy of the shepherd is eased through a recurrent play on literal and metaphorical uses of words: *acerba, enodis, recta, complico, simplex, sinuosus.*[47] Hints of personification play around the edges of the metamorphosis narrative: Lucifer is impelled by both *superbia* and *invidia*, traditional motivations for Satan's attack on mankind. He shares his *tumor* (195) with *Superbia* in the *Psychomachia*: *quo se fulta iubis iactantius illa ferinis | inferret tumido despectans agmina fastu. | turritum tortis caput adcumularat in altum / crinibus, extructos augeret ut addita cirros | congeries* ('that she might make a more imposing figure as she looked down on the columns with swelling disdain. High on her head she had piled a tower of braided hear, laying on a mass to heighten her locks and make a lofty peak over her haughty brows', 181–5).[48] The serpent is a standard attribute, and sometimes embodiment, of *Invidia*.[49] Satan is the fount of the vices (*natale caput vitiorum*), as God is the *virtutum sublime caput* (*Hamartigenia* 32): the metamorphosis of Lucifer is also the birth of psychomachia.[50] These close connections between metamorphosis, metaphor, and personification are Ovidian; they are also Nonnian.

The three-pointed tongue of the Vergilian snake (*G.* 3.439 = *Aen.* 2.475) becomes the forked tongue of Satan, the source of lies and slander.[51] The moral corruption of Satan, manifested in his serpentine metamorphosis, is at the same time the corruption of language. Several of the terms in the passage also have a stylistic application: *tumor, enodis, sinuosus.*[52] Martha Malamud explores Prudentius' account of the fall, of Satan and of man, under the aspect of the fall of language, and points out that the linguistic division

---

venenis, | tresque vibrant linguae, triplici stant ordine dentes, 'The serpent, sacred to Mars, had a wondrous golden crest; fire flashed from his eyes; his body was all swollen with venom; his triple tongue flickered out and in and his teeth were ranged in triple row', 77–8, *ipse modo inmensum spiris facientibus orbem | cingitur, interdum longa trabe rectior adstat*, 'Now he coils in huge spiral folds; now shoots up, straight and tall as a tree.' Other intertexts are footnoted above.

[47] *Complico* of convoluted thought: Cic. *Off.* 3.76, *si qui voluerit animi sui complicatam notionem evolvere.*

[48] Translation by H. J. Thomson (Loeb).

[49] Envy and snakes: cf. Meskill (2009: 53–5); Dunbabin and Dickie (1983: 18, 24–5, 32–3).

[50] Cf. Palla 1981 on *Hamartigenia* 203. Marcion's god (*Hamartigenia* 129–41) is a composite of Vergilian and Ovidian monsters, *Invidia, Fama*, and Allecto.

[51] Cf. Giotto's 'Envy' in the Arena Chapel, with a snake coming out of her mouth to sting her own eyes: cf. Gellrich (2000).

[52] *Enodis*: of speech, 'clear, plain': Plin. *Epist.* 5.17.2, *scripta elegis erat fluentibus et teneris et enodibus, sublimibus etiam*, Ambros. *Epist.* 1.12, *Comm. in Luc.* 7.136 init. *sinuosus* of style, 'diffuse', full of digressions': Quint. *Inst.* 2.4.3, *narrandi … ratio … neque rursus sinuosa et arcessitis descriptionibus* and Gell. 14.2.13 *sinuosae quaestionis.*

brought about by the devil's sin is immediately followed by the poem's first
extended simile, a postlapsarian staining of the transparency of language.[53]
This is not so much a proto-metamorphosis as a post-metamorphosis
innovation in the use (or misuse) of language. Satan is the author of a *varia
ars loquendi*, a *poikilia* valued negatively.[54]

Prudentius himself is hardly immune to the temptations of varied and
complicated poetic language. This passage, and the account of the metamorphosis of Lot's wife, are the kind of thing that Antonio Salvatore had in mind
when he claimed that 'Prudentius shows himself to be even more an *amator
ingenii sui* ['lover of his own genius'], even more intemperate than Ovid.'[55]

I shall end as I began, with Nonnus. From a Christian point of view,
there are aspects of Nonnus' Dionysus that would align him not with a
saviour-god who comes to transform the world, but rather with forces that
seem more hellish than heavenly. Wolfgang Fauth, in a chapter on
Dionysiac miracles in Nonnus, emphasises the duality in the *Dionysiaca*
between creative and destructive, between paradisal and infernal landscapes (a duality that is of course deeply rooted in the Dionysiac, and
central to Euripides' *Bacchae*).[56] The imagery of Maenads is often associated with the imagery of Furies.

When Hera sends Megaira, the ποικιλόμορφος Ἐρινύς 'manyshaped
Erinys', to madden Dionysus (*Dion.* 32.100–9), the Fury uses her serpentine whip and snaky locks as weapons and appears in the metamorphic
disguise of a lion; she inflicts φάσματα ποικιλόμορφα (121) on the god.
These are Dionysus' own weapons and shifts. Nonnus' Hellish Fury comes
close to being a dark double for the Olympian god-to-be[57] – and for the
poet himself. Nonnus practises something like a poetics of infuriation,
continuing a long tradition of figuring poetic inspiration as μανία or *furor*
(on μανία as poetic inspiration, cf. Verhelst in Chapter 7). One may also
think of the convergence in the *Aeneid* of a *furor* with Hellish origins and
associations and the frenzy of the Bacchant. Allecto provokes Amata and

[53] Malamud (2011: 102–4) 'Seeing and saying: Satan and the fall of language'.
[54] For ἁπλότης of literary style, cf. Dion. Hal. *Rhet.* 9.14.   [55] Salvatore (1958: 50).
[56] Fauth (1981: chapter 6, 'Dionysische Mirakel'; chapter 7, 'Manische Metamorphosen –
   mänadischer Wahnsinn'). The duality of Dionysus: Eur. *Bacch.* 860–1, Διόνυσον, ὡς πέφυκεν ἐν
   μέρει θεός | δεινότατος, ἀνθρώποισι δ' ἠπιώτατος, 'how Dionysus is a god by turns most terrible,
   and most gentle to men'; Plut. *Demetr.* 2.3; Nisbet and Hubbard on Hor. *Carm.* 2.19.27–8.
[57] Fauth (1981: 122), Megaira as 'eine pathologische Variante der dem Gott von vornherein vom
   Dichter zugeordneten elementaren Syzygie von Feuchte und Hitze'; her φάσματα ποικιλόμορφα as
   'krankhafte Auswüchse in jenem Kosmos von Farben, Gebilden und Tönen, von Phantasmagorie
   und Metamorphose, den die Dichtung nach dem Prinzip der ποικιλία um den Gott in der
   buntscheckigen Nebris zu errichten bestrebt ist.'

the Italian matrons to the *maior furor* of a fake Maenadism.[58] Vergil's Allecto is a Hellish monster of metamorphosis and illusion: *tot sese vertit in ora,* | *tam saevae facies, tot pullulat atra colubris* ('she changes herself into so many faces, such fearsome shapes she has, her head sprouts so many black serpents', *Aen.* 7.328–9); Juno praises her for her multiplicity, *tibi nomina mille,* | *mille nocendi artes* ('you have a thousand names, a thousand ways of causing harm', 337–8). Nonnus' Furies are also polymorphic and metamorphic demons.

The person and agency of Vergil's Allecto are frequently the model for Satan and his demons in Christian poetry from Late Antiquity to the Renaissance. What associations would Nonnus' Christian readers have made with the polymorphic perversity of his Megaira? Nonnus' Dionysus has features in common with Christ as a saviour-god appearing on earth; he also has a dark and Satanic side to him.

Metamorphosis as a subject continues to fascinate the poets of Late Antiquity, both Greek and Latin, speaking both to their innovative engagement with the writers of earlier antiquity and to the forces unleashed by the new religion of Christianity – as well as, in the case of Nonnus – by a paganism that has found a renewed imaginative, at least, vigour, a vigour that is arguably fuelled by its cohabitation with Christian culture and belief. I have privileged the Ovidian tradition of metamorphosis, not just because I am myself a Latinist, but because the Hellenistic poems of metamorphosis that might (but might not) have matched and inspired Ovid's remarkable construction of a world and a poetics of changes survive only in meagre fragments. But I leave open the question of whether the similarities between the Ovidian and the Nonnian poetry of metamorphosis are a matter of genealogy or convergence.

---

[58] *Aen.* 7.385–7, *quin etiam in silvas simulato numine Bacchi* | *maius adorta nefas maioremque orsa furorem* | *evolat,* 'she even flies out into the woods, feigning the possession of Bacchus, attempting a greater crime and starting out on a greater madness.'

Bibliography

Accorinti, D. (1996) *Parafrasi del Vangelo di San Giovanni: Canto XX*. Pisa.
    (ed.) (2016) *Brill's Companion to Nonnus of Panopolis*. Leiden.
    (2016) 'The poet from Panopolis: an obscure biography and a controversial
    figure', in *Brill's Companion to Nonnus of Panopolis*, ed. D. Accorinti. Leiden,
    Boston: 11–53.
    (2020) 'Did Nonnus really want to write a "gospel epic"? The ambiguous genre
    of the Paraphrase of the Gospel According to John', in *The Genres of Late
    Antique Christian Poetry: Between Modulations and Transpositions*, eds F.
    Hadjittofi and A. Lefteratou. Berlin, Boston: 225–47.
Accorinti, D. and Chuvin, P. (eds) (2003) *Des géants à Dionysos*. Alessandria.
Acosta-Hughes, B. (2016) 'Composing the masters: an essay on Nonnus and
    Hellenistic poetry', in *Brill's Companion to Nonnus of Panopolis*, ed. D.
    Accorinti. Leiden, Boston: 507–28.
Adler, E. (2003) *Vergil's Empire: Political Thought in the Aeneid*. Lanham, MD.
Agosti, G. (2001a) 'L'epica biblica nella tarda antichità greca', in *La scrittura
    infinita: Bibbia e poesia in età medievale e umanistica: atti del Convegno di
    Firenze, 26–28 giugno 1997*, ed. F. Stella. Tavarnuzze: 67–104.
    (2001b) 'Late antique iambics and *iambikè idéa*', in *Iambic Ideas: Essays on a
    Poetic Tradition from Archaic Greece to the Late Roman Empire*, eds A.
    Cavarzere, A. Aloni and A. Barchiesi. Lanham, MD: 219–55.
    (2003) *Nonno di Panopoli. Parafrasi del Vangelo di S. Giovanni. Canto V*.
    Florence.
    (2006) 'La voce dei libri. Dimensione performativa dell'epica Greca tardoan-
    tica', in *Approches de la Troisième Sophistique. Hommages à Jacques Schamp*,
    eds E. Amato, A. Roduit and M. Steinruck. Brussels: 35–62.
    (2008) 'Le Dionisache e le arti figurative', in *Nonno e i suoi lettori*, ed. S.
    Audano. Alessandria: 17–32.
    (2012) 'Greek poetry', in *The Oxford Handbook of Late Antiquity*, ed. S. F.
    Johnson. Oxford: 361–404.
    (2014) 'Contextualising Nonnus' visual world', in *Nonnus of Panopolis in
    Context: Poetry and Cultural Milieu in Late Antiquity with a Section on
    Nonnus and the Modern World*, ed. K. Spanoudakis. Berlin: 142–74.
    (2015) 'Chanter les dieux dans la société chrétienne: les *Hymnes* de Proclus
    dans le context culturel et religieux de leur temps', in *Fabriquer du divin: les*

constructions et ajustements de la représentation des dieux dans l'Antiquité, eds
N. Belayche and V. Pirenne-Delforge. Liege: 183–211.

(2016) 'Nonnus and late antique society' in *Brill's Companion to Nonnus of Panopolis*, ed. D. Accorinti. Leiden: 644–68.

(2020) 'Nonnus and Coptic literature: further explorations', in *Nonnus of Panopolis in Context III. Old Questions and New Perspectives*, eds F. Doroszewski and K. Jażdżewska. Leiden: 139–57.

Allen, W. (1940) 'The epyllion: a chapter in the history of literary criticism', *TAPhA* 71: 1–26.

(1958) 'The non-existent classical epyllion', *SPh* 55: 515–18.

Ambühl, A. (2007) 'Children as poets – poets as children? Romantic constructions of childhood and Hellenistic poetry', in *Constructions of Childhood in Ancient Greece and Italy*, eds A. Cohen and J. B. Rutter. Princeton: 373–83.

Andronikos, M. (1984) *Vergina: The Royal Tombs and the Ancient City*. Athens.

(1994) *Vergina II: The 'Tomb of Persephone'*. Athens.

Ayres, L. (2010) *Augustine and the Trinity*. Cambridge.

Bakke, O. M. (2005) *When Children Became People: The Birth of Childhood in Early Christianity*. Minneapolis.

Bal, M. (1991) *Reading 'Rembrandt': Beyond the Word-Image Opposition: The Northrop Frye Lectures in Literary Theory*. Cambridge.

Baldi, I. (2012) *Gli inni di Sinesio di Cirene: vicende testuali di un corpus tardoantico*. Berlin.

Bandinelli, R. B. (1955) *Hellenistic-Byzantine Miniatures of the Iliad*. Olten.

Bär, S. (2007) 'Quintus Smyrnaeus und die Tradition des epischen Musenanrufs', in *Quintus Smyrnaeus: Transforming Homer in Second Sophistic Epic*, eds M. Baumbach and S. Bär. Berlin: 29–64.

(2012) '"Museum of words": Christodorus, the art of ekphrasis and the epyllic genre', in *Brill's Companion to Greek and Latin Epyllion and Its Reception*, eds M. Baumbach and S. Bär. Leiden: 447–71.

(2015) 'Inventing and deconstructing epyllion. Some thoughts on a taxonomy of Greek hexameter poetry', *Thersites* 2: 23–51.

Bär, S. and Baumbach, M. (2015) 'The Epic Cycle and imperial Greek epic', in *The Greek Epic Cycle and Its Ancient Reception. A Companion*, eds M. Fantuzzi and C. Tsagalis. Cambridge: 604–22.

Barchiesi, A. (2001) 'The crossing', in *Texts, Ideas and the Classics*, ed. S. J. Harrison. Oxford: 142–63.

(2002) 'Narrative technique and narratology in the *Metamorphoses*', in *The Cambridge Companion to Ovid*, ed. P. Hardie. Cambridge: 180–99.

(2005) *Ovidio. Metamorfosi I–II*. Milan.

Barkan, L. (1986) *The Gods Made Flesh. Metamorphosis and the Pursuit of Paganism*. New Haven, London.

Barnes, T. D. (2006) 'An urban prefect and his wife', *CQ* 56: 249–56.

Bartels, A. (2004) *Vergleichende Studien zur Erzählkunst des römischen Epyllion*. Göttingen.

Barton, M. (2000) *Spätantike Bukolik zwischen paganer Tradition und christlicher Verkündigung: Das Carmen De mortibus boum des Endelechius*. Trier.

Bartsch, S. and Elsner, J. (2007a) 'Introduction: eight ways of looking at an ekphrasis', *CPh* 102: i–vi.

(ed.) (2007b) 'Ekphrasis', special issue *CPh* 102.1. Chicago.

Basson, A. (1996) 'A transformation of genres in late Latin Literature: classical literary tradition and ascetic ideals in Paulinus of Nola', in *Shifting Frontiers in Late Antiquity*, eds R. W. Mathisen and H. S. Sivan. Aldershot: 267–76.

Baumbach, M. (2007) 'Die Poetik der Schilde: Form und Funktion von Ekphraseis in den *Posthomerica* des Quintus Smyrnaeus', in *Quintus Smyrnaeus: Transforming Homer in Second Sophistic Epic*, eds M. Baumbach and S. Bär. Berlin: 107–44.

Baumbach, M. and Bär, S. (eds) (2007) *Quintus Smyrnaeus: Transforming Homer in Second Sophistic Epic*. Berlin.

(2012) *Brill's Companion to Greek and Latin Epyllion and Its Reception*. Leiden.

Bažil, M. (2009) *Centones Christiani: métamorphoses d'une forme intertextuelle dans la poesie latine chrétienne de l'Antiquité tardive*. Paris.

Beatrice, P. F. and Pouderon, B. (eds) (2016) *Pascha nostrum Christus: Essays in Honour of Raniero Cantalamessa*. Paris.

Beckby, H. (1965²) *Anthologia Graeca: Griechisch-Deutsch*, 4 vols., 2nd rev. ed. Munich.

Belayche, N. and Pirenne-Delforge, V. (eds) (2015) *Fabriquer du divin: les constructions et dynamises de ses representations*. Liège.

Benedetti, F. (1980) *La tecnica del 'vertere' negli epigrammi di Ausonio*. Florence.

Benediktson, D. T. (2000) *Literature and the Visual Arts in Ancient Greece and Rome*. Norman, OK.

Benelli, L. (2016) 'The Age of Palladas', *Mnemosyne* 69: 978–1007.

Bergman, I. (1926) *Aurelii Prudentii Clementis Carmina*, Corpus Scriptorum Ecclesiasticorum Latinorum 61. Vienna.

Bezantakos, N. P. (2015) Νόννου Πανοπολίτου Διονυσιακά. Τόμος πρῶτος. Βιβλία πρῶτο καὶ δεύτερο. Athens.

Bing, P. and Bruss, J. S. (eds) (2007) *Brill's Companion to Hellenistic Epigram down to Philip*. Leiden, Boston.

duBois, P. (1982) *History, Rhetorical Description and the Epic: From Homer to Spenser*. Cambridge.

Bolmarcich, S. (2002) 'Hellenistic sepulchral epigrams on Homer', in *Hellenistic Epigrams*, Hellenistica Groningana 6, eds M. A. Harder, R. F. Regtuit and G. C. Wakker. Leuven, Paris, Sterling: 67–83.

Borg, M. and Miles, G. (eds) (2013) *Approaches to Genre in the Ancient World*. Newcastle.

Bouquet, J. (1995) 'Introduction', in *Dracontius, Poèmes profanes III*, ed. E. Wolff. Paris.

Bouquet, J. and Wolff, E. (eds) (1995) *Dracontius. Oeuvres. Tome III*. Paris.

Bowie, E. (2005) 'Metaphor in *Daphnis and Chloe*', in *Metaphor and the Ancient Novel*, Ancient Narrative, Suppl. 4, eds S. J. Harrison, M. Paschalis and S. Frangoulidis. Groningen: 68–86.

Bowra, C. M. (1959) 'Palladas and Christianity', *PBA* 45: 255–67.

Braden, G. (1974) 'Nonnos' Typhoon: *Dionysiaca* books I and II', *Texas Studies in Literature and Language* 15: 851–79.

(1979) 'Claudian and his influence: the realm of Venus', *Arethusa* 12: 203–31.

Braune, J. (1935) *Nonnos und Ovid*. Greifswald.

(1948) 'Nonno e Claudiano', *Maia* 1: 176–93.

Bretzigheimer, G. (2010) 'Dracontius' Konzepzion des Kleinepos *De Raptu Helenae (Romul. 8)*', *RhM* 153: 361–400.

Bright, D. F. (1984) 'Theory and practice in the Vergilian cento', *ICS* 9: 79–90.

(1987) *The Miniature Epic in Vandal Africa*. Norman, OK.

Brocca, N. (2003) 'A che genere letterario appartiene il de *reditu* di Rutilio Namaziano?', in *Forme letterarie nella produzione latina di IV–V secolo*, ed. F. E. Consolino. Rome: 231–55.

Brown, P. R. L. (1971) *The World of Late Antiquity from Marcus Aurelius to Muhammad*. London.

Brown, J. (2007) *The Persistence of Allegory: Drama and Neoclassicism from Shakespeare to Wagner*. Philadelphia.

Buffière, F. (1956) *Les mythes d'Homère et la pensée grecque*. Paris.

Burkert, W. (1985) *Greek Religion: Archaic and Classical*, translated by John Raffan. Oxford.

(2005) 'Hesiod in context: abstractions and divinities in an Aegean-Eastern koiné', in *Personification in the Greek World: From Antiquity to Byzantium*, eds J. Herrin and E. Stafford. Aldershot: 3–20.

Burrow, C. (1999) '"Full of the maker's guile": Ovid on imitating and on the imitation of Ovid', in *Ovidian Transformations. Essays on Ovid's Metamorphoses and Its Reception*, eds P. Hardie, A. Barchiesi, S. Hinds. Cambridge: 271–87.

Butterfield, D. (2013) *The Early Textual History of Lucretius' De rerum natura*. Cambridge.

Buxton, R. (2009) *Forms of Astonishment: Greek Myths of Metamorphosis*. Oxford.

Byre, C. (1982) 'Per aspera (et arborem) ad astra: ramifications of the allegory of *Arete* in Quintus Smyrnaeus *Posthomerica* 5.49–68', *Hermes* 110: 184–95.

Cadau, C. (2015) *Studies in Colluthus' Abduction of Helen*. Leiden.

Cairns, F. (2016) *Hellenistic Epigram: Contexts of Exploration*. Cambridge.

Cameron, A. (1970a) *Claudian: Poetry and Propaganda at the Court of Honorius*. Oxford.

(1970b) 'PAP. ANT. III. 115 and the iambic prologue in late Greek poetry', *CQ* 20: 119–29.

(1982) 'The empress and the poet: paganism and politics at the court of Theodosius II', in *Later Greek Literature*, eds J. J. Winkler and G. Williams. Cambridge: 217–90.

(1993) *The Greek Anthology: From Meleager to Planudes*. Oxford.

(1998) 'Basilius, Mavortius, Asterius', in *Aetos: Studies in Honor of Cyril Mango*, eds I. Ševčenko and I. Hutter. Stuttgart: 28–39.

(2004a) *Greek Mythography in the Roman World.* Oxford.

(2004b) 'Poetry and literary culture in Late Antiquity', in *Approaching Late Antiquity: The Transformation from Early to Late Empire*, eds S. Swain and M. J. Edwards. Oxford: 327–54.

(2011) *The Last Pagans of Rome.* Oxford.

(2016a) *Wandering Poets and Other Essays on Late Greek Literature and Philosophy.* Oxford.

(2016b) 'The date of Palladas', *ZPE* 198: 49–52.

Cameron, Averil and Cameron, Alan (1966) 'The *Cycle* of Agathias', *JHS* 86: 6–25.

Cameron, Averil (2002) 'The "long" late antiquity: a late twentieth-century model', in *Classics in Progress*, ed. T. P. Wiseman. Oxford: 165–91.

Campbell, M. (1985) *A Lexicon to Triphiodorus.* Hildesheim.

Caprara, M. (2005) *Nonno di Panopoli: Parafrasi del Vangelo di San Giovanni, Canto IV.* Pisa.

Carvounis, K. (2014) '*Peitho* in Nonnus' *Dionysiaca*: the case of Cadmus and Harmonia', in *Nonnus of Panopolis in Context: Poetry and Cultural Milieu in Late Antiquity with a Section on Nonnus and the Modern World*, ed. K. Spanoudakis. Berlin, Boston: 21–38.

(2019) *A Commentary on Quintus of Smyrna, Posthomerica 14.* Oxford.

Carvounis, K. and Hunter, R. (eds) (2008) *Signs of Life? Studies in Later Greek Poetry* (= *Ramus* 37.1–2). Bendigo.

Cavarzere, A., Aloni, A. and Barchiesi, A. (eds) (2001) *Iambic Ideas: Essays on a Poetic Tradition from Archaic Greece to the Late Roman Empire.* Lanham, MD.

Celoria, F. (1992) *The Metamorphoses of Antoninus Liberalis.* London, New York.

Charlet, J.-L. (1988) 'Aesthetic trends in late Latin poetry', *Philologus* 132: 74–85.

Chuvin, P. (1992) *Nonnos de Panopolis: les Dionysiaques, Tome III, Chants VI–VIII.* Paris.

(2014) 'Revisiting old problems: literature and religion in the *Dionysiaca*', in *Nonnus of Panopolis in Context: Poetry and Cultural Milieu in Late Antiquity with a Section on Nonnus and the Modern World*, ed. K. Spanoudakis. Berlin, Boston: 3–18.

(2016) 'Nonnus, from our time to his. A retrospective glance at Nonnian Studies (notably the *Dionysiaca*) since the 1930s', in *Nonnus of Panopolis in Context II. Poetry, Religion and Society*, eds H. Bannert and N. Kröll. Leiden: 1–18.

Clark, E. A. and Hatch, D. F. (1981) *The Golden Bough, the Oaken Cross: The Virgilian Cento of Faltonia Betitia Proba.* Chico, CA.

Cohen, D. (1991) *Law, Sexuality, and Society: The Enforcement of Morals in Classical Athens.* Cambridge.

Coleman, K. (1999) 'Mythological figures as spokespersons in Statius' *Silvae*', in *Im Spiegel des Mythos. Bilderwelt und Lebenswelt*, eds F. de Angelis and S. Muth. Wiesbaden: 67–80.

Combeaud, B. (2010) *Ausonius, D. Magnus. Opuscula omnia.* Bordeaux.

Conant, J. (2012) *Staying Roman: Conquest and Identity in Africa and the Mediterranean, 439–700.* Cambridge.

Consolino, F. E. (2003) 'Metri, temi e forme letterarie nella poesia di Ausonio', in *Forme letterarie nella produzione latina di IV–V secolo*, ed. F. E. Consolino. Rome: 147–94.

(ed.) (2003) *Forme letterarie nella produzione latina di IV–V secolo.* Rome.

(2005) 'Il senso del passato: generi letterari e rapporti con la tradizione "parafrasi biblica" latina', in *Nuovo e antico nella cultura greco-latina di IV–VI secolo*, eds I. Gualandri, F. Conca and R. Passarella. Milan: 447–526.

Conte, G. B. (1991) *Generi e lettori: Lucrezio, l'elegia d'amore, l'enciclopedia di Plinio.* Milan.

(1992) 'Proems in the middle', in *Beginnings in Classical Literature*, eds F. Dunn and T. Cole. Cambridge: 147–59.

(1994) *Genres and Readers: Lucretius, Love Elegy, Pliny's Encyclopedia.* Baltimore.

Copeland, R. and Struck, P. (2010) 'Introduction', in *The Cambridge Companion to Allegory*, eds R. Copeland and P. Struck. Cambridge: 1–14.

Coşkun, A. (2002) *Die gens Ausoniana an der Macht: Untersuchungen zu Decimius Magnus Ausonius und seiner Familie.* Oxford.

Crawford, M. R. (2014) *Cyril of Alexandria's Trinitarian Theology of Scripture.* Oxford.

Cribiore, R. (2001) *Gymnastics of the Mind: Greek Education in Hellenistic and Roman Egypt.* Princeton, Oxford.

Cristante, L. (1999) *Reposiani concubitus Martis et Veneris.* Rome.

Crump, M. M. (1931) *The Epyllion from Theocritus to Ovid.* Garland.

Cuartero i Iborra, F. J. (1992) *Collut, El Rapte d'Hèlena.* Barcelona.

Culpepper, R. A. (1983), *Anatomy of the Fourth Gospel: A Study in Literary Design.* Philadelphia.

Cunningham, M. P. (1966) *Aurelii Prudentii Clementis Carmina*, Corpus Christianorum Series Latina 126. Turnhout.

D'Alessio, G. B. (1997) 'Pindar's *Prosodia* and the classification of Pindaric papyrus fragments', *ZPE* 118: 23–60.

D'Ippolito, G. (1962) 'Il fulmine minore in Ovidio e in Nonno', *RFIC* 40: 299–300.

(1964) *Studi Nonniani. L'epillio nelle Dionisiache.* Palermo.

(2007) 'Nonno di Panopoli e i poeti latini', in *De Grecia a Roma y de Roma a Grecia: un camino de ida y vuelta*, eds A. Sánchez-Ostiz, J. B. Torres Guerra en R. Martínez. Pamplona: 311–31.

De Lorenzi, A. (1928) 'Il proemio del Ratto di Elena di Colluto', *Rivista Indo-Greco-Italica* 13: 28–58.

De Prisco, A. (1977) 'Osservazioni su Draconzio Romul. VIII, 11–23', *Vichiana* 6: 290–300.

De Stefani, C. (2002) *Nonno di Panopoli. Parafrasi del Vangelo di S. Giovanni, Canto I.* Bologna.

(2016) 'Brief notes on the manuscript tradition of Nonnus' Works', in *Brill's Companion to Nonnus of Panopolis*, ed. D. Accorinti. Leiden: 671–90.

Del Mastro, G. (2014) *Titoli e annotazioni bibliologiche nei papiri Greci di Ercolano*. Naples.

Den Boeft, J. (1993) 'Ambrosius lyricus', in *Early Christian Poetry: A Collection of Essays*, eds J. den Boeft and A. Hilhorst. Leiden: 77–89.

(2007) '*Cantatur ad delectationem*: Ambrose's lyric poetry', in *Poetry and Exegesis in Premodern Latin Christianity: The Encounter between Classical and Christian Strategies of Interpretation*, eds W. Otten and K. Pollmann. Leiden: 81–97.

Den Boeft, J. and Hilhorst, A. (eds) (1993) *Early Christian Poetry: A Collection of Essays*. Leiden.

Depew, M. (2000) 'Enacted and represented dedications: genre and Greek hymn', in *Matrices of Genre: Authors, Canons, and Society*, eds M. Depew and D. Obbink. Cambridge, MA: 59–79.

Depew, M. and Obbink, D. (2000) 'Introduction', in *Matrices of Genre: Authors, Canons, and Society*, eds M. Depew and D. Obbink. Cambridge, MA: 1–14.

(eds) (2000) *Matrices of Genre: Authors, Canons, and Society*. Cambridge, MA.

Dewar, M. (2002) '*Si quid habent ueri uatum praesagia*: Ovid in the 1st–5th centuries A.D.', in *Brill's Companion to Ovid*, ed. B. W. Boyd. Leiden, Boston, Cologne: 383–412.

Díaz de Bustamente, J. M. (1978) *Draconcio y sus carmina profana. Estudio biográfico, introducción y edición crítica*. Santiago de Compostela.

Diggle, J. (1970) *Euripides. Phaethon*. Cambridge.

Dijkstra, R. (2016) *The Apostles in Early Christian Art and Poetry*. Leiden, Boston.

Dixon, S. (1992) *The Roman Family*. Baltimore, MD.

Dorfbauer, L. J. (2010) 'Die praefationes von Claudian und von Prudentius', in *Text und Bild*, eds V. Zimmerl-Panagl and D. Weber. Vienna: 195–222.

(2012) 'Claudian und Prudentius: verbale Parallelen und Datierungsfragen', *Hermes* 140: 45–70.

Dörrie, H. (1972) 'Une exégèse néoplatonicienne du prologue de l'Évangile de Saint Jean (Amélius chez Eusèbe, Prép. Év. 11, 19, 1–4)', in *EPEKTASIS. Mélanges patristiques offerts au cardinal J. Daniélou*, eds J. F. and C. Kannengiesser. Paris: 75–85.

Dover, K. J. (1978) *Greek Homosexuality*. London.

Duff, J. W. and Duff, M. A. (eds) (1934) *Minor Latin Poets, vol. 2: Florus. Hadrian. Nemesianus. Reposianus. Tiberianus. Dicta Catonis. Phoenix. Avianus. Rutilius Namatianus. others*. Cambridge, MA.

Dummler, N. N. (2012) 'Musaeus, *Hero and Leander*: between epic and novel', in *Brill's Companion to Greek and Latin Epyllion and Its Reception*, eds M. Baumbach and S. Bär. Leiden: 411–45.

Dunbabin, K. M. D. and Dickie, M. (1983) '*Invida rumpantur pectora*. The iconography of Phthonos/Invidia in Graeco-Roman art', *JbAC* 26: 7–37.

Eagan, M. C. (1965) *The Poems of Prudentius*, vol. 2. Washington, DC.

Eck, B. A. (2001) 'Nudity and framing: classifying art, pornography, information, and ambiguity', *Sociological Forum* 16: 603–32.

(2003) 'Men are much harder: gendered viewing of nude images', *Gender and Society* 17: 691–710.

Edwards, M. J. (1995) 'Chrysostom, Prudentius, and the fiends of Paradise Lost', *N&Q* 42.4: 448–51.

(2004) 'Dracontius the African and the fate of Rome', *Latomus* 63: 151–60.

Elderkin, G. W. (1906) *Aspects of the Speech in the Later Greek Epic*. Baltimore.

Eller, K. H. (1982) 'Die Metamorphose bei Ovid und Nonnos. Mythische Poesie im Vergleich.' *AU* 25: 88–98.

Elsner, J. (1995) *Art and the Roman Viewer: The Transformation of Art from the Pagan World to Christianity*. Cambridge.

(1998) *Imperial Rome and Christian Triumph: The Art of the Roman Empire A.D. 100–450*. Oxford.

(2002) 'Introduction: the genres of ekphrasis', *Ramus* 31: 1–18.

(2007a) 'Viewing Ariadne: from ekphrasis to wall painting in the Roman world', *CPh* 102: 20–44.

(2007b) *Roman Eyes: Visuality and Subjectivity in Art and Text*. Princeton.

Elsner J. and Hernández Lobato, J. (eds) (2017) *The Poetics of Late Latin Literature*. Oxford.

Espinar Ojeda, J. L. (2005) 'Algunas notas sobre las metamorfosis en las "Dionisíacas" de Nono de Panópolis', in *Actas del XI congreso español de estudios clásicos* (Santiago de Compostela, del 15 al 20 de septiembre de 2003), eds J. F. González Castro, A. Alvar Ezquerra, A. Bernabé et al. Madrid: 2.269–76.

Evelyn White, H. G. (1919) *Ausonius*. vol. 1: *books 1–17*. Cambridge, MA.

Evenepoel, W. (1993) 'The place of poetry in Latin Christianity', in *Early Christian Poetry: A Collection of Essays*, eds J. den Boeft and A. Hilhorst. Leiden: 35–60.

(1994) 'The early Christian poets Gregory Nazianzen and Prudentius', in *Philohistôr: Miscellanea in Honorem Caroli Laga Septuagenarii*, eds A. Schoors and P. Van Deun. Leuven: 87–101.

Faber, R. A. (ed.) (2016) 'Nonnus and the poetry of ekphrasis in the *Dionysiaca*', in *Brill's Companion to Nonnus of Panopolis*, ed. D. Accorinti. Leiden, Boston: 443–59.

Fairclough, H. R. and Goold, G. P. (1999) *Virgil*, 2 vols. Cambridge, MA.

Falcone, M. J. (2020) 'Some observations on the genre of Dracontius' Satisfactio', in *The Genres of Late Antique Christian Poetry: Between Modulations and Transpositions*, eds F. Hadjittofi and A. Lefteratou. Berlin, Boston: 125–38.

Fantuzzi, M. (1998/2004) 'Epyllion', *BNP* 4 (2004): 1170–2. Originally published in German. *DNP* 4 (1998): 31–3.

Fantuzzi, M. and Hunter, R. 2004. *Tradition and Innovation in Hellenistic Poetry*. Cambridge.

Fantuzzi, M. and Papanghelis, T. (eds) (2006) *Brill's Companion to Greek and Latin Pastoral*. Leiden.

Färber, H. (1937) 'Die Termini der Poetik in den Odenüberschriften der Horazoden', *Philologus* 92: 349–74.
Farrell, J. (2003) 'Classical genre in theory and practice', *New Literary History* 34: 383–408.
Faulkner, A. (2014) 'Faith and fidelity in biblical epic. The Metaphrasis Psalmorum, Nonnus, and the theory of translation', in *Nonnus of Panopolis in Context: Poetry and Cultural Milieu in Late Antiquity with a Section on Nonnus and the Modern World*, ed. K. Spanoudakis. Berlin, Boston: 195–210.
    (2020) 'Davidic didactic hexameters: the generic stance of the *Metaphrasis Psalmorum*', in *The Genres of Late Antique Christian Poetry: Between Modulations and Transpositions*, eds F. Hadjittofi and A. Lefteratou. Berlin, Boston: 265–74.
Fauth, W. (1974) '*Cupido Cruciatur*', *GB* 2: 39–60.
    (1981) *Eidos poikilon. Zur Thematik der Metamorphose und zum Prinzip der Wandlung aus dem Gegensatz in den Dionysiaka des Nonnos von Panopolis*. Göttingen.
Feeney, D. (1991) *The Gods in Epic: Poets and Critics of the Classical Tradition*. Oxford.
Feldman, L. H. (1953) 'The character of Ascanius in Virgil's *Aeneid*', *CJ* 48 (8): 303–13.
Felgentreu, F. (1999) *Claudians Praefationes. Bedingungen, Beschreibungen und Wirkungen einer poetischen Kleinform*. Stuttgart.
Fielding, I. (2014) 'A poet between two worlds: Ovid in Late Antiquity', in *A Handbook to the Reception of Ovid*, eds J. F. Miller and C. E. Newlands. Chichester: 100–13.
    (2017) *Transformations of Ovid in Late Antiquity*. Cambridge.
Fisher, E. (2011) 'Ovid metempsychosis', in *Ovid in the Middle Ages*, eds J. G. Clark, F. T. Coulson and K. L. McKinley. Cambridge: 26–47.
Fitzgerald, J. and White, M. (1983) *The Tabula of Cebes*. Chico.
Fo, A. (1989) 'Ritorno a Claudio Rutilio Namaziano', *MD* 22: 49–74.
Fontaine, J. (1975) 'Le mélange des genres dans la poésie de Prudence', in *Forma futuri: studi in onore del Cardinale Michele Pellegrino*. Turin: 755–77, reprinted in Fontaine (1980): 1–23.
    (1976) 'Prose et poésie: l'interférence des genres et des styles dans la création littéraire d'Ambroise de Milan', in *Ambrosius episcopus*, vol. 1, ed. G. Lazzati. Milan: 124–170, reprinted in Fontaine (1980): 84–130.
    (1977) 'Unité et diversité du mélange des genres et des tons chez quelques écrivains latins de la fin du IVe siècle: Ausone, Ambroise, Ammien', in *Christianisme et formes littéraires de l'antiquité tardive en occident*, ed. M. Fuhrmann. Geneva: 425–82, reprinted in Fontaine (1980): 25–72.
    (1980) *Études sur la poésie latine tardive d'Ausone à Prudence*. Paris.
    (1981) *Naissance de la poésie dans l'occident chrétien: esquisse d'une histoire de la poésie latine chrétienne du IIIe au VIe siècle*. Paris.
    (1988) 'Comment doit-on appliquer la notion de genre littéraire à la littérature latine chrétienne du IVe siècle?', *Philologus* 132: 53–73.

Formisano, M. (2007) 'Towards an aesthetic paradigm of Late Antiquity', *An Tard* 15: 277–84.

Formisano, M. and Sogno, C. (2010) 'Petite poésie portable: the Latin cento in its late antique context', in *Condensed Texts – Condensing Texts*, eds M. Horster and C. Reitz. Stuttgart: 375–92.

Formisano, M. and Fuhrer, T. (eds) (2014) *Décadence: 'Decline and Fall' or 'Other Antiquity'?* Heidelberg.

Fowler, A. (1982) *Kinds of Literature: An Introduction to the Theory of Genres and Modes*. Oxford.

Franchi, R. (2013) *Parafrasi del Vangelo di Giovanni: canto Sesto*. Florence.

   (2016) 'Approaching the "spiritual gospel": Nonnus as interpreter of John', in *Brill's Companion to Nonnus of Panopolis*, ed. D. Accorinti. Leiden, New York: 240–66.

Frangoulis, H. (2003) 'Les Pierres magiques dans les Dionysiaques de Nonnos de Panopolis', in *Des géants à Dionysos*, eds D. Accorinti and P. Chuvin. Alessandria: 433–5.

Fränkel, H. (1945) *Ovid: A Poet between Two Worlds*. Berkeley, Los Angeles.

Franzoi, A. (2002) *Decimo Magno Ausonio. Cupido messo in croce*. Naples.

Fredericks, B. R. (1977) 'Divine wit vs. divine folly: Mercury and Apollo in *Metamorphoses* 1–2', *CJ* 72: 244–9.

Fredouille, J.-C. et al. (eds) (1997) *Titres et articulations du texte dans les oeuvres antiques*. Paris.

Freund, S. (2016) 'Der Psalmus responsorius: missing link in der Entwicklung der christlichen lateinischen Dichtung?', in *Pascha nostrum Christus: Essays in Honour of Raniero Cantalamessa*, eds P. F. Beatrice and B. Pouderon. Paris: 121–36.

Friderici, R. (1911) *De librorum antiquorum capitum divisone atque summariis*. Marburg.

Fuhrmann, M. (ed.) (1977) *Christianisme et formes littéraires de l'antiquité tardive en occident*. Geneva.

Fux, P.-Y. (2005) 'Le Romanus de Prudence (Peristephanon 10), tragédie chrétienne?', in κορυφαίῳ ἀνδρί: *Mélanges offerts à André Hurst*, eds A. Kolde, A. Lukinovich and A.-L. Rey. Geneva: 87–96.

Gabathuler, M. (1937) *Hellenistische Epigramme auf Dichter*. PhD Dissertation: University of Basel.

Gador-Whyte, S. (2013) 'Playing with genre: Romanos the melodist and his kontakion', in *Approaches to Genre in the Ancient World*, eds M. Borg and G. Miles. Newcastle: 159–76.

Galand-Hallyn, P. (1994) *Le reflet des fleurs: description et métalangage poétique d'Homère à la Renaissance*. Geneva.

Galinsky, K. (1996) *Augustan Culture. An Interpretive Introduction*. Princeton.

Garambois-Vasquez, F. and Vallat, D. (eds) (2017) *Varium et mutabile: mémoires et métamorphoses du centon dans l'Antiquité*. Saint-Étienne.

Garani, M., Michaelopoulos, A. N. and Papaioannou, S. (eds) (2020) *Intertextuality in Seneca's Philosophical Writings*. London, New York.

Garipzanov, I. (2015) 'The rise of graphicacy in Late Antiquity and the early Middle Ages', *Viator* 46: 1–21.

Gärtner, U. (2005) *Quintus Smyrnaeus und die 'Aeneis': zur Nachwirkung Vergils in der Griechischen Literatur der Kaiserzeit.* Munich.

(2007) 'Zur Rolle der Personifikationen des Schicksals in den Posthomerica des Quintus Smyrnaeus', in *Quintus Smyrnaeus: Transforming Homer in Second Sophistic Epic*, eds. M. Baumbach and S. Bär. Berlin: 211–40.

(2014) 'Schicksal und Entscheidungsfreiheit bei Quintus Smyrnaeus', *Philologus* 58.1: 97–129.

Garuti, P. (2005) *Prudentius. Apotheosis.* Modena.

Garzya, A. (1984) 'Retorica e realtà nella poesia tardoantica', in *La poesia tardoantica: tra retorica, teleologia e politica*, ed. S. Costanza. Messina: 11–49.

Gellrich, J. M. (2000) 'The art of the tongue: illuminating speech and writing in later medieval manuscripts', in *Virtues and Vices: The Personifications in the Index of Christian Art*, ed. C. Hourihane. Princeton: 93–119.

Gelzer, T. (1975) *Musaeus. Hero and Leander.* Cambridge, MA.

Genette, G. (1982) *Palimpsestes. La littérature au second degré.* Paris.

(1987) *Seuils.* Paris.

Gerbeau, J. and Vian, F. (1992) *Nonnos de Panopolis. Les Dionysiaques, Tome VII, Chants XVIII–XIX.* Paris.

Gerlaud, B. (1982) *Triphiodore, La Prise d'Ilion.* Paris.

Geyer, A. (1989) *Die Genese narrativer Buchillustration. Der Miniaturenzyklus zur Aeneis im Vergilius Vaticanus.* Frankfurt am Main.

Giangrande, G. (1969) 'Review of Livrea 1968', *JHS* 89: 149–54.

Gianotti, G. F. (1991) 'Sulle tracce della pantomima tragica: Alcesti tra i danzatori?', *Dioniso* 61: 121–49.

Gigli Piccardi, D. (1985) *Metafora e poetica in Nonno di Panopoli.* Florence.

(2003) *Nonno di Panopoli. Le Dionisiache. Canti I–XII.* Milan.

Gildenhard, I. and Zissos, A. (eds) (2013) *Transformative Change in Western Thought. A History of Metamorphosis from Homer to Hollywood.* London.

Gilka, M. (2014). *Like Mother like Daughter? Hermione in Colluthus' 'Abduction of Helen'.* MSt Dissertation: University of Oxford.

(2020) 'Destiny's child: Hermione in Colluthus' *Abduction of Helen*', in *Myth, Religion, Tradition and Narrative in Late Antique Greek Poetry*, Wiener Studien Beiheft 41, ed. N. Kröll. Vienna: 187–209.

Gioseffi, M. (2012) '"Introducing Virgil": Forme di presentazione dell'Eneide in età tardoantica', in *Ways of Approaching Knowledge in Late Antiquity and the Early Middle Ages*, eds P. F. Alberto and D. Paniagua. Nordhausen: 120–43.

Glei, R. (2006) 'Vergil am Zeug flicken. Centonische Schreibstrategien und die Centones ex Virgilio des Lelio Capilupi', in *'Parodia' und Parodie: Aspekte intertextuellen Schreibens in der lateinischen Literatur der Frühen Neuzeit*, eds R. Glei and R. Seidel. Tübingen: 287–320.

Goldberg, S. M. and Manuwald, G. (2018) *Ennius. Fragmentary Republican Latin, vol. 1: Ennius, Testimonia. Epic Fragments.* Cambridge, MA.

Goldhill, S. (2007) 'What is ekphrasis for?' *CPh* 102: 1–19.

(2020) *Preposterous Politics: The Politics and Aesthetics of Form in Late Antiquity*. Cambridge.

Golega, J. (1930) *Studien über die Evangeliendichtung des Nonnos von Panopolis*. Breslau.

Gow, A. S. F. (1952) *Theocritus: Edited with a Translation and Commentary*, 2 vols., 2nd ed. Cambridge.

Gow, A. S. F. and Scholfield, A. F. (1953) *Nicander. The Poems and Poetical Fragments*. Cambridge.

Greatrex, G. and Elton, H. (2015) *Shifting Genres in Late Antiquity*. Farnham.

Greco, C. (2004) *Nonno di Panopoli: Parafrasi del Vangelo di S. Giovanni, canto tredicesimo*. Alessandria.

Green, R. P. H. (1991) *The Works of Ausonius*. Oxford.

(1997) 'Proba's introduction to her Cento', *CQ* 47: 548–59.

(1999) *Decimi Magni Ausonii Opera*. Oxford.

(2004a) 'Approaching Christian epic: the preface of Juvencus', in *Latin Epic and Didactic Poetry: Genre, Tradition, and Individuality*, ed. M. Gale. Swansea: 203–22.

(2004b) 'Refinement and reappraisal in Vergilian pastoral', in *Romane Memento: Vergil in the Fourth Century*, ed. R. Rees. London: 17–32.

(2006) *Latin Epics of the New Testament: Juvencus, Sedulius, Arator*. Oxford.

(2008) 'Which Proba wrote the cento?', *CQ* 58: 264–76.

Greensmith, E. (2018) 'When Homer quotes Callimachus: allusive poetics in the proem of the *Posthomerica*', *CQ* 68: 257–74.

(2020). *The Resurrection of Homer in Imperial Greek Epic: Quintus Smyrnaeus' Posthomerica and the Poetics of Impersonation*, Greek Culture in the Roman World. Cambridge.

Gregory, J. (1985) 'Some aspects of seeing in Euripides' '*Bacchae*'', *G&R* 32: 23–31.

Griffith, M. (1983) *Aeschylus. Prometheus Bound*. Cambridge.

Griffiths, J. G. (1960) 'The flight of the gods before Typhon: an unrecognized myth', *Hermes* 88: 374–6.

Grillo, A. (ed.) (2010²) *La Aegritudo Perdicae rivisitata*. Messina.

Grillone, A. (2008) *Blossi Aem. Draconti Orestis Tragoedia. Introduzione, testo critico e commento a cura di Antonino Grillone*. Bari.

Gruber, J. (2013) *D. Magnus Ausonius, Mosella: Kritische Ausgabe, Übersetzung, Kommentar*. Berlin, Boston.

Gualandri, I., Conca, F. and Passarella, R. (eds) (2005) *Nuovo e antico nella cultura greco-latina di IV–VI secolo*. Milan.

Guichard, L. A. (2017) 'From school to desacralization, or how Palladas read Homer', in *Traditions épiques et poésie épigrammatique: présence des épopées archaïques dans les épigrammes grecques et latines*, Hellenistica Groningana 22, eds Y. Durbec and F. Trajber. Louvain, Paris, Walpole: 157–70.

Gurd, S. A. (2012) *Work in Progress: Literary Revision as Social Performance in Ancient Rome*. Oxford.

Gutzwiller, K. J. (1981) *Studies in the Hellenistic Epyllion*. Königstein.

(2006) 'The herdsman in Greek thought', in *Brill's Companion to Greek and Latin Pastoral*, eds M. Fantuzzi and T. Papanghelis. Leiden, Boston: 1–23.

Haas, C. (1997) *Alexandria in Late Antiquity: Topography and Social Conflict*. Baltimore, London

Hadjittofi, F. (2020) 'Nonnus' *Paraphrase of the Gospel According to John* as didactic epic', in *The Genres of Late Antique Christian Poetry: Between Modulations and Transpositions*, eds F. Hadjittofi and A. Lefteratou. Berlin, Boston: 249–64.

Hadjittofi, F. and Lefteratou, A. (eds) (2020) *The Genres of Late Antique Christian Poetry: Between Modulations and Transpositions*. Berlin, Boston.

Hall, E. (2008) 'Is the "Barcelona Alcestis" a Latin pantomime libretto?' in *New Directions in Ancient Pantomime*, eds E. Hall and R. Wyles. Oxford: 258–82.

Hall, J. B. (1969) *Claudian, De Raptu Proserpinae*. Cambridge.

Hardie, P. R. (1986) *Virgil's Aeneid: Cosmos and Imperium*. Oxford.

(2002) *Ovid's Poetics of Illusion*. Cambridge.

(2005) 'Nonnus' Typhon: the musical giant', in *Roman and Greek Imperial Epic*, ed. M. Paschalis. Rethymnon: 117–30.

Hardie, P. R. (ed.) (2009) *Paradox and the Marvellous in Augustan Literature and Culture*. Oxford, New York.

(2019) *Classicism and Christianity in Late Antique Latin Poetry*. Oakland, CAL.

Harich-Schwarzbauer, H. (2009) 'Von Aeneas zu Camilla. Intertextualität im Vergilcento der Faltonia Betitia Proba', in *Jeux de voix: enonciation, intertextualité et intentionnalité dans le littérature antique*, ed. D. van Mal-Maeder. Bern: 331–46.

Harries, B. (1994) 'The pastoral mode in the *Dionysiaca*', in *Studies in the Dionysiaca of Nonnus*, ed. N. Hopkinson. Cambridge: 63–85.

(2006) 'The drama of pastoral in Nonnus and Colluthus', in *Brill's Companion to Greek and Latin Pastoral*, eds M. Fantuzzi and Th. Papanghelis. Leiden, Boston: 515–47.

Harrison, C., Humfress, C. and Sandwell, I. (eds) (2014) *Being Christian in Late Antiquity: A Festschrift for Gillian Clark*. Oxford.

Harrison, S. J. (ed.) (2001) *Texts, Ideas and the Classics*. Oxford.

(2007) *Generic Enrichment in Virgil and Horace*. Oxford.

(2013) 'Introduction', in *Generic Interfaces in Latin Literature*, eds T. D. Papanghelis, S. J. Harrison and S. Frangoulidis. Berlin, Boston: 1–15.

Haskell, F. and Penny, N. (1981) *Taste and the Antique: The Lure of Classical Sculpture, 1500–1900*. New Haven, London.

Häußler, R. (1998) 'Reposian und seine klassischen Helfer', in *Candide Iudex. Festschrift für Walter Wimmel zum 75. Geburtstage*, ed. A. E. Radke. Stuttgart: 81–130.

Havelock, C. M. (1995) *The Aphrodite of Knidos and Her Successors: A Historical Review of the Female Nude in Greek Art*. Ann Arbor, MI.

Hawkins, T. (2014) *Iambic Poetics in the Roman Empire*. Cambridge.

Hecquet-Noti, N. (1999–2005) *Avit de Vienne: histoire spirituelle*, 2 vols. Paris.

Heitsch, E. (1963–1964) *Die Griechischen Dichterfragmente der römischen Kaiserzeit*. Göttingen.

Henderson, W. (2009) 'Palladas of Alexandria on women', *AClass* 52: 83–100.

Henke, R. (1985) 'Die Nutzung von Senecas (Ps.–Senecas) Tragödien im Romanus–Hymnus des Prudentius', *WJA* 11: 135–50.

Hershkowitz, P. (2017) *Prudentius, Spain, and Late Antique Christianity: Poetry, Visual Culture, and the Cult of Martyrs*. Cambridge.

Herter, H. (1981) 'Ovidianum Quintum. Das Diluvium bei Ovid und Nonnos', *ICS* 6: 319–55.

Herzog, R. (1975) *Die Bibelepik der lateinischen Spätantike: Formgeschichte einer erbaulichen Gattung*. Munich.

(1977) 'Probleme der heidnisch-christlichen Gattungskontinuität am Beispiel des Paulinus von Nola', in *Christianisme et formes littéraires de l'antiquité tardive en occident*, ed. M. Fuhrmann. Geneva: 373–423.

(1979) 'Exegese – Erbauung – Delectatio. Beiträge zu einer christlichen Poetik der Spätantike', in *Formen und Funktionen der Allegorie. Symposion Wolfenbüttel 1978*, ed. W. Haug. Stuttgart: 52–69.

Hexter, R. (1988) 'The metamorphosis of Sodom: the ps-Cyprian "De Sodoma" as an Ovidian episode', *Traditio* 44: 1–35.

Higbie, C. (2010) 'Divide and edit: a brief history of book divisions', *Harvard Studies in CPh* 105: 1–31.

Hilhorst, A. (1993) 'The cleansing of the temple (John 2,13–25) in Juvencus and Nonnus', in *Early Christian Poetry: A Collection of Essays*, eds J. den Boeft and A. Hilhorst. Leiden: 61–76.

Hill, D. E. (1992) *Ovid. Metamorphoses V–VIII*. Warminster.

Hinds, S. (1987) *The Metamorphosis of Persephone: Ovid and the Self-Conscious Muse*. Cambridge.

(2000) 'Essential epic: genre and gender from Macer to Statius', in *Matrices of Genre. Authors, Canons, and Society*, eds M. Depew and D. Obbink. Cambridge, MA: 221–44.

(2014) 'The self-conscious cento', in *Décadence: 'Decline and Fall' or 'Other Antiquity'?*, eds M. Formisano, T. Fuhrer and A.-L. Stock. Heidelberg: 171–97.

(2016) 'Return to Enna: Ovid and Ovidianism in Claudian's *De Raptu Proserpinae*', in *Repeat Performances: Ovidian Repetition and the Metamorphoses*, eds L. Fulkerson and T. Stover. Madison: 249–78.

Hoch, C. (1997) *Apollo Centonarius. Studien und Texte zur Centodichtung der italienischen Renaissance*. Tübingen.

Hollis, A. (1994) 'Nonnus and Hellenistic poetry', in *Studies in the Dionysiaca of Nonnus*, ed. N. Hopkinson. Cambridge: 43–62.

(2006) 'The Hellenistic epyllion and its descendants', in *Greek Literature in Late Antiquity: Dynamism, Didacticism, Classicism*, ed. S. F. Johnson. Aldershot: 141–57.

Hopkinson, N. (1994a) *Nonnos de Panopolis: les Dionysiaques, Tome VIII, Chants XX–XXIV*. Paris.

(1994b) 'Nonnus and Homer', in *Studies in the Dionysiaca of Nonnus*, ed. N. Hopkinson. Cambridge: 9–42.

(ed.) (1994c) *Studies in the Dionysiaca of Nonnus*. Cambridge.

(ed.) (2018) *Quintus Smyrnaeus, Posthomerica*. Cambridge, MA.

Horstmann, S. (2004) *Das Epithalamium in der lateinischen Literatur der Spätantike*. Munich.

Hose, M. (2004) *Poesie aus der Schule: Überlegungen zur spätgriechischen Dichtung*. Munich.

Humphries, M. (2017) 'Late Antiquity and world history: challenging conventional narratives and analyses', *Studies in Late Antiquity* 1: 8–37.

Hunter, R. L. (2005) 'Generic consciousness in the *Orphic Argonautica*', in *Roman and Greek Imperial Epic*, ed. M. Paschalis. Crete: 149–68.

(2012) 'The songs of Demodocus: compression and extension in Greek narrative poetry', in *Brill's Companion to Greek and Latin Epyllion and Its Reception*, eds M. Baumbach and S. Bär. Leiden: 83–109.

(2015) *Apollonius of Rhodes, Argonautica Book IV*. Cambridge.

Ingalls, W.B. (1998) 'Attitudes towards children in the *Iliad*', *EMC* 17.1: 13–34

Irigoin, J. (1997) 'Titres, sous-titres et sommaires dans les oeuvres des historiens grecs du Iᵉʳ siècle avant J.-C. au Vᵉ siècle après J.-C.', in *Titres et articulations du texte dans les oeuvres antiques*, eds J.-C. Fredouille et al. Paris: 127–34.

Jakobi, R. (2014) *Nemesianus, Cynegetica. Edition und Kommentar*. Berlin.

James, A. (2004) *The Trojan Epic*. Baltimore.

(2007) 'Quintus of Smyrna and Virgil – a matter of prejudice' in *Quintus Smyrnaeus: Transforming Homer in Second Sophistic Epic*, eds M. Baumbach and S. Bär. Berlin: 145–58.

James, A. and Lee, K. (2000) *A Commentary on Quintus of Smyrna, Posthomerica V*. Leiden.

Jansen, L. (ed.) (2014) *The Roman Paratext. Frame, Texts, Readers*. Cambridge.

Jeffreys, E. (2006) 'Writers and audiences in the early sixth century', in *Greek Literature in Late Antiquity: Dynamism, Didacticism, Classicism*, ed. S. F. Johnson. Aldershot: 128–39.

Johnson, S. F. (ed.) (2006) *Greek Literature in Late Antiquity: Dynamism, Didacticism, Classicism*. Aldershot.

Johnson, W. (2004) *Bookrolls and Scribes in Oxyrhynchus*. Toronto.

(2005) 'The Posidippus papyrus: bookroll and reader', in *The New Posidippus: A Hellenistic Poetry Book*, ed. K. Gutzwiller. Oxford: 70–80.

Jülicher, A. (1938) *Itala: das Neue Testament in altlateinischer Überlieferung. 4. Johannes-Evangelium*. Berlin.

Jülicher, A. and Aland, K. (1963) *Itala: das Neue Testament in altlateinischer Überlieferung. 1. Matthäus-Evangelium*. Berlin.

Jungck, C. (1974) *Gregor von Nazianz, De vita sua, herausgegeben, eingeleitet und erklärt*. Heidelberg.

Kakridis, P. I. (1962) Κόιντος Σμυρναῖος. Γενική μελέτη τῶν Μεθ᾽ Ὅμηρον καὶ τοῦ ποιητῆ τους. Athens.

Kaster, R. A. (1988) *Guardians of Language: The Grammarian and Society in Late Antiquity*. Berkeley, Los Angeles, New York.

Kaufmann, H. (2006) *Dracontius, Romul. 10 (Medea): Einleitung, Text, Übersetzung und Kommentar*. Heidelberg.

(2017) 'Intertextuality in late Latin poetry', in *The Poetics of Late Latin Literature*, eds J. Elsner and J. H. Lobato. Oxford: 149–75.

Kay, N. M. (2001) *Ausonius: Epigrams. Text with Introduction and Commentary*. London.

Keller, O. (ed.) (1904) *Pseudoacronis Scholia in Horatium vetustiora*, vol. 2. Leipzig.

Kelly, G. (ed.) (forthcoming) *The Cambridge History of Later Latin Literature*, eds G. Kelly and A. Pelttari. Cambridge.

Kessels, A. H. M. and van der Horst, P. W. (1987) '*The Vision of Dorotheus* (Pap. Bodmer 29), edited with introduction, translation and notes', *VChr* 41: 313–59.

Keydell, R. (1949–1950) 'Seneca und Cicero bei Quintus von Smyrna', *Würzburger Jahrbücher für die Altertumswissenschaft* 230: 41–161.

(1951) 'Ein dogmatisches Lehrgedicht Gregors von Nazianz', *ByzZ* 44: 315–21.

(1954) 'Quintus von Smyrna und Vergil', *Hermes* 82: 254–56.

Kirsch, W. (1989) *Die lateinische Versepik des 4. Jahrhunderts*. Berlin.

Knight, G. (2005) 'Friendship and erotics in the late antique verse epistle: Ausonius to Paulinus revisited', *Rheinisches Museum für Philologie* 148: 361–403.

Knox, P. E. (1988) 'Phaethon in Ovid and Nonnus', *CQ* 38: 536–51.

Köchly, A. (1850) *Quinti Smyrnaei Posthomericum XIV*. Leiden.

Kokorea, S. R. (2014) Έρωτας καὶ πόλεμος: πηγές καὶ ερμηνεία των Διονυσιακών του Νόννου. PhD Dissertation: National and Kapodistrian University of Athens.

Kolde, A., Lukinovich, A. and Rey, A.-L. (eds) (2005) κορυφαίῳ ἀνδρί: *Mélanges offerts à André Hurst*. Geneva.

Koster, S. (2002) 'Epos-Kleinepos-Epyllion? Zu Formen und Leitbildern spätantiker Epik', in *Leitbilder aus Kunst und Literatur*, eds J. Dummer and M. Vielberg. Stuttgart: 31–51.

Kost, K. (1971) *Musaios, Hero und Leander: Einleitung, Text, Übersetzung und Kommentar*. Bonn.

Kraus, T. (1957) *Die Aphrodite von Knidos*. Bremen.

Krevans, N. (1993) 'Ilia's dream: Ennius, Virgil, and the mythology of seduction', *HSPh* 95: 257–71.

(2005) 'The editor's toolbox. Strategies for selection and presentation in the Milan epigram papyrus', in *The New Posidippus: A Hellenistic Poetry Book*, ed. K. Gutzwiller. Oxford: 81–96.

Kristensen, T. M. (2016) 'Nonnus and the art of Late Antiquity', in *Brill's Companion to Nonnus of Panopolis*, ed. D. Accorinti. Leiden, Boston: 460–78.

Kröll, N. (2016) *Die Jugend des Dionysos: die Ampelos-Episode in den 'Dionysiaka' des Nonnos von Panopolis*. Berlin.

Kroll, W. (1924) *Studien zum Verständnis der römischen Literatur*. Stuttgart.

Kuhn-Treichel, T. (2016) *Die Alethia des Claudius Marius Victorius: Bibeldichtung zwischen Epos und Lehrgedicht*. Berlin, Boston.

(2020) 'Poetological name-dropping: explicit references to poets and genres in Gregory Nazianzen's poems', in *The Genres of Late Antique Christian Poetry: Between Modulations and Transpositions*, eds F. Hadjittofi and A. Lefteratou. Berlin, Boston: 93–108.

Lacombrade, C. (1978) *Synésios de Cyrène, vol. 1: Hymnes, texte établi et traduit*. Paris.

Ladner, G. B. (1959) *The Idea of Reform. Its Impact on Christian Thought and Action in the Age of the Fathers*. Cambridge, MA.

Laird, A. (1993) 'Sounding out ecphrasis: art and text in Catullus 64', *JRS* 83: 18–30.

(ed.) (2006) *Oxford Readings in Ancient Literary Criticism*. Oxford.

Larmour, D. H. J., Miller, P.A. and Platter, C. (eds) (1998) *Rethinking Sexuality: Foucault and Classical Antiquity*. Princeton.

Lasek, A. M. (2016) 'Nonnus and the play of genres', in *Brill's Companion to Nonnus of Panopolis*, ed. D. Accorinti. Leiden: 402–21.

Lattke, M. (1991) *Hymnus: Materialien zu einer Geschichte der antiken Hymnologie*. Göttingen.

Lazzati, G. (1976) *Ambrosius episcopus*, vol. 1. Milan.

Lefteratou, A. and Hadjittofi, F. (2020) 'Generic debates and late antique Christian poetry', in *The Genres of Late Antique Christian Poetry: Between Modulations and Transpositions*, eds F. Hadjittofi and A. Lefteratou. Berlin, Boston: 3–36.

Lightfoot, J. (2016) 'Nonnus and prophecy: between 'pagan' and 'Christian' voices', in *Brill's Companion to Nonnus of Panopolis*, ed. D. Accorinti. Leiden, Boston: 625–43.

Lipscomb, H. C. (1909) *Aspects of the Speech in the Later Roman Epic*. Baltimore.

Lissarrague, F. (1989) 'The world of the warrior', in *A City of Images: Iconography and Society in Ancient Greece*, ed. C. Bérard. Princeton: 39–52.

Liveley, G. (2010) *Ovid's Metamorphoses: A Reader's Guide*. London.

Livrea, E. (1968) *Colluto, Il ratto di Elena. Introduzione, testo critico, traduzione e commento*. Bologna.

(1989) *Nonno di Panopoli. Parafrasi del Vangelo di S. Giovanni, Canto XVIII*. Naples.

(2000) *Nonno di Panopoli. Parafrasi del Vangelo di S. Giovanni, Canto B*. Bologna.

Llewellyn-Jones, L. (2003) *Aphrodite's Tortoise: The Veiled Woman of Ancient Greece*. Swansea.

Lovatt, H. (2013) *The Epic Gaze: Vision, Gender and Narrative in Ancient Epic*. Cambridge.

Lowden, J. (1999) 'The beginnings of Biblical illustration', in *Imaging the Early Medieval Bible*, ed. J. Williams. University Park, PA: 9–59.

Lowe, D. (2008) 'Personification allegory in the *Aeneid* and Ovid's *Metamorphoses*', *Mnemosyne* 61: 414–35.

Lubian, F. (2014) '*I Tituli Historiarum a tema biblico della tarda antichità latina. Ambrosii Disticha, Prudentii Dittochaeon, Miracula Christi, Rustici Helpidii Tristicha*'. PhD Dissertation: Macerata.

Ludwich, A. (1887) *Homeri Iliadis et Odysseae periochae metricae.* Königsberg.

Ludwig, W. (1977) 'Die christliche Dichtung des Prudentius und die Transformation der klassischen Gattungen', in *Christianisme et formes littéraires de l'antiquité tardive en occident*, ed. M. Fuhrmann. Geneva: 303–72.

Luiselli, R. (1993) 'Contributo all' interpretazione delle Argonautiche orfiche: studio sul proemio', in *Orfeo e l'orfismo: Atti del seminario nazionale (Roma-Perugia 1985–1991)*, ed. A. Masaracchia. Quaderni Urbinati di Cultura Classica: 265–307.

Lyne, R. O. A. M. (1987) *Further Voices in Vergil's Aeneid.* Oxford.

Maas, P. (1935) 'Review: Nonnus und Ovid', *ByzZ* 35: 385–7.

Maciver, C. (2007) 'Returning to the mountain of *Arete*: reading ecphrasis, constructing ethics in Quintus Smyrnaeus' *Posthomerica*', *Quintus Smyrnaeus: Transforming Homer in Second Sophistic Epic*, eds M. Baumbach and S. Bär. Berlin: 259–84.

(2011) 'Reading Helen's excuses in Quintus Smyrnaeus' *Posthomerica*', *CQ* 61.2: 670–703.

(2012a) *Quintus Smyrnaeus' Posthomerica: Engaging Homer in Late Antiquity.* Leiden, Boston.

(2012b) 'Representative bees in Quintus Smyrnaeus' *Posthomerica*', *CPh* 107.1: 53–69.

(2012c) 'Flyte of Odysseus: allusion and the *Hoplon Krisis* in Quintus Smyrnaeus, *Posthomerica* 5', *AJPh* 133.4: 601–28.

(2016) 'A Homeric afterlife in Quintus Smyrnaeus' Posthomerica?', in *Reading the Way to the Netherworld. Education and Representations of the Beyond in Later Antiquity*, eds A. Lefteratou, K. Stamatopoulos and I. Tanaseanu-Döbler. Göttingen: 123–37.

(2020) 'Triphiodorus and the poetics of imperial Greek epic', *CPh* 115: 164–85.

Maehler, H. (2004) *Bacchylides. A Selection.* Cambridge.

Magnelli, E. (2008) 'Colluthus' "Homeric" epyllion', in *Signs of Life? Studies in Later Greek Poetry*, eds K. Carvounis and R. Hunter (= *Ramus* 37.1–2) Bendigo: 151–72.

Mahoney, A. (1934) *Vergil in the Works of Prudentius.* Washington, DC.

Mair, A. W. (1928) *Oppian, Colluthus, Tryphiodorus.* Cambridge, MA.

Malamud, M. A. (1989) *A Poetics of Transformation: Prudentius and Classical Mythology.* Ithaca.

(2011) *The Origin of Sin. An English Translation of the Hamartigenia, with an Interpretive Essay.* Ithaca, London.

Malick-Prunier, S. (2017) 'De "l'ode" latine à l'hymne chrétien: métamorphoses d'un genre, d'Horace à Prudence', *Camenae* 20: 1–11.

Mallan, C. T. (2016) 'The book indices in the manuscripts of Cassius Dio', *CQ* 66: 705–23.

Mansfeld, J. (1994) *Prolegomena: Questions to Be Settled before the Study of an Author, or a Text*. Leiden.

Manuwald, G. (2011) *Roman Republic Theatre*. Cambridge.

Marcone, A. (2008) 'A long Late Antiquity? Considerations on a controversial periodization', *JLA* 1: 4–19.

Margoni-Kögler, M. (2001) 'Women promoting literary inculturation: a case study of the aristocratic Roman matron Faltona Betitia Proba and her biblical epic', in *Gender and Religion: European Studies*, ed. K. E. Børresen, S. Cabibbo and E. Specht. Rome: 113–41.

Mastrandrea, P. (2001) 'L'epigramma dedicatorio del 'Cento Vergilianus' di Proba (AL719dRiese): Analisi del testo, ipotesi di datazione e identificazione dell'autore', *Bollettino di Studi Latini* 31: 565–78.

Mathisen, R. W. and Sivan, H. S. (eds) (1996) *Shifting Frontiers in Late Antiquity*. Aldershot.

Matthews, J. (1992) 'The poetess Proba and fourth-century Rome: questions of interpretation', in *Institutions, société et vie politique dans l'Empire romain au IVe siècle après J.-C. Actes de la table ronde autour de l'oeuvre d'André Chastagnol*, ed. M. Christol. Paris: 277–304.

Matzner, S. (2016) *Rethinking Metonymy: Literary Theory and Poetic Practice from Pindar to Jakobson*. Oxford.

Maurice, L. (2013) *The Teacher in Ancient Rome: The Magister and His World*. Plymouth.

Maxwell, D. R. and Elowsky, J. C. (2013–2015) *Cyril of Alexandria: Commentary on John*, 2 vols. Downers Grove, IL.

McCail, R. C. (1969) 'The *Cycle* of Agathias: new identifications scrutinized', *JHS* 89: 87–96.

McDonald, J. (2020) 'The significance of metre in the biblical poems of Gregory Nazianzen (carmina I.1.12–27)', in *The Genres of Late Antique Christian Poetry: Between Modulations and Transpositions*, eds F. Hadjittofi and A. Lefteratou. Berlin, Boston: 109–23.

McGill, S. (2005) *Virgil Recomposed: The Mythological and Secular Centos in Antiquity*. Oxford.

   (2007) 'Virgil, Christianity, and the *Cento* Probae', in *Texts and Culture in Latin Antiquity. Inheritance, Authority, and Change*, ed. J. H. D. Scourfield. Swansea: 173–93.

   (2009) 'The rights of authorship in Symmachus' *Epistulae* I.31', *CPh* 104: 229–32.

   (2014) 'Ausonius at night', *AJPh* 135: 123–48.

   (2016) *Juvencus' Four Books of the Gospels. Evangeliorum libri quattuor*. London, New York.

   (2018) 'Minus opus moveo: verse summaries of Virgil in the Anthologia Latina', in *Marginality, Canonicity, Passion*, eds M. Formisano and C. Kraus. Oxford: 263–86.

McGill, S. and Pucci, J. (eds) (2016) *Classics Renewed: Reception and Innovation in the Latin Poetry of Late Antiquity*. Heidelberg.

McGill, S. and Watts, E. J. (eds) (2018) *A Companion to Late Antique Literature*. Oxford.

McLynn, N. (2014) 'Julian and the Christian professors', in *Being Christian in Late Antiquity: A Festschrift for Gillian Clark*, eds C. Harrison, C. Humfress and I. Sandwell. Oxford: 120–34.

McNally, S. (1985) 'Ariadne and others: images of sleep in Greek and early Roman art', *ClAnt* 4: 152–92.

Merriam, C. U. (2001) *The Development of the Epyllion Genre through the Hellenistic and Roman Periods*. Lewiston, NY.

Merrils, A. and Miles, R. (2010) *The Vandals*. Chichester.

Meskill, L. S. (2009) *Ben Jonson and Envy*. Cambridge.

Miguélez-Cavero, L. (2008) *Poems in Context: Greek Poetry in the Egyptian Thebaid 200–600 AD*. Berlin, New York.

   (2009) 'The appearance of the gods in the *Dionysiaca* of Nonnus', *GRBS* 49: 557–83.

   (2010) 'Invective at the Service of Encomium in the Dionysiaca of Nonnus of Panopolis', *Mnemosyne* 63.1: 23–42.

   (2013a) 'Rhetoric for a Christian community: the poems of the *codex visionum*', in *The Purpose of Rhetoric in Late Antiquity: From Performance to Exegesis*, ed. A. J. Quiroga Puertas. Tübingen: 91–121.

   (2013b) *Triphiodorus, The Sack of Troy: A General Study and a Commentary*. Berlin.

   (2013c) 'Cosmic and terrestrial personifications in Nonnus' *Dionysiaca*', *GRBS* 53: 350–78.

   (2019) 'The re-creation of a narrator: Nonnus of Panopolis' *Paraphrase of the Gospel of John* 1:1–45', *Symbolae Osloenses*, 93.1: 209–33.

Miles, R. (2017) 'Vandal North Africa and the fourth Punic war', *CPh* 112.3: 384–410.

Miller, F. J. and Goold, G. P. (1984) *Ovid. Metamorphoses*, 2 vols., 2nd ed. Cambridge, MA.

Milovanovic-Barham, C. (1997) 'Gregory of Nazianzus, *Ars poetica* (*In suos versus*: Carmen 2,1,39)', *JECS* 5: 497–510.

Mindt, N. (2013a) *Martials 'epigrammatischer Kanon'*. Munich.

   (2013b) 'Griechische Autoren in den Epigrammen Martials', *Millennium Jahrbuch* 10: 501–56.

Moloney, F. J. (2005) *The Gospel of John: Text and Context*. Boston.

Morales, H. (2016) 'Rape, violence, complicity: Colluthus's Abduction of Helen', *Arethusa* 49.1: 61–92.

Morelli, C. (1912) 'Studia in seros latinos poetas', *SIFC* 19: 82–120.

Moretti, P. F. (2008) 'Proba e il Cento nuptialis di Ausonio', in *Debita dona: studi in onore di Isabella Gualandri*, eds P. F. Moretti, C. Torre, G. Zanetto and I. Gualandri. Naples: 317–47.

Moreschini, C. and Sykes, D. A. (1997) *St Gregory of Nazianzus: Poemata Arcana*. Oxford.

Moore, S. D. (ed.) (1989) *Literary Criticism and the Gospels.* New Haven, London.

Morwood, J. (1999) 'Catullus 64, Medea, and the François Vase', *G&R* 46: 221–31.

Most, G. (2010) 'Hellenistic allegory and early imperial rhetoric', in *The Cambridge Companion to Allegory*, eds R. Copeland and P. Struck. Cambridge: 26–38.

Munari, F. (1956) 'Ausonio e gli epigrammi greci', *SIFC* 27–8: 308–14.

Murgatroyd, P. (2001) 'Ovid's Syrinx', *CQ* 51: 620–3.

Murray, A. T. and Dimock, G. E. (1999) *Homer. Odyssey*, vol. 1: *books 1–12.* Cambridge, MA.

Murray, A. T. and Dimock, G. E. (1999) *Homer. Odyssey*, vol. 2: *books 13–24.* Cambridge, MA.

Murray, A. T. and Wyatt, W. F. (1999) *Homer. Iliad*, vol. 1: *books 1–12.* Cambridge, MA.

Murray, A. T. and Wyatt, W. F. (1999) *Homer. Iliad*, vol. 2: *books 13–24.* Cambridge, MA.

Mynors, R. A. B. (1991) *Collected works: Adages 2.1.1 to 2.6.100: Desiderius Erasmus*, vol. 33. Toronto.

Naas, V. (2011) 'Imperialism, mirabilia, and knowledge: some paradoxes in the *Naturalis Historia*', in *Pliny the Elder: Themes and Contexts*, eds R. K. Gibson and R. Morello. Leiden, Boston: 57–70.

Newbold, R. F. (2010) 'Mimesis and illusion in Nonnus: deceit, distrust, and the search for meaning', *Helios* 37: 81–106.

Newby, Z. (2002) 'Testing the boundaries of ekphrasis: Lucian *On the Hall*', *Ramus* 31: 126–35.

Nicastri, L. (1999) 'Paolino di Nola lettore di Ovidio', in *Ovid: Werk und Wirkung. Festgabe für Michael von Albrecht*, ed. W. Schubert. Frankfurt: ii.865–910.

Nisbet, G. (2002) 'Barbarous verses: a mixed-media narrative from Greco-Roman Egypt', *Apollo* 156.485: 15–19.

  (2011) 'An ancient Greek graphic novel', in *Classics and Comics*, eds G. Kovacs and C. W. Marshall. Oxford: 27–42.

Noetzel, H. (1960) *Christus und Dionysos. Bemerkungen zum religionsgeschichtlichen Hintergrund von Johannes 2,1–11.* Stuttgart.

Nugent, S. G. (1985) *The Structure and Imagery of Prudentius' 'Psychomachia'.* Frankfurt.

Nünlist, R. (2009) *The Ancient Critic at Work. Terms and Concepts of Literary Criticism in Greek Scholia.* Cambridge.

O'Daly, G. (2004) '*Sunt* etiam Musis sua ludicra: Vergil in Ausonius', in *Romane Memento: Vergil in the Fourth Century*, ed. R. Rees. London: 141–54.

  (2012) *Days Linked by Song: Prudentius' Cathemerinon.* Oxford.

O'Hogan, C. (2016) *Prudentius and the Landscapes of Late Antiquity.* Oxford.

Oberg, B. (1973) 'Das Lehrgedicht des Amphilochius von Ikonion', *JbAC* 16: 67–97.

Orsini, P. (1972) *Collouthus: l'enlévement d'Hélène.* Paris.

Otlewska-Jung, M. (2014) 'Orpheus and Orphic hymns in the *Dionysiaca*', in *Nonnus of Panopolis in Context: Poetry and Cultural Milieu in Late Antiquity with a Section on Nonnus and the Modern World*, ed. K. Spanoudakis. Berlin, Boston: 77–96.

Otten, W. and Pollmann, K. (eds) (2007) *Poetry and Exegesis in Premodern Latin Christianity: The Encounter between Classical and Christian Strategies of Interpretation*. Leiden.

Palla, R. (ed.) (1981) *Prudenzio Hamartigenia: introduzione, traduzione e commento*. Pisa.

Palmer, A.-M. (1989) *Prudentius on the Martyrs*. Oxford.

Panofsky, E. (1939) *Studies in Iconology: Humanistic Themes in the Art of the Renaissance*. New York, Oxford.

Papanghelis, T. D., Harrison, S. J. and Frangoulidis, S. (eds) (2013) *Generic Interfaces in Latin Literature*. Berlin, Boston.

Papaioannou, S. and Marinis, A. (2021) *Elements of Tragedy in Flavian Epic*. Berlin, Boston.

Papaioannou, S., Serafim, A. and Edwards, M. (eds) (2021) *Brill's Companion to the Reception of Ancient Rhetoric*. Leiden, Boston.

Parker, H. N. (1997) 'The teratogenic grid', in *Roman Sexualities*, eds J. P. Hallett and M. B. Skinner. Princeton: 47–65.

Paschalis, M. (1997) *Semantic Relations and Proper Names*. Oxford.

(2005) 'Pandora and the wooden horse: a reading of Triphiodorus' Ἅλωσις Ἰλίου', in *Roman and Greek Imperial Epic*, ed. M. Paschalis. Herakleion: 91–115.

(2008) 'The *Abduction of Helen*: a reappraisal', *Ramus* 37: 136–50.

(2014) 'Ovidian metamorphosis and Nonnian *Poikilon Eidos*', in *Nonnus of Panopolis in Context: Poetry and Cultural Milieu in Late Antiquity with a Section on Nonnus and the Modern World*, ed. K. Spanoudakis. Berlin: 97–122.

Pavlovskis, Z. (1989) 'Proba and the semiotics of the narrative Virgilian cento', *Vergilius* 35: 70–84.

Paxson, J. (1994) *The Poetics of Personification*. Cambridge.

Pellegrino, M. (ed.) (1975) *Forma Futuri: studi in onore del Cardinale Michele Pellegrino*. Turin.

Pelttari, A. (2011) 'Symmachus' *Epistulae* 1.31 and Ausonius' poetics of the reader', *CPh* 106: 161–69.

(2014) *The Space That Remains: Reading Latin Poetry in Late Antiquity*. Ithaca.

(2019) *The Psychomachia of Prudentius. Text, Commentary, and Glossary*. Norman, OK.

Penwill, J. L. (1978) 'Men in love: aspects of Plato's Symposium', *Ramus* 7: 143–75.

Pieri, M.-P. (1979) 'L'incontro d'amore di Marte e Venere secondo Reposiano', *SIFC* 51: 200–20.

Platt, V. (2002) 'Viewing, desiring, believing: confronting the divine in a Pompeian house', *Art History* 25: 87–112.

Platnauer, M. (1922) *Claudian: on Stilicho's Consulship 2–3; Panegyric on the Sixth Consulship of Honorius; The Gothic War; Shorter Poems; Rape of Proserpina.* Cambridge, MA.

Pollmann, K. (1991) *Das Carmen adversus Marcionitas.* Göttingen.

(2001) 'Das lateinische Epos in der Spätantike', in *Von Göttern und Menschen erzählen: Formkonstanzen und Funktionswandel vormoderner Epik*, ed. J. Rüpke. Stuttgart: 93–129.

(2004) 'Sex and salvation in the Vergilian *cento* of the fourth century', in *Romane Memento: Vergil in the Fourth Century*, ed. R. Rees. London: 79–96.

(2012) 'Tradition and innovation: the transformation of classical literary genres in Christian late antiquity', in *Invention, Rewriting, Usurpation: Discursive Fights over Religious Traditions in Antiquity*, eds J. Ulrich, A.-C. Jacobsen and D. Brakke. Frankfurt a. M.: 103–20. Reprinted in (2017) *The Baptized Muse: Early Christian Poetry as Cultural Authority*, ed. K. Pollmann. Oxford: 19–36.

Pratt, L. (2007) 'The parental ethos of the *Iliad*', in *Constructions of Childhood in Ancient Greece and Italy*, eds A. Cohen and J. B. Rutter. Princeton: 25–40.

Prauscello, L. (2008) 'Colluthus' pastoral traditions: narrative strategies and bucolic criticism in the Abduction of Helen', *Ramus* 37: 173–90.

Prieto Domínguez, Ó. (2010) *De alieno nostrum: el centón profano en el mundo griego.* Salamanca.

Pucci, J. (2016) 'Ausonius on the lyre: *De Bissula* and the traditions of Latin lyric', in *Classics Renewed: Reception and Innovation in the Latin Poetry of Late Antiquity*, eds S. McGill and J. Pucci. Heidelberg: 111–31.

Pusey, P. E. (translator) (1874) *Cyril of Alexandria, Commentary on John*, vol. 1. Oxford, London.

Quiroga Puertas, A. J. (ed.) (2013) *The Purpose of Rhetoric in Late Antiquity: from Performance to Exegesis.* Tübingen.

Rank, R. G. (1966) 'The *Apotheosis* of Prudentius: a structural analysis', *Classical Folia* 20: 18–31.

Rees, R. (ed.) (2004) *Romane Memento: Vergil in the Fourth Century.* London.

Rey, A.-L. (1998) *Centons homériques (Homerocentra): Patricius, Eudocie, Optimus Côme de Jerusalem.* Paris.

Richardson, N. J. (1974) *The Homeric Hymn to Demeter.* Oxford.

Riemschneider, M. (1957) 'Der Stil des Nonnos', *Berliner Byzantinische Arbeiten* 5: 46–70.

Riggsby, A. M. (2019) *Mosaics of Knowledge: Representing Information in the Roman World.* Oxford.

Roberts, M. (1985a) *Biblical Epic and Rhetorical Paraphrase in Late Antiquity.* Liverpool.

(1985b) 'Paulinus poem 11, Virgil's first *Eclogue*, and the limits of *Amicitia*', *Transactions of the American Philological Association* 115: 271–82.

(1989) *The Jeweled Style: Poetry and Poetics in Late Antiquity.* Ithaca.

(1994) 'St Martin and the leper: narrative variation in the Martin poems of Venantius Fortunatus', *Journal of Medieval Latin* 4: 82–100.

(2001) 'Rome personified, Rome epitomized', *AJP* 122: 533–63.

(2002) 'Ovid's *Metamorphoses* and the Latin poets of Late Antiquity', *Arethusa* 35: 403–15.

(2017) 'Lactantius' *Phoenix* and late Latin poetics', in *The Poetics of Late Latin Literature*, eds J. Elsner and J. Hernández Lobato. Oxford: 373–90.

Roca-Puig, R. (1965) *Himne a la Verge Maria: Papir llatí del segle IV.* Barcelona.

Rodari, O. (1985) 'La métaphore de l'accouchement du cheval de Troie dans la literature grecque', *PP* 40: 81–102.

Romano, D. (1959) *Studi Draconziani.* Palermo.

Rondholz, A. (2012) *The Versatile Needle: Hosidius Geta's Cento 'Medea' and Its Tradition.* Berlin, Boston.

Rosen, R. M. (2012) 'Satire in the republic: from Lucilius to Horace', in *A Companion to Persius and Juvenal*, eds S. Braund and J. Osgood. Malden, Oxford, Chichester: 19–40.

Rosenmeyer, T. G. (1985) 'Ancient literary genres: a mirage?', *Yearbook of Comparative and General Literature* 34: 74–84, reprinted in *Ancient Literary Criticism*, ed. A. Laird (2006): 421–39.

Rossi, L. E. (1971) 'I generi letterari e le loro leggi scritte e non scritte nelle letterature classiche', *BICS* 18: 69–94.

Rotstein, A. (2010) *The Idea of Iambos.* Oxford.

Rouse, W. H. D. (1940) *Nonnos. Dionysiaca*, 3 vols. Cambridge, MA.

Rubenson, S. (2000) 'Philosophy and simplicity. The problem of classical education in early Christian biography', in *Greek Biography and Panegyric in Late Antiquity*, eds T. Hägg and P. Rousseau. Berkeley, London: 110–39.

Rüpke, J. (ed.) (2001) *Von Göttern und Menschen erzählen. Formkonstanzen und Funktionswandel vormoderner Epik.* Stuttgart.

Russell, D. (ed. and translator) (2001) *Quintilian: The Orator's Education.* Cambridge, MA.

Salvatore, A. (1958) *Studi Prudenziani.* Naples.

Sandnes, K. O. (2011) *The Gospel 'According to Homer and Virgil': Cento and Canon.* Leiden.

Scafoglio, G. (1999) 'Intertestualità e contaminazione dei generi letterari nella *Mosella* di Ausonio', *AC* 68: 267–74.

Scheindler, A. (1881) *Nonni Panopolitani Paraphrasis S. Evangelii Joannei.* Leipzig.

Scheijnen, T. (2018) *Quintus of Smyrna's Posthomerica: A Study of Heroic Characterization and Heroism.* Leiden.

Schelske, O. (2011) *Orpheus in der Spätantike: Studien und Kommentar zu den Argonautika des Orpheus: ein literarisches, religiöses und philosophisches Zeugnis.* Berlin.

Schembra, R. (2006) *La prima redazione dei centoni omerici: traduzione e commento.* Alessandria.

(2007a) *La seconda redazione dei centoni omerici: traduzione e commento.* Alessandria.

(2007b) *Homerocentones.* Turnhout.

Schierl, P. (2016) 'A preacher in Arcadia? Reconsidering Tityrus Christianus', in *Classics Renewed: Reception and Innovation in the Latin Poetry of Late Antiquity*, eds S. McGill and J. Pucci. Heidelberg: 241–64.

Schindler, C. (2009) *Per carmina laudes: Untersuchungen zur spätantiken Verspanegyrik von Claudian bis Coripp*. Berlin, New York.

Schmalzgruber, H. (2016) *Studien zum Bibelepos des sogenannten Cyprianus Gallus mit einem Kommentar zu gen. 1–362*. Stuttgart.

Schmid, W. (1953) 'Tityrus Christianus: Probleme religiöser Hirtendichtung an der Wende vom vierten zum fünften Jahrhundert', *RhM* 96: 101–65.

Schmidt, P. L. (1997) 'Paratextuelle Elemente in lateinischer Fachprosa', in *Titres et articulations du texte dans les oeuvres antiques*, eds J.-C. Fredouille, M.-O. Goulet-Cazé, P. Hoffmann and P. Petitmengin. Paris: 223–32.

Schottenius Cullhed, S. (2010) 'Typology and the cento of Proba', *Quaderni Urbinati di Cultura Classica* 95: 43–51.

  (2014) 'Proba and Jerome', in *Décadence: 'Decline and Fall' or 'Other Antiquity'?*, eds M. Formisano, T. Fuhrer and A.-L. Stock. Heidelberg: 199–222.

  (2015) *Proba the Prophet: The Christian Virgilian Cento of Faltonia Betitia Proba*. Leiden.

Schröder, B.-J. (1999) *Titel und Text*. Berlin.

Schubert, P. (2013) 'L'apport des papyrus grecs et latins d'Égypte romaine', in *Les Grecs héritiers des Romains*, eds P. Schubert, P. Ducrey and P. Derron. Vandoeuvres-Geneva: 243–71.

Schulze, J.-F. (1985) 'Nonnos' Dionysiaka 11,356–359 und Ovids Remedia 483–486', *WZHalle* 34.6: 78–82.

Scourfield, J. H. D. (ed.) (2007) *Texts and Culture in Late Antiquity: Inheritance, Authority, and Change*. Swansea.

Shanzer, D. (1986) 'The anonymous Carmen Contra Paganos and the date and identity of the Centonist Proba', *Revue des Études Augustiniennes* 32: 232–48.

  (1994) 'The date and identity of the Centonist Proba', *Recherches Augustiniennes* 27: 75–96.

Shapiro, H. A., Iozzo, M. and Lezzi-Hafter, A. (eds) (2013) *The François Vase: New Perspectives*. Zurich.

Sherry, L. F. (1991) *The Hexameter 'Paraphrase of Saint John' Attributed to Nonnos of Panopolis: Prolegomenon and Translation*. PhD Dissertation: Columbia University.

Shorrock, R. (2001) *The Challenge of Epic: Allusive Engagement in the Dionysiaca of Nonnus*. Leiden.

  (2011) *The Myth of Paganism: Nonnus, Dionysus and the World of Late Antiquity*. London.

  (2014) 'A classical myth in a Christian world: Nonnus' Ariadne episode (Dion. 47.265–475)', in *Nonnus of Panopolis in Context: Poetry and Cultural Milieu in Late Antiquity with a Section on Nonnus and the Modern World*, ed. K. Spanoudakis. Berlin: 313–32.

Simelidis, C. (2016) 'Nonnus and Christian literature', in *Brill's Companion to Nonnus of Panopolis*, ed. D. Accorinti. Leiden, Boston: 289–307.

Simons, R. (2005) *Dracontius und der Mythos. Christliche Weltsicht und pagane Kultur in der ausgehenden Spätantike*. Leipzig.

Sivan, H. (1993) 'Anician women. The cento Proba, and the aristocratic conversion in the fourth century', *Vigiliae Christianae* 47: 140–57.

Skiadas, A. D. (1965) *Homer im griechischen Epigramm*. Athens.

Small, J. P. (2003) *The Parallel Worlds of Classical Art and Text*. Cambridge.

Smolak, K. (1989) 'Reposianus', in: *Handbuch der lateinischen Literatur der Antike. Fünfter Band*, ed. R. Herzog. Munich: 247–49.

(2000) 'Der Hymnus für jede Gebetsstunde (Prudentius, *Cathemerinon* 9)', *WS* 113: 215–36.

(2001) 'Die Bibeldichtung als "verfehlte Gattung"', in *La scrittura infinita: Bibbia e poesia in età medievale e umanistica: atti del Convegno di Firenze, 26–28 giugno 1997*, ed. F. Stella. Tavarnuzze: 15–29.

Sowers, B. P. (2016) 'Amicitia and late antique Nugae: reading Ausonius' reading community', *AJPh* 137: 511–40.

(2020) *In Her Own Words: The Life and Poetry of Aelia Eudocia*. Washington, DC.

Spanoudakis, K. (2007) 'Icarius Jesus Christ? Dionysiac passion and biblical narrative in Nonnus' Icarius episode (*Dion.* 47.1–264)', *WS* 120: 35–92.

(2014a) *Nonnus of Panopolis: Paraphrasis of the Gospel of John XI*. Oxford.

(ed.) (2014b) *Nonnus of Panopolis in Context: Poetry and Cultural Milieu in Late Antiquity with a Section on Nonnus and the Modern World*. Berlin.

(2016), 'Pagan themes in the *Paraphrase*', in *Brill's Companion to Nonnus of Panopolis*, ed. D. Accorinti. Leiden, New York: 601–24.

Speck, P. (1997) 'Sokrates Scholastikos über die beiden Apolinarioi', *Philologus* 141: 362–69.

Spatharakis, I. (2004) *The Illustrations of the Cynegetica in Venice, Codex Marcianus Graecus Z 139*. Leiden.

Springer, C. P. E. (1988) *The Gospel as Epic in Late Antiquity: The Paschale Carmen of Sedulius*. Leiden.

(1993) 'Jerome and the Cento of Proba', *Studia Patristica* 27: 96–105.

(2013) *Sedulius, the Paschal Song and Hymns, Translated with an Introduction and Notes*. Atlanta.

Squire, M. (2009) *Image and Text in Graeco-Roman Antiquity*. Cambridge.

(2011a) *The Art of the Body: Antiquity and Its Legacy*. London.

(2011b) *The Iliad in a Nutshell*. Oxford.

Squire, M. and Wienand, J. (eds) (2017) *Morphogrammata / The Lettered Art of Optatian: Figuring Cultural Transformations in the Age of Constantine*. Paderborn.

Stella, F. (ed.) (2001) *La scrittura infinita: Bibbia e poesia in età medievale e umanistica: atti del Convegno di Firenze, 26–28 giugno 1997*. Tavarnuzze.

Stettiner, R. (1895–1905). *Die illustrierten Prudentiushandschriften*, 2 vols. Berlin.

Stevenson, J. (2005) *Women Latin Poets: Language, Gender, and Authority from Antiquity to the Eighteenth Century.* Oxford.

Stoehr-Monjou, A. (2014) 'Les comparaisons épiques dans le *De Raptu Helenae* (*Romul.* 8) de Dracontius', *Bollettino di Studi Latini* 1: 83–106.

Stramaglia, A. (2007) 'Il fumetto e le sue potenzialità mediatiche nel mondo greco-latino', in *Escuela y Literatura en Grecia Antigua*, eds J. A. Fernández Delgado et al. Cassino: 577–643.

Swain, S. and Edwards, M. J. (eds) (2004). *Approaching Late Antiquity: The Transformation from Early to Late Empire.* Oxford.

Szelest, H. (1976) 'Die Spottepigramme des Ausonius', *Eos* 64: 33–42.

Thatcher, T. (2008) 'Anatomies of the fourth Gospel: past, present, and future probes', in *Anatomies of Narrative Criticism: The Past, Present, and Futures of the Fourth Gospel as Literature*, eds T. Thatcher and S. D. Moore. Atlanta: 1–35.

Thomson, H. J. (1949) *Prudentius. Preface. Daily Round. Divinity of Christ. Origin of Sin. Fight for Mansoul. Against Symmachus 1.* Cambridge, MA.

Thraede, K. (2001) 'Iuvencus', *Reallexikon für Antike und Christentum* 19, 881–906.

Tilg, S. (2012) 'On the origins of the modern term "epyllion": some revisions to a chapter in the history of classical scholarship', in *Brill's Companion to Greek and Latin Epyllion and Its Reception*, eds M. Baumbach and S. Bär. Leiden: 29–54.

Tissol, G. (1997) *The Face of Nature. Wit, Narrative, and Cosmic Origins in Ovid's Metamorphoses.* Princeton.

Tissoni, F. (2016) 'The reception of Nonnus in Late Antiquity, Byzantine, and Renaissance literature', in *Brill's Companion to Nonnus of Panopolis*, ed. D. Accorinti. Leiden, Boston: 691–713.

Tompkins, I. (1999) 'Review of Moreschini and Sykes 1997', *BMCR* 1999.06.19. Available online https://bmcr.brynmawr.edu/1999/1999.06.19/ (last consulted on 24/01/2022).

Trapp, M. B. (1997) 'On the *Tablet of Cebes*', in *Aristotle and After*, B.I.C.S. Supplement 68, ed. R. Sorabji. London: 159–80.

Trimble, G. (2012) 'Catullus 64: the perfect epyllion?', in *Brill's Companion to Greek and Latin Epyllion and Its Reception*, eds M. Baumbach and S. Bär. Leiden: 55–79.

Ulrich, J., Jacobsen, A.-C. and Brakke, D. (eds) (2012) *Invention, Rewriting, Usurpation: Discursive Fights over Religious Traditions in Antiquity.* Frankfurt am Main.

Usher, M. (1997) 'Prolegomenon to the Homeric centos', *AJPh* 118: 305–21.

(1998) *Homeric Stitchings: The Homeric Centos of the Empress Eudocia.* Lanham, MD.

(1999) *Homerocentones Eudociae Augustae.* Stuttgart.

Van den Berg, R. M. (2001) *Proclus' Hymns: Essays, Translations, Commentary.* Leiden.

van der Laan, P. W. A. T. (1993) 'Imitation créative dans le *Carmen Paschale* de Sédulius', in *Early Christian Poetry. A Collection of Essays*, eds J. den Boeft and A. Hilhorst. Leiden: 135–66.

Van Dyke, C. (1985) *The Fiction of Truth: Structures and Meaning in Narrative and Dramatic Allegory.* Ithaca.

Van Rompay, L. (1993) 'Romanos le Mélode: un poète syrien à Constantinople', in *Early Christian Poetry: A Collection of Essays*, eds J. den Boeft and A. Hilhorst. Leiden: 283–96.

Van Rossum-Steenbeek, M. (1998) *Greek Readers' Digests? Studies on a Selection of Subliterary Papyri.* Leiden.

Verhelst, B. (2017) *Direct Speech in Nonnus' Dionysiaca: Narrative and Rhetorical Functions of the Characters' 'Varied' and 'Many-Faceted' Words.* Leiden.

    (2018) '"Narres, si poteris narrare" (Ov. Met. 3.192–193): Nonnus' (Dion. 5.287–551) response to Artemis' challenge to Actaeon in Ovid', *Latomus*, 77.3: 773–86.

    (2019) 'Six faces of Odysseus: genre and characterization strategies in four late antique Greek "Epyllia"', *Symbolae Osloenses* 93.1: 132–56.

    (2020) '"Breaking the Fourth Wall': on literariness and metalepsis in Nonnus" Dionysiaca', in *Nonnus of Panopolis in Context III: Old Questions and New Perspectives*, vol. 438, eds F. Doroszewski and K. Jazdzewska. Leiden, Boston: 45–66.

    (forthcoming) *Nonnus of Panopolis in Context IV. Poetry at the Crossroads.* Leuven.

    (forthcoming) 'The voice of the narrator. Speech introductions in Nonnus' Paraphrase', in *Studies in Nonnus' Paraphrase*, eds A. Rotondo and G. Agosti. Berlin, Boston.

Vian, F. (1959) *Recherches sur les 'Posthomerica' de Quintus de Smyrne.* Paris.

    (1963, 1966, 1969) *Quintus de Smyrne, La Suite d'Homère*, 3 vols. Paris.

    (1976) *Nonnos de Panopolis: les Dionysiaques, Tome I, Chants I–II.* Paris.

    (1997) 'Μάρτυς chez Nonnos de Panopolis. Étude de sémantique et de chronologie', *Revue des Études Grecques* 110: 143–60.

    (2002) *Les Argonautiques Orphiques.* Paris.

    (2003) *Nonnos de Panopolis: les Dionysiaques, Tome XVIII, Chant XLVIII.* Paris.

    (2008) 'Echoes and imitations of Apollonius Rhodius in late Greek epic', in *Brill's Companion to Apollonius Rhodius*, eds T. D. Papanghelis and A. Rengakos. Leiden, Boston: 387–411.

    (2011) 'Echoes and imitations of Apollonius Rhodius in late Greek epic', in *Brill's Companion to Apollonius Rhodius*, 2nd rev. ed., eds T. D. Papanghelis and A. Rengakos. Leiden, Boston: 387–412.

Viljamaa, T. (1968) *Studies in Greek Encomiastic Poetry of the Early Byzantine Period. Commentationes humanarum litterarum* 42.4. Helsinki.

Walsh, P. G. (1966–1967) *Letters of St. Paulinus of Nola.* Ancient Christian Writers 35–36. Newman Press.

Ward-Perkins, B. (1997) 'The cities', in *The Cambridge Ancient History, vol. 13: The Late Empire, AD 337–425*, eds Averil Cameron and P. Garnsey. Cambridge: 371–410.

Ware, C. (2012) *Claudian and the Roman Epic Tradition.* Cambridge.

(2016) 'Dreams of genre and inspiration: multiple allusion in Claudian (*VI Cons., praefatio*)', in *Classics Renewed: Reception and Innovation in the Latin Poetry of Late Antiquity*, eds S. McGill and J. Pucci. Heidelberg: 171–94.

Wasyl, A. M. (2011) *Genres Rediscovered: Studies in Latin Miniature Epic, Love Elegy, and Epigram of the Romano-Barbaric Age*. Kraków.

Watts, E. (2010) *Riot in Alexandria: Tradition and Group Dynamics in Late Antiquity in Late Antique Pagan and Christian Communities*. Berkeley.

Way, A. (translator) (1913) *Quintus Smyrnaeus Fall of Troy*. Cambridge, MA.

Webb, R. (1999) 'Ekphrasis ancient and modern. The invention of a genre', *Word and Image* 15: 7–18.

(2009) *Ekphrasis, Imagination and Persuasion in Ancient Rhetorical Theory and Practice*. Farnham.

Weitzmann, K. (1970²) *Illustrations in Roll and Codex: A Study of the Origin and Method of Text Illustration*. Princeton.

Welsh, J. T. (2010) 'Quintilian's judgement of Afranius', *CQ* 60: 118–26.

Wenglinsky, M. (2002) *The Representation of the Divine in the Posthomerica of Quintus of Smyrna*. PhD Dissertation: Columbia University.

West, M. L. (1966) *Hesiod. Theogony*. Oxford.

(1974) *Studies in Greek Elegy and Iambus*. Berlin, New York.

(1982) *Greek Metre*. Oxford.

(2003) 'The flood myth in Ovid, Lucian, and Nonnus', in *Mitos en la literatura griega helenística e imperial*, ed. J. A. López Férez. Madrid: 245–59.

(2013) *The Epic Cycle: A Commentary on the Lost Troy Epics*. Oxford.

Whitby, M. (1994) 'From Moschus to Nonnus: the evolution of the Nonnian style', in *Studies in the Dionysiaca of Nonnus*, ed. N. Hopkinson. Cambridge: 99–155.

(2007) 'The Bible Hellenized: Nonnus' *Paraphrase* of St John's Gospel and 'Eudocia's' Homeric centos', in *Texts and Culture in Late Antiquity: Inheritance, Authority, and Change*, ed. J. H. D. Scourfield. Swansea: 195–231.

(2016) 'Nonnus and biblical epic', in *Brill's Companion to Nonnus of Panopolis*, ed. D. Accorinti. Leiden: 215–39.

White, H. (2003) 'Anomalies of genre: the utility of theory and history for the study of literary genres', *New Literary History* 34: 597–615.

Whitman, J. (1987) *Allegory: The Dynamics of an Ancient Tradition*. Oxford.

Wiesen, D. S. (1971) 'Virgil, Minucius Felix and the Bible', *Hermes* 99: 70–91.

Wilcock, M. (1976) *A Companion to the Iliad*. Chicago.

Wilkinson, K. W. (2012) *New Epigrams of Palladas: A Fragmentary Papyrus Codex (P.CtYBR inv. 4000)*. Durham, NC.

(2015) 'More evidence for the date of Palladas', *ZPE* 196: 67–71.

Williams, C. A. (2010²) *Roman Homosexuality: Ideologies of Masculinity in Classical Antiquity*, 2nd rev. ed. New York, Oxford.

Woodruff, H. (1929) 'The illustrated manuscripts of Prudentius', *Art Studies* 7, 33–79.

Wright, D. (1993) *The Vatican Vergil. A Masterpiece of Late Antique Art*. Berkeley.

(2001) *The Roman Vergil and the Origins of Medieval Book Design*. Toronto.

(2006) *The Lost Late Antique Illustrated Terence*. Biblioteca Apostolica Vaticana.

Wyss, B. (1949) 'Gregor von Nazianz: ein griechisch-christlicher Dichter des 4. Jahrhunderts', *MH* 6: 177–210.

Young, F. M. (1997) *Biblical Exegesis and the Formation of Christian Culture*. Cambridge.

(2004) 'Classical genres in Christian guise: Christian genres in classical guise', in *The Cambridge History of Early Christian Literature*, eds F. M. Young, L. Ayres and A. Louth. Cambridge: 251–8.

Young, F. M., Ayres, L. and Louth, A. (eds) (2004) *The Cambridge History of Early Christian Literature*. Cambridge.

Zanker, G. (2004) *Modes of Viewing in Hellenistic Poetry and Art*. Madison, WI.

Zeitlin, F. (2013) 'Figure: ekphrasis', *Greece and Rome* 60: 17–31.

Zerwes, W. (1956) *Palladas von Alexandrien: ein Beitrag zur Geschichte der griechischen Epigrammdichtung*. PhD dissertation: Tübingen.

Ziogas, I. (2010) 'The permanence of Cupid's metamorphosis in the *Aeneid*', *Trends in Classics* 2: 150–74.

(2013) *Ovid and Hesiod: The Metamorphosis of The Catalogue of Women*. Cambridge.

Zissos, A. (1999) 'The rape of Proserpina in Ovid, *Met.* 5.341–661: internal audience and narrative distortion', *Phoenix* 53: 97–113.

Zöllner, F. (1892) *Analecta Ovidiana*. PhD Dissertation: Leipzig.

Zuenelli, S. (2016) 'Die Perioche der Dionysiaka als Mittel der Selbstinszenierung', *Mnemosyne* 69: 572–96.

Zumbo, A. (2007) 'PVindob 29788a: Λόγος ἐπιβατήριος (GDRK 28 Heitsch)', in *Proceedings of the 24th International Congress of Papyrology*, 2 vols., eds J. Frösén, T. Purola, and E. Salmenkivi. Helsinki: 2.1063–75.

Zymner, R. (2003) *Gattungstheorie: Probleme und Positionen der Literaturwissenschaft*. Paderborn.

General Subject Index

metamorphosis, 241–59
  and illusion, 259
  and metaphor, 245, 252
  and novelty, 251, 253
  landscape, 246
Metanoea, 34
metaphor, 105
  of implosion, 91–104, 114
Metaphrasis Psalmorum, 110, 174
metapoetics, 39, 46
metonymy, 155
metre, 95, 103–6, 134
  distichon, 43
  hemistichs, 115
  hexameter, 107, 113, 133, 137, 150
    didactic, 138
    heroic, 138
    orphic, 138
  iambic, 107, 137
  iambic dimeter, acatalectic, 113
  stichic telesilleans, 113
  trochaic tetrameter, catalectic, 103
  ἀπόκροτα, 113
mime, 149
mimesis, 243
Minerva, 223. See also Athena
mise-en-abyme, 134, 146, 149, 156
Morpheus, 244
Moses, 102
Musaeus
  Hero and Leander, 133, 142
Muse, 96, 141–6
  as guardian of poetic memory, 29
  invocation, 63, 66, 134, 150
  of epic. See Calliope
  of tragedy. See Melpomene
musician, 147
mythological, 134

Namatianus
  De reditu suo, 91
narratee, 137
narrative, 188, 196
  allegorical, 163
  frame, 213
  speed, 144
narrativity, 140
narrator, 134, 136, 144
  as a jockey, 144
  internal, 172
Nausicaa, 211
Nemesis, 157
Neoplatonic, 79
Niobe, 48, 51
Nola, 41

nominatim reference, 32–3, 49
Nonnus, 94, 100–1, 169, 174–7, 223, 236, 241.
  See also song contests: in Nonnus
  Dionysiaca, 13–30, 81, 105, 108–9, 142, 158,
    227, 230–5, 242
  and interfusion of genres, 21
  Paraphrase of the Gospel of John, 73, 111,
    174–7, 180–5, 189–95, 198–204, 242
  Hymn of the Logos, 180–5, 190
nonreferentiality, 52, 57
nymph, 229

objectification, 222–40
Occasio, 34
Odysseus, 43, 45–8
  anti-, 148
Oeagrus' song. See song contests: in Nonnus
Olympus, 45
omen, 217
Opium des Volkes, 218
Oppian of Apamea
  Cynegetica, 83–8
orality, 130
Orpheus, 136–8
  character vs. narrator, 146
Orphic Argonautica, 133–8. See also song
  contests: in *Orphic Argonautica*
Ovid, 33, 36, 48, 241. See also song contests: in
  Ovid
  Amores, 96
  and Late Antiquity, 14–15
  Fasti, 105
  Heroides, 39
  Metamorphoses, 13–30, 36, 38, 223, 244

Pactolus, 247
paganism
  gods, 255
  idol, 218
  metamorphosis, 252
  myth, 220
  philosophers, 204
  poets, 110
  statues, 230
  tradition, 212
paideia, 150, 180
Palladas of Alexandria, 31–3, 41–2
  and Homer, 41–2
  and misogyny, 42–5, 49
  and *persona*, 33, 41–4
  as a *grammaticus*, 49
Pandora, 46
panegyric, 98, 101, 107, 111
pantomime, 149, 245
paradigm, 44, 49

Index Locorum

For EU product safety concerns, contact us at Calle de José Abascal, 56–1°,
28003 Madrid, Spain or eugpsr@cambridge.org.

www.ingramcontent.com/pod-product-compliance
Ingram Content Group UK Ltd.
Pitfield, Milton Keynes, MK11 3LW, UK
UKHW020358140625
459647UK00020B/2540